BOOKS BY CHARLES W. SASSER

NONFICTION

Always a Warrior

Arctic Homestead (with Norma Cobb)

At Large

Back in The Fight (with Joe Kapacziewski)

Blood in The Hills (with Bob Maras)

The Collective

Crosshairs on The Kill Zone (with Craig Roberts)

Devoted to Fishing: Devotionals for Fishermen

Doc: Platoon Medic (with Daniel E. Evans)

Encyclopedia of Navy SEALs

Fire Cops (with Michael Sasser)

First SEAL (with Roy Boehm)

God in The Foxhole

Going Bonkers: The Wacky World of Cultural Madness

Hill 488 (with Ray Hildreth)

Homicide!

In Cold Blood: Oklahoma's Most Notorious Murders

Last American Heroes (with Michael Sasser)

Magic Steps to Writing Success

The Night Fighter (with Bill Hamilton)

None Left Behind

One Shot–One Kill (with Craig Roberts)

Patton's Panthers

Predator (with Matt Martin)

Raider

The Shoebox: Letters for the Seasons (with Nancy Shoemaker)

Shoot to Kill

CHARLES W. SASSER

CRUSHING

the

COLLECTIVE

THE LAST CHANCE TO KEEP AMERICA FREE AND SELF-GOVERNING

 WND Books

CRUSHING THE COLLECTIVE

Published by WND Books, Washington, D.C. WND Books is a registered trademark of WorldNetDaily.com, Inc. ("WND")

Unless otherwise indicated, Scripture quotations are from the Holy Bible, King James Version (public domain).
Scripture quotations marked ESV are taken from The Holy Bible, English Standard Version. ESV® Permanent Text Edition® (2016). Copyright © 2001 by Crossway Bibles, a publishing ministry of Good News Publishers.
Scripture quotations marked NIV are taken from the Holy Bible, New International Version®, NIV® Copyright © 1973, 1978, 1984, 2011 by Biblica, Inc.® Used by permission. All rights reserved worldwide.

Book designed by Mark Karis

WND Books are available at special discounts for bulk purchases. WND Books also publishes books in electronic formats. For more information call (541) 474-1776, e-mail orders@wndbooks.com, or visit www.wndbooks.com.

Hardcover ISBN: 978-1-944229-70-2
eBook ISBN: 978-1-944229-71-9

Library of Congress Cataloging-in-Publication Data on file

Printed in the United States of America
17 18 19 20 21 22 LBM 9 8 7 6 5 4 3 2 1

To all who seek and preserve liberty

CONTENTS

America will never be destroyed from the outside. If we falter and lose our freedoms, it will be because we destroyed ourselves.

—ABRAHAM LINCOLN

INTRODUCTION

I GREW UP through perhaps the last best age of the American experience. World War II had ended, the boys were home, the Great Depression was over, and everybody had an opportunity to live the "American dream."

There was a feeling of hope, of family, of things being right with the world. No tax agents, with their pointy-toed shoes and squinty eyes, came snooping around. Human Services minded its own business instead of sending out social workers to declare us "disadvantaged" and taking us under government's smothering wing. Schools taught reading, 'riting and 'rithmetic rather than self-esteem, gender studies, "social justice," and income redistribution.

Not that everything was lollipops and roses. I grew up in cotton fields and corn patches. I was following furrows behind a mule by the time I was seven. My dad could neither read nor write. For us, poverty was a step up. At various times, the family lived in a dirt-floored former chicken house, an old barn, and the back room of Gran'pa's little farmhouse.

But we were free, we *felt* free, and we were obligated to no one. Not to government, not to man, only to God. My old farmer-overalled Gran'pa said it best: "All I want from guv'ment is to be left alone."

I grew up independent, with a strong work ethic: You should work for what you get. Other folks aren't obliged to care for you. If you were capable and able-bodied and refused to work, then you were too worthless to eat. It's not my fault if you're a drunk or a doper, lazy, homeless, a bum. . . It was on you if you got syphilis, went to jail for stealing, couldn't hold down a job, wouldn't go to school, and hadn't enough sense to save for a rainy day.

I learned life's most important lesson when I was twelve. That year must have been an exceptionally tough one. Otherwise, Dad would never have contemplated accepting what he called "gimpy groceries"— government surplus commodities, such as cheese, beans, and powdered milk. He was too proud to go down to the county barn himself and ask for charity. He sent me.

I lined up with other poor folk who had had crop failures. For some reason, one of the petty government workers doling out free government food pushed me. I was a scrapper, a tough little quarter-breed Indian hill kid. I bristled for a fight.

"Boy," the worker snarled, "if the government feeds you, it'll do what it damn well pleases."

I went out into the world bold and unafraid when I was eighteen. I was a cop for fourteen years in two major cities—Miami, Florida; and Tulsa, Oklahoma, where Oklahoma governor David Boren once referred to me as "perhaps the best homicide detective in the nation." I served in the military for twenty-nine years, active-duty and reserve, four as a Navy journalist and much of the rest in the Army as a Green Beret. I attended university when I was nearly thirty, earning degrees in history and anthropology. I taught high school, university, and was director of criminal justice at American Christian College. Along the way I have published more than sixty books and more than three thousand magazine articles.

After I became reasonably successful as an author, a radio talk show host who knew my humble background asked me how it was possible I could have accomplished so much in life. What he meant was, how could I have done it on my own?

"I couldn't have done it today," I conceded. "You see, the first thing that happens to a poor kid today is that government welfare workers show up, tell him he's disadvantaged, that it's not his fault, and that he'll accomplish nothing in life without government's help. The kid believes it and gives up his independence, his will to succeed, his self-respect. Next thing you know, he's dependent on government to take care of him while he's living in government housing slums in Detroit or Chicago and blaming 'the rich' for keeping him down."

Years ago, I ran across a profound piece of insight attributed to a Scottish professor named Alexander Tytler. It is commonly referred to as the "Tyranny-Liberty Cycle." According to it, humankind historically and endlessly goes around and around through the same cycle: from bondage to spiritual faith; from spiritual faith to great courage; from great courage to liberty; from liberty to abundance; from abundance to complacency; from complacency to apathy; from apathy to dependence; and thereon from dependence back to bondage.[1]

In these few short phrases, Tytler described the process whereby one relinquishes his or her individual freedom and succumbs to the allure of the Collective State that will guide, direct, and command that individual through life.

I challenge you to name one empire in history, ancient or modern, that has not traveled, or is not currently traveling, Tyler's cycle: the Byzantines, Persians, Rome, Greece, Germany, Russia, the United States . . .

My great fortune is to have lived through what may well have been some of America's best times. My great misfortune is that I am now witnessing what can only be the cultural, political and economic decline of the United States of America and the fall of Western civilization.

"A really efficient totalitarian state," Aldous Huxley wrote in his

1930s classic, *Brave New World*, "would be one in which the all-powerful executive of political bosses and their army of managers control a population of slaves who do not have to be coerced, because they love their servitude."[2]

In this book, I explore the history of how humankind from our most primitive days has evolved away from the individual toward the collective—and how such societies always end, *always,* in tyranny.

A book such as this could not have been born without contributions from previous authors, historians, social commentators, and scholars. The selected bibliography at the back of this book acknowledges, in part, the exhaustive body of work I have been privileged to utilize and which has laid the foundation for the study of—and survival of—liberty in a world where the individual is struggling to remain free. I have referenced many other sources in the notes section and in the book itself. I owe a debt of gratitude to each of you.

"We will preserve for our children this, the last best hope for man on earth," Ronald Reagan once observed, "or we will sentence them to take the first step into a thousand years of darkness."

1

BEGINNINGS

So the story of man runs in a dreary circle, because he is not yet master of the earth that holds him.

—WILL DURANT

BEASTS OF BURDEN

Collectivism is the insidious belief that the group is of more worth than the individual and that the standard of value lies in the tribe, the race, the community, the state. Personal liberty throughout most of humankind's stay on earth is the exception.

Early nomads were likely the freest people to have ever lived on the planet. H. G. Wells described nomads as "communities of will," meaning a hunting, fighting community with individual self-reliance and discipline. Chiefs were leaders, not masters. If you didn't like the way things were going, you packed up your atlatl and arrows and stones or whatever and went out on your own or joined some other wandering group that was less apt to crimp your style.

Agriculture came along. People began settling down with their goats and sheep. That was the beginning of the "collective state," which H. G. Wells referred to as "communities of obedience."[1] It appears collectivism, the roots of which are subservience and obedience, may rest within the human soul. The state demands authority over and subjugation of its citizens in exchange for assuming responsibility for them. If there is a bad crop year and the rain gods need to be mollified, why shouldn't rulers take your virgins and sacrifice them for the good of the people?

That was the way the rhythm of history went for thousands of years—"civilized" peoples raising their goats and giving up much of their freedom, the nomadic folk relying on their own personal will. Gradually, however, the nomads gave up their old ways and blended into "civilization" for the security of walls.

Civilization or community is not a bad thing in itself. It only becomes so when taken to the extreme.

"Civil tyranny is usually small in its beginning, like 'the drop in the bucket,'" observed American minister Jonathan Mayhew (1720–1766), "till at length, like a mighty torrent or the raging waves of the sea, it bears down all before it and deluges whole countries and empires."[2]

Call it communism; call it fascism; call it the welfare state—it's all the same thing. The Collective takes precedence over the individual, who must be subordinated through deception, persuasion, and coercion, consumed by predators like Adolf Hitler and Joseph Stalin. "The vintage of history is forever repeating," noted E. A. Bucchianeri, "same old vines, same old wines!"[3] The same "Liberty to Tyranny" playbook.

When I was a kid, we farmed with horses and mules broken to the harness and the plow, bent to the will of the master, who had no patience or tolerance for disobedience or independence. A mule without spirit readily succumbs to numbly pulling a plow hour after hour, day after day, down one identical furrow after another.

Same thing applies to the mule's human counterpart. Once dispirited, he melds into the great One All. In effect, he becomes a beast of burden, equal with other beasts of burden, while the master rewards him with just enough essentials to keep him in harness. He must serve and, if necessary, be sacrificed for the "common good" and the "general welfare."

"We're going to take things away from you on behalf of the common good," boldly promised the indomitable 2016 Democratic presidential candidate, Hillary Rodham Clinton, in a 2004 fund-raising event.[4]

Adolf Hitler might have defined collectivism best: "It is thus necessary that the individual shall come to realize that his own ego is of no importance in comparison with the existence of his nation; that the position of the individual ego is conditioned solely by the interests of the nation as a whole. . . that above all the unity of a nation's spirit and will are worth far more than the freedom of the spirit and will of an individual."[5]

When will the world learn that a million men are of no importance compared with one man?

—HENRY DAVID THOREAU

MOBS FOR UTOPIA

Utopianism is as old as tyranny itself. Ideas of a collectivist paradise, of happy and well-behaved sheep kept flocked by enlightened shepherds, have permeated all societies. Every dictator and would-be despot from Pharaoh through Stalin and Fidel Castro have tried, *unsuccessfully,* to implement its tenets.

Plato (429–347 BC) might rightly be considered the father of collectivism. He was the first major thinker to formulate a systematic view of collective humanity. He stressed that no one, not even the ruling classes, should own private property, that everything should be equally shared.

"The first and highest form of the state and of the government and of the law . . . [is a condition] in which the private and individual is altogether banished from life," he stated in the *Laws.*[6]

According to him, the function and authority of the state should be unlimited and entrusted to a small intellectual elite—"Philosopher Kings"[7] especially bred and trained to comprehend great ideas and concepts. The masses would be assigned roles matching their humble capabilities and aspirations. They would have no political voice. They would be indoctrinated through schools controlled by the elite. Art and literature would be carefully censored to ensure the herd remained in the pasture. Regulations would be imposed and strictly enforced to maintain the orderly society.

Others throughout the ages have echoed Plato.

Jean-Jacques Rousseau (1712–1778) inspired radicals of the French Revolution with his assertion that all the vices of civilization stemmed from the concept of private property. "You are undone if you once forget that the fruits of the earth belong to us all, and the earth itself to nobody," he wrote.

Georg Hegel (1770–1831) espoused how the state "has supreme right against the individual, whose supreme duty is to be a member of the state . . . Hence, if the state claims life, the individual must surrender it."

German idealist J. G. Fichte (1762–1814) is often regarded as the father of modern socialism. As did Plato, he yearned for an elite corps of idealists, philosophers, and scholar-dictators to rule over the ignorant masses. "The individual life has no real existence since it has no value of itself," he preached.[8]

In a radical little book entitled *The Communist Manifesto,* Karl Marx (1818–1883) coalesced collectivist doctrine of previous centuries into a plague that has claimed more lives than the Black Death—and continues to do so. His ruddy, bearded countenance might well pass for "Big Brother" in the posters of George Orwell's *1984.*

Skip to the twenty-first century and we discover the dogma of Plato, Kant, Rousseau, Marx, and the other collectivist philosophers. With little understanding of history and no sense of irony, we seem to want to become peasants again, with our lives ordered and controlled by "Philosopher Kings." "Social and economic justice," "equality," and "redistribution of wealth" are synonymic with the desire for a strong man to take over and run things. And always, *always,* envy and fear of and resentment against individual freedom is the common denominator that ultimately ends in a stronger and more ruthless state.

Modern "mobs for Utopia" campaign for "change" through a collectivist, socialist mold. The Occupy Wall Street (OWS) movement that began in 2011 touted itself as a grassroots representation of the "99 percent" who were supposedly exploited by the "evil 1 percent."

As an undercover journalist, I "scruffed up" and lived with OWS protestors in New York's Zuccotti Park. Maybe four hundred people squatted there. The specter of Karl Marx hung over the park like smog. Passengers flying over in airliners must have gotten dizzy from marijuana smoke.

A half block in area, it had perhaps the highest crime rate in the nation. Drug overdoses, rapes, thefts, brawls, people taking leaks in the foliage . . . That was just my first night in the park.

Several "community organizers" set up a table to roll and distribute reefers.

Stoned out of his mind, a six-foot-two transvestite with the arms of a weight lifter and wearing a miniskirt, long bleached hair, and fake boobs went around hitting on nerds from Harvard or NYU.

"Philosophers" with red bandannas and black berets, à la Che Guevara, huddled like baby chicks around a sign that read, "The Youth Will Dig Capitalism's Grave."

A "nerve center" staffed by professional agitators, whom CNN reported linked to funding by socialist billionaire and one-worlder George Soros, distributed professionally printed pamphlets and signs that touted OWS as "the latest in the proud thread of human dignity, this generation's selfless contribution to the struggle for liberty and justice. "

Human dignity? One of the pamphleteers got arrested for toking and taking a leak on a police car.

Periodic marches prattled down Wall Street, with demonstrators chanting and shouting in righteous indignation, placards bobbing above scruffy heads.

SMASH IMPERIALISM

TAX THE RICH

SOCIALISM NOW

A plain-looking woman with no makeup and uncombed hair, the better perhaps to identify with the proletariat, displayed a huge sign enumerating OWS demands:

FREE BICYCLES

FREE MASS TRANSIT

FREE MEDICAL CARE

FREE COLLEGE EDUCATION

FREE HOUSING

FREE VACATIONS

Notice the operative word: *free.* Out of pure cussedness, I kept asking, "But who pays for it?"

They looked at me as if I were not from planet Earth.

"The rich, of course. And government."

Praise and support for these cupcakes poured in from all sides.

"God bless them for their spontaneity," raved then House Majority Leader Nancy Pelosi. "It's young, it's spontaneous, and it's focused. And it's going to be effective."[9]

President Barack Obama declared how OWS would "express itself politically in 2012 and beyond."[10]

The NAACP extended its support. SEIU (Service Employees International Union) and burned-out entertainer/socialist Harry Belafonte teamed up with OWS to cohost a civil rights event.

Paradoxically, movements calling for "freedom" invariably evoke the spirit of collectivism, of the submission of the individual to the mentality of the mob—and the mob calls for bigger government to sanction those deemed unworthy to be part of the mob. It used to be called slavery when government seized your wealth and distributed it to someone else. Today, it's called "social justice."

Posterity: you will never know how much it has cost my generation to preserve your freedom. I hope you will make good use of it.

—JOHN QUINCY ADAMS

CANNIBALISM AND COMMUNISM

Ironically enough, the first settlers to what became the United States of America experimented with communism long before Karl Marx made his philosophy the wet dream of every collectivist who thought he knew best how to place the individual into harness for the common good. New World colonial plantation companies assumed that survival in such a harsh and unforgiving environment required everyone working in concert for the good of all.

In 1584, and again in 1587, Sir Walter Raleigh attempted to found a settlement on Roanoke Island. Both failed. However, two other settlements survived—Jamestown in Virginia in 1607, and Plymouth in New England in 1620. Both were based on an agricultural economy; both initially turned to what today would be called communism. No private ownership of land, all work done in common.

Some 80 percent of Jamestown's population perished during the first two years. In 2013, researchers for the Smithsonian Museum of Natural History found physical evidence that survivors of the winter famine of 1609 resorted to cannibalism. The skull and shinbone of a fourteen-year-old girl dubbed "Jane" revealed obvious signs of having been butchered and presumably consumed.[11]

Colonist George Percy provided an eyewitness account of the "Starving Time," recording how "nothing was spared to maintain life and to do those things which seem incredible, as to dig up dead corpses out of graves and to eat them, and some have licked up the blood which hath fallen from their weak fellows."[12]

Even after England infused fresh supplies and replacements, the communal nature of Jamestown's workload remained inconsistent—until Governor Thomas Dale defied the settlement company and the British government by assigning plots of land to individuals. Prosperity arrived only after the relaxation of collectivist practices, making Jamestown the first successful colony in the New World.

Plymouth Colony faced similar hardships after the *Mayflower*, with 102 pilgrims and 30 crew members, dropped anchor off the coast of Massachusetts in 1620. Governor William Bradford assumed Plymouth would best thrive if each settler received an equal share of whatever the group produced without regard to individual contribution. "All profits & benefits that are got by trade, working, fishing, or any other means," he mandated, must be forfeited to a common storehouse and that "all such persons as are of the colony, are to have meat, drink, apparel and all provisions out of the common stock."[13]

In theory, it should have worked out splendidly. In application, however, they were one step away from eating their dead before they discovered the truth of Aristotle's statement from 350 BC: "That which is common to the greatest number has the least care bestowed upon it."[14]

Bradford, to his credit, was quick to learn. He began to ponder "how they might raise as much corn as they could, and obtain a better crop than they had done, that they might not still thus languish in misery . . . At length after much debate of things, [I] (with the advice of the chiefest amongst them) gave way that they should set corn every man for his own particular, and in that regard trust to themselves . . . [a]nd so assigned to every family a parcel of land."

And the result?

"This had very good success," Bradford said, "for it made all hands very industrious, so as much more corn was planted than otherwise would have been by any other means[15] . . . Any general want or famine hath not been amongst them since to this day."[16]

Bradford's turnabout toward free enterprise resulted in the colony celebrating its first Thanksgiving in America with a bountiful harvest.

Later colonies declined to learn from the early mistakes of Jamestown and Plymouth. In 1717, trustees in England contracted to build a colony in Georgia based on silkworms and mulberry trees. The colony proved little competition for China, however, since the mulberry trees were the wrong sort. Worms died of starvation. Colonists might have done likewise except for the largesse of their benefactors, who continued to shovel good cash into a losing enterprise.

The colony bore all the earmarks of a modern welfare state. Bureaucrats administered everything while settlers lived on charitable donations and government appropriations from England. Rigid rules governed virtually every aspect of communal life, severely limiting private ownership of land and how it could be used. Predictably, the structure of the colony bred dependency and discontent.

A docile, dependent, and subservient population with no incentive to produce will not long endure. The Georgia colony, on the dole all the way, finally gave up the "worm" and collapsed in 1751.

Lessons learned from these first colonists lingered on in America for much of the next two centuries. Only in recent times, historically speaking, have free citizens forgotten or overlooked these lessons and once more clamored for servitude. The same old Tyranny-Liberty Cycle continues. We all should know by now how it ends.

I have no reason to suppose, that he, who would take away my liberty, would not, when he had me in his power, take away every thing else.

—JOHN LOCKE

NATURAL LAWS

By the middle of the eighteenth century, European foundations were crumbling under the pressure of demands for revolutionary change in the relationship between those who governed and those who were governed. The increase and distribution of knowledge with the invention of the printing press vastly expanded human horizons and expectations. Rulers quaked at new developments in science and travel to and exploration of far-flung lands that broadened the mind of common citizens and instilled in them a craving for more freedom.

Although philosophers and thinkers such as Hegel and Rousseau argued that humankind could only ever be "free" through immersion in the collective, others spoke out for the natural rights of the individual. Among the most influential political thinkers of the Enlightenment, which eventually produced the United States of America, were Thomas Hobbes (1598–1679), John Locke (1632–1704), and Charles Montesquieu (1689–1744).

Hobbes, author of *Leviathan*, established the principle that government legitimacy stems from the rights of the governed rather than the divine right and natural superiority of kings and rulers. The primary purpose of government, he further assessed, was to protect those natural rights of the individual. Expositions on "self-evident" rights of life, liberty, and the pursuit of happiness in the American Declaration of Independence might well have been written by Hobbes himself.

In John Locke, the Founding Fathers found a patron saint. Whereas collectivists of his time operated on the assumption that individuals must be managed by masterminds for the greater good, Locke opposed authoritarianism in all its various utopian forms. Men, he contended, are "by Nature all free, equal and independent."[17] They submit to government only because of a convenience for good order and not because rulers might claim divine rights or natural superiority.

In *The Spirit of the Laws*, Charles Montesquieu lamented how most men continue to live under tyranny. Excessive taxation and wealth redistribution produces destructive consequences, he argued, adding, "The poor can better their circumstances (through freedom), whereas they have little hope in a despotic state. Every lazy nation is a grave, for those who do not work regard themselves as sovereigns of those who work."[18]

Nearly three centuries later, Occupy Wall Street protesters claimed "the rich" owe them a living, that society is obligated to provide for their needs regardless of whether they work or not. A self-described anarchist in Zuccotti Park, with perhaps more candor than he intended, said of his fellows, "A lot are on the dole, on welfare and social assistance. Some are trying to find work while a lot of others are avoiding work. I mean, man, let's be honest here. Work sucks."

Montesquieu's central contribution to the nation that later became the United States was the idea of checks and balances, of power divided into three branches. "When the legislative and executive powers are united in the same person, or in the same body of magistrates, there can be no liberty," he explained. "Again, there is no liberty, if the judiciary power be not separated from the legislative and executive."[19]

Total central power and liberty must always run counter to each other; one or the other will prevail. The American Revolution succeeded because, rather than power, it selected liberty as its goal. The Declaration of Independence, signed in 1776, reflects the Enlightenment in the British colonies and a follow-through of the growing philosophy that humankind derives its liberty from "the Creator" and not from man.

We hold these truths to be self-evident, that all men are created equal, that they are endowed by their Creator with certain unalienable rights, that among these are Life, Liberty, and the Pursuit of Happiness.

The individual, not some mythical collective, is the center of a just society. Rights precede government. Individuals cannot be denied their rights, nor can rights be undermined by political authority. This was revolutionary philosophy—and it produced a successful revolution in individual liberty.

The colonists' disdain for lawyers is an indication of their widespread distrust of centralized government and its bureaucratized law. They looked to common law, with its trial by jury, instead of to bureaucracy and a central administration.

Virginia excluded lawyers from its courts. No lawyer profession existed in South Carolina until 1699, when Nicholas Trott appeared and was widely shunned. It was said that in Pennsylvania, "they have no lawyers. Everyone is to tell his own case, or some friend for him . . . 'Tis a happy country."[20]

Skip to today, when hordes of lawyers in the United States, one for every three hundred citizens, descend like locusts to right every wrong—and collect the big dough in cases ranging from a cup of spilled hot coffee to a "victim" offended by some perceived slight. Politics is full of lawyers quibbling over our liberties like flocks of vultures. First thing we hear is, "I'll call my lawyer!"

The thirteen English colonies fought a bitter war of rebellion against the mother country and won independence. The nation that arose out of conflict was the first in human history predicated upon the premise that government works for the people, not the other way around.

"The grand end of civil government," declared Samuel Adams, "from the very nature of its institution, is for the support, protection, and defence of [individual liberty]." In other words, the state is the servant of the individual.

The individual has reigned long enough.

—LESTER F. WARD

THE HAUNTING

Hairy and bearded, looking as if he may have emerged from the Louisiana bayous instead of Germany, Karl Marx (1818–1883) might in appearance well be one of the Robertson clan from the popular reality series *Duck Dynasty* were he alive today. Except the Robertsons would probably drown his fat butt in the swamps over his claptrap about Christianity being the "opiate of the masses" and how there should be no private property, not even a duck call or a coon dog.

Directly or indirectly, the *Communist Manifesto*, penned by Marx and Friedrich Engels (1848), has dealt more death and destruction than any other single social/political philosophy in the history of the world. Like Satan, it keeps on haunting generation after generation.

While studying law at the University of Berlin, Karl Marx, son of a Jewish lawyer who converted to Christianity, got caught up in Hegel's dialectic, the idea that all things are in continuous conflict due to innate contradictions. From that, he drew his theory of "objective economic development," which he termed the "dialectical process."

The earliest stage of economic activity, he believed, is primitive communism, in which tribes and clans share for the common good. Primitive communism passes into the slave system of ancient Greece and Rome, which in turn gives way to the feudal system and then to capitalism. Theoretically, capitalism evolves into the final stage of the "dialectic," this being "pure" Communism. Each transition to a more advanced stage is inevitably punctuated by intense class warfare and political revolution.

For Marx, economics was the primary engine, if in fact not the *only* engine, that powered all social systems. He saw the main division in modern society as being between those who own the means of production, the *bourgeoisie,* and those who do not, the *proletariat,* who are exploited by the bourgeoisie. In their competition for jobs, the vast armies of the proletariat keep wages down to subsistence levels and allow wealth to accumulate at the top. The only way out is through violent revolution that places workers in charge of the economy.

Pure Communism, he stressed, will not immediately prevail following revolution. Instead, a socialist transition period, a "dictatorship of the proletariat," will rule until men learn how to live together and the state "withers away."[21] This transition, Marx insisted, is *not* a dictatorship in the conventional sense. It is a democracy in which the proletariat exercises dictatorship over the remnants of the bourgeoisie. Society's producers will be caged for the benefit of society and the common good.

Once the state and government become unnecessary and wither away, everything will be owned in common—a Communist utopia in which all humankind is equal in outcome, private property is abolished, and everyone lives happily ever after, chanting *Kumbaya.*

Trouble with Marxism is that it never advances beyond the "dictatorship of the proletariat" stage.

Marx's radical proselyting in Germany soon caught the attention of the authorities. He sought refuge in Paris, only to have his welcome wear out there as well. He fled to London, where he acquired himself a "sugar daddy" named Friedrich Engels to support him and his growing family. Most revolutionaries throughout history would rather plot than work as long as someone else pays the bills. Thus the *Manifesto* began, "A spectre is haunting Europe—the spectre of communism."[22]

It concluded with "Let the ruling classes tremble at a Communistic revolution. The proletarians have nothing to lose but their chains. They have a world to win. Working Men of All Countries, Unite!" Elsewhere we read: "The proletariat will use its political supremacy to wrest, by degrees, all capital from the bourgeoisie, to centralize all instruments of production in the hands of the state, i.e., of the proletariat organized as the ruling class; and to increase the total of productive forces as rapidly as possible."

Marx and Engels listed the objectives of Communism once the proletariat take over the state:

Abolition of property in land and application of all rents of land to public purposes.

A heavy progressive and graduated income tax.

Abolition of all rights of inheritance.

Confiscation of the property of all emigrants and rebels.

Centralisation of credit in the hands of the state, by means of a national bank with state capital and an exclusive monopoly.

Centralisation of the means of communication and transport in the hands of the state.

Extension of factories and instruments of production owned by the state . . .

. . . Establishment of industrial armies, especially for agriculture.

Combination of agriculture with manufacturing industries; gradual abolition of the distinction between town and country by a more equitable distribution of the population over the country.

Free education for all children in all public schools . . .

"The theory of the Communists," Marx concluded, "may be summed up in the single sentence: Abolition of private property."

Although the roots of Marxism may be withered and stunted, they run deep and continue to resist eradication. Notice how the monster in so many horror movies refuses to die. No matter how many times the good guys knock him down, there he is in the next scene, as big and mean and hairy as ever.

2

COLLECTIVISM: THE EXPANSION

Our worst enemies . . . are not the ignorant and the simple, however cruel; our worst enemies are the intelligent and corrupt.

—GRAHAM GREENE

THE TWENTIETH CENTURY brought the modern police state and the communal economy, mass mobilization and mass propaganda, routine terror and mechanized murder. From about 1920 to 1954, the Soviets and Nazis together exterminated more than 30 million people, mostly from the ranks of their own citizens. Gassed, shot, starved, or worked to death.

In *Life Expectancy,* novelist Dean Koontz perhaps best expressed the advent of Marxist collectivism: "We feel the pull of the mindless herd, the allure of the pack, but we resist the extreme effects of this influence—and when we do not, we drag our societies down into the bloody wreckage of failed utopias led by Hitler or Lenin, or Mao Tse-tung. And the wreckage reminds us that God gave us our individualism and that to surrender it is to follow a dark path."[1]

LENIN: THE DARK PATH

The *Communist Manifesto* was already making its devil's mark upon the world by the time Vladimir Ilyich Lenin arrived on the revolutionary scene. Born in 1870 to a well-educated and cultured family, he was seventeen when his older brother was hanged for conspiring to assassinate Tsar Alexander. That event undoubtedly influenced Vladimir's radicalization and involvement in the revolutionary unrest and discontent that plagued Russia in the first few years of the twentieth century.

Young Vladimir became steeped in Marxist doctrine while studying to become a lawyer. He subsequently published a small pamphlet in 1902 entitled *What Is to Be Done?* In it, he regurgitated the Marxist dogma that the proletariat would spontaneously rise up to destroy capitalism. However, he added, in order to be successful, the proletariat required leadership to create, recruit, and train a vanguard of professional revolutionaries to incite and lead the workers' revolt. Marxists into the twenty-first century stand by his insight. "Spontaneous peoples movements" always need professional "community organizers" to show them the way.

The social upheaval of World War I provided the catalyst that bred Lenin's Communist revolution. The viciousness of the trenches spilled over into the cities and countryside of Europe, inciting political violence, coups and attempted coups, and the rise of various groups and dictators backed by zealots and young "idealists" striving to turn the general crisis to their own advantage.

In Russia, Lenin's professional revolutionaries infiltrated cells into existing social, political, educational, and economic structures to subvert and agitate—schools, labor unions, churches, political parties, police, armed forces, and the tsar's own government. Lenin emphasized that *nothing* must stand in the way of achieving utopia.

In April 1917, Lenin; his new right-hand man, Joseph Stalin; and the Bolsheviks set events into motion to force Tsar Nicholas II to abdicate. Riots in the tsarist capital of Petrograd, fomented in large part by Lenin and his gangsters, led to food shortages, the closing of factories, and hordes of worker-rioters thrown onto city streets.

Lenin and Stalin convinced the Communist Central Committee

that it was time for the armed uprising. On October 21, the Bolsheviks' Military Revolutionary Council took over the Petrograd Army garrison, seized the famous Peter and Paul Fortress, deposed the tsar, murdered most of the royal family, and installed a provisional government under moderate socialist Aleksandr Kerensky.

Three days later, Lenin called in the Red Guard and tossed Kerensky out on his butt. Lenin's short reign (1917–1924) became noted for brutality that only Stalin's later exceeded. He immediately began imposing socialism by force and terror through a state secret police far more brutal than any under the tsar. He was prepared, he wrote in an article for *Pravda*, to use terror where necessary in "the interests of the workers, soldiers and peasants."[2]

Lenin's policies followed the Marxist formula: abolishment of private property; dissolution of the family unit and its replacement by government; destruction of religion; and nationalization of banking and all means of production.

He issued a "decree of the press" to close down all newspapers published by the bourgeoisie. Any other "worker" presses that incited resistance to the new regime would also be shut down and their publishers, editors, and reporters likely hung.

John Reed, an American Communist who chronicled Lenin's rise, included the Declaration of the Rights of the Peoples of Russia in his *Ten Days That Shook the World*. One phrase read: "We Bolsheviki have always said that when we reached a position of power we would close the bourgeois press. To tolerate the bourgeois newspapers would mean to cease being a Socialist. When one makes a Revolution . . . one must always go forward—or go back. He who now talks about the 'freedom of the Press' goes backward, and halts our headlong course toward Socialism."[3]

On January 20, 1918, Lenin issued another decree banning religion from the socialist state by ordering separation of church and state and church and school. Religious symbols were torn from all public buildings, church holdings confiscated. The Unified State Political Directorate (OGPU), the secret police, began rounding up monks, nuns, priests, and other Orthodox believers and sending them either into exile or to concentration camps.

Religious education of children became a political crime. Parents could be arrested for openly declaring their convictions or for bringing up children on religious principles.

"You can pray freely," poet Tanya Khodkevish noted, "but just so God alone can hear."[4]

On July 22, 1918, another decree—what might today be called an "executive order"—bluntly informed the nation's farmers that they and whatever they produced were being nationalized and that "those guilty of selling, or buying up, or keeping for sale in the business of food products what have been placed under the monopoly of the Republic (will receive) imprisonment for a time of not less than ten years, combined with the most severe forced labor and confiscation of all property."[5]

The measure led to peasant revolts and retaliatory repression that resulted in the Great Famine of 1920–21. Hundreds of thousands of peasants starved to death while their harvests were seized for city workers and industrialization.

"The good of the revolution," Lenin proclaimed, "the good of the working class, is the highest law."[6]

Critics could be arrested simply for speaking out in private conversations. Parents hid in closets or went into the woods to talk for fear their own children would denounce them.

Concentration camps, soon to be known as the *gulag*, were established to imprison hundreds of thousands of "enemies of the people." Entire families, from granny down to toddlers and babes in arms, were sent into exile.

Presumably, there would be no need for prison or police once the state dissolved itself into pure Communism and people became accustomed to complete happiness and earthly salvation.

A Russian general who opposed the Bolshevik takeover of Russia shocked the West when he disclosed the source of funds that supported the revolution.

"The main purveyors," Arsene de Goulévitch wrote in *Czarism and the Revolution*, "were neither the crackpot Russian millionaires nor the armed bandits of Lenin. The 'real' money primarily came from certain British and American circles which for a long time past had lent their support to the Russian revolutionary cause."[7]

Vladimir Lenin's Communist utopia had not yet arrived when he died at age fifty-three on January 21, 1924. Joseph Stalin stepped in from the wings to take over. Lenin might be considered only the warm-up act for what followed.

Wherever justice is uncertain and police spying and terror are at work, human beings fall into isolation, which, of course, is the aim and purpose of the dictator state.

—CARL JUNG

THE SUPERFLUOUS MAN

The key to comprehending collectivism is in understanding its ability to deprive human beings crushed by mass society and totalitarian regimes of their right to be regarded as humans. Hannah Arendt proffered the uncomfortable idea of the "superfluous man," meaning in this context "unnecessary, expendable."[8]

After Vladimir Lenin died, Joseph Stalin declared war on superfluous man to either break him to the harness or eliminate him. In *Road to Serfdom*, Friedrich A. Hayek deliberated over why it seems the worst people end up atop the political heap. "There will be special opportunities for the ruthless and unscrupulous. . . . The readiness to do bad things becomes a path to promotion and power."[9]

Iosif Vissarionovich Dzhugashvili, who assumed the "revolutionary" name "Joseph Stalin," was born December 21, 1879. He came up a troubled kid in the Russian province of Georgia, the youngest of three children born to a drunken, abusive cobbler named Vissarion Dzhugashvili and his wife, Ekaterina. The two firstborn sons of the couple died in infancy, leaving Joseph doted on by his mother and whipped and belittled by his sottish father. Vissarion sometimes thrashed his son so soundly that the kid peed blood.

Remarkable how often tyrants start out in abusive and dysfunctional households.

Stalin was a committed Marxist by the time he fell under the blood-thirsty spell of Vladimir Lenin. The two Bolshevik leaders utilized three classic methods of gaining power that have often been replicated.

First, they presented themselves as populists, members of a "people's party" dedicated to liberty, democracy, and "social justice."

Second, they employed dirty tricks, influence, and persuasion to infiltrate and control political parties, trade unions, and other social institutions.

Finally, there was always force, if all else failed. Lenin is said to have remarked how the Bolsheviks stood for acquiring power through the ballot but would reconsider their stand once they obtained guns.

Stalin held delusions that under his leadership the entire globe would turn Communist. The year Lenin died and Stalin took power, he published *Foundations of Leninism*, in which he divided the world into utopian socialism on the one side and evil capitalism and imperialism on the other. The Soviet Union would lead a coalition of Communist countries in overthrowing capitalism and attaining global domination. The only way capitalist countries could avoid war was to realize the hopelessness of resistance and surrender preemptively.

Stalin ruled for nearly thirty years with almost unlimited power to starve, execute, or work to death millions of his own countrymen. Not content with seizing only economic and political power, he exerted dictatorial control over virtually every aspect of Soviet life. Jobs, education, medical care, housing—*everything* came under the purview of Stalin and the Party. The individual became completely dependent upon the state. The human mind is collectivism's most dangerous enemy. It must therefore be dominated or destroyed. It is not possible to achieve utopia if individuals are free to go their own way.

"Socialism," Chuck Morse wrote in *Was Hitler a Leftist?* "replaces the virtues of self-interest, love, loyalty, integrity, honesty, family, the right to trade goods and ideas freely, the right to free association and voluntary community, representative government, national sovereignty, and, indeed, individual identity itself with measures that the socialist believes will march human society forward in the utopian direction of world collectivism and absolute equality which is viewed by the socialists as the ultimate virtue."[10]

Faced with a faltering economy three years before he died, Lenin had relaxed his stranglehold on Russia enough to allow some free enterprise through his New Economic Policy (NEP). Stalin did away with NEP in order to put Communist principles into immediate practice. His Five-Year Plan for rapid industrialization included nationalizing all means of production, taking over private banks, farms, retail shops, and other businesses and enterprises. If you were a cobbler, local Party bosses told you how many shoes to manufacture, to whom you must sell them, and how much they were worth. If you objected, you were arrested as "socially dangerous," and your business and equipment were confiscated. Only skilled essential workers, civil servants, and Party members felt relatively safe from "Special Citizens Boards" established to keep questionable people under surveillance and to imprison or exile them on the slightest pretense.

The entire Soviet system sat on a bedrock of police coercion and repression, on forced labor, manipulation, and perversion of law into an instrument solely of power. The Party strove constantly to keep different ethnic and class groups at each other's throats. A divided nation cannot concentrate on the real problems.

Secret police and the army formed interlocking agencies to run the state at the dictator's bidding. Those who refused to believe they were living in Paradise had to be converted by force. Resistance brought a midnight knock at the door and a bullet to the back of the head in the basement of the Lubyanka, the Moscow headquarters of the state police.

Family and religion were considered Communism's greatest threats.

Stalin's Soviet Union set about to wreck the family unit by incrementally stripping it of all means of social support in order to substitute in its place "the State." Women were encouraged to leave home and take jobs that required communal living in dormitories. Those conscripted into the labor force aborted most children and placed the survivors in day care. The average woman aborted between five and ten children in her lifetime.

Life was equally hostile to the new Soviet family man. He, too, was simply a worker ant in a colony that became increasingly superfluous to women and children.

Soviet Communists considered belief in God to be backward and even counterrevolutionary. Religion had to be broken to the socialist harness on the way to establishing utopia. Merely talking to a priest could get you arrested. During the twenty-year period ending in 1937, the Soviets executed some two hundred thousand clergy and believers, an average of nearly three people a day. Over half the existing clergy in Russia was murdered.

Article 19 of the Criminal Code stated that no overt action had to actually take place in order for a crime to occur; mere *intent* was sufficient. People were not only incarcerated and executed for having *done* something; they were imprisoned and executed to *keep them from doing something.* For example, one could be imprisoned or executed if he displayed "social hostility" or held "suspicious sentiments."

Formerly successful people and the educated, those who might actually *think*, were some of the first to fall. Citizens were arrested for crimes such as "concealment of social origins." If you graduated from a university, you might be guilty of "individual nobility."

Writers and journalists vanished so quickly no one bothered erasing old names off the doors of the offices of newspapers and other publications to put up new ones. Only fifty of the seven hundred writers who attended the First Congress of Soviet Writers in 1934 survived the terror. The lesson was clear: "If you think, don't speak. If you speak, don't write. If you write, don't publish. If you publish, recant immediately."

More than five thousand leading Ukrainians—scholars, scientists, and cultural and religious leaders—were arrested and falsely accused of being "wreckers" or of plotting counterrevolution. Most were deposited in prison camps or shot without trial.

Intellectuals, restless students, and a variety of eccentrics, truth seekers, and fools, those who were thorns in the buttocks of a well-ordered regime, accompanied them. The most minor "crimes" got you sent to the labor camps.

Late for work on three separate occasions—down for three years. Stealing a radish left in a field to rot after harvest—ten years. A really *serious* crime, like cracking a joke about a Party official—twenty-five years.

Aleksandr Solzhenitsyn, future author of *The Gulag Archipelago,* was arrested and sent to Butyrkie Prison. His crime? Corresponding with a suspicious school friend.

"For several decades," he later wrote, "political arrests were distinguished in our country precisely by the fact that people were arrested who were guilty of nothing and were therefore unprepared to put up any resistance whatsoever."[11]

In 1936 alone, Stalin and the Communist Party sent five million "rich farmer" kulaks, two million artisans, and one million merchants to forced labor. The gulag eventually included 476 institutions, some of which contained more than twenty thousand prisoners each. Four million inmates vanished without a trace.

The gulag provided cheap labor to support Stalin's Five-Year Plan. Like the Egyptian slaves who built the pyramids, these more-contemporary slaves constructed giant canals, built roads and factories, and worked in mines to modernize the Soviet Union. Estimated camp deaths range from a low of about 15 million up to 30 million. The exact number will never be known.

"You are not brought here to live," an NKVD "camp doctor" is reported to have lectured inmates, "but to suffer and die. If you live, it means that you are guilty of two things: Either you worked less than assigned, or you ate more than your proper due."[12]

Russian author Varlam Shalamov survived twenty years in the gulag. "Each time they brought in the soup," he recalled, ". . . it made us all want to cry. We were ready to cry for fear that the soup would be thin. And when a miracle occurred and the soup was thick, we couldn't believe it and ate it as slowly as possible. But even with thick soup in a warm stomach there remained a sucking pain; we'd been hungry for too long. All human emotions—love, friendship, envy, concern for one's fellow man, compassion, longing for fame, honesty—had left us with the flesh that had melted from our bodies."[13]

Prison commandants were given free rein to execute at the slightest slowdown in production. At the Kolyma concentration camps, death could be dealt for saying the work was too hard, for not responding quickly enough to a guard's order, or merely for remaining silent when a crowd of prisoners was required to shout in unison "Long live Stalin!"

Above the entire system of socialist "transformation" stood Joseph Stalin, "Father of Nations, Brilliant Genius of Humanity, Gardener of Human Happiness, Great Architect of Communism."[14] Huge images of him appeared everywhere—on the sides of public buildings, in numerous Roman-like statues in public parks, where pigeons caught crapping on his noble bronze head were undoubtedly trapped and executed.

While George Orwell may have popularized the slogan "Big Brother is watching you," Stalin put it to practical use. Propaganda posters stuck on the walls of Soviet buildings depicted a large eye watching over a work camp. The caption below stated in cold terms: "GPU—The Unblinking Eye of The Proletarian Dictatorship."

"What would Comrade Stalin do?" people asked each other before making any of the few important decisions left to them about their lives.

People all but prayed to his image.

"I write books . . . All thanks to thee, O great educator Stalin," effused Russian author A. O. Avidenko. "I love a young woman with a renewed love and shall perpetuate myself in my children—all thanks to thee, great educator Stalin. Everything belongs to thee, chief of our great country. And when the woman I love presents me with a child the first word it shall utter will be: Stalin."[15]

In spite of the mass deaths, starvation and wholesale incarceration of Russian citizens, many intellectuals and journalists in the West continued to blindingly support Stalin's efforts to mold a new socialist world.

New Masses magazine in the United States drooled admiration for the "noble experiment" Comrade Stalin had undertaken: "As long as the Red Flag waves over the Kremlin, there is hope in the world. There is something in the air of Soviet Russia that throbbed in the air of Pericles' Athens, the England of Shakespeare, the France of Damon, the America of Walt Whitman. . . . This is the first man learning in agony and joy how to think. Where else is there hope in the world?"[16]

Walter Duranty of the *New York Times* preached that the concentration camps were not *actually* concentration camps. In his words, they only existed to "remove subversive individuals from their familiar milieu to a remote spot where their potentially harmful activities will be mollified . . .where such misguided persons will be given a chance to regain by honest toil their lost citizenship in the Socialist fatherland . . . They are fed and housed gratis and receive pay for their work . . . They are certainly not convicts in the American sense of the word."

Aleksandr Solzhenitsyn, who had experienced the reality of the superfluous man system, was not enamored. "Communism is irredeemable," he warned. ". . . It cannot survive as an ideology without using terror, and that, consequently, to coexist with communism on the same planet is impossible. Either it will spread, cancer-like, to destroy mankind, or else mankind will have to rid itself of communism."[17]

If you clung to the truth even against the whole world, you were not mad.
                                                            —GEORGE ORWELL

CRACKING EGGS

Most of the outside world ignored what was happening in the Soviet Union during the Lenin and Stalin period, partly because of the secrecy and subterfuge under which it occurred, partly because much of the West was enamored with Marxism and didn't *want* to see it. Willful blindness became the twentieth century's default position when it came to collectivist activities.

"You can't make an omelet without breaking eggs," cryptically remarked *New York Times* reporter Walter Duranty, whose sympathies lay unabashedly with Communism.[18]

Horrendous as the Great Terror was that purged Stalin's government of thousands of prospective enemies from the ranks of government officials, army officers, Soviet Security officials, and others whom Stalin viewed as suspicious, it was no match for the largest mass killings in world history—the Stalin-directed famine between 1928 and 1933 during which at least ten million of Russia's own citizens starved to death. Millions of others were deported to labor camps in Siberia, where another large percentage died from starvation, disease, and labor.

Although himself a Communist sympathizer, British journalist Malcolm Muggeridge smuggled back to England one of only a few honest reports about Stalin's efforts to collectivize agriculture by forcing more than 25 million farm households to give up their land and move onto communal farms called *kolkhozes*.

"The novelty of this particular famine," he confessed, "what made it so diabolical, is that it was not the result of some catastrophe like a drought or an epidemic. It was the deliberate creation of a bureaucratic mind which demands the collectivization of agriculture . . . without any consideration whatever of the consequences in human suffering."[19]

Initially, peasants resisted giving up the family goat. They slaughtered livestock and destroyed crops rather than turn everything over to the state. Bolder peasants even attacked Stalin's enforcers with pitchforks and shotguns. Stalin responded with overwhelming force, exorbitant taxation, and calculated class warfare against *kulaks*—"rich farmers" who had worked hard and prospered. A farm family with even two cows and a mule might be considered kulaks.

He declared that the kulaks "as a class" must be eliminated with a new Soviet "offensive . . . We have passed from the policy of restricting the exploiting tendency of the kulaks to the policy of eliminating the kulaks as a class."[20]

While the Great Depression raged around the globe, the Soviet Union eliminated millions of its best producers for ideological purposes. Peasants whose labors had fed the nation were uprooted by Young Soviets and other "officials" sent in from the outside. Like raging predators, these representatives of the "workers" rounded up the very best farmers and their families and exiled them, stripped of their possessions, into the northern wastes. Fifteen million peasants were arrested in 1929–30 alone, and either forcibly transported to labor camps or executed.

According to article 58 of the Russian Soviet Federative Socialist Republic (RSFSR) Penal Code, any action or *absence* of action directed toward the weakening of state power was deemed counterrevolutionary.

A little girl caught hiding a single potato during harvest was sentenced to a labor camp for "stealing from the people."

A peasant with six children devoted himself so diligently to collective farm work, the better to avoid censure, that he was presented a special award at an assembly. He rose to declare his gratitude.

"Now, if I could just have a sack of flour instead of this decoration . . ." he began haltingly. "Couldn't I somehow?"[21]

He was arrested as a counterrevolutionary and sent into exile with his wife and children.

"It took a famine to show the peasants who is the master here," declared Mendel Khataevich, a Stalin lieutenant. "It cost millions of lives, but the collective farm system is here to stay."[22]

As famine and mass starvation swept the land, it was said the good people died first—those who refused to steal, to prostitute themselves, who gave food to others.

"The first who died were the men," wrote a Soviet author, "later on the children. And the last of all, the women. But before they died, people often lost their senses and ceased to be human beings."[23]

An official document by State Security recorded how "families kill their weakest members, usually children, and use the meat for eating." At least twenty-five hundred people were sentenced for cannibalism in the Ukraine during the two years of 1932–33. The actual rate of cannibalism was certainly much higher. Black markets dealt in human flesh.[24]

One mother cooked her son for herself and her daughter in order to survive.[25] Older children often relayed this message to their siblings: "Mother says that we should eat her if she dies."

Women who ran an orphanage in the Kharkiv region recalled Little Petrus: "One day the children suddenly fell silent. We turned around to see what was happening, and they were eating the smallest child, little Petrus. They were tearing strips from him and eating them. And Petrus was doing the same, he was tearing strips from himself and eating them. . . . The other children put their lips to his wounds and drank his blood. We took the child away from their hungry mouths and we cried."[26]

Horrifyingly enough, foreign Communists somehow reconciled themselves to the idea that the purges, the executions, the starvation were all signs of human progress, that the deaths of the "superfluous" were part of creating a higher civilization.

Walter Duranty of the *New York Times* published a piece in September 1933 that falsely asserted how "the use of the word 'famine' in connection with the North Caucasus is a sheer absurdity. There a bumper crop is being harvested as fast as tractors, horses, oxen, men, women, and children can work. There are plump babies in the nurseries and gardens of the collectives. . . . Village markets are flowing with eggs, fruit, poultry, vegetables, and butter at prices far lower than in Moscow."[27]

In the middle of this tragic period, President Franklin Roosevelt granted the Soviet Union diplomatic recognition and opened an American embassy in Moscow.

Aleksandr Solzhenitsyn issued a warning to the world once he managed to free himself from the gulag and make his way to the United States. "In keeping silent about evil," he said, "in burying it so deep within us that no sign of it appears on the surface, we are *implanting* it, and it will rise up a thousandfold in the future. When we neither punish nor reproach evildoers, we are not simply protecting their trivial old age, we are thereby ripping the foundations of justice from beneath new generations. . . . It is going to be uncomfortable, horrible, to live in such a country."[28]

Heaven . . . was brought to earth . . . in Russia.
—AMERICAN POET TILLIE OLSEN

CAPTURED AMERICANS

The Great Depression convinced many Americans driven off their land by hunger and drought that capitalism was a tired horse starved down to bones and unable to provide jobs and economic progress. Thirteen million Americans, a quarter of the workforce, were unemployed. Bread lines and soup kitchens drew millions all over the nation. Half the country, it seemed, was on the move. Ragged hobos rode the rails and shuffled along dusty roads. Looking for a "hand up," they said, but they'd settle for a "hand out."

President Franklin Roosevelt's first inaugural address to a radio audience of 60 million sounded as if he too had lost faith in free enterprise.

The rulers of the exchange of mankind's goods have failed, through their own stubbornness and their own incompetence, have admitted their failure, and abdicated. Practices of the unscrupulous money changers stand indicted in the court of public opinion, rejected by the hearts and minds of men. . . .

A host of unemployed citizens face the grim problem of existence, and an equally great number toil with little return. Only a foolish optimist can deny the dark realities of the moment. . . .

The money changers have fled from their high seats in the temple of our civilization. We may now restore that temple to the ancient truths.

The measure of the restoration lies in the extent to which we apply social values more noble than mere monetary profit.[29]

According to historian Dennis J. Dunn, FDR subscribed to the theory of "convergence." Capitalism and Communism would each take on some characteristics of the other and "converge" so that neither remained pure in its doctrine. The "welfare state" that began in America during Roosevelt's administration, and exists today in an even more encompassing capacity, is an example.[30]

Either ignorant of or ignoring the reality of purges, famine, concentration camps, and forced labor in the Soviet Union, scores of Western newspapers in their enthusiasm for Stalin's "brave experiment in socialism" celebrated his successes at planning a society that placed workers at its very center and protected them from the greed of capitalists.

"Naturally, the contempt of the Russians for us is enormous," playwright George Bernard Shaw broadcast a lecture that was printed in the *New York Times* on October 11, 1931. "You fools, they are saying to us, why can you not do as we are doing? You cannot employ nor feed your people. . . . [E]very intelligent Russian [who] has been [to] America . . . didn't like it because he had no freedom there. . . . There is hope everywhere because those evils are retreating there before the spread of Communism as steadily as they are advancing upon us before the last desperate struggle of our bankrupt Capitalism to stave off its inevitable doom."[31]

Russia, largely a rural, peasant society, needed skilled industrial workers along with professionals in engineering, medicine, and other occupations. Desperate and out-of-work Americans were lured by the English translation of *New Russia's Primer: The Story of the Five-Year Plan*, whose glowing promise was published and distributed all over the United States:

> All this will be written about us a few decades hence. [The worker] will work less and yet accomplish more. During seven hours in the factory, he will do what now requires eleven and a half hours . . .

Instead of dark, gloomy shops with dim, yellow lamps there will be light, clean halls with great windows and beautiful tile floors. Not the lungs of men, but powerful ventilators will suck in and swallow the dirt, dust and shavings of the factories . . . Socialism is no longer a myth, a phantasy of science . . . We ourselves are building it . . . and this better life will not come as miracle; we must create it. But to create it we need knowledge; we need strong hands, yes, but we need strong minds too.[32]

Drawn by the prospect of work, the American migration to the Soviet Union was the least-heralded in U.S. history. Daily steamships pulled out of New York harbor, bound for Leningrad, each packed with auto workers, laborers, tradesmen, artisans, and others clasping their hopes of a bright new world, ready to *believe* in the promise of socialism and trust their lives to Uncle Joe and Karl Marx. During the first eight months of 1931 alone, the Soviet Trade Agency headquartered in New York processed more than a hundred thousand American applications for emigration to the USSR.[33]

Edmund Burke, the eighteenth-century philosopher, famously noted that "the people never give up their liberties but under some delusion."

Disillusionment set in among the American expatriates as soon as they arrived in the USSR, where their passports were seized and they were advised they had become Soviet citizens.

While the Soviet Union claimed to be a classless society with equality from the humblest pig farmer on a collective farm to Comrade Stalin luxuriating in his Moscow dacha, an American auto worker in Moscow counted six different classes of retail shops catering goods of varying quality to customers according to their social status. The best of everything, of course, was reserved for those on the highest rung of the classless ladder. As many as seventeen different categories of food and goods were rationed and issued in these retail shops to "citizens" according to their standings.[34]

Workers of the world unite—and then divide yourselves into categories of privilege!

In 1935, immigrant John Match smuggled a handwritten letter to the U.S. State Department through the American Embassy in Moscow.

"After 8 months of work I decided to go back to the United States," he wrote. "They told me they are not going to give [me] my papers, because they need me as a specialist in the factory . . . They scared me with threats to put me in jail. They kept asking me why I wanted to go to the States, as there is starvation. I told them that I would rather be in jail in America than an employee in the Soviet Union. This made them angry . . . They told me they would rather kill a person like me than let him out of the country."[35]

Thousands of Great Depression–era workers and their families who fled to the "workers paradise" to find jobs never returned to the USA. Not because they didn't *want* to return. They were either executed as "spies" and "reactionary elements" or shipped off to the gulag, where most of them perished from starvation and overwork. This is a fact never fully acknowledged by the American government, truly one of the most egregious cover-ups of the era.

All-American football great Paul Robeson, a Communist fellow traveler, made a celebrated sojourn to the shrine of the USSR in 1934. He expressed no sympathy for the plight of the so-called captured Americans.

"From what I have already seen of the workings of the Soviet Government," he confided in the *Daily Worker*, "I can only say that anybody who lifts his hand against it ought to be shot! It is the government's duty to put down any opposition to this really free society with a firm hand . . . It is obvious that there is no terror here, that all the masses of every race are contented and support their government."[36]

Uncle Joe Stalin and his Marxist state rode high over the world. His was the future of humankind—never mind that the future would soon expose Communism as least likely to resemble Utopia and most apt to meet George Orwell's assessment of collectivism in his novel *1984:* "If you want a picture of the future, imagine a boot stamping on a human face—for ever."[37]

The world is a dangerous place to live, not because of the people who are evil, but because of the people who don't do anything about it.

—ALBERT EINSTEIN

THE CAGE

The objective of totalitarianism that emerged in the twentieth century was not merely to snatch individual freedom but to cage the bird for the "greater good" and make him fear freedom and favor the security of the cage.

"He who is conceived in a cage yearns for the cage," observed Russian poet Yevgeny Yevtushenko.

Both Communism and fascism bloomed in the twentieth century and are frequently described as two separate phenomena, Communism being far left on the political scale while fascism represents the Far Right and the opposite of Communism. Actually, both are simply different forms of socialism. Both promote essentially the same agenda—supremacy over the individual, with freedom being on the other end of the scale from either.

The only major difference is how each divides the spoils. Communist socialism advocates state ownership of all means of production while fascist socialism demands that government oversee and run the economy. Citizens may continue to hold title to property, or *claim* it, but the state reserves the unqualified right to regulate it and use it as the state sees fit.

Classically, Communism advocates the violent overthrow of the existing structure by "workers" in order to build a new society; it is typically a product of pre-democratic and preindustrial societies in poor and underdeveloped nations. Fascism, on the other hand, rises in *post*-democratic and *post*industrial societies. Put simply, Communism is the totalitarian method of industrializing a backward society, fascism the totalitarian way of organizing a more industrial nation. The modern welfare state is more akin to fascism than to Communism, but is actually a mixture of both.

Both rise to power promising "fairness," "social justice," and "equality." Free education, free health care, free housing, a guaranteed income . . . Like pigs at feeding time, people rush squealing and grunting and running over each other to get to the trough. It has been declared over and over that those who would give up liberty for security ultimately end up bacon.

In the 1930s as the Great Depression gripped Germany, the Weimar Republic began collapsing like a grass hut in a flood. Six million Germans lost their jobs. Civil services and public salaries were reduced, war pensions cut, foreign debt climbed, inflation consumed the German mark. Small business blamed big business; big business blamed labor unions; labor wanted to soak the rich; the unemployed demanded action. Street fighting erupted between Communists and fascists, each of whom offered almost identical solutions.

Austere times called for dramatic measures. Hitler liked to point out that he gained power legally and not at gunpoint in the election of 1932. "One man, one vote, one time" is the political credo of all modern totalitarians. By 1934, the National Socialist German Workers Party (Nazi) had unchallenged rule of Germany. The little man with the Charlie Chaplin mustache and the biggest ego on the continent other than Stalin's was telling the world he intended to change Germany in his own image.

"The [Nazi] Party . . . must not become a servant of the masses, but their master," he blustered in his inimitable style. "The unity of a nation's spirit and will are worth far more than the freedom of the spirit and will of an individual. . . . We are socialists, we are enemies of the capitalist economic system . . . and we are all determined to destroy this system under all conditions."[38]

In 2011, Austrian-born Kitty Werthman, a witness to the Nazi era, chronicled Hitler's ascendency in a Tea Party Rally speech she delivered at Woodstown, New York:

> You might ask, "How could a Christian nation elect a monster like Hitler?" The truth is, at the beginning Hitler didn't look like or talk

like a monster at all. He talked like an American politician. . . . It was a gradual process starting with national identification cards, which we had to carry with us at all times. We could not board a bus or train without our ID cards. Gun registration followed . . . Since the government . . . knew who owned firearms, confiscation followed under threat of capital punishment.[39]

Hitler counted on the triad of irrationalism (lack of common sense), altruism (personal sacrifice), and collectivism (one for all, all for the State) to liberate humanity from its individuality. The Party imposed authority above all personal rights, the group over the individual, sacrifice over happiness, nihilism above morality, feelings above facts, obedience above logic. Human intelligence and progress seemed to stand still, replaced by a strange world where virtually anything would be believed and accepted.

"Hear nothing that we do not wish you to hear," explicated Joseph Goebbels, Hitler's propaganda minister. "See nothing that we do not wish you to see. Believe nothing that we do not wish you to believe. Think nothing that we do not wish you to think."

Germany exploded with occult crazes, medieval rituals, orientalist sects, theosophy, immorality, and debauchery to further seduce citizens away from reality and better accept his cage.

Historical observer Walter Laqueur explained: "The phenomenal revival of astrology and various quasi-religious cults, the great acclaim given to prophets of doom, the success of highly marketable Weltschmerz in literature and philosophy, the spread of pornography and the use of drugs, the appearance of charlatans of every possible description and the enthusiastic audiences welcoming them—all these are common."[40]

"I am freeing man from the restraints of an intelligence that has taken charge," Hitler sermonized, "from the dirty and degrading self-mortifications of a chimera called conscience and morality, and from the demands of a freedom and personal independence which only a few men can bear."[41]

Perhaps not surprisingly, the main source of fascist support came from the lower middle classes, while at the same time its most ardent supporters were college and university students and professors and the general run of so-called intellectuals.

"[Nazi] death camps," the *New York Times* noted, "were conceived, built and often administered by Ph.D.s."[42]

Women provided major Nazi support. George Orwell in *1984* noted this curiosity when it came to women and collectivism. "It was always the women, and above all the young ones, who were the most bigoted adherents of the Party, the swallowers of slogans, the amateur spies and nosers-out of unorthodoxy."[43]

Women in the United States today are a major voter group when it comes to supporting socialist programs and movements. "We don't need men," a young female at Occupy Wall Street in New York scolded. "Government takes care of us better."[44]

Hitler consolidated his power, as Stalin had, by purging his ranks of possible traitors, by massive searches and seizures of firearms, through suspension of civil liberties and restricting basic rights, such as freedom of the press, freedom of speech, and freedom of assembly. Privacy and rule of law were likewise suspended as police ransacked houses and offices for subversive literature and weapons.

Nationalist Socialist Utopia also produced an imposed planned economy, work camps for dissidents; the corralling of labor, sports, and culture through propaganda and coercion; racial purity laws; elimination of Jews from most professions; and, finally, the attempted elimination of Jews and other "undesirables" altogether.

The ominous parallel seeds of Communism and fascism continue to grow weed patches of socialism throughout the world—and always with the same outcome.

All animals are equal but some animals are more equal than others.
—GEORGE ORWELL IN *THE ANIMAL FARM*

A LESSER FORM

Left unchecked, collectivism has a penchant for taking dark and dangerous roads. One such road traced through Adolf Hitler's extermination camps.

I became acquainted with Charles Darwin's *On the Origins of the Species* and *The Descent of Man* as a kid growing up half-wild in the Ozark Mountains of Arkansas and Oklahoma. Living among animals both domesticated and wild, I found natural selection for the health of the species to be perfectly reasonable. A coyote's survival quotient dropped to about zero if he were born defective. A cow prone to throwing deformed calves had to be eliminated from the herd.

Why then, I asked myself, did we allow the breeding of unfit humans?

"With savages," Darwin wrote, "the weak in body or mind are soon eliminated; and them that survive commonly exhibit a vigorous state of health. We civilised men, on the other hand, do our utmost to check the process of elimination; we build asylums for the imbecile, the maimed, and the sick; we institute poor-laws; and our medical men exert the utmost skill to save the life of every one to the last moment . . . Thus the weak members of civilised societies propagate their kind."[45]

My flirtation with eugenics, the definition of which was influenced by Darwin as the science of improving the physical and mental qualities of human beings, lasted for a very brief period—until even my juvenile mind realized I myself might well be selected as one of the undesirables whose line could be marked for extinction. As I continued to study, I learned that many of the so-called great minds that view humankind in the collective and not as individuals never evolve beyond the juvenile stage.

Social planners in both Britain and the United States, with their utopian visions of a perfect world, rallied around "social Darwinism." By the beginning of the twentieth century, the theory of eugenics, of building superior men through proper breeding, had spread throughout the West. To writers and intellectuals such as Thomas Huxley, George Bernard Shaw, and D. H. Lawrence, it seemed perfectly logical that "superiors" should contemplate action against "inferiors" for the greater good of society.

In England, the ideas of Francis J. Galton helped launch a world-wide crusade to abolish human inferiority. The problem, he concluded, "was so clear cut and so dire, as to warrant state intervention of a coercive nature in human reproduction."[46]

Social planning methods he suggested included segregation, depor-tation, castration, prohibition of marriage, and compulsory sterilization. Ultimately, he admitted, it might be necessary to include wholesale extermination of the unfit.

With the rise of Progressivism in the United States, America's finest universities and most reputable scientists piled into the crusade, along with trusted professional, charitable, political, and corporate foundations, such as the Rockefeller Foundation, the American Medical Association, the American Museum of Natural History, and the U.S. State Department's Vital Statistics Bureau. The movement recruited "progressive" advocates from child welfare, prison reform, education, clinical psychology, world peace, immigration rights, and dozens of other groups.

More than forty major educational institutions offered eugenics instruction. *A Civic Biology*, a popular high school text by George William Hunter, railed against unfit families "spreading disease, immo-rality, and crime to all parts of the country. . . . They take from society, but they give nothing in return. They are true parasites."[47]

The Eugenics Records Office (ERO) was established to identify defective and undesirable Americans, estimated to be at least 10 percent of the population, who should be subjected to appropriate remedies to terminate their bloodlines.

Voluntary sterilization, the first step in the eugenics process, soon became involuntary. In 1907, Indiana became the first jurisdiction in the world to enforce sterilization against the mentally impaired, poor-house residents, and prisoners. Three more states ratified similar laws in 1909. In 1911, New Jersey governor Woodrow Wilson, who would become president of the United States the following year, signed a sterilization bill into law.

Wilson was not the only U.S. president to support eugenics. In 1913, former president Theodore Roosevelt privately announced his backing: "Society has no business to permit degenerates to reproduce their kind."[48]

The United States upheld the legality of forced sterilization in 1927 when the Supreme Court ruled against a hapless, feeble-minded teenager named Carrie Buck. "Three generations of imbeciles are enough," Justice Oliver Wendall Holmes Jr. decided.[49]

More than sixty thousand Americans would be involuntarily sterilized in the 1930s. Legalizing a matter goes a long way in persuading people of the moral acceptability of immoral actions.

Eugenicist Margaret Sanger, founder of Planned Parenthood, which gradually evolved into the nation's major abortion provider, referred to the lower classes and "Negroes" as "human waste." She was also one of the first, in 1927, to take eugenics to its logical next step—euthanasia.

"The most merciful thing that the large family does to one of its infant members is to kill it," she wrote.[50] "Nature eliminates the weeds, but we turn them into parasites and allow them to reproduce."[51]

Other eugenicists followed Sanger's lead.

Physician Duncan McKim, author of *Heredity and Human Progress*, decided that the "surest, the simplest, the kindest and most humane means for preventing reproduction among those whom we deem unworthy of that high privilege, is a gentle, painless death. In carbonic acid gas, we have an agent which would instantaneously fulfill the needs."[52]

New York urologist William Robinson in *Eugenics, Marriage and Birth Control*, likewise thought it appropriate to gas children of the unfit. "The best thing would be to gently chloroform these children or to give them a dose of potassium cyanide."[53]

In prewar Germany, the emerging dictator Adolf Hitler developed his own interest in eugenics.

"I have studied with great interest the laws of several American states concerning prevention of reproduction of people whose progeny would in all probability be of no value or be injurious to the racial stock," he told a fellow Nazi.[54]

Individuals and institutions in the United States encouraged and supported his absorption before the outbreak of the war. The Carnegie Institute's Cold Harbor Eugenics Enterprise enthusiastically propagandized for the Nazis. The Rockefeller Foundation provided financial grants to German science. Hitler and his Nazi doctors regularly communicated with American eugenicists and relied extensively on their studies and experiments. Leon Whitney, president of the American Eugenics Society, and Madison Grant, author of *The Passing of A Great Race*, received personal letters from Hitler congratulating them for their studies in eugenics.

As the United States had done over two decades previously, Germany made sterilization compulsory for all people "who suffered from allegedly hereditary disabilities including feeble mindedness, schizophrenia, epilepsy, blindness, severe drug or alcohol addiction, and physical deformities that seriously interfered with locomotion or were grossly offensive."[55]

Hitler's application of social Darwinism was directed toward eliminating unfit humans of all sorts—not only Jews and the mentally and physically unfit, but also homosexuals, Gypsies, Slavs, and other "inferior racial groups," a genocide program that became known as the Holocaust. The full horror of it would not become widely known until after the end of World War II.

What occurred during the Holocaust represented the collective will as much as it did decisions made by one man or any group of men. As with a lynch mob, no one whose individuality is smothered within the collective feels guilty or responsible for deeds committed by the whole.

Doctor David Herbert, in his foreword to Jerry Bergman's *Hitler and the Nazi Darwinian Worldview*, warned that the same naturalistic, collectivist impulse that spawned the atrocities of the World War II era thrive today among Progressive intellectuals and social planners throughout the world.

In 2012, a coalition of scientists representing multiple fields of study in ecology, agriculture, biology and economics met in Washington, D.C., to study the best methods by which to save the planet from overpopulation. The coalition concluded that one-third of the planet's population, at least two billion humans, must die to prevent wide-scale depletion of the earth's resources. Having exceeded earth's sustainable population size, one in three humans must either choose how he wants to die or governments can mandate liquidation programs.

"The earth's carrying capacity will no longer be able to keep up with population growth, and civilization will end unless large swaths of human beings are killed," Cambridge University ecologist Dr. Edwin Peters told *Science & Technology* "So, the question is: How do we want to do this? Do we want to give everyone a number and implement a death lottery system? Incinerate the nation's children? Kill off an entire race of people? Give everyone a shotgun and let them sort it out themselves?"[56]

3

STRUGGLE FOR INDIVIDUALISM

"Freedom is government divided into small fragments."

—THOMAS HOBBES

AS A KID GROWING UP ON THE OKLAHOMA–ARKANSAS BORDER, I roamed the Ozarks with an old shotgun and a hound, fishing and hunting and living off the land, sleeping nights on the ground next to a campfire. A free spirit, with no one to regulate, spindle, fold, or mutilate. It was the sort of environment that molded early American character and led to the Declaration of Independence, the Constitution, and the idea that individual liberty is the natural order of things and comes from God and not man.

THE BEGINNING STRUGGLE

Privileged classes in Old World Europe rarely had the guts and incentive to climb aboard leaky wooden ships to set sail for a wild and unknown land on the other side of a vast and turbulent ocean. They stayed home and powdered their wigs. Those who set off to build new homes in the wilderness were a hardy and adventurous lot, ranging from religious zealots and opportunity seekers to stowaways and indentured servants. What they possessed in common was a dream that they might escape the bonds of the onerous and suffocating collectivism that dominated the rest of the world and start fresh by virtue of determination and their own wits.

Historian Frederick Jackson Turner believed the frontier was the reason there was almost no socialism in America before the twentieth century, with the exception of the earliest colonies, such as Plymouth Rock and Jamestown. If a man didn't like the way things were being run in his settlement, he could always pack his bags, saddle his cayuse, and ride off into the sunset.

"The tendency [of the frontiersman] is anti-social," Turner elaborated. "It produces antipathy to control, and particularly to any direct control."[1]

"West is where we all plan to go some day," Robert Penn Warren wrote in *All the King's Men.* "It is where you go when the land gives out and the old-field pines encroach."[2]

The New Americans brought little of their European baggage with them: none of the aristocrats, guilds, old monopolies, or hereditary titles. What they packed with them instead were ideas from the Enlightenment and classic liberalism.

Classical liberalism, history professor Ralph Raico explained, "is the term used to designate the ideology of advocating private property, an unhampered market economy, the rule of law, constitutional guarantees of freedom of religion and of the press, and international peace based on free trade and strength."[3]

While it may have been the foundation of the American republic, it was an entirely different animal from today's "liberalism" and "Progressivism."

Adam Smith (1727–1790), author of *Wealth of Nations,* was one of the most influential of the early classic liberals. His "invisible hand" formulation in economics laid the groundwork for laissez-faire capitalism. He, along with those who came after him of a like mind, such as Ludwig von Mises and Milton Friedman, attributed the growth of wealth to the production of goods according to the demands of an open marketplace. In seeking their own wealth, men who freely compete in the market with minimal interference from government enrich the entire society as if being directed by the "invisible hand" of nature.[4] People form relationships for mutual benefit on the basis of voluntary exchanges.

The system is based on private ownership of the means of production; free competition in an open market; personal risk taking leading to profit or loss; success or failure based on the quality of one's decisions. In all this, government is designed to play but a minimal role.

"According to the system of natural liberty," Smith wrote, "the sovereign [government] has only three duties to attend to: . . . first, the duty of protecting the society from violence and invasion of other independent societies [national defense]; secondly, the duty of protecting, as far as possible, every member of the society from the injustice and oppression of every other member of it, or the duty of establishing an exact administration of justice (police and courts based on rule of law); and, thirdly, duty of erecting and maintaining certain public works and certain public institutions [roads and bridges], which it can never be for the interest of any individual, or small number of individuals to erect and maintain."[5]

Conflict between the individual and the state, between liberty and tyranny, is present in every political venue. Italy's Benito Mussolini, who formed the third arm of the Axis power during World War II, evaluated this constant strain between individual and state: "There is the great, silent, continuous struggle: the struggle between the State and the Individual; between the State which demands and the Individual who attempts to evade such demands. Because the Individual, left to himself, unless he be a saint or hero, always refuses to pay taxes, obey laws, or go to war."[6]

America's Founding Fathers faced this conundrum long before Mussolini came along to solve it in favor of the State. Their solution was to place the lives of citizens as much as possible out of the grasp of predatory politicians by, as Charles Montesquieu recommended, fracturing and dividing government into three branches—executive, legislative, and judicial, each of which would jealously guard its power against encroachment from the other branches and thereby never surrender to centralized control.

The Constitution "is not an instrument for the government to restrain the people, it is an instrument for the people to restrain the government." So goes a quote often misattributed to Patrick Henry.

In spite of the Founders' distrust of government, tendencies to engorge the future Leviathan began almost before the ink dried on the ratified Constitution. It is a testament to the insidious growth of state power that no less than George Washington was president when the process began.

The tea tax imposed against the colonies by Britain remained fresh in the minds of citizens of the new United States in 1791 when Washington listened to treasury secretary Alexander Hamilton and levied a tax on whiskey that farmers brewed from leftover grain and used for trading. Farmers in western Pennsylvania responded with the so-called Whiskey Rebellion and began tarring and feathering tax collectors. Jesus had once tossed tax collectors out of the temple (see Matthew 21:12–13 NIV)—and now Pennsylvania was running them out of the state. Tax collectors throughout history have enjoyed a reputation somewhere between that of snakes and alley cats.

At Hamilton's urging, Washington dispatched armed federal troops to suppress the rebellion so that, as Hamilton put it, "the authority of the national government shall be visible."[7]

Fallout from the rebellion contributed to the formation of political parties in the United States. Thomas Jefferson, a member of the new Republican Party and an opponent of Hamilton's Federalist Party, repealed the whiskey tax when he took the presidency in 1801.

The second major step toward extending the reach of the federal government took place under President Abraham Lincoln during the Civil War. As with all disasters and threats, war provides justification for a nation to consolidate under collective management in response to "an enemy at the gate." Although Lincoln's actions may have been necessary in order to preserve the Union, they demonstrate how fragile democracy can be under pressure.

Lincoln imposed an income tax to finance the war; suspended due process of law and tossed thousands of New Yorkers and Ohioans in jail for opposing the war; shut down some three hundred independent newspapers because they disagreed with him; censored all telegraph communications; arrested the mayor of Baltimore and a majority of the Maryland legislature when they opposed the war; disarmed everyone in states that bordered the Confederacy; and sent federal troops to New York City to battle opponents of his policies.

"The national government that emerged victorious from the conflict dwarfed in power and size the minimal Jacksonian State that had commenced the war," historian Jeffrey Rogers Hummel noted in *Emancipating Slaves, Enslaving Free Men: A History of The American Civil War.*[8]

The old federation of sovereign states was shattered forever as the national government began its surge into realms not established in the U.S. Constitution.

America lasted less than a century before collectivism encroached even more significantly upon the individual. By the middle of the twentieth century, few practical remnants of classical liberalism survived as it deteriorated into the "new liberalism" of the Progressive Era that canonized central government power, federal "tax and spend" policies, federal meddling in local and economic matters, and opened new boundaries for the arrival of the welfare state and the interventionist state.

You couldn't see Big Brother, but he waited just over the horizon, and you could hear him chortling and flirting with Karl Marx.

*The shaft of the arrow has been feathered with one of the eagle's own
plumes. We often give our enemies the means of our own destruction."*

—AESOP

PROGRESSIVE OR REGRESSIVE

The rugged frontier mentality, with its belief in free enterprise and individual initiative with a minimum of government interference, lingered
on in America longer than in the rest of the Western world. Still, by the
advent of the "Progressive Era" in the early twentieth century, public
opinion had become susceptible to accepting increased participation
and interference by a central government. "Progressivism" might be best
defined as the ascendency of government over the individual.

"The Victorian and Progressive Period movements," wrote David
Wagner in *The New Temperance: The American Obsession with Sin and
Vice,* "were characterized by what scholarly observers consider an exaggerated . . . notion of their ability to change behavior by a huge faith in
government's ability to regulate every aspect of private life."[9]

Quite a step removed from the intentions of America's Founding
Fathers. Thus began the underlying assumption of the budding
Progressive Movement that government *allowed.* Government was
always the final authority.

"You didn't build that," presidential candidate Barack Obama
scolded in a 2012 election campaign speech, the implication being that
government *allowed* business to be built.

Chancellor Otto von Bismarck may be credited with originating the
modern welfare state in imperial Germany in the 1880s when he established "welfare" programs such as compulsory accident, health, and old
age insurance, a pragmatic rather than an altruistic move since his goal
was to nip Marx's socialism in the bud by buying the loyalty of workers.

American social scientists such as Richard T. Ely and Henry Carter
Adams brought the Germanic doctrine to America, infused it with
Progressive idealism, and an incipient welfare state began to emerge.

Alexis de Tocqueville (1805–1859) had previously warned of the consequences in *Democracy in America.*

The despotism democratic nations must fear, he wrote, was "an immense and tutelary power . . . absolute, minute, regular, provident, and mild . . . like the authority of a parent if, like that authority, its object was to prepare men for manhood; but it seeks on the contrary to keep them in perpetual childhood . . . It compresses, enervates, extinguishes, and stupefies a people, till each nation is reduced to being nothing better than a flock of timid and industrious animals, of which the government is the shepherd."[10]

American students in the 1880s and 1890s were the first college generations to be taught the new collectivist theories. Student generations to come would subsequently study how increasing the power of the state was the solution to most of humankind's problems.

"The national government must step in and discriminate," urged Herbert Croly (1819–1930), cofounder of the *New Republic* magazine, "but it must discriminate not on behalf of liberty and the special individual, but on behalf of equality and the average man."[11]

"Social needs," echoed U.S. Supreme Court justice Oliver Wendell Holmes Jr. (1841–1935), "must be supreme over all laws and abstract principles."[12]

American intellectuals at the break of the twentieth century increasingly turned against America's founding principles to begin the long grind to undermine the Constitutional system, discredit its premises, and erode its institutions, thereby "fundamentally transforming the United States of America," as Barack Obama would famously promise when he ran for his first term as president in 2008.[13]

Progressives such as Woodrow Wilson believed "Progressive" thinking resolved the conflict over fundamental principles of the relationship between government and the individual. To him, Plato had it right in determining that only the intellectual elite were qualified to rule. Five motivating factors for Progressives emerged as its tentacles reached deeper into the souls of the American people.

PATERNALISM. Father (government) knows best, because the common people are too stupid to act responsibly and look after themselves.

GREED. Give the people stuff and they'll give you their votes in return.

GOOD INTENTIONS. Progressivism begins with the noble conviction that its intentions are supremely moral, no matter the outcome.

LINEAR THINKING. Progressives with a goal in mind—say, redistribution of wealth—see only one way to get there: through government action.

UTOPIANISM. "If we just do it right this time, we can create heaven on earth"—no matter how many times it has previously failed.

Known as the "Sage of Baltimore," author and journalist H. L. Mencken (1880–1956) was one of the most influential proponents of the Progressive movement. Representative democracy, he warranted, was the "worship of jackals by jackasses," a system whereby inferior men dominated their superiors. He considered the "booboisie," as he referred to the reprehensible middle class, to be vulgar and irresponsible. Thus, he, like many in the Progressive movement, contended scientific experts free from the constraints of the Constitution should run government. Only that could save America from the appalling slovenliness of middle-class capitalism.

Although Progressivism is often associated with the Democratic Party and traces its lineage back to Woodrow Wilson, its roots entwine both major political parties. Theodore Roosevelt and Robert "Fighting Bob" La Follette, both Republicans, are considered founders of the modern Progressive movement and predate Wilson.

Theodore Roosevelt was the first major opponent of pure capitalism to occupy the White House (1901–1909). The Sherman Antitrust Act of 1890 provided him "trust-busting" ammunition to rein in and control the economy by prohibiting and sanctioning business activities that government regulators deemed anticompetitive.

Henry Demarest Lloyd, a leader of the antitrust movement, made no bones about how he viewed the act. The principle of self-interest, he avowed, was "one of the historic mistakes of humanity." What America needed, he added, was a system "in which no man will have the right to do with his own what he will, but only a right to do what is right."[14]

"What is right" would naturally be determined by government.

The University of Wisconsin, which La Follette attended, was an early cauldron of Progressivism whose goal was to reorder society outside the Constitution. As governor of Wisconsin (1901–1906) and U.S. senator (1906–1925), La Follette campaigned ceaselessly for a variety of Progressive causes—a federal income tax; government ownership of public transportation and utilities; tariffs; and more control over businesses.

Americans in the nineteenth and twentieth centuries were not yet conditioned to doling out substantial shares of their income and wealth to government. Supreme Court justice John Marshall had even equated the power to tax with the power to destroy. Nonetheless, the idea of a universal federal income tax first initiated by Lincoln did not die following the Civil War.[15]

In 1893, President Grover Cleveland proposed a "small tax" on incomes at a flat rate of 2 percent above an exemption of $4,000. The Supreme Court declared the bill void the following year.

Nonetheless, the door had been opened. Eventually, as much as 90 percent of a citizen's income could be seized as his "fair share." The Internal Revenue Service administering a graduated income tax became the largest branch of government outside the military and certainly its most feared. Although government claims the tax system is based on voluntary compliance, the only way it works is through massive government surveillance, penalties, and ruthless criminal sanctions. In spite of Al Capone's career of murder, extortion, and pillage, it was the IRS that finally sent him to prison.

Regulations follow taxation as surely as eggs follow chickens. The bill that created the Interstate Commerce Commission, the nation's first regulatory agency, born in 1887, opened the way for the "Regulation

Nation." Created to protect railroads, the ICC has expanded over the years to regulate everything from highways and frozen chickens to mattresses and a little girl's lemonade stand. Thousands of rules and regulations are added to the *Federal Register* each year.

To hell with law when you can regulate what you cannot legislate.

Many historians contend that "the Progressive Era" thrived between 1900 and 1916. On the contrary, it continues to thrive in the modern age, blending through the New Deal and the Great Society into the "Transformational Society" of the twenty-first century.

4

LEVIATHAN EMERGES

Each generation of Americans is being conditioned to accept less freedom than the generation before.

—DONNA SUE SASSER

WOODROW WILSON (1856-1924) was perhaps the most prominent figure responsible for launching America on its long trek toward a collectivist nation. U.S. president from 1913 to 1921, he viewed the Constitution as cumbersome and outdated, a "living organism" that must grow and change with the times.

"Living political constitutions must be Darwinian in structure and in practice," he contended. "The trouble with the theory of [limited government] is that government is not a machine, but a living thing. . . . It is modified by its environment, necessitated by its tasks, shaped to its function by the sheer pressure of life. No living thing can have its organs offset against each other as checks, and live."[1]

THE LIVING CONSTITUTION

During his tenure in the White House, Wilson pushed through a Progressive legislative agenda that included planks from Marx's *Communist Manifesto* and which redefined the relationship between government and the individual. Marx's theories had made such inroads into American society by this time that a member of the Socialist Party had even won a seat in the House of Representatives in 1910.

Marx had laid out ten planks that must be nailed in place in order to turn a country socialist. A huge progressive or graduated income tax was so important that he made it his second plank. One of Wilson's first efforts in the White House was to ram through the Sixteenth Amendment to the Constitution to allow a graduated income tax, which three-fourths of the states ratified on February 25, 1913. Great government activism requires the means to fund it.

The *Manifesto's* fifth plank reads "Centralisation of credit in the hands of the state, by means of a national bank with State capital and an exclusive monopoly."[2]

Vladimir Lenin said a central bank and control of a nation's currency was 90 percent on the way toward communizing a country.

Largely due to mismanagement, several U.S. banks had collapsed and prompted a short-lived banking panic three years before Wilson assumed the presidency. Grasping onto the presumed crisis as a Progressive opportunity, Senator Nelson Aldrich of Rhode Island, chairman of the National Monetary Commission, called a secret conference of millionaire bankers and economic scholars to review the possibility of creating a central bank. The conference that convened in November 1910 at Georgia's plush Jekyll Island Resort was so hush-hush that attendees used only first names.

These giants of finance and academia denned up for ten days before they emerged with a plan to establish a national bank of which Marx would have approved—a plan which, incidentally, benefited them and others like them immensely.

As Baron von Rothschild once purportedly pointed out, "Let me control the currency, its issuance and value, and I care not who makes the laws."

Wilson shoved through Congress the Jekyll Island plan that became the Federal Reserve Act of 1913, "an Act to provide for the establishment of Federal reserve banks, to furnish an elastic currency, to afford means of rediscounting commercial paper, to establish a more effective supervision of banking in the United States, and for other purposes."[3]

For other purposes was the catch-all that included manipulating interest rates, loan and mortgage rates, printing money, and issuing credit to the United States government at rates set by the independent central bank.

"In the United States today we have in effect two governments," observed Congressman Wright Patman, then chairman of the housing banking committee. ". . . We have the duly constituted Government. Then we have an independent, uncontrolled and uncoordinated government in the Federal Reserve System."[4]

To this date, the Federal Reserve has never been audited and has no accountability other than to itself. It totally controls the dollar, which has lost 98 percent of its value since passage of the act. Government borrows money from the Fed at an interest rate set by the Fed, which amounts to a staggering unreported percentage of the nearly $20 *trillion* national debt reported in 2016.

Culturally, economically, and politically, World War I launched the United States out of isolationism and into its new role as leader of the free world. As with all dramatic upheavals, whether natural, like the Black Death, or caused by humans, the war precipitated dramatic changes in the structure of government. As had Lincoln during the Civil War, President Wilson assumed certain dictatorial liberties in the lives of citizens and their institutions on the grounds that it was necessary in order to protect the nation in a dangerous world.

His expansion of government power included new taxes, the first military draft since 1862, and a series of measures called the Espionage and Sedition Acts of 1917 to suppress anti-American, antiwar opinion and quash pro-German sympathizers.

The Acts suspended habeas corpus so that foreign-born "radicals" could be arrested in huge numbers and deported without due process. Hundreds of citizens were tossed behind bars for merely criticizing Wilson and his administration. Robert Goldstein, for example, was sentenced to ten years in prison for producing a film about the Revolutionary War that the Wilson administration considered critical of Britain, an ally.

Government propaganda accompanied widespread censorship. U.S. post offices under government orders refused to carry materials deemed critical of the war effort. More than sixty newspapers were banned from using the mail due to antiwar content.

Power can be a heady master. Surges in the use of government power are rarely recalled once the crisis is over. Even after the war ended, Wilson continued to attack dissenters with the Palmer Raids, headed by attorney general A. Mitchell Palmer, that rounded up some ten thousand so-called anarchists and labor activists. Massachusetts district judge George Anderson ordered them halted in 1920.

"A mob is a mob," he rebuked the administration, "whether made up of government officials acting under instruction from the Department of Justice, or of criminals, loafers, and the vicious classes."[5]

In the aftermath of war, Wilson and leaders from Britain and France succeeded in establishing the League of Nations, a first effort toward creating a world government. It died a slow death, to be eventually replaced by the United Nations following World War II.

Wilson received the Nobel Peace Prize for his work in building the League, even though it ended in failure. Like most Progressive institutions, the Nobel Committee seems more impressed with intent than results. Only four other U.S. presidents or vice presidents, all of whom were Progressives, have made the Nobel Peace Prize list as of 2016—Theodore Roosevelt, Jimmy Carter, Vice President Al Gore, and Barack Obama. Obama, a career "community organizer," was awarded the 2009 Nobel almost as soon as he assumed office "for his extraordinary efforts to strengthen international diplomacy and cooperation between peoples."[6]

"For doing nothing, you're supposed to get a Nobel Peace Prize[?]"

cracked former senator Fred Thompson.[7]

Under Wilson, the political trend in America moved further toward the heavily interventionist path governments in Europe had trod for decades. When Austrian economist Ludwig von Mises toured American in 1926, he warned against the populist clamor that the economic system of the United States was not "rational" or "democratic" enough and that government should assume more authority to influence the direction of industry and business.

"Both political parties," he said, "the Republicans as well as the Democrats, are ready to take radical steps in this direction [interventionism], in order to retain the votes of the electorate."[8]

A liberal paradise would be a place where everybody has guaranteed employment, free comprehensive healthcare, free education, free food, free housing, free clothing, free utilities, and only law enforcement has guns. And believe it or not, such a place does, indeed, exist; it's called prison.

—ARIZONA SHERIFF JOE ARPAIO

A RAW DEAL

Catastrophe invaded the first half of the twentieth century: depressions, two world wars, uprisings and coups, holocausts, the rise of fascist-socialist and Communist-socialist regimes in Germany and Russia and around the world. Parliamentary democracies failed; economies collapsed. The globe went into emergency overdrive to cope.

It is a rule of nature, like the law of gravity or the order of the universe, that governments exploit national and international emergencies to expand power. Between 1929 and 1943 the United States experienced a constitutional Revolution that changed the character of the nation and its people.

"No constitutional government," historian Clinton Rossiter noted, "ever passed through a period in which emergency powers were used without undergoing some degree of permanent attrition, always in the direction of an aggrandizement of the power of the state."[9]

Wall Street crashed on "Black Tuesday," October 29, 1929, about eight months after Herbert Hoover advanced to the presidency, precipitating the longest, deepest, and most widespread depression of the twentieth century. The stock market lost $30 billion within three weeks. Millionaires who became paupers almost overnight were shooting themselves and jumping out windows. People sang "Twentieth-Century Blues" and anticipated the collapse of the Western world.

The Great Depression was soup kitchens; "Okies" caravanning to California to find work; the Dust Bowl; skinny little kids with big, haunted eyes; families living in lean-tos and barns and sod houses; desperation; hunger; hopelessness; unrest; and "Brother, can you spare a dime?"

President Hoover fought to overcome the crisis with new, government-enforced efforts—massive public works projects such as the Hoover Dam; tariffs; increased welfare programs; taxes on the "rich" and new corporate taxes; farm price support; emergency loans to businesses; and so forth. He advocated unionization of industry and supported regulations to control air transport, railroads, and the media.

"It was Mr. Hoover," wrote columnist Walter Lippman, "who abandoned the principles of *laissez faire* in relation to the business cycle and established the conviction that prosperity and depression can be publicly controlled by political action."[10]

Hoover's initiatives failed to produce recovery. Makeshift slums were referred to as "Hoovervilles." He would be forever blamed for causing the depression. Voters turned him out of office in 1932 and replaced him with Franklin D. Roosevelt, who campaigned on the theme of a popular song, "Happy Days Are Here Again."

Roosevelt received credit for ending the depression and became an enduring Progressive icon, although he merely continued actions that Hoover had begun, only on steroids. He blamed the crisis on the capitalist system and its profit motive.

For many nations, socialism and the ideas of Marx and Lenin seemed an answer to the crisis. Roosevelt bent the United States in that direction.

Philosopher-psychologist John Dewey (1859–1952), who became a major voice in Progressive education, agreed with Roosevelt's course of action and explained that what America needed was "organized action in behalf of the social interest . . . organized planning . . . some kind of socialism."[11]

Roosevelt, asserting that the nation must act "as a trained and loyal army to sacrifice for the good of a common discipline," introduced the "New Deal" and what supporters termed "government interventionism."[12]

Economist Ludwig von Mises warned that only the threat of force would make people follow courses of action different from the ones they would take without government intervention. He explained by enumerating eight points to describe an interventionist economy:

1. Private ownership of the means of production is either limited, regulated, or outright prohibited.

2. The use of the means of production by private owners is either limited, regulated, or outright prohibited.

3. Users of the means of production are prevented from relying on consumer demand.

4. Government influences or controls prices and elements of production.

5. Government uses artificial means such as price controls, production regulations, subsidies, protected markets, and other means to reduce market supply and demand on certain enterprises.

6. Foreign rivals into the domestic market are discouraged or outlawed by the use of tariffs.

7. Government regulates the monetary system to affect employment, economic output and growth.

8. The role of government expands beyond the constitutional limits of protecting life, liberty, and property.

The crisis of the Great Depression demanded action. The American people expected government to do *something*—and so it did.

Roosevelt's first order of business two weeks after he assumed office was to criminalize the private possession of gold. Congress passed a bill making it a felony to possess as much as a gold necklace or a keepsake twenty-dollar gold piece. Forty years later, my grandpa was still pissed off that he'd had to turn in a ring that his mother had passed down to him.

"Why didn't you hide it?" I asked.

"Boy"—he always called me "boy"—you don't understand them times. Government was *everywhere*. For all folks knowed, they'd break in our houses and search unless we turned something in."

In 1929, federal spending constituted 2.5 percent of the nation's gross domestic product (GDP); the percentage more than tripled during FDR's first term in office. His policies entailed heavy costs and burdens, not only financially but also in the profusion of restraints on private property and individual rights.

"It was during those years," asserted political commentator Paul R. Hollrah, "that Democrats initiated the long process of assembling a diverse coalition of special interests—each wanting something from government that they were unable to acquire through free and open competition."[13]

Muddy New Deal footprints stomped all over the Constitution with a multitude of federal projects, entitlements, regulations, new laws and new agencies. Beginning with the National Recovery Act, the New Deal regimented agriculture, imposed more controls over financial institutions, more closely supervised the stock market, enforced antitrust policies, attempted to restrict private business, increased taxes to fund welfare programs, created huge public works projects, and established guaranteed pensions and unemployment programs.

The Public Works Administration (PWA) was looked upon as one of the administration's most significant accomplishments during the first cluster of welfare programs. Under the generalship of Secretary of Interior Harold L. Ickes, all but thirty-three of the three thousand counties in the United States received PWA grants to build bridges and buildings, upon each of which appeared permanent plaques eulogizing the secretary. Politicians' names are still plastered on most public works projects.

In an attempt to alleviate an unemployment rate of 14 percent, the Emergency Relief Appropriations Act created the WPA (Works Progress Administration) to hire the unemployed. It turned into a notoriously corrupt scheme for Democrats to buy votes for the upcoming 1935–36 election. Journalists, photographers, artists, sculptors, and actors on Washington's payroll developed blatant forms of propaganda to support Roosevelt and his administration.

For example, a WPA-produced Marxist play titled *Power* caricatured private-sector utilities executives as greedy, rich old men who exploited American families. The intent and theme of the play was to encourage towns and cities to use government power instead of private power.

In rounding out the busy election campaign year, Congress passed the Social Security Act to provide federal unemployment insurance and "old age" pensions. Roosevelt promised participation in the program would be completely voluntary and that no one would ever have to pay in more than 1 percent of his susceptible income. Today, the rate of pay for participants has risen to nearly 8 percent and there is nothing voluntary about it.

The economy stubbornly refused to rebound in spite of government's efforts. By Roosevelt's second term, government was about the only entity in the United States not begging, "Brother, can you spare a dime?"

Along came a plethora of other "emergency" measures: Home Owners Loan Corporation; Deposit Insurance Corporation; Securities and Exchange Commission; Fair Labor Standards Act establishing a national minimum wage; the GI Bill . . . American society was rapidly coalescing into a "mixed economy," part free enterprise, part socialist. While, strictly speaking, the economy was not controlled by government, it *was* regulated and restricted.

Senator Arthur Vanderburg of Michigan called government spending "four or five billion [dollars'] worth of lost liberty."[14]

Roosevelt wasn't through yet. He lifted his eyes to more distant horizons and offered people a "Second Bill of Rights" chillingly similar to Karl Marx's tenets for a Communist state:

FRANKLIN ROOSEVELT'S SECOND BILL OF RIGHTS[15]

We have accepted, so to speak, a second Bill of Rights under which a new basis of security and prosperity can be established for all regardless of station, race, or creed.

Among these are:
  • The right to a useful and remunerative job in the industries or shops or farms or mines of the Nation;
  • The right to earn enough to provide adequate food and clothing and recreation;
  • The right of every farmer to raise and sell his products at a return which will give him and his family a decent living;
  • The right of every businessman, large and small, to trade in an atmosphere of freedom from unfair competition and domination by monopolies at home or abroad;
  • The right to adequate medical care and the opportunity to achieve and enjoy good health;
  • The right to adequate protection from the economic fears of old age, sickness, accident, and unemployment;
  • The right to a good education.

"More and more we . . . debate what government should do," Garet Garnett wrote in the *Saturday Evening Post* in 1935, "[while] forgetting that though an omnipotent government were able to confer these blessings, it would be obliged at the same time to confer upon people also the status of servility."[16]

In his historical survey of socialism, Sidney Webb concluded that socialism becomes inevitable as societies mature—more like fascism in

Nazi Germany, however, than Communism in the USSR. Government takes one small step at a time until it takes over most of the free ground. By FDR's third term in office and his death in 1945, transformation of the nation's economy and its government gave every indication of being irreversible.

"It is not possible to experiment with society and just drop the experiment whenever we choose," William Graham Sumner observed. "The experiment enters into the life of the society and never can be got out again."[17]

For all Roosevelt's meddling in the economy and his alphabet of programs to pin the nation's institutions to government's coattails, for all that he still receives credit for "saving us all" from the Great Depression, the Brookings Institute found that "on the whole [the New Deal] retarded recovery."[18] At no time under Roosevelt did the unemployment rate drop below 14 percent until World War II began.

In fact, a 2004 study conducted by UCLA economists Harold L. Cole and Lee L. Ohanian resolved that Roosevelt's "ill-conceived stimulus policies" extended the Depression by seven years.[19] Only World War II rescued the United States while at the same time paving the way for even more government control.

Whittaker Chambers, a member of the Communist Party of the United States, a Soviet spy during World War II, and editor of *Time* magazine, later turned against both the New Deal and Communism. In *Condemned*, his 1952 autobiography, he wrote, "I had to acknowledge the truth of what its most forthright protagonists, sometimes unwarily, sometimes defiantly, averred: The New Deal was a genuine evolution, whose deepest purpose was not simple reform within existing traditions, but a basic change in the social, and above all, the power relationships within the nation."[20]

"He who sees the truth, let him proclaim it, without asking who is for it or who is against it."

—HENRY GEORGE

WAR: THE HEALTH OF THE STATE

Between the end of World War I in 1918 and the start of World War II in 1939, a period of a mere two decades, many of the major powers of continental Europe seemed ready to renounce liberty and democracy in favor of one of the two major brands of socialism—Nazism or Communism—each of which prepared to dominate the world. The USSR wanted a "world dictatorship of the proletariat": Nazi Germany envisioned a "Third Reich."

The ink wasn't even dry on the German–Soviet Non-Aggression Pact between the two dictatorships, which included a secret protocol that essentially agreed they divide up eastern Europe between them, before Germany invaded Poland. Two weeks later, on September 17, 1939, the Soviet Union also invaded Poland to share in the spoils. Their joint aim was to control—*conquer*—their individual spheres of influence.

The scheme might have worked, except Hitler got greedy, stabbed Stalin in the back, and invaded Russia. World War II lined out with the United States allied with England, France, and the USSR against Germany, Japan, and Italy.

In his 2008 book, *The Chief Culprit: Stalin's Grand Design to Start World War II*, Russian historian Viktor Suvorov marveled how "the world hated Hitler and commiserated with Stalin. Hitler conquered half of Europe, and the rest of the world declared war against him. Stalin conquered half of Europe, and the world sent him greetings."[21]

Randolph Bourne, in his essay "War Is the Health of the State," contended that in time of peace, "the sense of the state almost fades out of the consciousness of men. [However] with the shock of war . . . the state comes into its own again. The moment war is declared . . .the mass of the people, through some spiritual alchemy, becomes convinced that they have willed and executed the deed themselves. [They] proceed to allow themselves to be regimented, coerced, deranged in all the environment of their lives, and turned into a solid manufactory of destruction."[22]

Each of America's major wars beginning with the Civil War produced massive violations of human rights guaranteed under the Constitution and moved the nation further along the path to collectivism. No longer a bulwark to protect rights, the U.S. Constitution was essentially suspended each time to award unchecked powers to government officials.

Citing Woodrow Wilson's war measures as a precedent for radical federal intervention, FDR whipped virtually every sector of American society into line for the war effort. He began by nationalizing telephones, domestic, and international telegraphic cable industries and seizing entire industries, such as railroads, coal mines, and meatpacking plants. He took control of consumer prices and of most businesses and corporations while issuing new regulations over labor and management, international commerce, manufactured products, and markets for raw materials.

People were restricted in what they could say or do. Some newspapers and publications were denied use of the U.S. mail under the Espionage Act from World War I, while others were banned altogether. The Office of Censorship restricted press reports and radio broadcasts and censored personal mail leaving or entering the country.

Penalties for violating any of the new laws and regulations included heavy fines and jail. Warrantless searches and seizure became legal, as did blanket arrests through suspension of due process. You could go to jail for violating ration laws; speaking out against the draft, the war, or the government; buying and selling on the black market; and dozens of other infractions of law. Thousands of Americans served prison time for violating these measures.

One of Roosevelt's most egregious violations of civil rights occurred when, in the wake of the Japanese attack on Pearl Harbor, he signed Executive Order 9066 authorizing the military to relocate all Japanese Americans to detention centers, where they would be confined for the duration of the war. All Japanese—old, young, men, women, and children—were considered possible enemy subversives. FBI director J. Edgar Hoover was the only official in the Roosevelt administration to oppose internments as unconstitutional, but the Supreme Court upheld Roosevelt.

A few Germans were locked up, but not en masse, as with the Japanese.

Franklin Roosevelt died before the war ended. Vice President Harry Truman succeeded him and authorized dropping atomic bombs on Japan. Churchill announced the falling of an "iron curtain" over the Soviet Union and the east European satellites it conquered during the war. Stalin obtained the atom bomb in 1949. Allies during the war, the United States and Russia emerged as superpowers and as rivals in the Cold War—creating yet another pending "national emergency" for the further extension of government power.

While such "war measures" may have been warranted to some extent, they nonetheless resulted in permanent losses of economic and individual liberties in the United States. Government had imposed unprecedented taxation and economic controls over the population and accumulated an enormous national debt. Congress gained legislative power, including the right to delegate powers to the president for achieving social objectives and meeting further "emergencies"; the president took upon himself the duty and authority to stimulate the society for social outcomes; and in many instances the making and enforcement of laws, rather than their interpretation, slipped into the hands of the judiciary.

Today, it is considered "normal" for massive government intervention in private industry, communications, and transportation, and for government to spy on, control, and command individuals in ways that were unheard-of before Woodrow Wilson and Franklin Roosevelt.

5

COMMUNISM ARRIVES

The further a society drifts from truth the more it will hate those who speak it.

—GEORGE ORWELL

IN 1934, AT THE HEIGHT OF THE GREAT DEPRESSION, a school superinten-
dent named William Wirt attended a dinner party with a number of U.S.
government employees associated with FDR's New Deal. Apparently
assuming Wirt to be down with it, the gathering spoke openly about a
"concrete plan" for the "proposed overthrow of the established American
social order." Alarmed, Wirt volunteered to testify before a select house
committee about what he called the "secret revolution." His testimony
made headlines and the *Congressional Record*.

"The fundamental trouble with the Brain Trusters [as President
Roosevelt's cabinet of advisers was known] is that they start with a
false assumption," Wirt testified. "They insisted that the America of

Washington, Jefferson, and Lincoln must first be destroyed and then on the ruins they will reconstruct an America after their own pattern."[1]

THE SECRET REVOLUTION

No good deed goes unpunished. Wirt found himself ridiculed, falsely accused of various crimes and improprieties, and with his reputation besmirched in the national media. The *Miami Daily News* provided a tongue-in-cheek appraisal of the affair: "A nation needs a good laugh now and then. . . . Laughing again, the country can resume its march again, not to revolution but to prosperity."[2]

Brain Truster Donald Richberg contributed his wit to the hilarity:

Cuttle-fish squirt;

Nobody hurt.

And that's the end

Of Dr. Wirt.[3]

Wirt slumped off into obscurity, his warning unheralded and his reputation soiled while Communists in America laughed at him and promised to humiliate anyone else who spoke out.

Americans were attracted to the ideas of a "class struggle," thanks in large part to the apparent failure of the capitalist system manifested in the Great Depression and to a U.S. media and intellectual community sympathetic to the USSR's "workers' paradise." It seemed Americans so badly *wanted* to believe in Stalin that they were willing to blind themselves to the reality of Russian Communism. The 1930s became "America's Red Decade," followed by other "Red decades" for the rest of the century. Belief in Communism became a fashionable expression of "class consciousness."

"Several of the best friends I have are communists," President Roosevelt declared.[4]

Friedrich Hayek (1899–1992), a Nobel Prize winner in economics and author of *The Road to Serfdom*, argued that the socialist philosophies of Germany and Russia were becoming a guiding light for American and British statesmen.

"In the United States . . ." he wrote, "the most extreme kind of economic planning had been seriously advocated and the model of Russia held up for imitation by men who were soon to play an important role in public affairs."[5]

A former captain in the Soviet Army named Victor Kravchenko (1905–1966) was one of the earliest defectors from the USSR to alert the United States to the dangers of Communism.

"Someone somewhere had manipulated the surge of fellow-feeling for Russians for Stalin's benefit," he wrote in his autobiography, *I Chose Freedom*. "Americans seemed intent on explaining everything in *Stalin's favor*, to the discredit of the democracies. . . . What the communists had not yet succeeded in doing in their own country—as the purges and the millions of political prisoners indicate—they had succeeded in doing in America! . . . The greatest Soviet triumph, it was borne in upon me, was in the domain of foreign propaganda. . . . Stalin's grip on the American mind, I realized, was almost as firm as his grip on the Russian mind."[6]

Having become disillusioned with Communism and having sought asylum in the United States, Kravchenko spent the remainder of his life paranoid and hiding out from Russia's Secret Police, who were under orders to assassinate defectors wherever they were found. He died in New York of a gunshot wound, apparently another victim of Soviet agents.

In 1919, Vladimir Lenin had invited the left wing of the Socialist Party of America to join the Russian Comintern, out of which contact sprouted the Communist Party of the United States (CPUSA), which promptly grew into a membership of about sixty thousand. Like a Trojan horse, CPUSA presented itself as a peaceful, democratic group of patriots merely championing a vision of widely held Progressive notions. Throughout the 1930s, it helped shape crusades to change the nature of American life by promoting industrial unions and forging coalitions with other Progressive groups to lend support to New Deal policies. History would much later reveal how leaders of CPUSA often served as Soviet couriers or recruited spies to steal U.S. secrets for Russia. Such individuals were even more dangerous than ordinary spies since they acted out of the conviction that Stalin and Communism were "enlightened" and offered a genuine alternative to failed American and British capitalism.

In 1938, the House Un-American Activities Committee (HUAC) headed by Democratic representative Martin Dies of Texas launched an investigation into possible Communist or fascist infiltration of the U.S. government.

"Before Joe McCarthy, there was Martin Dies," journalist M. Stanton Evans noted in *Blacklisted by History: The Untold Story of Senator Joe McCarthy and His Fight Against America's Enemies*. ". . . Virtually everything that would later be said about Joe McCarthy was said first of Martin Dies, that he was conducting 'witch hunts,' smearing innocent victims, using the Communist issue to advance his own malign agenda, spreading hysteria about a nonexistent menace."[7]

Dies's committee lasted until 1944 before it folded from lack of interest and from attacks and ridicule directed at his character the same as those launched against schoolteacher William Wirt. By this time, after all, Stalin was solidly in the Allied camp after Hitler double-crossed him.

Republican senator Joe McCarthy and his Senate Permanent Subcommittee on Investigations took up Dies's mantel in 1950. McCarthy would not be so easily dissuaded.

"A nation can survive its fools, and even its ambitious," mused Rome's Marcus Tullius Cicero in 40 BC in "The Traitor." "But it cannot survive treason from within. An enemy at the gates is less formidable, for he is known and carries his banner openly. But the traitor moves amongst those within the gates freely, his sly whispers rustling through all the alleys, heard in the very halls of government itself."

The Communist Party [of the United States] will systematically and persistently propagate the idea of the inevitability of and necessity for violent revolution, and will prepare the workers for armed insurrection as the only means of overthrowing the capitalist state.

ORIGINAL CPUSA CONSTITUTION, 1919

WITNESS

February 9, 1950. A bombastic senator from Wisconsin delivered a startling speech to the Republican Women's Club of Wheeling, West Virginia, during which he brandished a list of what he claimed to be the names of known Communists working for the U.S. government.

"The State Department is infested with communists," thundered Joseph McCarthy (1908–1957). "I have here in my hand a list of [the exact number he cited is in dispute, ranging from 57 to 205] that were made known to the Secretary of State as being members of the Communist Party and who nevertheless are still working and shaping policy in the State Department."[8]

With that speech, McCarthy's lot, due to his abrasive and straight-forward manner, was to become the public face of a period during which Cold War tensions fueled fears of pervasive Communist subversion. The U.S. Senate promptly voted to investigate further, as did the FBI and the House Un-American Activities Committee (HUAC), which was already involved in investigations since before FDR's death.

"It has become increasingly clear in the investigation of this case," FBI special agent Guy Hottel wrote in a memo to director J. Edgar Hoover, "that there are a tremendous number of persons employed in the United States Government who are communists and who strive daily to advance the cause of communism and destroy the foundations of this government. Today, nearly every department or agency of the government is infiltrated with them in varying degrees. To aggravate the situation, they appear to have concentrated most heavily in those departments which make policy, particularly in the international field."[9]

Through their investigations, McCarthy and the various probe committees suggested hundreds, perhaps thousands, of Communists were hired by the U.S. government during the 1930s and 1940s, their "sly whispers rustling through all the alleys."[10] Whittaker Chambers (1901–1961) and Elizabeth Terrill Bentley (1908–1963) turned out to be two of the most important witnesses to this infestation.

Chambers, a journalist and writer, became a Marxist in 1924 after reading Vladimir Lenin's *Soviets at Work*. In 1925, he joined the Communist Party of the United States and wrote for a number of Communist publications, such as the *Daily Worker* and the *New Masses*, before he became editor of *Time* magazine.

He began his seditious career in the Communist underground by working for a Soviet apparatus led by Alexander Ulanovsky. His job was to act as a courier for stolen government documents between New York and Washington, D.C.

Elizabeth Bentley was a Vassar-educated alcoholic who turned Soviet spy for a network centered on Nathan Silvermaster; his wife, Helen; and his stepson, Anatole Volkov. Silvermaster, an economist with the United States War Production Board during World War II, was head of one of the largest Soviet espionage operations in the United States.

Chambers broke with the Soviets in 1939. Shocked by the Hitler–Stalin Pact to divide up Poland, he approached assistant secretary of state Adolf Berle with names of prominent spies implanted within the halls of the U.S. government.

When Berle repeated Chamber's allegations to the president, FDR laughed them off and told Berle "[Go] f--- yourself."[11]

Among those named by Chambers as spies were Alger Hiss, a notable official in the State Department, and his brother Donald, also employed at State.

Not discouraged by Roosevelt's rebuff, Adolf Berle next discussed Chambers with Dean Acheson, undersecretary of the Treasury. Acheson responded that he had known the Hiss family "and those two boys since childhood and could vouch for them absolutely."

Acheson subsequently advanced to assistant secretary of state and took Alger Hiss with him as his assistant. Later, during the war, Roosevelt selected Hiss to advise him at Yalta.

"Other ages have had their individual traitors," Chambers wrote later in his autobiography, *Witness*, "men who from faint-heartedness or hope of gain sold out their causes. But in the twentieth century, for the first time, men banded together by the millions in movements like fascism and communism, dedicated to the purpose of betraying the institutions they lived under. In the twentieth century, treason became a vocation whose modern form was specifically the treason of ideas."[12]

The matter seemed closed. Little further was done about subversion during the Roosevelt administration.

In 1945, after World War II ended, Elizabeth Bentley defected from the Communists and went to the FBI. She named more than one hundred people in government who were, or had been, Soviet assets. Two dozen of them still held official jobs, most of whom Whittaker Chambers had tried to expose six years earlier. Among the most significant of these were Alger and Donald Hiss; assistant secretary of Treasury Harry Dexter White; White House assistant Lauchlin Currie; Harry Hopkins, who had been FDR's most intimate adviser; and Julius and Ethel Rosenberg, whose cloak-and-dagger activities provided secrets to Stalin that allowed him to build nuclear warheads.

Alger Hiss was one of the Soviet Union's most trusted secret agents, in addition to being a leading member of the U.S. liberal establishment and a significant figure in the State Department during the war years.

Harry Hopkins was the most highly placed government official to take up a spy career. He had been so tight with President Roosevelt that he actually lived in the White House for over three years. American diplomat Robert Murphy said of him, "Few men of this century have exerted more influence upon American politics, domestic or foreign, than Hopkins." (92)

His sympathies should have been obvious. In 1942, he addressed a pro-Russian rally of twenty thousand at Madison Square Garden, declaring, "I believe we are fighting for a new world. . . . The world can be freed from the economic oppression that has nourished misery among hundreds of millions of people . . . but no Utopia was ever won without struggle."[13]

President Harry Truman appointed Harry Dexter White American director of the International Monetary Fund, where he assisted Soviet espionage by sponsoring or facilitating the hiring of a number of other Communist spies into the government. Some of the spies reported directly to him.[14]

Lauchlin Currie was yet another highly placed Soviet source in Washington. As deputy administrator of FDR's Foreign Economics Administration, he began undermining free markets by championing a new macroeconomic policy known as "stimulus spending," the public expenditure of funds to "stimulate" the private economy. Accusers later described the policy he advocated as a Red plot to destroy America.

Decades later, "stimulus spending" became a major part of President Barack Obama's economic recovery package to battle the 2007–2008 recession.

Like Hopkins, Currie eventually moved into the White House as a member of FDR's executive staff.

If you have a bunch of rats living in your kitchen and the cheese keeps getting compromised, then you are either blind, incredibly naïve— or you are one of the rats.

Julius Rosenberg, along with wife, Ethel, and Ethel's brother, David Greenglass, supplied the Soviets with vital information on atomic weapons in his capacity as an engineer with a Top Secret clearance working in laboratories at Monmouth, New Jersey. Greenglass worked on the Manhattan Project at the Los Alamos National Laboratory.

Nothing further would likely have been done with information Chambers and Bentley supplied were it not for the upstart Joseph McCarthy and a young Congressman from California named Richard M. Nixon, a member of HUAC.

Hearings by Nixon, HUAC, and McCarthy's Senate Permanent Subcommittee on Investigations brought on a defensive storm to block investigators from pursuing the probe. Democrats in Congress, Progressives, intellectuals, and much of the media lashed back viciously at those who had the audacity to try to expose Communists. Every time a name came up in the investigation, the usual suspects galloped in to lambast the investigators.

Reports issued by Democrats on the Subcommittee labeled charges of Communist spies in government as a "fraud and a hoax . . . to confuse and divide the American people."[15] They accused investigators who disagreed as engaging in "witch-hunts"[16] and seeing "Reds under the bed."[17] Rumors to discredit FBI director J. Edgar Hoover, who took the Communist hearings seriously, began to circulate that he was a cross-dressing drag queen getting it on with his deputy director.

On December 2, 1948, Whittaker Chamber had provided HUAC indisputable proof against Alger Hiss when he produced highly classi-fied documents from the Navy and State departments that had come from Hiss's office and were intended to be delivered to Soviet handlers. Hiss's exposure promised to be dangerous to his Soviet sponsors and to worldwide subversives. His defenders now rallied to attack Chambers, Nixon, McCarthy, and anyone else involved in taking down the ring.

The press vilified Chambers as a "vulgar imposter" who had snowed congressional investigators. HUAC was composed of "the least intel-ligent in Congress . . . uncouth, underqualified, and ungrammatical."[18]

President Harry Truman deemed the investigation a "red herring, a cheap political ploy by . . . do nothing [Republicans] to distract from their sorry legislative record."[19] The Justice Department attempted to discredit Chambers by asking the FBI to investigate whether he had ever been institutionalized for mental illness.

Supreme Court justices Felix Frankfurter and Stanley Reed, both appointed to the bench by Roosevelt, testified for Hiss as character wit-nesses. So did future presidential candidate Adlai Stevenson.

Hiss was eventually convicted of two counts of perjury for denying under oath that he was a spy, the statute of limitations having run out on espionage. In January 1950, he was sentenced to five years in prison. Progressives, Marxists, Communist sympathizers, intellectuals, and fellow travelers have spent decades attempting to clear his name.

Journalist William Reuben called Hiss an "American saint."[20] Bard College named a chair in his honor. Up until his death in 1996, he was a steady fixture on the university lecture circuit, a hero among college audi-ences, faculty, and students. In 1972, the Massachusetts Bar Association reinstated his license to practice law, making him the first lawyer ever readmitted to the Massachusetts bar following a major criminal conviction.

Lauchlin Currie testified before HUAC in 1948, denied all accusations, and was never prosecuted. He fled to Colombia the following year, married, and died there in 1993.

Nathan Silvermaster, the leader of Elizabeth Bentley's coven, likewise denied Communist links and was never prosecuted. He died in New Jersey in 1964.

Harry Dexter White denied all charges and died of a heart attack three days after he testified.

Harry Hopkins died in 1946 before testifying about his possible clandestine activities.

Most of the others pleaded the Fifth and, except for Julius and Ethel Rosenberg, were never prosecuted. The Rosenbergs were brought down not only by Elizabeth Bentley's testimony but also because of Klaus Fuchs, a German refugee theoretical physicist working for the British mission on the Manhattan Project. Arrested on May 23, 1950, for having supplied key documents to the Soviets throughout the war, he snitched and helped expose the Rosenberg spy ring.

The Rosenbergs were indicted on eleven counts of espionage. Found guilty, they were sentenced to the death penalty and subsequently executed in the Sing Sing electric chair at sundown on June 19, 1953. They were the only civilians executed for espionage during the Cold War.

David Greenglass, Ethel's brother, served ten years in prison.

Soviet premier Nikita Khrushchev, who succeeded Joseph Stalin, praised Julius Rosenberg in his 1990 memoirs for "very significant help in accelerating the production of the atomic bomb. . . . Let my words serve as an expression of gratitude to those who sacrificed their lives to a great cause of the Soviet state at a time when the United States was using its advantage over our state to blackmail our state and undermine its proletarian cause."[21]

As with Alger Hiss, the Rosenbergs became a cause célèbre for international Progressives and Communists and thrust Joe McCarthy into position as the lightning rod for the "Red Scare" era. Lawyers and Progressive Democrats, aided by a media hostile to the investigations, succeeded in portraying McCarthy as bullying, reckless, and dishonest. Defense lawyer Joseph Nye Welch slapped the label on McCarthy that has been used ever since to slander him.

"Have you no sense of decency, sir, at long last?" Welch wailed. "Have you left no sense of decency?"[22]

Vehement attacks against McCarthy hounded him to his grave at the early age of forty-eight in 1957.

Subsequent developments were to prove beyond any doubt that McCarthy was right all along and that the internal Communist threat was real and that an organized "fifth column" of Progressives collaborated with the Soviets.

Colonel Carter Clarke, chief of the U.S. Army's Special Branch, had set up a unit in 1943 known as the Venona project to break the Soviet spy code. Neither Roosevelt nor Truman was let in on it, although FBI director J. Edgar Hoover was. Clarke did not believe Roosevelt or Truman could be trusted, considering the overwhelming number of spies inside their administrations.

On July 22, 1995, the U.S. government finally released a cache of Venona material that had languished at FBI headquarters since World War II. These cables verified the overwhelming truth of Joe McCarthy's charges. Hundreds of Americans—Alger Hiss, the Rosenbergs, Harry Dexter White, Lauchlin Currie, Harry Hopkins, and many others—were identified in the cables and confirmed as Soviet agents. McCarthy's "victims" were not so innocent after all.

If President Ronald Reagan had not brought down the Soviet Union and thereby allowed the eventual publication of the Venona papers, it is likely American Progressives would still be championing the innocence of "McCarthy's spies."

Wait a minute. They *are* still doing it.

We feared that the final victory of socialism would be hampered and hindered if the truth about Stalin's paradise was revealed to the public.

—HALLDÓR LAXNESS

PARTY LINE

To be labeled an anticommunist, to speak out openly against Communism in any of its subsequent "liberal" forms or disguises, is akin to having an STD or passing wind in a crowded room. American Progressives have successfully blamed everything from the Cold War to hangnails on paranoid anticommunists in the West, on their ignorance and irrational prejudices that prevent their understanding the peaceful intent of socialism. Anyone who disagrees with the Progressive party line has learned to hold his peace out of fear of being tar-brushed with the McCarthy label.

Journalist Eugene Lyons, himself a fellow-traveling Progressive, recorded how "thousands who do not hesitate to speak their minds vigorously about other social [or political] philosophies stop short, panic-stricken, when it comes to speaking their minds on communism."[23] Although Joe McCarthy has been dead for more than a half century, "McCarthyism" and the ghost of McCarthy live on as weapons with which to bludgeon anyone who dares question Progressive motives or the Progressive involvement with socialist collectivism. McCarthy has become a reviled and sinister symbol of political repression.

In 1985, Ohio representative George Crockett voted against a House resolution condemning Soviet Russia for shooting U.S. Army Major Arthur Nicholson in East Germany and denying him medical aid while he bled to death. A *Newsweek* article condemned conservatives who questioned Crockett's opposition, asking if their simply inquiring might not be "sort of McCarthyism."[24]

Two years later, according to the press, Crockett was practicing free speech in his enthusiasm for Communist Sandinistas in Nicaragua while conservatives who opposed his stand were employing "McCarthyism."

When Ronald Reagan became president in 1981, intelligence advisers briefed him that "the threat of internal security of the Republic is greater today than at any time since World War II." Senator Jeremiah Denton suggested launching a new subcommittee on Security and Terrorism. The *Washington Post* charged how this would "move the country back to the dark ages of McCarthyism."[25]

CRUSHING *the* COLLECTIVE

At the same time there was hardly a peep from the *Washington Post* and the rest of the media over a "Marxist Scholars Conference" held in Seattle by CPUSA, during which Professor Herbert Aptheker urged other professors to return to their campuses and support "imaginative actions . . . interfering with the armed forces, interfering with maneuvers, doing everything possible" to oppose efforts by the U.S. government to stop Communist advances in Latin America. For any in the media to have commented negatively against these Marxists would have constituted "McCarthyism."

Having suffered from "McCarthyism" became a badge of honor for the liberal establishment as the term invaded popular culture, schools and universities, and other major institutions. Dozens of books and magazines warned of the dangers of "right-wing extremism" and "McCarthyism." Instead of Reds under the bed, it was bourgeoisie under the sheets. You simply did not speak out against commies for fear of being labeled. Anticommunists were turned into boogeymen hiding in the closet.

Kenneth Lloyd Billingsley, author of *Hollywood Party: How Communism Seduced the American Film Industry in the 1930s and 1940s,* commented on how "not a single Hollywood film [of that era] has ever shown communists committing atrocities."[2] Instead, Hollywood regurgitated pro-Soviet propaganda such as *North Star* and *Mission to Moscow.*

In *A History of the United States,* a major high school text, McCarthy is depicted as "a liar. Not your ordinary small-time fibber. No. Senator Joe McCarthy was an enormous, outrageous, beyond-belief liar."[27]

Other history texts falsely asserted that McCarthy "did not discover a single communist anyplace" and that he was the mastermind behind a Red Scare that never actually existed.[28]

Authors of research and opinion departing from the Progressive Party line on McCarthy and Marxism had, and still have, difficulty reaching a publisher.

Historian and former Marxist Ronald Radosh (1937–) was blacklisted from nearly every university in the nation after he wrote *The Rosenberg File* (1983) expressing his opinion on the guilt of Soviet spies Julius and Ethel Rosenberg.

Author Diana West tells a similar story of how her father wrote an anticommunist novel in 1969. After he signed a deal for publication with Houghton Mifflin, a large segment of the firm's editors threatened to resign if the book with a viewpoint of which they did not approve remained on the list.[29]

It was removed.

In 2004 I was informed that my *Going Bonkers: The Wacky World of Cultural Madness*, lampooning political correctness, socialism, and the outrageous orthodoxy of collectivist Progressives, could never be published. One major New York house warned that I would never work again if I released it.

I published it with a smaller house—and have received threats and smears ever since.

And so it goes . . . *Playboy* magazine condemned the Meese Commission on Pornography as "sexual McCarthyism";[30] attempting to control AIDS at its source is the public health equivalent of "McCarthyism"; the *Journal of American Medicine* claims mandatory testing of welfare recipients for drug use amounts to "chemical McCarthyism"[31]

By the 1960s only a few obscure groups possessed the fortitude, the *cojones,* to stand up against the "McCarthyism" tidal wave. It got so bad that campaign donors to the Communist Party of the United States were uniquely exempt from complying with election law requirements to report such donations on the grounds that they might be subjected to "McCarthyism."

The Progressive attacks against "McCarthyism" never mellow. The *New York Times* expressed concern about another outbreak of "McCarthyism" after Islamic terrorists flew jetliners into the World Trade Center and the Pentagon on 9/11.

"I'm not sure which is more frightening," declared Columbia University professor Eric Foner, "the horror that engulfed New York City or the apocalyptic rhetoric emanating daily from the [Bush]

White House. . . . [It is] analogous to McCarthyism . . . self-appointed guardians engaging in private blacklisting [and] trying to intimidate individuals who hold different points of view."[32]

Following the fall of the Soviet Union, Soviet dissident Vladimir Bukovsky stated, "Because of the documents I recovered [the Venona papers from Soviet archives], we now understand why the West was so against putting the communist system on trial. It is not only that the West was infiltrated much deeper than we ever thought, but also there was ideological collaboration between left-wing parties in the West and the Soviet Union. This ideological collaboration ran very deep."[33]

Hollywood film director Edward Dmytryk, who was named in 1947 as one of the so-called blacklisted Hollywood Ten, later broke ranks to offer an evaluation of the period in his 1996 memoir *Odd Man Out*. "What thousands of confused liberals have believed" he wrote, ". . . was that one must allow a seditious Party to destroy one's country rather than expose the men or women who are the party."[34]

Those who cannot remember the past are doomed to repeat it.
—GEORGE SANTAYANA

PEACE FOR OUR TIME

In 1938, British prime minister Neville Chamberlain returned to England after his historic meeting with Adolf Hitler, stepped off the train in London, and delivered the speech for which he will forever be remembered as a naïve dupe: "My good friends, . . . [I have returned from Germany bringing peace with honor. I believe it is 'peace for our time . . ."[35]

Chamberlain was not the first, nor will he be the last, to fall for the deceitful rhetoric of the collectivist tongue. Diplomats and leaders repeatedly return from treks into the lion's lair—*"Don't eat me, Mr. Lion!"*—to announce peace for our time. Instead of peace, what we more often get are "wars and rumors of wars."[36]

After World War II ended, Johnny came marching home to the cities and countryside all over the United States. He, the common man, had sacrificed life and health to restore peace for the common good. The bad times were over, fascism destroyed.

Instead, Johnny got the Cold War, the arms race, "duck 'n' cover," mutually assured destruction (MAD) . . . The collectivist monster unleashed prowled the globe, spreading brutality, retribution, ethnic cleansing, civil war, suspicion, and brushfire wars by proxy. Its heavy footfall was felt all over Asia, Africa, Europe, South and Central America, bringing immeasurable suffering to millions.

In 1949, Communism under Mao Tse-tung conquered China. That same year, the Soviet Union under Stalin test-exploded its first atomic bomb. Inevitable war loomed beyond the next sunrise. Everyone lived with a certain ill-defined terror in his or her soul that, sooner or later, humankind would end with an "uh-oh!" and a bang.

The Berlin blockade in 1948–49 nearly brought the free world and the Iron Curtain to open hostilities. In 1950, North Korea invaded South Korea and generated a bloody conflict that directly pitted the West against Communism. Fidel Castro took over Cuba in 1959 in the name of Communism, only ninety miles from the United States. The Berlin Wall went up in 1961. In 1962, the Soviets secretly installed ICBMs in Cuba, precipitating the Cuban missile crisis, which hurtled the United States and Russia to the brink of nuclear war. The United States and Europe created NATO (the North Atlantic Treaty Organization) to resist Soviet expansionism; the Soviet Union and the nations of Eastern Europe acquired by Russia during World War II countered with the Warsaw Pact. In 1965, the United States sent Marines to South Vietnam to confront invading Communists from Hanoi. Anticolonial movements throughout the Third World began to embrace Communism.

The entire globe appeared ready to bow to the authoritarian superiority and "rightness" of the Communist socialist system. Nothing brings about collectivism faster than the threat of war. President Dwight

Eisenhower hinted that the U.S. government should assume a stronger posture in the lives of citizens in order to counter the Soviet Union's growing power.

"The demands of modern life and the unsettled status of the world," he said, "requires a more important role for government than it played in earlier and quieter times."[37]

Even though the world had fought a tragic war against the dragon of fascist socialism and now peered into the dragon's cave of Communist socialism, there were no shortages of Chamberlains ready, even eager, to appease and excuse the dragon.

Nor were there shortages of little Stalins ready to drive their people along Communist roads to famine, oppression, torture, and death in applying Stalin's first commandment: "If the workers and peasants do not wish to accept socialism, our reply will be: Why waste words when we can apply force . . .? If we do not apply terror and immediate executions, we will get nowhere. It is better that a hundred innocents are killed than that one guilty person escapes."[38]

The hottest place in hell is destined to those who adapt a neutral attitude in a moral conflict.

—ANCIENT DICTUM

THE COMMON MAN

The common man, whether the Ukrainian kulak or the campesino in Latin America, is always a target for collectivists. It is in his name, that of the "worker," that collectivism characteristically consumes a state. The small nation of Nicaragua in Central America in the 1980s is a prime example of Communism in action. It is even better as an example of how so much of the Progressive political establishment in the United States is willing to kowtow, enable, and applaud Marxists as they carry out their plans.

In 1979, the *Frente Sandinista de Liberación Nacional* (FSLN), under the leadership of Daniel Ortega, ousted the nation's current dictator,

Anastasio Somoza, and set about the "total transformation" of Nicaragua along Marxist lines.

"You are either with the Soviets or you are against them," warned Humberto Ortega, minister of defense and Daniel's brother. "We are with the Soviets. . . . [T]herefore, our political force is Sandinism and our doctrine is Marxist-Leninism."[39]

The Ortega brothers transplanted Joseph Stalin's Five-Year Plan to their own country and set about nationalizing means of production, redistributing wealth, and initiating land reform. When Miskito Indian farmers resisted being relocated to collective farms similar to the kolkhozy Stalin established in the 1930s, Ortega's Sandinistas surrounded their villages with tanks and troops and opened fire, burning the houses and leaving bodies where they fell.

During this period I was a freelance combat correspondent. One night in Honduras, at a U.S. Army Special Forces aid station, I watched a five-year-old boy expire from starvation and exposure. The kid's dad and mom were murdered south of the border by FSLN thugs who were attempting to round up recalcitrant campesinos. The little boy had wandered off into the jungle, where Hondurans rescued him. He weighed fewer than twenty pounds, his head a skull with skin stretched over it, his eyes closed, his body revealing every bone. He opened his eyes once, looked at me, and then he died.

At least 400,000 people out of a population of approximately 2,900,000 fled Nicaragua to escape Communism. Most of them were poor—the working class, peasants, factory workers, white-collar day workers, the *proletariat* over which Marxists like to say they anguish.

A couple of thousand Nicaraguan refugees huddled in a UN camp near Jacaleapa in Honduras, where they suffered from rampant malnutrition, neglect, and a variety of diseases that left sores and scabs on their bodies. Pigs lived under better conditions. Homes were three-sided wooden hovels, one room, open to the south, a ground fire for cooking, a communal outhouse toilet nearby. Stench from the camp was detectable more than a mile downwind.

Armed UN guards at the gates kept people from escaping. No field agents from human rights organizations such as Amnesty International had made an appearance at the camp for at least the past three years.

"We are not communists," said a mother with two daughters and a five-year-old son who had been born in the camp after the FSLN killed his rebel *Contra* father, "so the United Nations doesn't care about us. They hide us out here so the world won't know."

Under Nicaragua's new Communist rulers, supermarket shelves where food was once abundant went bare. Poultry, beef, pork, and staples such as rice and beans were rationed and often unobtainable. People hoarded cooking oil. Homemakers stood in lines all day for a bag of tainted cornmeal. Ragged, half-naked children fighting for scraps prowled the streets with their gaunt expressions and distended bellies.

A military draft made it illegal for a teenager to leave the country for any reason other than advanced military training in Cuba or some other Soviet bloc nation. Mail was censored, telephones calls monitored, and "block captains" organized to report directly to the Sandinista Defense Committee in a system of "people control" modeled after Cuba's.

Block captains were charged with maintaining files on all residents within their purview and making notes on possible counterrevolutionaries. If they uncovered a suspect—that night came a knock at the miscreant's door. Thousands vanished into Managua's infamous El Chipote prison.

Liberation theology was the going philosophy throughout Latin America, spread by nuns, priests, and Jesuits who claimed Jesus advocated the violent overthrow of capitalist systems and their being replaced by loving Communism. The official head of the Human Rights Office in Nicaragua was an American nun who assumed the moniker Sister Mary Hartman. She assured nosy reporters that no political prisoners were being held in the nation. Not a single one.

"Your problem is that you don't understand the poor," she chided. "I think the U.S. is evil. I am afraid to go back home very often because I fear an outbreak of fascism in the streets."[40]

According to James Hitchcock in *The Pope and the Jesuits*, the U.S. government, through its Agency for International Development (AID), funded a Jesuit named Peter Marchetti to help the Nicaraguan people. Marchetti, a big-time proponent of Marxism, participated in anti-U.S. demonstrations in Managua while operating on the American taxpayer's dime.

What was happening in Nicaragua couldn't have been clearer from the very beginning. It wasn't as though American Progressives and the politicians they championed had gotten drunk at a Managua cantina, picked up a lovely senorita, and awakened the next morning to find themselves in bed with a slut. They should have known she was a slut from the time they entered the bar.

President Jimmy Carter, for all his naïveté, could have been Neville Chamberlain reincarnated. He jumped right into bed with the slut.

"During the first eighteen months of the new government," reported Lane Johnson in the *Constitution*, "the Carter administration provided Nicaragua with 100,000 tons of food, $118 million in economic assistance, and $24.6 million in emergency food, medical and reconstruction assistance. . . . The United States also helped the Sandinista government arrange for $1.6 billion from international lending institutions and other Western governments."[41]

Even while the Carter administration was helping the new collective state get on its feet, the CIA discovered a combat brigade of Soviet troops setting up in Cuba. The president took a strong line by calling the presence of the troops "unacceptable." In a major address to the nation shortly thereafter, however, he said he was "[satisfied by] assurances . . . from the highest level of the Soviet Government . . . that the Soviet personnel in Cuba are not and will not be a threat to the United States or any other nation."[42]

The brigade remained on the island.

As part of President Carter's legacy, the United States gave up control of the Panama Canal, ceding it in essence to the People's Republic of China. Nicaragua as well as a half dozen other Latin American nations either went Communist or became embroiled in "wars of liberation" that left them with socialist despots at their helms to destroy economies and the morale of their citizens.

Hours after Ronald Reagan supplanted Carter and moved into the White House, he was greeted with news that Carter was being awarded that year's Nobel Peace Prize. The award to Carter, said Peace Prize chairman Gunnar Berge, "should be interpreted as a criticism of the [anticommunist] line the current [Reagan] administration has taken. It's a kick in the leg to all that follow the same line [as Reagan]."[43]

Predictably, U.S. Progressives and the press that supported them fell right into harness with the Nobel Peace Board. MSNBC's Brian Williams asked history professor Marshal Frady if he were justified in calling Carter "the best former President in, at minimum, modern American history, and perhaps, well, I guess, the last 200 years."

"Absolutely," Frady replied.[44]

President Reagan continued to pinch the tails of Progressives and the mainstream press for the rest of his two terms in office by openly supporting anticommunist forces around the world—in Angola, Afghanistan, Africa, Ethiopia, El Salvador, Poland, Cuba, and Nicaragua. His policies preordained that *he* would certainly never receive the Nobel Peace Prize considering those who received it were mostly Progressives or terrorists such as Yasser Arafat.

Nicaragua remained a contention point between Reagan and congressional Democrats, who blocked his efforts to fund anticommunist guerrillas—contras—who were training and organizing in Honduras along the border. Even while campesinos were being slaughtered, Democratic senator Tom Harkin of Iowa and Massachusetts senator John Kerry, later a presidential candidate and then secretary of state under Barack Obama, met with Danny Boy Ortega to proclaim him "a misunderstood democrat rather than a Marxist autocrat."[45]

The Democratic leadership in the House of Representatives dispatched a "Dear Commandant" letter to Ortega, commending his efforts to install "democracy" in his country and pledging the Congressmen's support for the Sandinistas. The letter was signed by Representative Michael Barnes of Michigan, House Majority Leader Jim Wright of Texas, and eight other congressmen.

The latest tin-pot socialist dictators are always up for show-and-tell in Hollywood and in the multimillion-dollar mansions of the limousine liberals and defenders of the proletariat. Dozens of stars and celebrities threw lush, poolside fund bashes for Ortega, the humble Nicaraguan "man of the people." While at the same time "the people" were back home starving their asses off and being spied on by block captains.

The wife of the former mayor of Beverly Hills hosted an event and declared the Marxist campaign to destroy the rich no concern of hers. "I don't regard them as a threat to my way of life."[46]

American Progressives swarmed into Managua to witness the rise of Utopia, sniffing about, noses in the air, wearing compassion and condescension like cheap aftershave or perfume, supporting "the people." Celebrities flew in to donate blood for commies injured by campesinos who fought back, then returned to the United States, singing joyous hallelujahs to Marxism.

Alvin Guthrie, a Miskito Indian, described American "Sandalistas" who came south to support FSLN and the Ortega boys: "They come down in their buses, these Americans, and chant 'We are Sandinistas too.' The Sandinistas roused everybody. 'Come on, get up, the gringos are here for a little solidarity.'"[47]

Historian Ronald Radosh was in the bar of the Intercontinental Hotel in Managua, a favorite watering hole for leftist American journalists and politicians. American University professor William Leogrande, an "expert commentator" for CBN News, and Robert Borosage, president of the Institute for Policy Studies, were explaining to the chief of the Nicaraguan foreign ministry, Alejandro Bendana, how he should play things to keep the American media in the Communist corner.

All the Sandinistas had to do to survive, they assured him, was to outlast the Reagan administration, the implication being that another Jimmy Carter was bound to come along.

How about instead of term limits (for politicians), there's a mandatory prison term after so many years in office for everything we didn't catch them at?

—HUMORIST FRANK J. FLEMING

A NEW PRIESTHOOD

America's understanding of liberty, what it means and what it requires to sustain it, has declined sharply during the roughly two and a quarter centuries since the advent of the Declaration of Independence and the Constitution. Modern Americans have been conditioned to passively submit to abuses and intrusions by government against which Paul Revere would have mounted up to ride.

Progressives bearing the Wilson–Roosevelt legacy entered the twenty-first century with a strong conviction that people like them were born to rule, that in their intellect and natural superiority they would save the planet from the heathen common folk. Naturally, it would all be done "for the people." Progressives, after all, are good, caring people, generous, peace-loving, enlightened. And Big Mama always knows best.

Those who disagree with them, on the other hand, are selfish, greedy, ignorant, warmongering gun nuts who hate women, gays, and minorities and don't give a damn if Granny gets pushed off a cliff. If you don't believe it, ask any university student, media personality, celebrity, college professor, social worker, or Hillary Clinton. People who oppose them are not only misguided but also evil.

"[Americans] are the dumbest people on the planet. . . . [Their] stupidity is embarrassing," opined left-wing documentary filmmaker Michael Moore.[48]

David Carr of the *New York Times* described conservative Midwesterners as having "low, sloping foreheads."[49]

It was up to the "Enlightened Ones" to save such people from their own stupidity. The solution, of course, was more government.

"United States capitalism and imperialism remain absolute horrors for the poor and people of color of the world, and ultimately hazardous to the health of the rest of us," self-righteously proclaimed University of Michigan professor Allan Wald, adding that "an effective oppositional movement in the United States remains the most rewarding, and the most stimulating task for radical cultural workers . . . resurrecting models of cultural practice that can contribute to the development of a seriously organized, pluralistic, democratic, and culturally rich left-wing movement."[50]

"At a time when most of their fellow citizens were ignorant and uninterested, Communists knew about the world and cared about it," asserted Professor Ellen Wolf Schrecker.[51]

Actress Jane Fonda, who traveled to North Vietnam to declare American soldiers "war criminals," is said to have exhorted, "I would think that if you understood what communism was, you would hope, you would pray on your knees that we would someday become communists."[52]

While most of us were busy living our lives, raising families, and working, a permanent political class, a *new priesthood*, arose in Washington, D.C., with the unprecedented power to tax and to use that money to control and corrupt the entire fabric of society—and to push it toward collectivism.

The United States was not founded by career politicians. Washington, D.C., enjoyed a high turnover in the nineteenth century because people were first farmers and tradesmen and only secondarily politicians. They hopped on their horses and rode to Washington, debated, passed what few laws were necessary, and then returned home to live under those laws the same as their neighbors.

President Calvin Coolidge, the vice president who took over the executive after President Warren G. Harding died in office in 1923, refused to run for reelection in 1928 because he believed it dangerous to remain too long in the White House surrounded by flattery and isolated from reality.

Modern politicians no longer serve and go home. They spend their entire lives in government in one capacity or another, turnover having been reduced to almost nothing. They only return to their home districts in order to get reelected. Political alliances, rampant corruption, and a vast bureaucracy with a vested interest in seeing their party picks stay in office make reelection for most a foregone conclusion. It seems the only time anyone is ever kicked out of office is due to some scandal, such as getting a Lewinsky in the White House toilet.

Wait! He *didn't* get kicked out, did he?

"Leaders and gangsters have much in common," author F. G. Bailey noted, "except politicians are much more ambitious than gangsters."[53]

Politics! Poly meaning "many." *Ticks,* "blood-sucking parasites."

As a result of the professional political class, Big Government has every incentive to create even bigger government. "When I took up my little sling and aimed at communism," said Whittaker Chambers, former Communist spy during the FDR years, "I also hit something else. What I hit was the forces of the great socialist revolution, which, in the name of liberalism, spasmodically, incompletely, somewhat formlessly, but always in the same direction, has been inching its ice cap over the nation for two decades."[54]

The perennial socialist candidate for president, Norman Thomas, while on his sixth campaign for the presidency, concluded that "The difference between Democrats and Republicans is: Democrats have accepted the ideas of socialism cheerfully, while Republicans have accepted them reluctantly."

In the 1970s, Walter Trohan, political columnist for the *Chicago Tribune,* asserted, "It is a known fact that the policies of the government today, whether Republican or Democratic, are closer to the 1932 platform of the Communist Party than they are to either of their own party platforms. . . . Conservatives should be realistic enough to recognize that their country is going deeper into socialism and will see expansion of federal power, whether Republicans or Democrats are in power."[55]

Rafael Cruz, father of 2016 presidential contender Senator Ted Cruz of Texas, fled Cuba in 1956 when he was eighteen after having been imprisoned and tortured by the Batista dictatorship. He landed in Austin, Texas, with a hundred-dollar bill sewn into his underwear and not speaking a word of English. He obtained a job washing dishes for fifty cents an hour. He worked seven days a week to pay his way through the University of Texas. Eventually, he started a successful business before becoming a pastor in Dallas.

"I cannot tell you," he said, "how many times I've thanked God that some well-meaning liberal didn't greet me when I landed in Austin and put his arm around me and say, 'Let me take care of you. Let me make you dependent on government. Let me sap your self-respect . . .' Living in Cuba, I always knew I had somewhere to go if I could escape—America. But if we lose our freedom here, we have no place else to go."[56]

Freedom is never more than one generation away from extinction . . . It must be fought for, protected, and handed on for [our children] to do the same, or one day we will spend our sunset years telling our children . . . what it was once like in the United States where men were free.

—RONALD REAGAN

DRAWING THE LINE

In his 1952 autobiography *Witness,* Whittaker Chambers, who had forsaken Communism to expose its agents skulking inside FDR's administration, expressed his belief that Communism would ultimately triumph because of the "intensity of faith" Communists invested in their cause. To overcome the dark cloud of socialist collectivism, he wrote, the free world must discover "a power of faith which will provide man's mind, at the same intensity, with the same two certainties: a reason to live and a reason to die."[57]

A Hollywood actor named Ronald Reagan credited *Witness* for his switching from a New Deal Roosevelt Democrat to a conservative anticommunist Republican. By the time he broke onto the international scene, much of the world was sealed behind an iron curtain of oppression, an impenetrable barrier that impounded at least one billion people while untold others were killed, tortured, and imprisoned with no hope of rescue or outside help. The free West seemed prone to hunker down in fear to accept the inevitable, like Churchill's story of the monkey who makes a deal with the crocodile on the condition that he be the last one eaten.

Harry Hopkins, FDR's former adviser and suspected Soviet agent, presented a policy paper (author unknown) to Roosevelt at the end of World War II that predicted "Russia's post-war position in Europe will be a dominant one. With Germany crushed, there is no power in Europe to oppose her tremendous military forces. The conclusions from the foregoing are obvious. Since Russia is the decisive factor in the war, she must be given every assistance and every effort must be made to obtain her friendship."[58]

In other words, play doggie. Turn over with paws in the air, whimper, and play dead. America discarded proven values in favor of becoming an old whore ready to spread her legs for appeasement and peace. After all, socialism *was* the future. America's withdrawal from the moral arena left an international power vacuum that Communism and its forces were eager to fill.

Author/political commentator Ann Coulter charted the advance of Communism through U.S. presidential administrations:

WOODROW WILSON (1913–21): The October 1917 Russian Revolution brings the Bolsheviks to power. Lenin starves millions of his own people and adds territory by seizing that of his neighbors.

CALVIN COOLIDGE (1923–29): Becomes president after Warren G. Harding dies in office. Soviets acquire five more nations.

HERBERT HOOVER (1929–33): Soviets continue to capture new territory. Stalin starves to death some 10 million of his own people during the Great Famine.

FRANKLIN ROOSEVELT (1933–45): Officially recognizes the USSR diplomatically. Sells out Eastern Europe at Yalta with Stalin's agent Alger Hiss at his side. Promises the USSR three votes in the General Assembly of the newly organized United Nations. Soviets take over six more neighboring nations, murder an estimated 12 million to 20 million people, and force at least 10 million into slave labor.

HARRY TRUMAN (1945–53): Stalin consolidates control over Eastern Europe. The Korean War begins and then ends with Communists digging in. Red Chinese Communists seize China, the most populous nation on earth, and occupy Tibet. Over the next forty years, Chinese Communists will murder as many as 60 million of their own people, along with one million Tibetans. Ho Chi Minh announces Communism in Vietnam.

DWIGHT EISENHOWER (1953–61): Cuba turns Communist under a Castro takeover, the first Soviet-backed regime in the Western Hemisphere. Soviet- and Chinese-backed Viet Cong instigate insurrections to conquer South Vietnam. The United States refuses to intervene in the 1956 Hungarian uprising against Soviet rule. Russians explode the world's first thermonuclear weapon, successfully test the first intercontinental ballistic missile, almost a year ahead of the United States, and enter space first with *Sputnik.*. Soviet premier Nikita Khrushchev, who succeeded Stalin upon his death in 1953, warns the West, "We will bury you."

JOHN F. KENNEDY (1961–1963): The United States is humiliated at the Bay of Pigs fiasco in Cuba and loses a standoff with the Soviet Union that results in the United States pulling missiles out of Turkey. Kennedy, however, backs down Khrushchev during the Cuban missile crisis. East Germany erects the Berlin Wall. The Soviet Union detonates a thermonuclear bomb that is the largest man-made explosion in history, and wins another leg of the space race by successfully orbiting the first man.

LYNDON B. JOHNSON (1963–69): Sends combat troops into Vietnam. Communist regimes established in South Yemen and in the African Congo. China explodes its first hydrogen bomb.

RICHARD M. NIXON (1969–74): Continues America's first serious resistance to Communist encroachment by holding off Communism in Vietnam until he is impeached for Watergate.

GERALD FORD (1974–77): South Vietnam, Cambodia, and Laos fall to Communism, as do four more nations in Africa. Communist Khmer Rouge leader Pol Pot murders half of the seven million inhabitants of Cambodia. Hundreds of thousands of Vietnamese flee South Vietnam, while an equal number end up executed or in labor and "reeducation" camps. Secretary of State Henry Kissinger proposes détente with Russia by proclaiming, "We cannot prevent the growth of Soviet power."

JIMMY CARTER (1977–81): Marxists come to power in Nicaragua, Seychelles, and Grenada and initiate "popular front" uprisings all over Latin America. The Soviet army invades Afghanistan. Carter lifts the ban on travel to Cuba and North Korea and gives a speech on May 22, 1977, exhorting Americans to abandon their "inordinate fear of communism."

Many in the West actually cheered for a world Communist victory. Willfully blind or ignorant of Communism's history of terror and death, Americans remained susceptible to its false promises of a collectivist utopia. Even if socialism has its faults, went the argument, its *intent* was noble. Progressives cradling the Communist agenda under their bonnets insinuated themselves into the heart of American democracy, claiming to have glimpsed the future in which, with a few breaking of eggs, an omelet could be made. More and more political leaders, primarily among Democrats, turned up associated with those in the Progressive-Communist tent.

Henry Wallace, FDR's first vice president, split with the Democratic Party in 1948 to head the Communist-dominated

Progressive Party. Democrat George McGovern noted that he, McGovern, ran for president in 1972 on a platform similar to Wallace's, with the help of Yale Law School grad Bill Clinton.

Socialist Bernie Sanders, who later, in 2016, became a Democratic presidential contender, flew the Soviet flag in his office when he was mayor of Burlington, Vermont. He collaborated with Soviet and East German "peace committees" to oppose anticommunist movements in the United States.

RONALD REAGAN (1981–89): The first president to put up any significant resistance to the advance of world Communism. His bold, straightforward attack against Soviet collectivism and the socialist system shocked American Progressives as much as it did the Soviets. After all, most previous U.S. presidents had made a policy of pussyfooting and kowtowing.

His firm belief that Communism was not only an impossible economic system but also an evil one abandoned completely the "sweet talk" temerity of the Cold War free world. Drawing the proverbial line in the sand, he executed an ideological, economic, and geopolitical offense to leave Communism, as he described it, on "the ash heap of history" by drawing the Soviets into a battle of systems they could not win. No political figure since the American Revolution had so boldly expressed the tone of what freedom entailed as he did in his famous "Evil Empire" speech delivered to the National Association of Evangelicals in Orlando, Florida, on March 8, 1983:

> Let us pray for the salvation of all of those who live in that totalitarian darkness, pray they will discover the joy of knowing God. But until we do, let us be aware that while [Communists] preach the supremacy of the State, declare its omnipotence over individual man, and predict its eventual domination of all peoples on the earth, they are the focus of evil in the modern world. . . . I've always maintained that the struggle now going on for the world will never be decided

by bombs or rockets, by armies or military might. The real crisis we face today is a spiritual one; at root, it is a test of moral will and faith.[59]

Such a wailing and gnashing of teeth all over the left-wing world! Progressives in the United States went insane with fury, referring to Reagan as "reckless" and accusing him of "unconsciously provoking the Soviets into war."[6] Variously through the media he was "dangerous . . . simplistic . . . crazy . . . illiberal and provocative." House Speaker Tip O'Neill charged him with "Red baiting." Dr. Henry Commagen, history professor at Amherst College, said it was "the worst presidential speech in American history." The freshman history textbook *American Journey* subsequently mocked him, saying Reagan "considered the Soviet Union not a coequal nation with legitimate world interests, but an 'evil empire,' like something from the *Star Wars* movies." The *Washington Post* shouted "McCarthyism!" The Law Center for Constitutional Rights, notorious for its support of socialist causes, echoed with, "A move back to the dark ages."[61]

Although Progressives and Communist sympathizers at home opposed Reagan at every turn, his speech filtering into the Soviet gulag was "incredibly popular."[62]

"Finally," exclaimed Natan Sharansky, a Jewish dissident inmate at Permanent Labor Camp 35, "the leader of the Free World had spoken the truth—a truth that burned inside the heart of each and every one of us."[63]

Sovietologist Seweryn Bialer said Reagan's speech "stunned and humiliated the Soviet leaders. . . . [He seemed] determined to deny the Soviet Union nothing less than its legitimacy and status as a global power [which] they thought had been conceded once and for all by Reagan's predecessors."[64]

Henry Kissinger, who had previously championed détente, now praised Reagan as the first American president to present a "direct moral challenge" to the Soviet Union. "An enormous difference," he added, between Reagan and prior administrations.[65]

As for Reagan, he unflinchingly stated that détente "is what a farmer has with his turkey—until Thanksgiving Day."[66]

Although the global influence of the Soviet Union had grown dramatically under the eighteen-year rule of General Chairman Leonid Brezhnev, mostly due to military expansion, Russia found itself hampered by economic and social stagnation. Socialism had, in fact, collapsed in Russia on a number of occasions, revived each time only because, for brief interludes, such as Lenin's New Economic Policy in the 1920s, the free market was allowed to rescue it.

Relentlessly, Reagan kept up the pressure by aiding anticommunist efforts everywhere in the world. Reagan and Pope John Paul II, "one of the great secret alliances of all times," cooperated in destabilizing the Communist regime in Poland to eventually win the little nation its freedom.[67]

The United States installed Pershing missiles in Europe as a deterrent to further Russian expansion, began a massive military buildup at home, and proposed the Strategic Defense Initiative (SDI), or "Star Wars," which terrified the Soviets who thought it would make their nuclear weapons obsolete.

Mikhail Gorbachev, who rose to become secretary general in 1984, realized that the Soviet Union's efforts to counter the U.S. military threatened to wreck the Soviet economy and overwhelm its technological capabilities. He put out feelers for a negotiated arms control. Twice, arms summits failed when Reagan walked away from the table because of Soviet intransigence. The U.S. media, U.S. intellectuals, and U.S. college hordes furiously attacked him.

On June 12, 1987, Reagan delivered his famous speech at Berlin's Brandenburg Gate, which led to the dismantling of the Berlin Wall:

> We welcome change and openness; for we believe that freedom and security go together, that the advance of human liberty can only strengthen the cause of world peace. General Secretary Gorbachev, if you seek peace, if you seek prosperity for the Soviet Union and Eastern Europe, if you seek liberalization, come here to this gate. Mr. Gorbachev, open this gate. Mr. Gorbachev, tear down this wall![68]

The same predictable elements inside the U.S. were wildly enthusiastic in their support of the Soviet News Agency's accusation that
Reagan had delivered an "openly provocative, war-mongering speech."

Gorbachev, backed into a corner, agreed to an arms reduction
treaty, signing the Intermediate Range Nuclear Forces (INF) treaty in
December 1987.

Gorbachev was also being forced to make social changes within the
USSR, with unintended consequences, as a result of pressure from six
years of economic decline in his fierce competition with the United
States. Reagan's victory over the "evil empire" was all but complete
as the USSR began to fall apart internally and satellite slave nations
declared their independence and broke away. By the end of Reagan's
presidency, the USSR was negotiating its own surrender.

"In the Cold War," wrote Reagan biographer Dinesh D'Souza,
"Reagan turned out to be our Churchill; it was his vision and leadership
that led us to victory."[69]

The Soviet Union formally dissolved itself on Christmas Day,
1991. Boris Yeltsin (1931–2007) became the first president of the New
Russian Federation. The Cold War was over.

But by no means did the fall of the Soviet Union mean the collapse
of Communism. Although the Marxist doctrine had exploited, impoverished, and murdered millions of people, there were more than enough
Communists and neo-Communists remaining to meld into respectable
societies and launch new crusades for collectivizing the world, refusing
to consider the stark reality that if socialism actually worked, barriers
of secret police would not have to maintain control and keep people
in their pens.

Socialism still dominates the thinking of intellectuals and public
policy makers around the globe. It is proving more difficult to take
socialism out of nations and out of peoples than it is to take peoples
and nations out of socialism.

By the way, the Nobel Peace Prize went to Mikhail Gorbachev.
Ronald Reagan got the raspberry.

Man is born free, but is everywhere in chains.

—JEAN-JACQUES ROUSSEAU

DOWN THE YELLOW BRICK ROAD

Some dark corner must exist within society and the human psyche that succumbs over and over again to the siren call of the all-powerful state. Knowing the horror of the collectivist state, seeing how socialist nations such as the USSR always end in tyranny and ultimately in failure, why does humankind give up liberty so easily in order to continue down the Yellow Brick Road toward a speculative future utopia that has never been created on earth and, what's more, can *never* be created?

Supreme Court Justice Joseph Story in 1829 suggested *dry rot*.

"Governments," he said, "are not always overthrown by direct and open assaults. They are not always battered down by the arms of conquerors, or the successful daring of usurpers. There is often concealed the dry rot which eats into the vitals, when all is fair and stately on the outside."[70]

America was an entirely different country as recently as the 1950s. A *Leave It To Beaver* world where almost no one locked his front door. Theft and lying and so many other vices now common in modern America were looked upon with the disapproval they deserve. People were basically confident, full of life, full of hope, inspired by a land of opportunity. Government was relatively small and kept its nose out of the people's personal business. The culture was strong and largely moral, the people robust and independent.

Today, bars on windows, burglar alarms, electrified fences, armed guards, gated communities, and suspicion are needed to keep crime and evil at bay. Prayers are not allowed in public, the American flag has been ripped from classrooms, men marry men and sex with children and animals is about to be considered acceptable, drugs are legalized, politicians lie, and no one is embarrassed at being a layabout, a cheat, or a mooch. Cultural insanity has led to rampant divorce and the breakdown of families, sexual anarchy, widespread corruption, passive citizens, and political correctness to silence dissenters.

Young people "educated" at the end of the twentieth century and certainly now into the twenty-first century are fed the unwitting philosophy that the United States is not a force for good in the world. A generation of the ignorant and self-absorbed don Che Guevara T-shirts and demand "safe spaces."

Newsweek and George Mason University conducted recent polls in which it asked a group of American citizens some basic questions about the United States. The group failed in nearly every category: 29 percent could not name the vice president; 43 percent were unable to define the Bill of Rights; 40 percent did not know that Germany and Japan were our enemies during World War II; 67 percent did not realize that capitalism was the basis of the U.S. economy; and 73 percent did not understand that Communism was the main contention during the Cold War.[71]

Further, 20 percent thought the sun revolves around the earth; a majority failed to pick out New York on a map; and only 25 percent could name one of the five freedoms guaranteed by the First Amendment—but many more than that could name the reality-TV show characters of *The Housewives of . . .* wherever, and the winners of *Dancing with the Stars.*

Even when Americans vote—those dwindling numbers who even bother—they vote for what they can get, not what is right or best for society and the nation. A free "Obama phone," another "99 weeks" of unemployment pay, free contraceptives, free college . . . on and on, all of which buys political parties a lifetime of loyalty. Look at the three candidates who led the 2016 race for the U.S. presidency: an avowed socialist-Marxist; a socialist who tries to cover it up; and a populist. Like sheep, the ignorant and unaware can be easily corralled and led to the slaughter.

For decades, oracles such as Ludwig von Mises have attempted to warn America of a future rapidly closing in around us. In his book *The*

Naked Communist, former FBI agent Cleon Skousen itemized forty-five separate goals that a socialist-Communist movement must score in order to take over a nation. The United States has already left many of these signposts in the rearview mirror.

GOALS OF A COMMUNIST MOVEMENT[72]

Capture one or both political parties.

Use technical decisions of courts to weaken American institutions.

Infiltrate the press. Gain control of book-review assignments, editorial writing, and policy-making positions.

Gain control of key positions in radio, TV, and motion pictures.

Control art critics and directors of art museums with plans to promote ugliness and repulsive and meaningless art.

Break down cultural standards of morality by promoting pornography and obscenity in books, magazines, motion pictures, radio, and TV.

Present homosexuality, degeneracy and promiscuity as normal, natural, and healthy.

Infiltrate churches and replace them with social religion. Discredit the Bible and emphasize the need for intellectual maturity which does not need a religious crutch.

Eliminate prayer or any religious expression in schools that violates "separation of church and state."

Discredit the American Constitution by calling it inadequate, old-fashioned, out of step with modern needs, and a hindrance to cooperation between nations on a worldwide basis.

Support socialist movements to give centralized control over culture, education, social agencies, welfare, etc.

Infiltrate and gain control of big business.

Transfer some powers of arrest from the police to social agencies.

Treat all behavior problems as psychiatric disorders, which no one but psychiatrists can understand and treat.

Dominate the psychiatric profession and use mental health laws to gain coercive control over those who oppose Communist goals.

Discredit the family as an institution. Encourage promiscuity and easy divorce.

Emphasize the need to raise children away from negative influence of parents. Attribute prejudices, mental blocks, and retarding of children to suppressive influence of parents.

Create the impression that violence and insurrection are legitimate aspects of American tradition; that students and special-interest groups should rise up and use "united force" to solve economic, political, or social problems.

In 2009, author and commentator Mark Steyn summarized and contributed to this list his Four Stages to the Loss of Freedom:

FOUR STAGES TO THE LOSS OF FREEDOM

STAGE ONE: Government takes over health care. Once this occurs, government can justify almost any restraint on freedom, including regulating who receives it. If the State cures you, it has a vested interest in preventing your needing treatment in the first place.

STAGE TWO: Government increasingly regulates personal behavior. Since the State guarantees all your basic needs, it is increasingly comfortable with regulating your behavior.

STAGE THREE: Lure people into becoming wards of the State. Once they are dependent, it is only a matter of degree to begin regulating their thoughts as well as their behavior.

STAGE FOUR: Control dissenting ideas and words by declaring them "hate speech" or politically incorrect.[73]

Aldous Huxley, in his revised 1947 foreword to *Brave New World*, was not optimistic about the future toward which the Yellow Brick Road was leading.

"It seems quite possible," he wrote, "that the horror [of totalitarianism] may be upon us within a single century. . . . We have only two alternatives to choose from: either a number of national, militarized totalitarianisms, having as their root the terror of the atomic bomb and as their consequence the destruction of civilization; or else one supranational totalitarianism, called into existence by the social chaos resulting from rapid technological progress in general and the atomic revolution in particular, and developing under the need for efficiency and stability, into the welfare-tyranny of Utopia."[74]

6

FUNDAMENTAL TRANSFORMATION OF CULTURE AND INSTITUTIONS

Those who see their lives as spoiled and wasted crave equality and fraternity more than they do freedom.

—ERIC HOFFER

POOR OLD VLADIMIR LENIN. Toward the end of his life, he lamented the fact that socialism, no matter what he tried—from propaganda and forced reeducation to imprisonment and execution—could not completely rid the world of every remnant of individuality. There was always a stubborn minority of holdouts.

"All our lives," he said, "we fought against exalting the individual, against the elevation of the single person, and long ago we were over and done with the business of the hero, and here it comes again: the glorification of the one personality."

"Society is the end, individuals the means," said Hitler spokesman Alfred Rocco, "and its whole life consists of using individuals . . . for its social ends."[1]

THE BEGINNING OF THE DESCENT

A growing mainstream sentiment in the United States seems obsessed with knocking the individual back into the herd, with government regulating all personal behavior, protecting us from every catastrophe, including ourselves, and nurturing us from day care to old age care. Under attack, the nation's cultural foundations, its institutions, are devolving along the line of some futuristic apocalyptic novel and producing social, moral, and economic dry rot that will only lead to chaos and ruination. A survey of the breakdown of American institutions toward collectivism can be a troubling glimpse into the future of democracy and the descent of free men.

> *Woe unto them that call evil good, and good evil; that put darkness for light, and light for darkness; that put bitter for sweet, and sweet for bitter.*
> —ISAIAH 5:20

THE BODY SNATCHERS

The 1978 sci-fi movie thriller *Invasion of the Body Snatchers* plotted around a health inspector who discovers human beings are being replaced by aliens. The duplicates appear as exact copies of the people they replace, except they are devoid of normal human characteristics as they conspire to install a conformist, collectivist society. Like a hive.

It almost seems modern America may have been taken over by body snatchers. And for the same reason—to destroy the culture and replace it with a distorted hive of collective conformity. Once we are seduced by the body snatchers, we invert good and evil and turn the world upside down.

"Counterculture" dominated after the 1960s. The pagan spirit released man from his own conscience. He looked up into the endless galaxies and saw—*nothing*. God, if He ever existed, was dead. Man was supreme, ruled only by his lusts and desires. There was little will to preserve the unique nation that America once was.

There is a vast difference between being free and being libertine. What better way to make people happy in their servitude, asked Aldous Huxley in *Brave New World*, than in reducing adults to infants in need of constant supervision while providing a hedonistic culture that keeps the masses drugged, sexed, and walking in intellectual and moral filth?

"In a society where anything goes, everything, eventually, will," journalist John Underwood decided. "A society that stands for nothing will fall for anything—and then, of course, will just simply fall."[2]

Artists, actors, writers, songwriters, pop singers, and other celebrities take to the dark side to shape young minds full of mush. The explosion of dope and free love launched new lows in vulgarity and moral anarchy.

Filmmaker Frank Capra, who produced or directed great classics such as *A Pocketful of Miracles* and *It's a Wonderful Life*, summed up the Hollywood ethos that took hold in the 1960s: "The winds of change blew through the dream factories of make-believe, tore at its crinoline tatters. . . . There was dancing in the streets among the disciples of lewdness and violence. . . . The hedonists, the homosexuals, the hemophiliac bleeding hearts, the God-haters, the quick-buck artists who substitute shock for talent all cried: 'Shake 'em! Rattle 'em! God is dead! Long live Pleasure! Nudity! Yea! Wife-swapping? Yea! Liberate the world from prudery. Emancipate our films from morality . . .'"[3]

TV and the big screen came up with titles such as *I Banged My Stepdad*; *Mom, Daughter, and Me*; *Teenie Boppers Gone Wild*.

Compare the difference in pop music between the 1930s top ten hit "The Way You Look Tonight," with the modern hit, "Big Man with a Gun."

THE WAY YOU LOOK TONIGHT

Yes you're lovely

With your smile so warm . . .

And the way you look tonight . . .[4]

BIG MAN WITH A GUN

I am a big man. . .

And I have a big gun . . .

against your forehead I'll make you suck it. . . .[5]

These are "tasteless times," *Ladies' Home Journal* decided. "The American people appear to be unshakable now, desensitized to genuine brutality—not to mention the lack of simple civility—and possessed of an insatiable appetite for whatever might once have been thought unsavory, crude, crass, and even decadent."[6]

The Internet hosts 4.25 million porn websites, 372 million pornographic pages, with search engine requests totaling 68 million per day, a substantial number of which are for kiddie porn, bestiality, or other perversions.[7]

Adding insult to injury, American taxpayers are compelled to subsidize much of this madness. "Every artist has a First Amendment right to [government] subsidy," ignorantly claimed Robert Brustein, whose theater is funded by the NEA (National Endowment for the Arts).[8]

A Northeastern Oklahoma State University professor received a $30,000 NEA grant that provided him "the leisure and opportunity to take off a year to write his novel." Marginal writers and artists like him have learned to manipulate the police powers of government to compensate for their lack of actual skills or talent. The professor's novel was never published—but he got to keep the money.

Here are other wonderful, culturally deteriorating projects funded by taxpayer cash:

An art show called "Sensation" at the Brooklyn Museum of Art featured obscenities such as the Virgin Mary adorned in elephant dung and a 3-D acrylic painting of women with erect penises for their noses.

Coincidently, during that same period, the NEA denied a modest grant to a small art academy teaching students to draw the human figure because "the human figure is revisionist and stifles creativity."[9] However, add a vagina, a few penises, a little elephant dung, or some guy masturbating and the academy would have received the dough.

A $30,000 NEA grant went to Robert Mapplethorpe at Philadelphia's Institute of Contemporary Art for his masterpiece exhibit termed "Homoerotic," which featured a self-portrait of the artist with a bullwhip sticking out of his anus and a photo of a man urinating into another man's mouth.

A Manhattan Theater called the Kitchen produced a live performance of a porn star masturbating on stage. "Usually," she quipped, "I get paid lots of money for this, but tonight it's government-funded."[1]

Nearly a quarter million dollars of NEA cash went to another New York theater, the Furnace, to fund a show starring an eighty-six-year-old woman bragging of her sexual exploits and a lesbian inserting her foot into another lesbian's vagina.

A "poet" named Aram Saroyan received tax monies totaling $2,250—a modest sum compared to what others receive—to underwrite the publication of his poem in the *Chicago Review* and the NEA-sponsored *American Literary Anthology*.

The poem consisted of one word: *Lighgt*. That's it. It won the *Chicago Review's* "New Poetry Award."

"You are from the Midwest," the editor of *American Literary Anthology* snapped when a rude congressman from flyover country questioned the NEA expenditure. "You are culturally deprived, so you would not understand it anyway."[11]

The rubes, hicks, and hillbillies wedged between the enlightened East and West coasts are simply too stupid to understand the nature of "true art" and "genius." Workers caused a furor at the Richard B.

Russell Federal Office Building in Washington, D.C., where millions of dollars have been spent on ugly welfare art, when they mistook a large, torn piece of canvas with paint splattered on it as an old painter's drop cloth and tossed it into the Dumpster.

"Skin art" and skin piercings have become the rage as today's strange pop culture reverts to humankind's primitive and paganist past. Tattoos, believed to be the mark of sailors on the high seas, were once virtually taboo for females. Then little hearts on feminine ankles and butts and pubic areas began to appear and spread like mold all over the body.

A young man in his early twenties working at a fast-food restaurant served a Big Mac and attempted to explain the bill to his customer. An inked blue-and-pink snake coiled on the fella's right cheek, balanced by a spider on his chin. Intricate colored designs crept up out of his shirt collar to below his earlobes. Both arms were similarly designed. He wore dangling earrings, a nose ring, a cheek ring, and a lip ring, in addition to the tongue ring that reduced speech to bursts of guttural grunts.

"If you'll take that ring out of your tongue," the customer scolded, "maybe people can understand you. Perhaps you can even find a better job."

Males began piercing their ears with diamond studs to express their feminine side. Soon, multiple disfiguring piercings for both males and females targeted noses, tongues, eyebrows, lips, nipples, genitals . . . Add lip-splitting, earlobe stretching, branding, hair dying, and amputation to the carnage—has the world truly gone bonkers?

Legalize drugs and contribute them to the fray. In *Brave New World,* Aldous Huxley noted how drugs and promiscuous sex are two primary ingredients marking a society on its way to subservience. In 2013, Washington and Colorado became the first states of the union to legalize marijuana for recreational use. Marijuana is now legal in one form or another in more than half the states—at the same time that smoking tobacco is being banned, trans fats are banished, and warning labels appear on soft drinks.

Ignored in the stampede to legalize weed are countless studies citing its ill effects on individuals and society and the unintended consequences of across-the-counter merchandising.

The use of pot has gone up 84 percent since legalization started. A report issued by the National Institute of Health warns that teens who use pot before the age of eighteen are four times more likely than other teens to develop psychosis. One in six will become addicted.[12]

Other research indicates that the *minimum* dangers of marijuana use include heart and lung complications, loss of mental acuity, car accidents, IQ loss, poor academic and job performance, and loss of quality of life. Crime rates rise, the rate of school dropouts increase, and youth unemployment and poverty rates go up, especially in inner cities. More than three hundred thousand people who enter drug treatment each year list marijuana as their drug of dependency.[13]

Even California's Progressive governor Jerry "Moonbeam" Brown in *Meet the Press* questioned the wisdom of opening up Pandora's box: "If there's advertising and legitimacy, how many people can get stoned and still have a great state or a great nation? The world's pretty dangerous, very competitive. I think we need to stay alert, if not 24 hours a day, more than some of the potheads might be able to put together."[14]

In addition, well over 100 million Americans, a third of the population, are dependent in one degree or another on powerful, mind-altering substances to get through life. Tens of millions are addicted to antidepressants; one in five boys is diagnosed with ADHD and treated with dangerous, psychostimulant drugs.[15] An out-of-control psychiatric drug bureaucracy labels almost everything a "mental illness" or "personality disorder" and writes hundreds of millions of prescriptions annually for mind-altering drugs.

By comparison, the drug culture of gangs and cartels, criminal pushers, and strung-out addicts may be a minor problem.

David Kupelian, editor of *Whistleblower*, expressed it nicely with "While America in the age of Obama spins spectacularly out of control—as the culture, morals, law, institutions, government, economy, and overall wellbeing continue to disintegrate before our eyes, and as the forces of evil worldwide wax stronger and get more menacing in the shadow of America's ever-growing feebleness—our solution is: *Get high!*"[16]

The late Senator Daniel Patrick Moynihan (1923–2003) referred to the decline of American culture as "defining deviancy down."[17]

"As part of the vast social project of moral leveling," added social commentator Charles Krauthammer, "it is not enough for the deviant to be normalized. The normal must be found to be deviant."[18]

So why would anyone want to drug our society into a stupor and subject it to what can only be termed cultural brutality? Consult Aldous Huxley, George Orwell, and the other sages who peered into the future of freedom and collectivism. A culture that rejects ageless truths, minds that become twisted in surrender, are soon absorbed into an unknown country that the body snatchers find easy to control.

A familiar TV ad may sum up the new age of advancing cultural collectivism: "This is the age of knowing what you're made of . . . Why let erectile dysfunction stand in your way?"[19]

It is not the business of government . . . to preserve the fool from the consequences of his folly.

—HENRY GEORGE

IT AIN'T FAIR

Progressives can only reach their vague socialist utopia beyond the rainbow by stripping people of their individuality and assigning them group identities according to race, ethnicity, gender, physical attributes, incomes, and so on. Subgroups then batter the hell out of each other in their quest for "equality." Not equality of opportunity but of outcome. Anyone who feels unequal for any of a variety of reasons considers himself or herself a victim of society. *It just ain't fair.*

Out of this has come a culture that worships helplessness, impotence, weakness, and frailty, whether it be real, perceived, contrived, or imagined. Since virtually everyone is worse off in some manner than somebody else, there are nearly unlimited opportunities for people to pander to their sense of victimhood and entitlement. You're healthy only if you're *not* healthy.

Everyone is afflicted with *something*—race, gender, alcoholism, obesity, flat feet, poor upbringing, or halitosis. It seems no one can cope with even life's minor uncertainties without unending whimpering, a dozen self-help books, a support group, and government intervention to level the playing field.

Support groups exist for virtually every affliction: Alcoholics Anonymous; Emotions Anonymous; Workaholics Anonymous; Overeaters Anonymous; Families of Sex Offenders (forum); Transsexual Anonymous (blog); the National Association to Advance Fat Acceptance Anonymous, and on and on it goes.

If you have more than one malady, you can always join Dual Disorders Anonymous. One man belonged to five different support groups. A woman named Nadean Cool required so much support that a psychiatrist convinced her she supported 120 distinct personalities, each of which required sustenance. She sued her shrink for malpractice after he charged her insurance company for *group therapy*.[20]

It is calculated that the number of victims in America reaches 374 percent of the population.[21] Yes, you read that right. Statistically, that means each of us belongs to 3.74 different victim categories. Just the thought of it is enough to make you feel sorry for yourself, whimper, seek a support group, and demand preference and deference and government entitlement.

Body snatchers continue their work in concocting ingenious new categories of suffering martyrs seeking their rightful share of victimhood spoils.

Merely being born white, over which you have no control, may be a fundamental racist act and a hate crime against all those not born with that privilege. Universities have hosted "White Awareness Weeks" to remind whites that, merely as a result of *being* white, they are consequently guilty of victimizing "persons of color."

Males who wear lipstick and skirts and "identify" as female are victimized if not allowed to use the ladies room.

Public schools no longer publish honor rolls in some schools since they represent "an unhealthy focus on grades" and victimize those who do not make the rolls.[22]

A grade school in Cañon City, Colorado, suspended a six-year-old boy for kissing a little girl on the hand, such act of affection making her a victim of "sexual harassment."[23]

Some feminist groups want to make it a crime of sexual harassment for a man to even *look* at a woman, as such an act "demeans" and "objectifies" her. Others want to make it an offense to refer to a group of mixed-gender people as "you guys," since the term may "traumatize" women.

Rob Long parodied the politically correct victim culture in a piece he wrote for *National Review* about a college commencement speaker trying to include all possible sex victims in his opening remarks.

He began with, "Greetings, agender, androgyne, androgynous, bigender, cis, cisgender, cis female, cis male, cis man, cis woman, cisgender female . . . cisgender woman, female to male . . . gender nonconforming, gender questioning, gender variant, genderqueer, intersex, male to female, MTF, neither . . ." On and on, for more than fifty terms, to cover every possible combination.[24]

You're behind the times and unsophisticated if you think there are only *two* genders.

"A wide range of subjective ailments are affected by attitude," reflected TV commentator John Stossel. "Labeling people victims, telling them they need help, teaches them to think like victims. Social scientists call that 'learned helplessness.'"[25]

"Victim" has become such a coveted title that people will go to extremes to acquire it. Take Rachel Dolezal, a white woman who so strongly identified with racism that she permed her hair, dyed her skin, affected a ghetto patois, called herself African-American, and became head of the NAACP in Spokane, Washington.

First came the "transgendered" and the "transracial." Now, along comes the "transabled." A Canadian university teacher, Professor Clive Baldwin, advocates amputating limbs from able-bodied, physically healthy "victims" who "identify" themselves as disabled.

Such procedures, he said, will provide "very much a deeply felt need to become this way because their bodies are wrong. [After their amputations, they] report physical feelings of relief. They feel more confident in themselves. They feel more at home in their bodies. They feel empowered."[26]

Chloe Jennings-White, a former research scientist, was unable to find a doctor willing to make her paralyzed. Even though she was healthy and could walk, she used a wheelchair and leg braces and lived the life of a disabled person. When young, she said, she was jealous of disabled kids and envious of an aunt required to use leg braces because of a biking accident.[27]

Is a rational society, one that still cherishes common sense, too much to hope for?

During Franklin Roosevelt's 1932 presidential campaign, he referred to the "forgotten man at the bottom of the economic pyramid."[28] As time went on, he refined "forgotten man" to include not only the poor but constituency victim groups. It was the duty of the "more fortunate" to pay Washington, which in turn would pay the "forgotten" ones.

The term "forgotten man" as coined by Yale professor William Graham Sumner, had an entirely different meaning than that used by Roosevelt and the Progressives who followed him.

"A and B want to help [victim] X," the professor explained. "This is the charitable impulse. The problem arises when A and B band together and pass a law that coerces C into co-funding their project for X. [The forgotten man] is the man who works, the man who prays, the man who pays his own bills, the man who is 'never thought of.'"[29]

Give me four years to teach the children and the seed I have sown will never be uprooted.

—VLADIMIR LENIN

PUBLIC EDUCATION: THE LITTLE ENGINE THAT COULDN'T

You might expect, with all the effort to protect little Johnny and Janie from the vagaries of school and the hazards of the playground, and with all the money pumped into public schools, that today's children would be the brightest and best-educated little whippets ever to go out to make a difference and save the world.

Wrong.

The United States currently ranks a pitiful thirty-sixth in the world in successfully educating children, about on the level of, say, North Korea or Cuba. Recently, 556 seniors from fifty-five of the nation's top-rated colleges and universities were tested on thirty-four questions they should have learned in high school. The results were abysmal. Four out of five flatly flunked the test.

But virtually all knew who Lady Gaga and Beyonce were.

"American high school graduates are among the most sensitive illiterates in the world," noted Allan Bloom in *The Closing of the American Mind.*[30]

Vladimir Lenin, once a schoolmaster himself, believed control of the educational system was the key to building socialism by instilling values and beliefs in students from a very young age. In education, he remarked, lay the struggle for the mind of the New Socialist Man.

In 1837, Horace Mann (1796–1859), commonly cited as "the father of the American public school system," was appointed secretary of the newly created Massachusetts Board of Education, the first such board in the United States. He believed universal education by government would end poverty and social injustice. He was so impressed with the Prussian education system, in which students were taught skills that made them productive workers, that he supported its adoption in Massachusetts. Other states soon followed. Children would be groomed in practical knowledge, not in knowledge for its own sake.

In 1905, Elwood Cubberly, future dean of education at Stanford, took up Mann's mantle by defining school as "factories . . . in which raw products, children, are to be shaped and formed into finished products—manufactured like nails; and the specifications for manufacturing will come from government and industry."[31]

John Dewey (1859–1952) defined education in his 1899 book, *The School and Society*, which became a bible for Progressive educators, as "a regulation of the process of coming to share in the social consciousness. . . . The adjustment of individual activity [on this basis] is the only sane method of social reconstruction. . . . The mere absorption of facts and truth is so exclusively an affair that it tends very naturally to pass into selfishness. There is no obvious social motive for the acquirement of mere learning, there is no social gain."[32]

Translated from pointy-head-speak, this means traditional schools promoted individualism, which Dewey and Progressives who followed him equated with "selfishness." The prescription for changing "self-ishness" into "social justice" was universal institutionalized schools controlled by government.

In 1923, Georg Lukacs, a member of the German Communist party, established an "Institute for Marxism" at Frankfurt University that became known as the Frankfurt School. He and others who followed began to translate Marxism into cultural terms rather than economic ones.

According to him, the enemy was not so much capitalism as it was Western culture. The Frankfurt School defined itself as "essentially destructive criticism of all the main elements of Western culture, including Christianity, capitalism, authority, the family, patriarchy, hierarchy, morality, tradition, sexual restraint, loyalty, patriotism, nationalism, heredity, ethnocentrism, convention, and conservatism."[33] Its goal was to bring down the West without a fight by destroying capitalist institutions and capturing culture and education, a process predicted to take decades of patience.

When Adolf Hitler brought fascism to Germany, the Communist-based Frankfurt School packed up its ideology, methodology, and copy of *Manifesto* and escaped to the United States, where Columbia University helped it set up in New York City. The Frankfurt School of thought found fertile soil on a foundation already being laid by Progressives such as Mann and Dewey. It was to exert major influence upon education, with little awareness by students that it was hatched in Weimar Germany by Marxists whose purpose was to subvert American culture and overturn democracy.

Ideas spread by the Frankfurt School became more important than learning history or math or how to construct a proper sentence. Teachers colleges in the 1940s and 1950s taught new teachers that their primary goal was to produce students displaying "correct attitudes." America subsequently surrendered her youth and their future to state-run educational institutes where they could be "reconstructed" in submission to the demands of the collective.

The modern public school in the United States that developed out of all this is about "feelings" and "social justice," about inclusion and diversity and multiculturalism. Core subjects are being dropped one after the other. In many instances, a student can graduate high school without ever having taken courses in American or world history, civics, economics, biology, or physics. Instead, political correctness, victimhood, and all the other trash of the feel-good society are inculcated in young minds from the first day of government day care through college. The new symbol of paternalism may well be the ignorant and infantile thirty-year-old playing video games in his parents' basement.

Fourth graders in Skokie, Illinois, are taught that government is the new family and that it will therefore take care of them. A worksheet handout states, "Government is like a nation's family. Families take care of children and make sure they are safe, healthy, educated, and free to enjoy life. Families encourage children to be independent, hardworking, and responsible. Families make and enforce rules and give appropriate punishments when rules are broken. Government does these things for citizens, too."[34]

In 1988, the Senate Committee on Education became concerned that children may actually be taught *too much.*

"We believe," stated the Committee's report, "that education is one of the principle causes of discontent of later years manifesting itself among the laboring classes."[35]

The sun doesn't rise in the east if that's not a call for dumbing down our children.

Further, some educational philosophers say education emphasizing the intellect places unnecessary burdens upon the child at the expense of his "inner experience." Whatever the hell that means. Little Johnny of the twenty-first century may not be able to read, write, spell, pick out Texas on a map, or define the concept of "liberty," but he learns to get in touch with his inner self, serve the state, obey his betters, and enjoy high self-esteem along the way.

Due to early educational indoctrination against free thought and expression, high schoolers exhibit powerful anti–free speech attitudes by the time they graduate. They are more likely than adults to think people should not be allowed to express unpopular opinions. A survey revealed that nearly three-quarters of high schoolers are ambivalent about the First Amendment. Not only do they accept the silencing of opinion considered unacceptable; they also deem it appropriate and even noble to do so.

In 1979, the National Endowment for Humanities and the U.S. Department of Education awarded a $2 million grant to UCLA to develop "new history standards" for middle school and high school textbooks. These new standards failed to mention Samuel Adams, Paul Revere, Thomas Edison, Alexander Graham Bell, the Wright Brothers, or even that George Washington was America's first president. On the other hand, they referenced Harriet Tubman and the founding dates of the Sierra Club and the National Organization of Women. The Soviet Union was commended for "great achievements in space exploration." Former Speaker of the House Tip O'Neill was cited for calling President Ronald Reagan a "cheerleader for selfishness."

In his *The Book of Laughter and Forgetting*, Milan Kundera wrote, "The first step in liquidating a people is to erase its memory. Destroy its books, its culture, its history. Then have someone write new books, manufacture a new culture, invent new history. Before long the nation will begin to forget what it is and what it was."[36]

A People's History of The United States is one of the most influential texts in many colleges and universities and some high schools. "I wanted my writing of history and my teaching of history to be part of the social struggle," explained Professor Howard Zinn, author of the book.[37]

A Stalinist in his youth, Zinn was a well-known radical who supported Fidel Castro and the Soviet Union during the Cold War and celebrated the victory of Communists in South Vietnam. His textbook, supposedly presented from the viewpoint of workers, American Indians, slaves, women, and other minorities, describes the United States as a repressive state run by a corporate ruling class for the benefit of the wealthy. Private property and private corporations, he alleges, support "social injustice" and the "world's greatest terrorist state."[38]

When Philadelphia approved bringing Zinn's magnus opus to the city's public schools, the city council resolution stated, with no intent at irony, "Council does hereby recognize the need for students to be taught an unvarnished, honest version of U.S. history that empowers students to differentiate between moments that have truly made our country great versus those that established systemic inequality, privilege, and prejudice which continue to reinforce modern society's most difficult issues."[39]

On June 2, 2010, the American Left ramped up its crusade to further nationalize and centralize public education by initiating so-called Common Core federal standards. With Common Core, the federal takeover of public education is virtually complete, as states appear willing to relinquish their tenuous hold on local education in exchange for stimulus funds, matching funds, and other bribes.

"The foundational philosophy of Common Core," explained Dean Kalahar in *American Thinker*, "is to create students ready for social action. . . . Nationalizing education via Common Core is about promoting an agenda of anti-capitalism, sustainability, white guilt, global citizenship, self-esteem, affective math, and culturally sensitive spelling and language. This is done in the name of consciousness raising, moral relativity, fairness, diversity, and multiculturalism."[40]

According to historian David Barton, Common Core history skips over or ignores references to topics such as World War II, Hitler, and the Nazis. It mentions briefly if at all Pearl Harbor and the Holocaust. It does, however, go into depth on America's dropping atomic bombs on Hiroshima and Nagasaki, with follow-up discussions questioning American values for having done so.

"A president's job is not easy," begins a third grade Common Core reading lesson. "A nation's people do not always agree. . . . The president's choices affect everyone. . . . He makes sure the country's laws are fair. . . . Government officials' commands must be obeyed by all. . . . An individual's wants are less important than the nation's well-being."[41]

The lesson plan for a little book called *The Jacket* explains, "This guide is for fourth grade teachers. The story centers around a young white boy named Phil who wrongly accuses an African American student of stealing his brother's jacket. It's a fun little book about racism and white privilege."[42]

Frankfurt School philosophy has been highly successful as a "change agent" in reprogramming Johnny into a drone carefully groomed for service in a future utopian socialist state.

"We're losing the culture in our own home and in our churches," asserted Pastor E. Ray Moore of Frontline Ministries, "and it's because of government education."[43]

"Community education is the plan, womb to tomb," declared social and educational commentator Charlotte Iserbyt. "Is it the value of the child that matters? No. It's the value of that person to the state."[44]

She cited a Carnegie Corporation study to draw conclusions on how education is helping transform America from a capitalist to a socialist country. "There is a notable waning of the once widespread popular faith in economic individualism," she said. "Leaders in public affairs, supported by a growing mass of the population, are demanding the introduction into economy of ever-wider measures of planning and control . . . Evidence supports the conclusion that, in the United States as in other countries, the age of individualism and laissez faire in economy and government is closing and that a new age of collectivism is emerging."[45]

Utopia must be right over the horizon.

Nowhere at present is there such a measureless loathing of their country by educated people as in America.

—ERIC HOFFER

TRAUMATIZED IN STUDENTVILLE

As a kid growing up in rural poverty, I harbored dreams of becoming a distinguished university professor and dedicating my life to the pursuit of knowledge. By the time I made it to Florida State University, I was a Vietnam-era veteran of both the Navy and the Army and an ex-cop. University was a big disappointment. Instead of scholarly, inquiring, open-minded people, I found spoiled brats who had known little hardship or discomfort. These were the *professors*.

As for the students, many were bored and affluent campus radicals living on Daddy's dime. Urban revolutionaries, potheads, hippie Marxists out to "make a difference." Florida State *mailed* me my degree. No way was I walking across a stage with that herd to shake the soft hands of people who had rarely worked real jobs with real-world consequences, who lived detached and protected on campus, convinced their "social justice" beliefs were universally held and anyone who questioned them was a dolt or a monster.

Things have gotten much worse since then.

It has been said, not totally in jest, that more Marxists occupy American college campuses than there are Communists in Russia after the collapse of the Soviet Union.

The first two words in the university textbook *Up Against the American Myth* are "Capitalism stinks." In its introduction, the book states, "We can only solve problems . . . by doing away with capitalism and the institutions that support it."[46]

Schools in totalitarian societies function as centers of indoctrination in the orthodoxy of the state. The disturbing trend in the United States to politicize the academic curriculum to "fundamentally transform" society is closer to an authoritarian society than a democratic one. Filling impressionable young minds with socialist ideas under the pretext of education, Charles C. W. Cooke wrote in *Revolution in Dotage,* has allowed Progressives to take over the university system and reshape the American mind. Their ultimate goal is to radicalize the citizenry at large and seize power to implement National Socialism.[47]

Like their high school counterparts, college students are being dumbed down to accept socialism by being fed a diet of inanity and insanity, of licentiousness and amorality in place of a body of knowledge designed to enable them to think for themselves and grow into citizens capable of self-government.

"Every year," concluded author and cultural commentator Ann Coulter, "another ten million graduates emerge, hating God, their parents, America, and Republicans."[48]

Some 90 percent of the faculties of most U.S. colleges and universities consider themselves "Progressive" or "liberal" as they push ideologies that are openly hostile to a free society.[49] Radicals, some of whom are very high-profile, teach on campuses across the United States. Coulter notes how 80 percent of the violent 1960s radicals known as the Weathermen are now full-tenured professors.

"That's all you need to know about the state of higher education today," she said.[50]

James Kilgore was a member of the Communist-inspired Symbionese Liberation Army, which kidnapped Patricia Hearst in the 1970s. He fled to Africa, where he remained in hiding for twenty-two years. Finally captured and convicted of murder, he served six years in prison before he was released to become a "distinguished" professor teaching art and African affairs at the University of Illinois.

Bill Ayers, a longtime friend and associate of President Barack Obama, was a cofounder of the 1960s-era Communist revolutionary group known as the Weather Underground that bombed public buildings. He went into hiding for years before he resurfaced. After avoiding conviction for his crimes on a legal technicality, he subsequently ended up as "Distinguished Professor of Education" at the University of Illinois–Chicago, from which position he recently retired.

Bernardine Dohrn, now Ayers's wife, back then his live-in, also came out of hiding, avoided prison, and became a professor at Northwestern University.

Professor Sami Al-Arian, the North American head of Palestine Islamic Jihad, taught at the University of South Florida until the FBI busted him and sent him to prison for raising funds in the United States to support the worldwide Islamic jihad.

Kathleen Cleaver, former communications secretary for the Black Panther Party, teaches at Emory University.

Professor Angela Davis teaches at the University of California following her acquittal in a murder plot centered on helping her lover, George Jackson, escape from prison. A recipient of the "Lenin Peace Prize," she was an active member of the Communist Party of the United States until at least 1991.

Professor Ron Karenga, inventor of the African-American holiday known as Kwanzaa, teaches at California State University–Long Beach after having been convicted in 1971 of falsely imprisoning and torturing two female members of his radical organization.

On and on it goes. The only way so many radicals end up teaching at universities is because of the education community's sympathetic acceptance of them and their radicalism. The Progressive Left on campus decides what is acceptable and unacceptable, what is welcome or unwelcome, offensive or safe, just or unjust, what is, in effect, *normal.* If the esteemed faculty and their lemming students determine that two lesbians, a male pedophile, a castrated transgender, and a gerbil in a loving relationship are normal, then by heavens, they *are* normal. Don't dare question it.

When the president of Harvard University made a politically

incorrect observation that men and women may have different aptitudes, the ladies took to their broomsticks and forced him to resign.

Steven Hayward was the first-ever visiting scholar in conservative thought at the University of Colorado–Boulder. He had the temerity to question the value of gender reeducation training for the faculty on the subject of male students who dress like women. The gender bender "community" rose up en masse to demand he be punished.

At Marquette University, teaching assistant Cheryl Abbate berated a student in class for opposing gay marriage because his position, she said, *offended* other students.

"You don't have a right in this class to make homophobic comments," she raged.[51]

Such actions, said tenured professor John McAdams, are "typical among liberals . . . Opinions with which they disagree are not merely wrong, and are not to be argued on their merits, but are deemed 'offensive' and need to be shut up."[52]

Modern higher education these days borders on the realm of cultural suicide.

Bard College of upstate New York established an "Alger Hiss Professor of Social Studies" in honor of the infamous Communist spy from the halcyon days of Franklin Roosevelt.

Columbia University has its "Corliss Lamont Chair of Civil Liberties." Lamont (1902–1995) was a socialism advocate and chairman of the National Council of American-Soviet Friendship.

The University of Washington boasts a "Harry Bridges Center for Labor Studies," which "showcases a celebration of communists in Washington [State] history as well as a condemnation of anyone who dared criticize communism."[53] Bridges (1901–1990) was a labor union leader convicted for perjury in the 1950s for falsely denying his membership in the Communist Party.

"The Star-Spangled Banner" and "God Bless America" were considered inappropriate for a University of California–Berkeley memorial service on the anniversary of 9/11. Explained Jessica Quindel, president of the graduate assembly, "Patriot songs may exclude and offend people because there are so many people who don't agree with the songs."[54]

The University of Dallas "will allow the theology of the Declaration [of Independence] to be taught in the classroom as long as it is understood that it belongs to a world that is dead and gone, that it has nothing to do with the world that we live in here and now."[55]

When it comes to educational goals deemed "most important," genuine scholarship bows to inclusiveness, diversity, tolerance, and multiculturalism through a curriculum of indoctrination and powder-puff "victimhood" courses that teach African-American studies, women's studies, Hispanic studies, gay and lesbian studies, and so on. Of course, there are also serious classes—on Harry Potter, Lady Gaga, and the Kardashians. "Nude Week" on campus is also a biggie, during which students are encouraged to strip down and reveal their *vulnerabilities.*

Many colleges provide "trigger warnings" on syllabi to prevent students stumbling upon controversial or difficult thoughts and issues that might upset or offend them. According to Rutgers student Philip Wythe, literary materials such as those of F. Scott Fitzgerald with "grotesque, disturbing and gruesome imagery" are potentially lethal to a student's psychological well-being and could even trigger an episode of PTSD.[56]

Students are sometimes so traumatized by national and international events that they are unable to function and, in fact, become secondary victims. Faculties often postpone exams to allow their fragile student bodies to "heal."

"In America today, particularly on university campuses," commented Jonah Goldberg in the *National Review,* "we reward victimhood with enormous emotional and political prestige."[57]

"One slip . . . even momentarily exposing [students] to any uncomfortable thought or imagery—and that's it," blogged a professor at Columbia, who understandably chose to remain anonymous. "Your classroom is triggering, you are insensitive, kids are bringing mattresses to your office hours, and there's a Twitter petition out demanding you chop off your hand in repentance."[58]

In her dystopian novel *The Giver*, Lois Lowery explores an authoritarian society that has eradicated all controversial, difficult, sad, or uncomfortable thoughts and memories from the world. People are happy robots protected from bad thoughts and choices because "when people have the freedom to choose, they choose wrong."[59]

Universities and colleges purport to restrict speech for the greater freedom of everyone. Take away the ability to express unpopular speech, as George Orwell pointed out in *1984*, and you take away the thought that produces such speech.

Nearly two-thirds of U.S. colleges, institutions that purport to champion free speech and free inquiry, have enacted speech codes to specify which types of speech are permitted and which may be offensive and therefore deserving of punishment.[60] The Foundation for Individual Rights in Education reported in 2014 that 60 percent of four hundred–plus colleges "seriously infringe upon the free speech rights of students."[61] Only sixteen of the colleges had no policies restricting political speech.[62]

New York University prohibits "insulting, teasing, mocking, degrading, or ridiculing another person or group."[63]

College of the Holy Cross prohibits speech "causing emotional injury though careless or reckless behavior."[64]

The University of Connecticut's Policy Statement on Harassment bans "actions that intimidates, humiliates, or demeans persons or groups, or that undermines their security or self-esteem."[65]

Virginia State covers everything at once by banning students from "offending a member of the university community."[66]

Some colleges designate "free speech zones" where students allegedly may discuss any topic. However, speech deemed offensive is still proscribed. If you want to talk about black-on-black crime in black neighborhoods, for example, shut your trap. Take a stand against abortion or gay marriage, here come the Thought Police.

Students at the University of Connecticut are required to register ten days in advance of a planned expression of free speech—or be charged with trespassing in a "free speech zone."

In other areas of campus life, however, the First Amendment knows no such restrictions.

As part of a "well-rounded education," the University of Michigan hosted a "Bondage, Dominance, Sadism and Masochism" class entitled "Kink for Beginners" to coincide with its three-day-long Sexpertise 2014. The stated objective was to teach "safety, communications and . . . basic concepts" of, presumably, beating each other with whips, naked paddling, and tying the little lady's arms and legs to bedposts.

There is bound to be a career opportunity somewhere in all this. Perhaps as an S and M porn star?

The University of California—Berkeley celebrated National Condom Week on the same day that scores of elementary and middle school students arrived to tour the campus. The little darlings received an education far beyond cutting out paper dolls, coloring, or reading *Johnny Has Two Daddies* when a giant penis came strutting around handing out Trojans.

Other attractions at the event included "sex-themed activities such as a vagina-anus condom toss, a vulva and anus 'pin the tail,' and a condom water balloon game." Also, kids were taught about "different types of lube and how each may enhance your next sexual experience," how to "properly use insertive condoms in a vagina or anus," and about "commercial and do-it-yourself barrier methods such as dental dams, gloves, and finger cots."[67]

Naturally, students must be protected from outside sources that might question or criticize what they are learning about S and M and "social justice." It is more difficult for a conservative professor to be admitted to a university faculty than it is for Dracula to get past a doorway festooned with garlic. Even when they are admitted, they are frequently hounded until they have no choice but to leave. One professor equated being the token conservative on campus to being a goose let loose in a fenced enclosure with a pack of foxes.

In a letter to *USA Today*, a "scholar" named Chris Wolfe defended his university's discrimination policy against conservative student groups on campus, saying that by doing so "school administrators are [merely] forbidding an environment where hate, individualism, and repression are encouraged."[68]

Few conservatives will ever be asked to deliver a commencement address—or any other address, for that matter—on most college campuses.

Singer Harry Belafonte, a fervent supporter of Fidel Castro's Cuba and Hugo Chavez's Venezuela, received an honorary degree without controversy from Brandeis University. Somalia-born Ayaan Hirsi Ali, a fierce advocate of women's rights in repressive Muslim societies, was likewise invited to speak and receive an honorary degree at Brandeis in 2014. The offer was withdrawn after the "Muslim community" objected. The Brandeis administrators explained that Ali, who had been genitally mutilated, beaten, and chased from her country, was simply not in line with the university's "core values."[69]

When David Horowitz, author of numerous books critical of collectivism, was invited to speak at Duke University, anthropology professor Diane Nelson led students in a noisy demonstration against his presence, even going so far as to urge students to strip naked to further disrupt the event.

That seems to be the modern intellectual's response to every challenge—strip naked, smoke a joint, hashtag on Twitter, and make a noise.

Judge Robert Bork, author of *Slouching Towards Gomorrah*, was once requested to make a tape about the judiciary to be used in a course on American government. He asked why a tape was necessary when students already had a textbook containing the information.

"They don't read," he was informed. "They don't even read for pleasure. If they are given a reading assignment, they feel agony—which is why textbooks are becoming shorter and dumber."[70]

They do, however, know how to read and spell *Trojan*.

In a poll of twenty-two countries conducted by the Organization for Economic Cooperation and Development, youth of the United

States from ages sixteen to thirty-four ranked sixteenth in literary skills and tied last in math and problem solving with countries such as Italy, Spain, Poland, and the Slovak Republic.[71]

Surveys by the Annenberg Public Policy Center found that a mere 36 percent of American adults could name all three branches of federal government and that only 58 percent of college grads knew that the document establishing separation of powers was the U.S. Constitution.[72]

Little wonder America's pampered darlings from the universities can't find a job and end up at age twenty-six on their parents' Obamacare, demonstrating at Occupy Wall Street against the "1 Percent," and spouting Marxist platitudes.

To disarm the people [is] the best and most effectual way to enslave them.
—GEORGE MASON, AMERICAN PATRIOT

BOILING THE GUN CONTROL FROG

"Before a standing army can rule," Noah Webster warned, "the people must be disarmed."[73]

In early Europe, rulers were reluctant to permit their subjects a means of revolting, meaning the citizenry must be kept unarmed and therefore subservient. It was different in the American colonies. Nearly every settler owned firearms for self-defense and hunting. Entire armed communities organized themselves against hostile Indians and potential enemies from French and Spanish settlements.

Armed, independent men out on the frontier understandably made the English crown nervous.

"When the resolution of enslaving America was formed by Great Britain," noted patriot George Mason during the Virginia Ratifying Convention in 1778, "the British Parliament was advised . . . to disarm the people, that it was the best and most effectual way to enslave them; but that they should not do it openly but weaken them, and let them sink gradually."[74]

"To preserve liberty," declared Richard Henry Lee in 1776, "it is essential that the whole body of the people always possess arms."[75]

That particular truth stretches far back into the history of humankind. Machiavelli in the early sixteenth century noted how "legally armed" citizens have kept governments "free and incorrupt . . . Rome remained free for four hundred years and Sparta eight hundred although their citizens were well armed at that time; but many other states that have been disarmed have lost their liberties in less than forty years."[76]

Foremost in the minds of the American Founding Fathers was the firm belief that people have the right to the *means* of resistance should government become oppressive. The Second Amendment to the Constitution of the United States contains only twenty-seven unequivocal words: *A well regulated Militia, being necessary to the security of a free State, the right of the people to keep and bear arms shall not be infringed.*

Today, any talk in the United States of possible defense against tyrannical government is met with mockery and ridicule. Tyranny cannot happen here, goes the argument. Therefore, individuals have no need to possess weapons, since we have the police and the military to protect us.

"No guns, period, except for those held by law enforcement officials and a few others." argued a *Los Angeles Times* editorial. "Without both strict limits on access to new weapons and aggressive efforts to reduce the supply of existing weapons, no one can be safe."[77]

But who, Second Amendment proponents respond, protects us from the protectors?

The first modern federal action against firearms in the United States occurred during President Franklin Roosevelt's administration with the National Firearms Act of 1934. In addition to requiring gun registration, the act took a page from the early rulers of Europe and enacted such heavy taxation on firearms that few people could afford a gun. A $200 tax, for example, was levied on registering a shotgun when a new shotgun only cost $6.95 from the 1938 Sears catalog.

Since then, momentum continues to build to further restrict private gun ownership: the Gun Control and Omnibus Crime Control and Safe Streets Act of 1968; the 1986 Firearms Owners Protection Act; the Brady Handgun Prevention Act of 1993; the 1994 Violent Crime Control and Law Enforcement Act . . . There are now twenty thousand laws in the United States restricting the Second Amendment, with more being added all the time. The more successful government becomes in disarming people, the more dependent people become on government for their security.

"The first problem [in disarming citizens]," averred Peter Shields, past president of the Brady Campaign, "is to slow down the increasing number of handguns being produced and sold in this country. The second is to get handguns registered. And the final problem is to make possession of all handguns and all handgun ammunition—except for the military, policemen, licensed security guards, licensed sporting clubs, and licensed gun collectors—totally illegal."[78]

Street crime and violence, along with mass shootings like the one that occurred in 2012 at Sandy Hook Elementary School in Connecticut (twenty-six murdered), the 2015 church shooting in Charleston (nine gunned down), and the Orlando night club massacre (forty-nine killed) provide gun control advocates every incentive to howl louder for the abolition of firearms while they yammer to give up liberty in attempts to buy security.

Ironically, the highest violent crime rates occur in metropolitan areas with the most restrictive gun laws. In Chicago or Los Angeles, for example, annual gang-related homicides are nearly twice as high as for the number of American soldiers killed in Iraq or Afghanistan during a comparative period. Sixty-seven percent of all firearms murders take place in the nation's largest fifty cities, with their strict gun laws, political corruption, high taxes, out-of-reach debts, bureaucratic regulations, antipathy toward capitalism, and general, all-around-devastating social, moral, and economic collapse.[79]

Nationwide gun registration, however, which the National Rifle Association contends will eventually lead to gun confiscation, is virtually a fait accompli in the United States. Wasn't that how Nazi Germany, Communist Russia, and other totalitarian states did it—first register, then confiscate?

In January 2014, Washington, D.C., officials required thirty thousand citizens with guns already legally registered to submit to a renewal process during which each owner was photographed, fingerprinted, and squeezed out of a $48 fee. Those who failed to comply had their registrations jerked and were considered in possession of an unregistered firearm, a felony carrying a $1,000 fine and a year in jail.

In Buffalo, New York, authorities cross-referenced the obituary pages with the names of those who had registered handguns. Said Alan Gottlieb, chairman of Citizens Committee for the Right to Keep and Bear Arms, "[Police] then send officers to take those guns while a family is still grieving their loss. . . . This is the kind of behavior one might expect in a police state. . . It proves that the anti-gun mindset knows no boundaries. . . . The final insult is that 16 days after someone dies, his or her survivors could become criminals simply because they didn't report a firearm, or maybe didn't even know it existed."[80]

Anti–Second Amendment gangsters are constantly creating more nefarious methods to disarm citizens. Government disregards the inconvenient fact that virtually no one arrested for a gun crime actually possesses a registered weapon; criminals don't register guns.

Totalitarian societies often rule insane or mentally impaired those who fail to see the light as reflected by government. The United States is following this path.

In 2014, the Obama administration issued executive orders to make it easier for a wide range of officials to rule a person unstable and report his or her name to the FBI as a "threat." Further, Congress passed legislation to restrict access to guns based on a person's *perceived* mental health, thus empowering police to seize guns from those they *believe* might use them to harm themselves or others.

Military veterans are particularly vulnerable. Some of us receive letters proclaiming, "A determination of incompetency will prohibit you from purchasing, possessing, receiving, or transporting a firearm or ammunition. If you knowingly violate any of these prohibitions, you may be fined, imprisoned, or both."[81]

"If more people can be classified as mentally unstable," clinical psychologist Dathan Paterno stated, ". . . fewer people will be able to legally own guns."[82]

Representative Carolyn Maloney (D-NY) and Senator Ed Markey (D-MA) went even further in introducing a bill granting $10 million a year to the Centers for Disease Control to study "gun violence" as a form of contagious public health malady requiring government attention.

President Barack Obama vowed to do whatever it takes, Constitution or no Constitution, to bring "sensible gun control to America . . . If Congress won't act, then I will."[83]

He issued a total of twenty-three executive orders following the Sandy Hook School incident to implement extralegal gun control.

In his never-ending assault on the Second Amendment, he ordered a direct attack on ammunition producers through the Environmental Protection Agency in a crackdown on sulfur dioxide and lead emissions. All domestically mined lead ore would have to be shipped overseas, refined, then shipped back, which meant the price of ammo would "necessarily skyrocket." There was even a suggestion that the market would be government-rigged so that any purchaser of ammo would first have to obtain permission from the authorities.

Intimidation is another method of gun control. In Bozeman, Montana, shortly after the EPA and OSHA officials inspected USA Brass, a company that recycles brass for ammo manufacturing, federal agents with weapons drawn raided the plant. They terrorized employees by locking them in a room and confiscating their cell phones. It turned out the company had violated no laws.

Gary Marbut, president of Montana Shooting Sports Association, explained the incident: "USA Brass managers didn't kneel quickly enough . . . to inspectors and offended them by not being subserviently cooperative. So, the subsequent raid by EPA, FBI, and others was conducted to teach them a lesson about federal power and proper cooperation."[84]

Another chilling raid occurred in 1988. On election eve, police forced their way into a gun owners' rights organization that opposed Maryland governor Donald Schaefer, who was campaigning for reelection on a platform to ban the sale of handguns. Although police produced no warrant, and no laws were broken, they still searched and shoved workers around.

"Police with political assignments are more dangerous than Saturday Night Specials," editorialized the *Baltimore Sun*.[85]

In 2014, in a move the Department of Justice called "Operation Choke Point," the Federal government attempted to dissuade banks from doing business with gun companies by informing them that the companies were being redefined as "high risk."[86]

Anything goes in the war on gun ownership. At the same time that government continues massive legal assaults against the Second Amendment, antigun Progressives are in full-court press to win culture to their point of view.

California has banned gun stores from putting up signs depicting handguns, or even using the word *handgun*. "It's . . . illegal for me to show customers that I sell handguns until after they walk in the door," said gun merchant Michael Baryla.[87]

The Eau Claire school district of Wisconsin canceled Veterans Day ceremonies involving military veterans because "guns are scary . . . and the shooting of guns . . . is something we don't feel is appropriate on school premises."[88]

A teenaged boy and girl were suspended from the Bristol Plymouth Regional School after they posed with an airsoft rifle in a Facebook photo.

Progressive politicians, the enlightened elites, Hollywood types, and limousine liberals employ armed guards to ride shotgun on their own hypocritical butts while they bay against the hoi polloi possessing guns to protect themselves. Chicago mayor Rahm Emanuel, recently of President Obama's White House staff and an antigun advocate, travels around in an armored car with gun-toting bodyguards. In New York, former mayor and "nanny state" nanny Michael Bloomberg, although well protected by men with guns, spent $50 million of his own dough in attempting to bring down the National Rifle Association and its opposition to state gun control.

While access to weapons is increasingly being denied the average citizen, government seems to be preparing for war against its own people. "We cannot rely on our military in order to achieve the national security objectives that we've set," famously declared Barack Obama in a 2008 campaign speech. "We've got to have a civilian national security force that's just as powerful, just as strong, just as well-funded."[89]

Janet Napolitano, head of the Department of Homeland Security in 2013, admitted that the federal government in its nonmilitary agencies was stockpiling millions of rounds of ammunition, including sniper rounds. Hoarding "something like a 24-year supply," according to U.S. Representative Jason Chaffetz.[90]

WND founder and CEO Joseph Farah termed all this "the biggest arms buildup in the history of the federal government—and [it was] not taking place in the Defense Department."[91]

"I'm going to tell you what I think is going on . . . ," conjectured radio talk show host and columnist Mark Levin. "I think they're simu- lating . . . the collapse of our financial system, the collapse of our society and the potential widespread violence, looting, killing in the streets, because that's what happens when an economy collapses."[92]

At the same time the federal government appears to be arming for battle, it is simultaneously increasing its nonmilitary force and expanding its authority. In 1997, 60,000 federal agents were tasked with enforcing some three thousand U.S. criminal laws. Two years later, the number of agents expanded to 80,000, then doubled to 160,000 in 2014.

Before the finals years of the twentieth century, SWATs (special weapons and tactics units) were relatively rare in most police depart- ments and seldom deployed. I was a member of a municipal SWAT and can count the number of times I was deployed on one hand.

Today, virtually every federal agency has its own SWAT armed and equipped for combat—Department of Agriculture; U.S. Fish and Wildlife Service; the Railroad Retirement Board; the Tennessee Valley Authority; the Consumer Product Safety Commission; Office of Personnel Management; the EPA; Army Corps of Engineers; Bureau of Land Management . . . Even the Department of Education has a SWAT, but for what purpose? To round up truants?

Ron Paul, then U.S. representative from Texas, warned America against arming federal agencies. "Under the [C]onstitution," he said, "there was never meant to be a Federal police force. . . . Yet today . . . intimidation with government guns, the threat of imprisonment, and the fear of harassment by government agents put fear into the hearts of millions of Americans."[93]

Although the posse comitatus law prohibits the use of military for domestic law enforcement, the federal government issued proposed rules in 2008 to expand the military inside U.S. borders to prevent "environmental damage," and as a response to "special events."[94] It also established policies for "military support for civilian law enforcement." Department of Defense Directive No. 301518 signed in 2010 provides the president of the United States authority to unilaterally declare martial law and use the military to enforce it.

In 2016, in response to unrest in American cities, the Obama administration began clandestine efforts to nationalize police through the use of federal funds and civil rights investigations of local police departments. The U.S. Justice Department has magnified its efforts to control local and state police. A "Safe Cities Proposal" even flirts with the prospect of "partnering" local U.S. law enforcement with international police through the United Nations in efforts against "violence" and "terrorism."[95]

As we have seen, the slide into tyranny is more often than not propelled by some crisis, whether natural or man-caused. Take a crisis and mix in discontented and disarmed citizens and you have the setting, sooner or later, for concentration camps. History has proven over and over again throughout the ages that the best safeguard against tyranny rests in the right of citizens to bear arms.

Loss of freedom, said Rafael Cruz, immigrant father of Senator Ted Crus (R-TX). "won't happen overnight like it did in Cuba. But it is happening slowly, like boiling a frog."[96]

Religion is the only ideal base of morals and . . . the only possible support of free governments.

—GOUVERNEUR MORRIS

WHEN GOD DIES

The rise of Christianity in the first century provided for the first time in human history a common moral education for the masses. The moral precepts of the Ten Commandments spread to every corner of the world. They were simple and easy to understand: You shall have no other gods before me; you shall not worship idols; you shall not take the name of the Lord in vain; keep the Sabbath holy; honor your father and mother; you shall not murder; you shall not commit adultery; you shall not steal; you shall not bear false witness; you shall not covet (from Exodus 20). Legal systems throughout the world have been constructed on these ten simple concepts.

The United States of America was the first nation in the world to base government and society upon the idea, as the Declaration of Independence states, that "all men are created equal . . . endowed by our Creator with certain inalienable rights." Liberty comes from God, not from man or man's governments.

Religion is looked upon as the enemy of the godless, all-powerful, and infallible State. Government in the United States, like governments in all socialist or soon-to-be-socialist countries, is in attack mode against Christianity. More surrender is demanded from each Christian generation until finally nothing remains to surrender.

In a report titled *Undeniable: The Survey of Hostility to Religion in*

America, the Texas-based Liberty Institute asked several what-if questions: "What if open and widespread expression of religion—in government, schools, workplaces, public places and more—is eliminated, driven into the shadows of society? What if religion becomes an opinion only to be expressed privately in your home or quietly in your church, if at all? What if religious liberty becomes a poor, subservient tenant of an arbitrary and imperious government landlord?"

If that occurs, concluded the report, "then government can erase any of your rights as it sees fit, since government, not the 'Creator' cited by the Founders, will be regarded as the ultimate definer, giver or taker of all rights."[97]

"Once abolish the God," declared author G. K. Chesterton, "and the government becomes the God."

The three most influential thinkers of the modern era who influenced and laid foundations for the secular state to free humankind from the constraints of God were Sigmund Freud, Karl Marx, and Charles Darwin. Freud assailed religion as an illusion and therefore a neurosis; Marx viewed it as a superstition that held down the working class; and Darwin helped provide a theory that left a Creator out of the equation. Under their influence, anarchists of the soul have spent the better part of the last half century vilifying, undermining, discrediting, marginalizing, and silencing faith.

Within the lifetime of many people still living, faith in America has suffered a long string of defeats both legally and culturally. Here are just a few:

voluntary religious instruction in public schools outlawed

school prayer ruled unlawful

reading a Bible in school deemed unconstitutional

the Ten Commandments banned from classroom walls and all public government venues

high school graduation prayers prohibited

students forbidden to pray during high school athletic games

veterans memorials not allowed to display the cross or the Ten Commandments

Bibles forbidden to be handed out on federal property

employers forced to pay for abortions despite their religious objections (thanks to President Obama's Affordable Care Act)

Christians forced to accept and endorse same-sex marriage

the Boy Scouts of America compelled to accept homosexual Scout leaders

All across the spectrum of the Brave New World that the United States is becoming, the war on Christianity rages in the courts, academia, the media, and the general secular culture. From their viewpoint, Progressives are justified in their persecution because Christianity is destructive, divisive, incompatible with democracy, intellectually unsupportable, and a clear and present threat to the American way of life. The Progressive objective is for people of faith to shut up, go to the back of the line, and accept that God is dead. And if you don't, Igor has ways of making you.

The culture war has split Americans into hostile camps. One camp, a growing minority, clings to "guns or religion," as Barack Obama termed it,[98] while the other demands socialism and dependency upon the New God in Washington, DC. Battles are erupting all over the countryside—and liberty and Christianity lose more often than they win.

At the 2012 Democratic National Convention in Florida that reaffirmed President Obama as the Democrats' "Man of Change," the platform was scrubbed of any mention of God. Delegates stood and booed when someone proposed that God be reinstated.

Incredibly, a year later, Democrats gathered for a proabortion rally in Iowa's capital. They bowed their heads while an activist delivered a prayer thanking God for "the blessing of choice" and for doctors "who provide quality abortion care." He then asked God to increase taxpayer funding for abortion and to deliver from fear women who had "been made afraid by their paternalistic religions."[99]

Talk about irony. They booed God, after which they thanked Him for helping them kill unborn babies.

The U.S. Supreme Court, in defiance of all major religions and the history of humanity all the way back to the garden of Eden, struck down traditional marriage laws and found in the Constitution a requirement that the United States recognize same-sex marriage. "We are a better people than what these [traditional marriage] laws represent," asserted U.S. district judge John E. Jones II in Pennsylvania. "It is time to discard them onto the ash heap of history."[100]

The issue is not whether in the privacy behind closed doors you have sex with your German shepherd or marry your gerbil. The problem is about destroying the ancient foundations of society, of civilization, in the name of "inclusiveness" and "diversity," about radically redefining marriage to satisfy less than 3 percent of the population.

Once, not so long ago, abortion and sodomy were crimes. Now, they are constitutional rights extolled and celebrated.

"Deep-seated cultural codes, religious beliefs and structural biases have to be changed," declared Hillary Clinton as she prepared to run in the 2016 presidential elections.[101]

American Christian youth in public schools and universities are grievously attacked in efforts to turn them away from God to the other god.

"We cannot win this [cultural] war . . . as long as we keep handing our children over to the enemy to educate," warned Pastor E. Ray Moore of Frontline Ministries. "The culture has turned against God, against our Constitution and against traditional values. . . . We estimate 70–80 percent of evangelical Christian children who are in public school for their entire educational career are abandoning the church and the Christian faith in their early adult years."[102]

Most never return.

Many campuses, said Frank Turek, author of *I Don't Have Enough*

Faith to Be an Atheist, are openly hostile to Christianity.[103]

The ACLU sued an Ohio high school football coach with an undefeated record because he refused to stop praying with his student players. Coach Dave Daubenmire was forced to resign. He returned to his hometown in 2014, where he came highly recommended to take over as the high school football coach. The school board folded and refused to give him the position after more than four thousand atheists, gays, and anti-Christians led by George Soros's Change.org demonstrated against his being hired.

During Christmas in the suburbs of Los Angeles, little Isaiah Martinez brought candy canes to hand out to his teacher and fellow pupils at Merced Elementary School. Each candy cane bore a brief religious message. The teacher ripped the messages from the canes and tossed them in the trash can while scolding, "Jesus is not allowed in school."[104]

The Supreme Court ruled that the Ten Commandments could not be posted on a schoolroom wall in Kentucky because seeing it "may induce children to read, meditate upon, perhaps to venerate and obey the Commandments."[105]

We mustn't permit *that!*

Federal courts in *Roberts v. Madigan* ruled against a teacher possessing a personal Bible in school. Later, the court ruled that the same school must remove titles dealing with Christianity from the classroom library containing 237 other books.

"In the last days," warned Jesus in 2 Timothy 3:1–4, "perilous times shall come. For men shall be lovers of their own selves, covetous, boasters, proud, blasphemous, disobedient to parents, . . . despisers of those that are good; traitors, heady, highminded, lovers of pleasure more than lovers of God."

More and more Americans are drifting toward the "dark side" as moral decay consumes the culture. But don't worry, offered Edward L. Rubin, Vanderbilt professor of law. We are merely shifting to a "new morality" based on a "concept of self-fulfillment."[106] New generations offended by a Christmas nativity scene or the Ten Commandments now embrace smut on TV, abortion on demand, Internet porn, casual hooking up, gay marriage, and more. Christians are commonly ridiculed and portrayed as old-fashioned, self-righteous, and ignorant.

Culture sets the scene for campaigns of defamation, bullying, and destruction from powerful anti-Christian organizations that have declared open season on Christianity. The National Endowment of Arts recently awarded a $20,000 government grant to an arts festival that arranged sex toys and Bibles together in a display. The display was titled "Bible Burn" because the Bibles were set afire as part of the so-called art.

The Far Left Southern Poverty Law Center (SPLC), which sees itself as a bulwark against prejudice and "hate," lists Christian groups that champion faith, family, and freedom as terrorists.

In 2013, the Christian Liberty Academy in Arlington Heights, Illinois, planned a banquet to honor pro-family activist Scott Lively, author of *The Pink Swastika*. A militant homosexual group of self-described Trotskyites, the Gay Liberation Network, took exception to the private ceremony by demonstrating and hurling chunks of concrete through the church windows.

Satanists, Wiccans, and anti-God "churches" spring up to counter Christianity and contribute to its downfall.

"It is high time," declares the Satanic Bible, "that human beings stopped fighting themselves and devoted their time to building temples designed for man's indulgences. . . . We are no longer supplicating weaklings trembling before an unmerciful 'god' who cares not whether we live or die. We are self-respecting, prideful people—we are Satanists."[107]

The Harvard Cultural Studies Club invited the Satanic Temple of New York City to conduct a Black Mass on-campus. So did "cultural groups" in Oklahoma City, where the temple was fighting to erect a seven-foot tall demonic statue at the Oklahoma state capitol. The statue depicted Baphomet, a goat-headed demon with horns, wings, and a long beard.

"The statue," explained temple spokesman Lucien Greaves, "will have a functional purpose as a chair where people of all ages may sit on the lap of Satan for inspiration and contemplation."[108]

Atheists and agnostics who profess to believe in nothing beyond global warming are constructing "churches" where they form political action committees that advocate for the "rights" of nonbelievers, champion the principles of secular government, and support political candidates who are humanists, atheists, or agnostics.

"When people see respected ethical humanists and atheists serve in public office," declared a statement from the Center for Humanist Activism, "they will begin to dispel many myths about nonbelievers. Humanism is a progressive philosophy of life."[109]

As practiced by such notable "humanists" as Stalin, Lenin, and Hitler.

Atheist Preston Smith demanded the right to deliver the invocation at the Lake Worth, Florida, City Commission meeting. "Mother Earth," he began, "we gather today in your redeeming and glorious presence to invoke your eternal guidance in the universe, the original Creator of all things. May the efforts of this council blend the righteousness of Allah with the all-knowing wisdom of Satan. May Zeus, the great god of justice, grant us strength. Jesus might forgive our shortcomings while Buddha enlightens us through His divine affection. We praise you Krishna for the sanguine sacrifice that freed us all. After all, if Almighty Thor is with us, who can ever be against us?"[110]

The U.S. military, a staunch defender of tradition, is also crumbling beneath the onslaught. The Military Religious Freedom Foundation, headed by activist Mikey Weinstein, compared evangelical Christians to terrorist groups like ISIS and demanded that Christian chaplains be court-martialed for "proselytizing." It was he who convinced the Air Force Academy to remove "so help me God" from the Cadet Honor Code.

In 2015, he insisted that two-star Air Force general Craig Olson be court-martialed for mentioning God in a speech he delivered for—and I'm not making this up—the National Day of Prayer Task Force. "Olson's highly-publicized, sectarian speech is nothing less than a brutal disgrace to the very uniform he was wearing," Weinstein ranted.[111]

Instructors during a U.S. Army training session declared that the

American Family Association (AFA), a well-respected Christian ministry, should be classified as a domestic terrorist group because of its stand on traditional family values. The AFA, according to instructors and briefers, does not "share our Army Values."[112]

Army Major Steven Firtko and Navy Lt. Commander Dan Klender were drummed out of a program that trained and distributed chaplains to VA medical centers—*because of their Christian faith.* Nancy Dietsch, a VA employee and the officers' training supervisor, warned them that the VA did not allow chaplains to pray in Jesus' name during public ceremonies and that they did not belong in the program if they held contrary beliefs on such issues as evolution and homosexuality.[113]

While Christianity loses ground, Satanists, witches, and assorted cults are going for the hill. Wiccan fertility rites are officially sanctioned on some military installations, while Satanists wait in the wings for their appointments as "chaplains."

Significantly, the U.S. government responds to attacks on Christianity not by defending the First Amendment right to freedom of religion but instead by launching its own assaults.

A gay, lesbian, bisexual, and transgender advocacy group attacked a Kentucky bill that would have helped protect sincere religious believers from government harassment. The group claimed the bill was an "endorsement of discrimination." The governor vetoed the bill while expressing his concern that protecting religious beliefs from government coercion may "threaten public safety, healthcare, and individual civil rights."[114]

Massachusetts officials prohibited "adults holding [destructive] traditional [conservative Christian] values" from adopting or becoming foster parents.[115]

Annise Parker, the openly lesbian mayor of Houston, subpoenaed the sermons, copies of speeches, and other materials from the city's ministers in an attempt to intimidate them and prove discrimination because they opposed her gay rights laws.

In 2009, the U.S. government apparently decided there might be members of church congregations who were not submitting to government's will and therefore were dangerous. It implemented a highly classified program to spy on, identify, and expose dissidents within churches who might be avid gun owners or belong to the Tea Party.

Government's notorious use of the Internal Revenue Service (IRS), has proved a major weapon in the ongoing battle against conservatives, including Christians. Surely by coincidence, the IRS targeted the Billy Graham Evangelistic Association for audit on the same day that the Association ran ads urging voters to vote biblical principles on North Carolina's amendment to permit same-sex marriage. The *Biblical Recorder* newspaper, which supports traditional marriage and published the Graham ads, was also tagged to be audited, the first time since it was founded in 1833.

Billy Graham's son Franklin protested in a letter to President Obama: "I do not believe that the IRS audit . . . is a coincidence—or justifiable. I believe that someone in the Administration was targeting and attempting to intimidate us. This is morally wrong and unethical."[116]

All across the landscape, churches are bowing to the pressure and growing reluctant to preach Jesus and redemption, morality and truth, sin and hell and the devil, as though these issues are no longer relevant in the modern, enlightened world. When social cultural issues conflict with religious liberty, religious liberty retreats. As Christianity retreats, it transforms itself to accommodate every conceivable worldview, everything from gay rights to abortion. The clergy has essentially become bystanders in a church going into full retreat with its tail tucked between its legs.

"The clergy in our nation," observed Dr. Ben Carson, noted pediatric brain surgeon and current US Secretary of Housing and Urban Development, "has largely adopted a go-along to get-along attitude. We don't want anyone to see us as bad guys. . . . What the word of God says [is] old stuff . . . The secular progressives . . . will never stop. So, if you have adopted a go-along to get-along attitude, then they win by default."[117]

While millions now reinterpret the Bible to make it more compatible with their particular moral beliefs or lifestyles, such as a gay Bible that does not proscribe homosexuality, or a PC feminist version in which God has undergone a trendy transgender surgery and is now a *she*, churches likewise reinvent themselves in order to be "compatible." A new "metropolitan" church caters to homosexuals. Others hold beer parties with high-voltage music to attract the young. A church in Indiana celebrates the use of marijuana.

In these "socially relevant" churches, *everybody* goes to heaven because there is no hell. Stalin, Lenin, Hitler, mass murderers, serial killers, none of them have to be redeemed. They all pass through the pearly gates to perhaps "fundamentally transform" heaven in their image.

"We will, I hope, raise our children to believe in human potentiality, not God," feminist activist Gloria Steinem declared.

The National Council of Churches (NCC), founded in New York in 1950, purports to be the major representative power of American Christianity. However, Jacob Laskin in "The Church of the Latter-Day Leftists" exposed NCC as a mole lurking underground to destroy Christianity and religious liberty.

The NCC has for more than half a century, he wrote, "remained faithful to the legacy of its forerunner, the Communist front-group known as the Federal Council of Churches. . . . The NCC has today recast itself as a leading representative of the so-called religious Left. . . . [It] has soft-pedaled its radical message [Marxist ideology disguised as Christianity], dressing up its demands for global collectivization and its rejection of democratic capitalism in the garb of religious teachings."[118]

In recent years, the NCC has received much of its funding from a handful of Progressive foundations, such as the Ford Foundation and organizations supported by multibillionaire atheist and One World Socialist George Soros.

The society-wide onslaught against Christianity is yielding astonishing and rapid results. Basic understanding of the Bible by a vast majority of Americans is mired in appalling ignorance. A recent poll disclosed that 30 percent of millennials think Noah was married to Joan of Arc.[119] A recent Pew survey reveals that the percentage of Americans who identify themselves as Christians dropped from 86 percent in 1990 to 70 percent in 2015.[120]

At the height of the Cold War, President Ronald Reagan famously labeled the Soviet Union a "Godless nation." Ironically enough, a quarter century later the leader of the Orthodox Church in Moscow, Patriarch Kirill I, accused Western countries of "spiritual disarmament." Although he was undoubtedly motivated by political considerations, what he said still made sense.

"[The Western political] elite," he said, "bears, without doubt, an anti-Christian and anti-religious character. . . . We have been through an epoch of atheism, and we know what it is to live without God. We want to shout to the whole world, 'Stop!'"[121]

Stop!

"The reason enemies of faith try to minimize people of faith is simple," said T. W. Shannon, speaker of the House of Representatives in Oklahoma. "If you create a godless society, the rights of the people can be manipulated at will. If we cease to believe that our natural rights are given to us by a divine creator, then our rights merely come from a document, a law, a president, or a government. Documents can burn, laws can be overturned, presidents can be overthrown, and governments can crumble. If we leave our freedom to the will of men, then that freedom will surely be stripped from us."[122]

Great civilizations and animal standards of behavior coexist only for short periods.

—JENKIN LLOYD JONES, LONGTIME PUBLISHER *TULSA TRIBUNE*

"I DON'T NEED A DUDE"

Progressive social engineers look upon the traditional family as a roadblock to perfecting human nature. To change the structure of society, they must first destroy old virtues and replace them with new ones that reflect a greater whole in which an individual's life outside the larger social unit is meaningless. In June 2000, a block of developing nations introduced to the United Nations Special Session for Human Rights a statement that read, "The family is the basic unit of society and is a strong force for social cohesion and integration and [its stability] should be strengthened."[123]

The United States *opposed* the statement.

Marriage—the family—has from the first day of history been considered the foundation of a civilized society upon which all other institutions are constructed. It is the strength of the family that ensures next generations will not wreck a nation and its social order. Again and again, great empires have risen and fallen on the moral strength of the family structure.

"It is a statistical fact that the institution of the family has been collapsing in America over the past forty-five years," wrote columnist Terence Jeffrey. "As the traditional family has receded from its historical role as the foundation of our society, what has taken its place? Government. If American continues to turn away from the traditional family, we will never turn back to limited government and the liberty that goes with it."[124]

According to a report issued by the Massachusetts Institute of Technology, the collapse of the marriage culture may be the "defining issue of our time." In 1960, only 12 percent of adults between the ages of twenty-five and thirty-four had never been married. Today, only 26 percent of so-called millennials born between 1980 and 1995 are married at an age when 36 percent of the previous generation and 50 percent of baby boomers, born after World War II, were wed.[125]

Instead of defending children, morality, and the traditional family as women heretofore have always done, the "modern American woman" has taken point in essentially aiding the Stalins and Lenins of today in dismantling the foundations of society. Radical feminism demands the abolition of monogamous families. After all, marriage as a lifestyle is a choice and, once the tradition is destroyed, can mean anything you say it means.

Kate Millet, author of *Sexual Politics*, is one of many Progressives who have bought into the notion that the traditional family is oppressive by nature. She and fellow liberals held a meeting during which they delivered their intent to "destroy the family" in order to "destroy the American Patriarchy."[126] Their method of accomplishing this is through redefining, minimizing, sidelining, and reducing marriage to something less than a lifelong construct.

After all, as pop singer Katy Perry informed *Rolling Stone* magazine, "I don't need a dude [to have and raise a baby]."[127]

Valeria Solanis, president of the Society for Cutting Up Men, brayed, "It is now technically possible to reproduce without the aid of males . . . and to produce only females. We must begin immediately to do so. . . . The male is a biological accident. . . ."[128]

"No woman," sneered Simone de Beauvoir in an interview with Betty Friedan, "should be authorized to stay at home and raise her children. . . . Women should not have that choice, precisely because if there is such a choice, too many women will make that one."[129]

That's the classic stance of authoritarian governments. *Force* people to obey by reducing their allowable choices.

In 1977, Hillary Clinton, 2016 presidential candidate, was hired as a research assistant for the Carnegie Council of Children, which ascertained that child rearing in the Soviet Union was superior to that in the United States. The published report essentially advocated that government replace the traditional family and "undermine the authority of parents whose values [are] considered outmoded." This would be necessary, the report stated, to "prevent parents from denying children certain privileges that society wants them to have."[130]

A society that once held up marriage and family as the ideal has turned into a rising tide of sexual anarchy reeking of decay and destroying the limits of trust and loyalty between men and women.

Divorce is no longer the trauma it once was. Remember when actress Gwyneth Paltrow and her husband, Coldplay's Chris Martin, announced they would undergo a "conscious uncoupling"? Explained the uncoupling couple's New Age guru, Habib Sadeghi, "[T]he drama of divorce . . . [can be avoided by releasing] the belief structure we have around marriage that creates rigidity in our thought practice."[131]

An article in the *Washington Post* introduced "wedlease" as an alternative to lifelong marriage—and to divorce.

"Why don't we borrow from real estate and create a marital lease?" the article posited. "Two people [presumably of whatever combination of sexes] commit themselves to marriage for a period of years . . . whatever term suits them. The marital lease could be renewed at the end of the term however many times a couple likes. . . . The messiness of divorce is avoided and the end can be as simple as vacating a rental unit."[132]

"Renting" a house, or a mate, is no-fault at its best. It's the *enlightened* way.

Old-fashioned marriage, with its idealistic lifelong monogamy and commitment, sets up too many people for failure, said coauthors Susan Pease Gadoua and Vicki Larson in *The New "I Do:" Reshaping Marriage for Skeptics, Realists and Rebels* (Berkeley, CA: Seal Press, 2014).

Not so long ago it was considered sluttish for a woman to appear publicly in her underwear. "Shacking up" was scandalous. People refrained from tossing around the f-word in mixed company. And young men didn't run around with their butt cracks showing.

Virtually anything now goes in today's relaxed social culture. "Hooking up" has become a pandemic where sex is performed as thoughtlessly as jogging or riding a bicycle. It has become cool for friends to use each other for casual sex.

"Some of us believe that friends with benefits can be mutually enjoyable and perfectly suited to our needs," D. A. Wolf wrote in a *Huffington Post* article. "In my opinion, especially as a mother, if you're looking for sex but not in a position to pursue something more, whatever exploring you undertake, you owe it to your kids (and of course yourself) to do it safely."[133]

Mommy's a tramp with spare condoms in her purse.

"Sexual freedom" means 85 percent of young men and about 50

percent of all young women watch pornography over the Internet at least once a month.[134] A significant number of boys and girls watch child porn; half of these kids peruse group and homosexual sex online, and an even higher percentage view bestiality and sexual bondage.

All of this conditions Americans to accept the idea of family as an artificial construct with no more profound meaning than a "friendship" on Facebook. "Consensuality" replaces "old-fashioned" notions of marriage and family. Two people—or three or four or six of various sexes and gender persuasions—can engage in whatever abominable behavior they desire as long as it is "consensual" and "doesn't hurt anybody else." A single mother is a complete family. So are three men and a gerbil, or a coupling of various degrees of "orientation."

A "throuple," explain its practitioners, is the same as a "couple"— only with three people. *New York* magazine introduced the term in 2012 in an article that made it sound so *domestic,* so *normal.*

"Their trouplehood," the article read, "is more or less a permanent arrangement . . . The three men work together, raise dogs together, sleep together, miss one another, collect art together, travel together, bring each other glasses of water, and, in general, exemplify a modern, adult relationship."[135]

Online magazine *Salon* provided an example of the new normal in an account of a woman who shared a life with her husband, boyfriend, and a daughter. "Everyone wants to know how my polyamorous family works. You'd be surprised how normal we are."[136]

Sexual exclusivity, contended the *New York Times*, "gives people unrealistic expectations of themselves and their partners." What is needed, the article continued, is a "more flexible attitude in marriage."[137]

Why even bother to keep sex between consenting adults—or even within the species—when it can be so much more flexible? What's wrong with a man and a woman in a throuple with a consenting Rottweiler?

In an interview of bioethicist Jacob Appel on whether "prostitution, polygamy, incest, and brutality" should be legalized, posted on the web portal Big Think, Appel responded, "I would argue that all of them should be legal. . . . People say they are concerned about the welfare of the individuals, but what they are really interested in doing is imposing their own social values."[138]

In a decision soon coming to a city near you, Australian judge Garry Nielson opined that incest should no longer be taboo. "A jury," he pontificated, "might find nothing untoward in the advance of a brother toward his sister once she had sexually matured, had sexual relationships with other men, and was now 'available.'"[139]

Even pedophilia is making inroads into the mainstream. An article in the *Guardian* entitled "Paedophila: Bringing Dark Desires to Light" argued that the desire to abuse children sexually is simply another "sexual orientation."[140]

"Adult-child sex," "intergenerational intimacy," and "minor-attracted persons" is rapidly gaining respectability. A Maryland conference hosted by a pedophile group known as B4U-ACT suggested that the *American Psychiatric Association's Diagnostic and Statistical Manual of Mental Disorders* should delete pedophilia as a mental disorder the same way it removed homosexuality in 1973. It should "focus on the needs" of the pedophile rather than "obsessing about the 'need to protect children.'"

One of the conference speakers maintained that since children can properly be "the object of our attraction," there was no need to have the child's consent for sex "any more than we need consent from a shoe to wear it."[141]

President Obama appeared unperturbed by the trend toward child-adult sex. He appointed Kevin Jennings to be his "safe schools czar." Jennings is the founder of GLSEN (Gay, Lesbian and Straight Education Network) and advocates child-adult sex through his recommended reading list for kids.

Safe schools?

Two recent decisions by the Supreme Court to legalize "same-sex marriage" opened up an entirely new avenue for assaults on traditional marriage. "Marriage equality" was never the end game. Tamara Metz, associate professor of political science at Reed College, penned an op-ed for the *Nation* in which she admitted that the next phase of "marriage equality" is to eliminate marriage altogether as an institution.[142]

Social pathologies expand as family structures disintegrate. Playing the slut and remaining uncommitted to exclusive relationships invariably produces more fatherless children and fragmented families, with a long trailer of consequences for "baby mama," society. and children. While neither men nor women thrive without marriage, men and boys appear to suffer most. Fatherless boys drop out of school at a much higher rate than girls and end up swaggering the streets with baggy pants and gangsta tattoos.

"Virtually every personal and social pathology can be traced to fatherlessness more than to any other single factor," stressed Stephen Baskerville, professor of political science at Howard University. "Fatherlessness far surpasses both poverty and race as a predicator of social deviance."[143]

In 1940, only 3.8 percent of American babies were born to unmarried mothers. The rate rose dramatically after that: 14.3 percent by 1975; 20 percent in 1983; 40.7 percent in 2011.[144] According to the U.S. Census Bureau, more than 33 percent of American kids—*24 million*—now live without fathers.[145] The social implications of these statistics are staggering in the lower classes, where kids, as William Tucker pointed out in *Marriage and Civilization*, are being taught that "marriage doesn't matter, that illegitimacy is no big deal, and that there's nothing wrong with being on the public dole."[146]

Further, he continued, "Children without fathers are more at risk for drug and alcohol abuse, dropping out of school, depression, delinquent behavior, crime, early sexual activity, and having illegitimate children in the next generation. They are more at risk for abuse, molestation, and incest."[147]

Seventy-two percent of all adolescent murderers grow up in homes without fathers.[148]

A survey contrasting the 1940s with 2015 illustrates the correlation between behavior and family. The 1940s survey listed the top seven disruptive problems in public schools as: talking; chewing gum; making noise; running in the hallway; getting out of line; wearing improper clothing; and not putting paper in the wastebasket.

Today, the top seven discipline problems in schools are: drug abuse; alcohol abuse; pregnancy; suicide; rape; robbery; and assault.[149]

Promiscuity, disintegration of family, and declining male influence all factor into the equation of the rise of collectivism and the loss of individual liberty as families are ripped apart and single mothers reduced to "marrying" government. Men having been diminished, it seems somehow more respectable, more acceptable, for women to depend on government than on husbands.

It's the *enlightened* way.

During President Obama's 2012 reelection campaign, he posted an interactive web ad titled "The Life of Julia" to attract female voters to the federal nanny state. Government, the site implied, would provide for "Julia" and her sisters through every step of their lives, from cradle to old age—if they but voted for Progressives.[150]

> *A state which dwarfs its men . . .will find that with small men no great thing can really be accomplished.*
>
> —JOHN STUART MILL

WUSSIFICATION

Traditionally, man was the hunter and defender warrior. He was stronger and more aggressive than his gatherer female counterpart. He protected and guided the family while she kept the cave and nurtured the children. Today, it seems society is blending sex roles and even turning them around.

I was a cop when women first began appearing in patrol cars. One night, a district car received a call to a barroom brawl. Minutes later, the stressed cop came back on the radio. "Get me backup! Hurry!"

Dispatch assigned a woman officer to assist.

"No, no. You don't understand!" shouted the frantic policeman over his radio. "They're killing each other down here. Get me a *real* cop."

He's slugging it out with several bruisers—and dispatch sends him a 110-pound woman to help him. Of course, not all female cops are petite, like the one dispatched that night, but in this case—and many more like it—unless Police Woman is a kung fu master, the male cop is going to get his ass kicked. She's simply not as strong as the male she's been called to back up. *That's* the reality—not the myth promoted by the new PC culture that pretends women can do *everything* a man can do and do it just as well or even better.

Women are depicted in the increasingly feminized Western world as strong, tough, and aggressive, as *leaders* and *commanders in chief.* One-hundred-ten-pound chicks beat the hell out of male mashers every night on primetime TV, in the movies, in popular novels, even in children's cartoons. Men stand by helplessly and marvel at their saviors' prowess.

A newspaper movie review of *300: Rise of the Empire* displayed a photo of a tough-looking woman accompanied by the caption "Eva Green steals the movie as Artemisia . . . stalking through scene after scene looking for men to threaten and belittle."[151]

Hollywood has built an industry on mocking men and portraying them as unimportant.

In the Bible, David admonished Solomon to "be strong, and show yourself a man" (1 Kings 2:2 ESV). There is little room in the Brave New World for *men.* Our increasingly female-dominated and gay-influenced culture strives to "socialize" males out of their aggressiveness. Make them gentle, sweet, more passive, and malleable. Perhaps even compel them to menstruate. After all, the UN Human Rights Office of Economic and Social Development called the stigma of menstruation a "violation of several human rights, most importantly the right to human dignity."[152]

Call it wussification.

I'm a troglodyte when it comes to manliness. I was a tough cop. I served thirteen years as an Army Special Forces (Green Beret) trooper.

As an Army first sergeant, I took my MP company to Desert Storm . . . Men and women interchangeable? Pardon the expression, but that's what a bull drops in the pasture. It simply *ain't* so.

With manhood under attack and the culture calling for men to "get in touch with their feminine side"—in other words, become more like women—it should be no surprise that "metrosexual" men are wearing earrings and pony tails, applying makeup, shaving hair off their bodies, wearing "Little Lord Fauntleroy" short-pants suits, carrying man purses, and sporting spandex and plastic helmets for leisurely bicycle jaunts through suburban parks.

Even the "generic American male accent," observed author and social commentator Victor Davis Hanson, "has all but disappeared, replaced by a particular nasal stress, a much higher note than one heard 50 years ago . . . a precious voice often nearly indistinguishable from the female."[153]

Wussification of young American males begins at a very early age. The author of an article on the *Slate* magazine blog *Outward*, entitled "Don't Let Your Doctor Do This to Your Newborn," argued that sex is a social construct rather than a biological reality. When the attending physician at birth announces "It's a boy!" or "It's a girl!" avers the author, "the newborn is instantly and brutally reduced from such infinite potentials down to one concrete set of expectations and stereotypes."

Treating "gender nonconforming" boys as boys and girls as girls, she went on, is the same type of "psychological abuse" as that doled out by a parent who sends a boy to school in a dress as punishment.[154]

The Toys R Us chain capitulated to threats of a "discrimination" lawsuit and dropped "sexist marketing and gender stereotyping of its [toy] products to girls and boys" because such marketing is the "root cause of narrow-minded adult gender roles."[155]

David Kemlo received a note from his six-year-old son's female teacher advising him that he needed to help his son "think of other ways to play nicely at recess" and stop playing "chasing games. . . . Chasing is dangerous because we lose control of our bodies."[156]

The Richland School District in Washington State barred swing sets from the playground because, as school spokeswussy Steve Aagard explained, "Swings have been determined to be the most unsafe of all equipment on the playground."[157]

Boy Scout rules ban water guns, paintball, potato guns, boomerangs, and any other "simulated firearms."[158] Needlepoint and making milk foam for lattes, however, have not been banned.

The World Health Organization and the American Heart Association complained that 80 percent of young people are not getting enough exercise, that heart-related fitness has declined by 5 percent each decade since 1975 for kids ages nine to seventeen, and that today's children take ninety seconds longer to run a mile than their counterparts of thirty years ago. Perhaps there is a good reason for such dismal statistics.[159]

Even competitive sports are becoming *non*competitive. A website for the Wisconsin T-Ball League maintains the league's goal is to "develop individual player skills in a noncompetitive environment. . . . There is no score keeping of any kind."[160]

Nobody wins; nobody loses. Little "metrosexuals" germinating.

Some high school football leagues that still keep score fine a coach up to $200 if his team scores too high over another. It's "insensitive" to win by such a margin. It's so . . . *male.*

Kids of previous generations learned to take their lumps and give them. They took care of bullies in their own way. I was of that generation. I bullied no one—and I would not be bullied. Recently, an elementary school distributed a flyer to its students, listing nine rules for dealing with a bully. In essence, the flyer proposed kids cringe and become compliant in their victimhood rather than fight back. Here are the rules:

Refuse to get mad.

Treat the person who is being mean to you as if they are trying to help you.

Do not be afraid.

Do not verbally defend yourself.

Do not attack.

If someone physically hurts you, just show you are hurt; do not get angry.

Do not tell on bullies.

Don't be a sore loser.

Learn to laugh at yourself and not get "hooked" by put-downs.[161]

To which might be added three more rules:

Give them all your lunch money.

Roll up into a fetal position.

Don't worry. The government will help you.

We may soon advance to the point of outlawing males completely in the manly sense. In fact, "man" as a definition is already being outlawed. Princeton University banned "man" in order to "foster a more inclusive community."[162] Gone are such useful terms as: *man and wife* (substitute *spouses* or *partners*); *workmanlike* (*skillful*); *businessman* (*business person*); *fireman* (*firefighter*); *layman* (*layperson*); and *mankind* (*human kind*).

Other universities are busy issuing similar guidelines. Anything is acceptable—except never *man.*

A story from Annapolis says a lot about twenty-first-century America and the state of manhood. A woman in child labor and her *boyfriend* were on their way to the hospital when they were accosted by three assailants. Boyfriend hauled ass, leaving his pregnant girlfriend to fend for herself. It is today's manly way. It's called *cowardice.*

One of the tenets of the so-called Frankfurt School that migrated to American shores from Germany to infuse academia with Marxist theology was the "androgyny" theory, in which male and female genders would be interchangeable and even reversed in order to weaken the capitalist society and bring it down.

In his 1985 novel, *The Time Machine*, H. G. Wells described the Eloi, a people whose sexes merged to the point that they were almost indistinguishable one from the other:

> I perceived that all had the same form of costume, the same soft hairless visage, and the same girlish rotundity of limb . . . In all the differences of texture and bearing that now mark off the sexes from each other, these people of the future were alike.[163]

Western civilization seems to be devolving into a distorted and grotesque version of Wells's image of the future. The distinction between male and female disappears and merges into the "freedom" to select from any number of "genders" ranging from male and female and gay to about thirty-two other combinations. After all, there is no need for the strength of maleness in a Utopia where all are equal, where "social justice" reigns, and where the collective hive controls everything.

> *Heather's favorite number is two. She has two arms, two legs, two ears, two hands—two mommies. Momma Jane and Momma Kate.*
> —FROM THE CHILDREN'S BOOK *HEATHER HAS TWO MOMMIES*

A GAY, GAY WORLD

More than four hundred years before the birth of Christ, Socrates wrestled with the question of right and wrong, justice and injustice, of the best way for an individual, and for a society, to live. In the modern era, we no longer reflect on questions that concern the essence of humankind and their nature. Instead, we seem to have given up on elevating humanity and have succumbed to our baser nature, as though the best we are capable of achieving is to wallow in the mud like pigs.

Over thousands of years, Western culture viewed homosexuality as unnatural and self-destructive. In recent years, however, we have been pressured to overcome the "yuck" factor and accept—to *believe*—that it is natural and normal to see two men passionately kissing each other at their *wedding.* That we allow ourselves to fall into this trap is testimony to how people may be compelled to accept and go along with virtually anything if properly conditioned to it.

What started off asking for tolerance soon sought acceptance, and now demands affirmation. Talk show guru Michael Savage warned of the connection between sexually deviant behavior and a negative view of the overall society. Deviant sexual behavior, he said, seems to trigger rejection of structure and authority, sinking society deeper into the doldrums of immorality and corruption that have destroyed empires from the dawn of history.

I learned one thing well in the Ozark Mountains where I grew up: You live and let live as long as the other fella doesn't try to knock down your fence. So, if two guys want to stuff gerbils, boa constrictors, or each other up their bums in the privacy of their boudoir, so be it. What tees me off, however, is when bearded, paunchy men prancing around in bras and high heels start stepping on my fence while demanding, through government coercion, that I accept and embrace their behavior. And if I don't, I'm a bigoted, closed-minded, homophobic, intolerant, judgmental redneck who should be tossed in jail or sent to a reeducation camp.

Until 1973, psychologists and psychiatrists classified cross-gender attractions and aberrant sexual behavior as a mental disorder often rooted in childhood trauma and family dysfunction. It was in that year that the American Psychiatric Association (APA) declared homosexuality "normal" and removed it from its manual of disorders.

In 2003 the U.S. Supreme Court struck down a Texas antisodomy law that might be looked upon as the beginning of legalizing virtually every form of aberrant behavior. The ruling not only made sodomy a "constitutional right," observed Justice Antonin Scalia; it also "decrees the end of all moral legislation [against] fornication, bigamy, adult incest, bestiality and obscenity."[164]

A mere eight years later, the Supreme Court ruled in *Obergefell v. Hodges* that bans on same-sex marriage are unconstitutional.

In December 2012, the APA again revised its *Diagnostic and*

Statistical Manual to find that transgender was also no longer a pathology.

"If you think there's something wrong with people who want to amputate parts of their body," social critic David Kupelian satirized, "you're intolerant, biased in favor of Western Culture and hung up on the outdated notion that there are just two genders. If you were more multiculturally enlightened, you would realize it is just your own prejudice and narrow frame of reference that is the real problem."[165]

In spite of efforts by "gender activists" and their enlightened Progressive supporters to suppress studies on sex pathologies and their harmful effects on society and the individual, research continues to emerge that paints the "gender lifestyle" in anything other than rainbow colors.

Contrary to the popular perception that being gay is a normal "choice" or a mix-up of genetic makeup, the National Institute of Health at Harvard and Columbia reported that "epidemiological studies find a positive association between childhood maltreatment and same-sex sexuality in adulthood, with lesbians and gay men reporting 1.6 to 4 times greater prevalence of sexual and physical abuse than heterosexuals."[166]

Statistics also show that hundreds of disorders ranging from bipolar conditions to schizophrenia disproportionately affect this "absolutely normal variant of human sexuality."[167]

During the height of the AIDS crisis, *Rolling Stone* magazine published an exposé on a nihilistic underground sex movement called "bug chasing." "Bug chasers" were men who sought the ultimate sexual experience by deliberately getting "knocked up," "bred," or "initiated into the brotherhood of AIDS."[168]

Sally Kohn, CNN political commentator and writer for the *Daily Beast*, announced that not only was she a lesbian but she also wanted her six-year-old daughter to grow up to be gay.[169]

Countless studies sound the alarm over high rates of disease and clinical depression within the gender communities. Gay sex, warned Dr. Paul Church, a veteran urologist at Beth Israel Deaconess Medical Center, is a dangerous lifestyle.[170] Half of all gay and bisexual men will be HIV-positive by age fifty.

The *International Journal of Epidemiology* issues even worse news—the life expectancy at age twenty for homosexual and bisexual men is eight to twenty years less than for all men. "That's a lifestyle shortening of life expectancy greater than obesity and tobacco use," stated the *Journal.*[171]

Dr. Paul R. McHugh, professor of psychiatry at John Hopkins Hospital, pointed to research indicating that the suicide rate among transgenders with reassignment surgery is twenty times higher than the suicide rate among non-transgenders.[172] Over 40 percent of transgenders living in the United States attempt to commit suicide after whacking off or adding to their parts.[173]

So, in lieu of all this, what happened in such a relatively short time to lead the nation from criminalizing sodomy to celebrating it and all its accessories?

The Gay Rights Movement has been wall-to-wall "in your face" since it came out of the closet. First came the public relations push, with clarion calls for "tolerance," "acceptance," and "equality." Gay Day celebrations. Gay Pride marches. Come "out of the closet." Be proud. Be visible. Raise awareness. Then, to speed up the process, came indoctrination and intimidation in an emotional campaign designed to overwhelm the average person's prior belief systems and reprogram him or her the "right" way.

"It's all done in the name of 'inclusion' and 'non-discrimination,'" remarked columnist Mona Charen. "[L]et's face it, there's an element of fashion in it. Non-traditional sexual behavior is 'in.' . . . We have elevated sexual appetites—especially unusual sexual tastes—to an exalted status."[174]

During the 2013 Christmas season, the Gay Day "Screw You" show went on the road out of New York and into the nation's hinterlands with *The Most Fabulous Story Ever Told.* In the basement of the Oklahoma City Civic Center Music Hall, homosexual characters satirized biblical stories and simulated homosexual sex as Adam encountered Steve in the garden of Eden and lesbian couples Jane and Mable insisted *they* were earth's original couple.

It seemed gay political correctness couldn't get much more flagrant than when the U.S. embassy in Israel celebrated LGBT Pride Week by hoisting a rainbow "gay pride" flag. It turned out political correctness *could* get more flagrant: President Obama lit up the entire White House in homosexual rainbow colors to celebrate the Supreme Court's ruling in favor of same-sex marriage.

Ostensibly as part of a campaign to prevent AIDS, the U.S. government turned pimp by funding an ad for a gay night club in the *Washington Blade*, a gay newspaper: *Tired of the bar scene? Tired of phonies? Want to go beyond type? Come and meet real men.*[175]

As part of the indoctrination and conditioning crusade, political correctness requires that popular culture portray homosexuals sympathetically and as more noble than heterosexuals. Gay characters on TV and in the movies are rarely if ever bad guys.

"Television and movie producers began to do stories promoting homosexuality as a legitimate lifestyle," said Dr. Charles Socarides of the British Health Services. "A gay review board told Hollywood how it should deal or not deal with homosexuality. Mainstream publishers turned down books that objected to the gay revolution."[176]

The popular media went absolutely nutty over Bruce Jenner when the former Olympic decathlon champion announced his transition to "womanhood." ESPN extended him a "courage" award, presumably for curling his hair, applying makeup, donning a bra and dress, and changing his name to "Caitlyn." Immediately, with that, *he* became a *she*, even though *he* retains male equipment. The *Washington Post* fawned over him: *Radiant in a white dress at the ESPY awards on Wednesday, Caitlyn Jenner seemed a woman on top of the world.*[177]

Public schools have fallen under the gay purview, teaching kids as young as five that being gay and transgender is normal and that to disagree means you are intolerant and mean. Bit by bit, school curricula proceed up the scale of burlesque. Enlightened "sexual health" courses teach that consensual sex, of whatever combination of performers, is "safe" as long as condoms are used. Pro-homosexual teachers counsel "sexually confused" children in the sixth grade to embrace the homosexual lifestyle. Never mind that most studies show that such children, left alone, sort things out for themselves the normal boy-girl way. Pardon the use of the word "normal," when *everybody* knows there is no such condition as *normal*.

Lincoln Public Schools in Nebraska instructed teachers to avoid abusive language such as "boys and girls" and "ladies and gentlemen," and similarly offensive gender expressions. In a document created by a group called "Gender Spectrums," teachers were provided 12 steps to avoid creating a "gendered space."[178]

Minnesota's State High School Athletic League, in addition to requiring "Transgender Sensitivity Training" of all students, teachers, parents, staff, and counselors, drafted a policy allowing "transgender" children who believe they are born in the wrong biological bodies to participate on sports teams according to their "perceived gender," regardless of "gender assignment at birth."[179]

Mount Holyoke, a women-only college, accepts any student who is "biologically born male but identifies as woman."[180] *The Vagina Monologues* were banned from campus because the performance "is demeaning to 'women' who have penises."[181]

"Those in academia who attempt to reveal the truth about sexual deviancy," said Dr. Charles Socarides, "were soon silenced at their own professional meetings. Our lectures were canceled inside academe and our research papers turned down in the learned journals."[182]

Formerly looked upon as moral and psychological deviants, homosexuals, transgenders, and others of the gender-bender bent are now honored, idealized, defended as "victims," and celebrated as role models. The search was on in early 2014 to locate heroes to hold up as "courageous" examples when the U.S. government established a team within the National Park Service to locate and preserve as national heritages locations of "'significance' to the 'history of lesbian, gay, transgender, and bisexual Americans . . . [an] 'important step to recognize the courageous contributions of LGBT Americans.'" One of these sites was a camera shop in San Francisco that had belonged to gay city official

Harvey Milk, who was killed in 1978 during a political dispute with a fellow assembly member.[183]

California proclaimed a state holiday in his name—Harvey Milk Day. A commemorative postage stamp was issued in his memory. President Obama posthumously awarded him the Presidential Medal of Freedom, and in 2016 named a U.S. Navy ship in his honor.

However, as is often the case, there is more to the story. Milk's biographer described this honored and venerated hero as a pedophile and "sexual predator of teenage boys, most of them runaways with drug problems, and an advocate of multiple sex relations at the same time."[184]

Research suggests promiscuity of strenuous proportions to be the norm among male homosexuals: 43 percent of gay men have had five hundred or more partners *each*.[185] Andrew Sullivan, an eloquent advocate of gayness, defends "the beauty and mystery and spirituality of sex, even anonymous sex."[186]

A recent Pew poll revealed that people believe gays, lesbians, and the rest of the "gender confused community" make up at least a quarter of the American population when the actual percentage is about 3 percent or less. This 3 percent, however, seems to have the strength of the Man of Steel when backed by a campaign of intimidation as pervasive and nefarious as stink on a Porta-Potty. Intimidation is tyranny's most effective weapon, which at its rawest in a politically correct society will shut up most dissenters and even force them to change their beliefs and become dead-eyed sheep willing to accept any indoctrination.

During the Miss America finals one year, judges trapped Miss California, Carrie Prejean, when they asked her opinion on same-sex marriage. Those less forthright would have spun like a top to avoid answering the question.

"I believe that a marriage should be between a man and a woman," she responded honestly. "No offense to anybody out there, but that's how I was raised."[187]

Outrageous! She was widely mocked and ridiculed. You're not *allowed* to think that way. The lesson was clear: Keep your mouth shut and go along to get along until you've given up the entire store down to the welcome mat at the front door.

National Football League's Tim Tebow was similarly mocked for his outspoken Christian faith. After the NFL cut him from its lineup, ostensibly because his high profile as a Christian was a "distraction," chiding remarks directed at him appeared in the *Huffington Post:*

"Awwwww! I bet this made the Baby Jesus weep. Tim should have prayed more."

"Hey, Tim are you getting the message now? Nothing fails like prayer."

"Where is your God now, Tebow?"[188]

On the other hand, when NFL draftee Michael Sam emerged from the closet as the league's first openly gay player, even passionately kissing his lover on national TV, nothing followed but fawning approval. President Obama personally called to congratulate him on his NFL selection.

Columnist/author David Limbaugh, among others, points out that there is no such thing as free speech if it's critical of the LGBT gang.[189] Or, for that matter, of any other Progressive sacred cow. Jobs are lost, careers wrecked through the pressure of intimidation by the noisy bearers of the rainbow flag.

Brendan Eich, CEO of Mozilla Technology, lost his position after it was discovered he'd donated to California's Proposition 8, which sought to confirm that marriage meant between a man and a woman.

Two New York radio hosts, Kimberly Ray and Barry Beck, were fired for satirizing the local government's paying for transgender counseling and surgery for its employees.

The Gay mafia and its supporters boycotted and marched against Chick-fil-A because the restaurant chain's CEO, Dan Cathy, opposed same-sex marriage. Chicago Mayor Rahm Emanuel, of the Obama White House staff, barred Chick-fil-A from his city. Several enlightened universities also banned Cathy's chicken.

On threat of losing their jobs, San Diego firefighters were forced to participate in the city's Gay Pride parade, where half-dressed men, women, and other "gender preferences" strutted their stuff and engaged in pretend sex with each other.

Natalie Johnson lost her job at Macy's for telling a teen cross-dressing male that he could not use the female fitting room.

New U.S. passport application forms require the names of "Parent One" and "Parent Two" rather than "Mother" and "Father."

In forty-seven states and Washington, D.C., a person can legally change his or her birth certificate to reflect sexual conversion or identity.

"How many legs does a dog have if you call the tail a leg?" Abraham Lincoln is credited with asking rhetorically. He reportedly answered his own rhetoric with simple common sense: "Four. Calling a tail a leg doesn't make it a leg."

"One last barrier to 'gay' cultural hegemony remains," declared pastor, activist, and evangelical attorney Scott Lively: "the Christian church." He wrote this in an open letter to Christian leaders in America as he recounted the story of the Stonewall riots and their inspiration, gay agenda founder Herbert Marcuse.[190]

In a brochure he published for pastors that explains what the Bible says about homosexuality, Lively warned, "A dangerous modern heresy called 'gay theology' is infiltrating the Christian church at an alarming pace. Many believers, fearful of being called 'haters,' are trivializing the threat by calling homosexuality *just another sin.*

"But from Genesis to Revelation," he continued, the Bible teaches that homosexuality is NOT 'just another sin.' It is a symbol of extreme rebellion against God and harbinger of His wrath."[191]

Like the Boy Scouts, Christians are folding to the onslaught of intimidation. Yes, *all* sinners are welcome in church—but sinners should not be welcome to change the church to accommodate their particular pet sin. Throughout the nation, churches are losing their congregations while they celebrate Gay Pride Week and appoint practicing gay pastors and priests to their podiums.

Jesus indeed taught love, but he never taught the acceptance of sin.

He taught change and redemption from sin.

Progressives of whatever ilk depend on the triad of *separate, intimidate, indoctrinate* to win their battles. And if that doesn't work, there are always gulags and bullets. While the gay rights movement has metastasized into a pervasive force, it is government that can turn it into totalitarianism that violates everything from free speech and free association to what ministers are allowed to say from the pulpit. It is to the point that speaking out in an unacceptable way on a controversial topic can land you in jail.

Government has initiated a number of mandates, laws, and regulations to ensure politically correct beliefs and behavior when it comes to gender. That these fail to strike most Progressives as dangerous or absurd speaks to their peculiar mind-set.

After U.S. House Minority Leader Nancy Pelosi (D-CA) failed at passing a coed bathroom bill to satisfy the fifty-eight gender identity options listed on Facebook, the Obama administration issued an executive order that accomplished what Congress would not. It deemed that "transgender individuals . . . once he or she has begun living and working full-time in the gender that reflects his or her identity, should [be allowed] access to restrooms and (if provided to other employees) locker room facilities consistent with his or her gender identity."[192]

San Antonio proposed a law to bar Christians from serving in government if they had ever demonstrated "bias" against LGBTs.

California was the first state in the nation to pass a law ordering that gay history be taught in public schools, along with a mandate that gay, lesbian, transgender, and bisexual individuals be extolled as role models.

A Denver court forbade a mother on threat of criminal contempt charges from telling her own child that homosexuality is wrong or from exposing the daughter to any idea "that can be considered homophobic."[193]

The tyranny of institutional insanity continues throughout the culture of the Brave New World. Rather than promoting democracy and individual freedom around the world, the United States now wants to advance Sodom and Gomorrah. In a tribute to globalism, a coalition of congressional Democrats led by Senator Ed Markey of Massachusetts contrived an effort called the "International Human Rights Act" that would compel the U.S. State Department to "make preventing and responding to discrimination and violence against the LGBT community a foreign policy priority and devise a global strategy to achieve these goals."[194]

U.S. district judge Michael Posner asserted that such discrimination issues ought to fall under the purview of the United Nations, while defense attorney Horatio Mihet took a step further to opine that anyone "opposing special designation for homosexuals [should be] considered an international human rights criminal."[195]

The end game for Progressives is to use the gay movement as another tool to dictate what you can and cannot say, what you can and cannot do, what you can and cannot *think*. What else is left once the last bastion of morality abdicates as a roadblock to mandatory acceptance of the Brave New World? Recalcitrants will end up in a padded room, where Big Nanny and Nurse Ratchet administer generous doses of social Prozac to make sure everyone behaves in, and believes in, a proper, *enlightened* manner.

> *It will avail us little if the members of our defeated force are all equal.*
> *History will treat us for what we were: a social curiosity that failed.*[196]
> —PROFESSOR RICHARD A. GABRIEL

THE FIGHTING ENGENDERED

Duke University law professor Madeleine Morris, a paid consultant to President Bill Clinton's secretary of the Army in 1997, wanted to change the "military culture from a masculinist vision of unalloyed aggressivity to an ungendered vision."[197]

Ungendered? Earth to Madeleine: The military exists to kill people and break things when the nation is threatened. That *requires* masculine aggression, men with balls, not eunuchs or those with balls acquired through sex-change surgery.

And change the military culture to what? One big, happy, diverse family with latrines shared by a dozen different genders and where there is so much niceness and sensitivity that guns have Elmer Fudd corks in their barrels?

One of the last bastions of conservatism and open manhood has now become ground zero for social experimentation.

President Bill Clinton's administration set the tone to rectify perceived discrimination. One of Clinton's first policy decisions was to declare the rights of gays and lesbians to serve in the military. He preferred allowing them to serve openly but settled for "Don't Ask, Don't Tell." If you were gay and kept it to yourself, no one would ask.

When the act was later lifted, President Obama stated, "I was proud to sign the Repeal Act into law . . . because I knew that it would enhance our national security, increase our military readiness, and bring us closer to the principles of equality and fairness that define us as Americans."[198]

What world is this man living in? Did he really think infusing gays into line units would "enhance national security" and "increase military readiness?" I served in the military twenty-nine years, active duty and reserve, and I can assure you that good order and discipline are absolutely essential in maintaining a capable fighting force, and this is not the way to do it.

After Obama's repeal of "Don't Ask," allowing gays to openly serve in the armed forces, he appointed a gay officer as secretary of the Army precisely *because* he was gay. Chaos took over, accompanied by dark comedy and virtual anarchy as order in uniform collapsed. Our enemies or potential enemies worldwide are laughing their butts off while we fill our soldier ranks with feminized men who double as hairdressers on the side.

"Because we repealed 'Don't Ask, Don't Tell,'" declared Obama's White House advisor Valerie Jarrett, "our military . . . is stronger and our country is safer" now that homosexuals may serve openly.[199]

"We're very proud of everything the gay and lesbian community has contributed and continue to contribute," chimed in then secretary of defense Chuck Hagel.[200]

Air Force acting secretary Eric Fanning praised a gay Marine captain who, said Jarrett, would be "taking his husband" with him the next time he deployed.[201]

"The truly sad story is that many of the brightest graduates of the three major service academies witnessing what the social experiment on diversity . . . is doing to the U.S. military, are leaving the service after five years," observed retired Navy captain Joseph John. "We are being left with an officer corps that can be made to be more compliant. . . . Social experiments . . . [have constituted] a massive assault to restructure the military mindset, destroyed unit cohesion, unit morale, and is negatively affecting combat effectiveness."[202]

Things went haywire immediately with the infusion of so much that is anathema to the establishment and maintenance of a fighting force. Only a fool fails to see the raw hypocrisy and insane contradiction of what now passes for "military readiness."

After the Missouri National Guard forbade troops to give a patriotic demonstration at the Bible Baptist Church in Carthage to avoid the appearance of government's approving a faith-based organization, President Obama appointed a military honor guard to march in a Washington D.C., Gay Pride parade. Apparently, it's not against foreign policy to prance with flamboyant gays strutting their stuff—but it is against policy to have the military seem to be associated with a church.

Under the Obama administration's gay policies, U.S. military bases began hosting gay marriage ceremonies and other gay socials. *Stars & Stripes* called it a "sign of the times" when six service members donned makeup, dresses, and wigs to perform as drag queens at Kadena Air Base in Okinawa for a fund-raiser in support of lesbian, gay, bisexual, and transgender troops.[203]

"The repeals of Don't Ask, Don't Tell [and] the Defense of Marriage Act . . ." *Stars & Stripes* stated, "have allowed gays and lesbians in the military to be open with their sexuality for the first time."[204]

Open it has become—and much more. Blatant, brassy, in-your-face. It is no longer that unusual to see military people returning from deployment beng met by their same-sex lovers.

After Obama's White House approved transgenders serving in the military, the Pentagon released written instructions on how a service member can change her or his sex—and Uncle Sam will pay for it, including time off.

Gay Army private Bradley Manning was sentenced in 2013 to thirty-four years in a military prison for violating the Espionage Act. A Kansas judge granted his petition to change his name to Chelsea Elizabeth Manning. "She," said the court, although Manning was still a male, with all the body parts that implies, "filed the court petition as a first step toward getting her army records changed."[205] Furthermore, the Pentagon approved paying for the convicted traitor's "gender treatment."

Wounded veterans are kicked around in VA hospitals to the point that some die waiting for treatment. Crippled vets have a tough time getting wheelchairs and therapy. Yet, *Chelsea* was promptly approved for sex-change surgery. It's the politically correct thing to do.

In early 2015, the Pentagon celebrated gay pride with a month of gay-themed events. Defense Secretary Ashley Carter was the keynote speaker at one event. Afterwards, Brigadier General Randy S. Taylor introduced his husband, Lucas, followed by a panel discussion featuring a gay Marine officer, a gay Army sergeant, a lesbian chaplain, and a transgender woman. All four introduced their same-sex wives, husbands, and one fiancé.

This is the U.S. military!

And if you disagree with the absurdity of such behavior, keep your mouth shut. Christian troops and military chaplains face punishment if they refuse to at least pay lip service to this insanity. The Obama gang has purged more than two hundred senior officers during the past five years because they expressed disagreement with his policies dealing with gays, women in combat, transgenders, and so forth.

"Morale is at an unprecedented low," said retired Army lieutenant General William J. "Jerry" Boykin. "Officers want to train for war but are not allowed to because of other distractions such as allowing openly homosexual personnel in the military . . . and rules of engagement that favor political correctness over our ability to fight and win."[206]

As a final example of how far the military has descended from common sense, take the case of combat pilot Lt. Col. Christopher Downey, who went onto the dance floor at an officers' club to caution two lesbian officers, one a lieutenant, the other a captain, against engaging in prolonged French kissing, buttocks grasping, and partial disrobing. They clearly violated Army rules against inappropriate displays of public affection while in uniform.

For having dared to notice it, Colonel Downey is being forced to resign and give up his military career.

The American society is well on its way to tyranny made palatable by sex, drugs, rock 'n' roll, and general debauchery when:

government chooses sides and picks winners and losers based on what is politically correct and culturally expedient;

the culture aided and abetted by corrupt and degenerate politicians increasingly debases itself;

the State restricts the rights and privileges of the majority while extending them to favored minorities;

we are afraid to stand up for common sense and basic morality;

national defense and the survival of the nation become susceptible to social experimentation and manipulation;

political correctness dictates that we accept "social justice" however it may be defined by growing mobs of malcontents, anarchists, socialists, and their "enlightened" supporters;

we passively accept greater and greater restrictions on personal liberty in deference to a variety of questionable "causes"; and

we know instinctively and from history that what happened to bring down previous hedonistic empires is occurring right now in the United States.

Facts are stubborn things; and whatever may be our wishes, our inclina-
tion, or the dictates of our passion, they cannot alter the state of facts and
evidence.

—JOHN ADAMS

THE ANDROGYNOUS WARRIOR

"We're about changing the culture," crowed Barbara Pope, secretary of Navy for manpower, as the military began integrating women into combat slots previously reserved for men.[207]

*Man*power in her title must have galled the hell out of her. In fact, to avoid offending female service members, new military rules dictate the term "man" will no longer be used.

The West Point class of 1978 proudly professes to be the "last class with balls" as feminist activists, sensitive "social justice" Progressives, and politicians without balls and who have never served in uniform began pushing for female "equality" throughout the armed forces.[208]

In 1992, the President's Commission on Assignment of Women in the Armed Forces approved "gender-normed scoring" (read "reduced standards") for women in basic, pre-commissioning and entry-level training, with the caveat that they not participate in direct ground battle.

In 2013, then defense secretary Leon Panetta and General Martin Dempsey, chairman of the Joint Chiefs of Staff, lifted the caveat to allow women to serve in direct combat. Spin claimed that integrating women into combat units was a positive advancement that did not reduce combat capabilities. Women, went this nonsense, were "integral . . . We can't go to war without them . . . They perform as well or better than men."[209]

Plus, they added "an air of civility to military service."[210]

"Now you've opened Pandora's box!" exclaimed Lt. Col. Bob Maginnis. "We're going against history and against psychology and all the physical differences. We're pushing in a direction that will jeopardize the very safety of our nation."[211]

Progressives tout Israel for drafting women to serve in combat with its Israeli Defense Forces. However, Israel learned its lesson when a handful of women saw combat with the Polmach against hostile Arabs in 1948. Their presence produced higher casualties on both sides. Israeli men risked their lives and their missions in protecting women while Arabs fought more fiercely to avoid the humiliation of being defeated by women. Since then, the IDF does *not* put women in front-line combat brigades mobilized to engage in direct heavy combat. A report in the *Israel National News* on females in IDF combat declared the experiment a complete failure.

"None of America's allies, much less potential adversaries, treat women like men in combat arms," pointed out Elaine Donnelly, director for the Center for Military Readiness.[212]

Although a small number of women disguised themselves as men to fight during the Civil War, women in U.S. military service became an institution only after the establishment of the Army and Navy Nurse Corps in 1901 and 1908 respectively. Nearly 50,000 women served in uniform during World War I as nurses, clerks, typists, telephone operators, and other similar occupations.

World War II brought 350,000 women into uniform between 1942 and 1945. Again, they were service and support, except for a few who served behind Nazi lines as spies and underground contacts.

Predictably, everything went totally nuts with the debut of the "androgynous warrior." Never mind that females repeatedly fail combat-tested standards. The argument changed from "You can't exclude them because of their gender" to "You can't exclude them just because they can't meet the standards . . . The standards aren't 'fair.'" In many instances, standards were reduced for both men and women to allow women to qualify without stigma.

At the instigation of President Obama, General Martin Dempsey called for a "critical mass" of women to be integrated into all-male ground combat units. Navy Secretary Ray Mabus set a goal calling for one in every four Marines to be women. The Marine Corps considered adopting a new unisex hat, tall and stylishly designed for the tough Marine sergeant's feminine side.

To accommodate women in these tough outfits, men are required to soften up. Manliness, toughness, and courage are controversial in today's "age of enlightenment." At West Point, some male cadets were required to participate in walkathons while wearing women's high-heeled shoes as part of the Army's mandatory Sexual Harassment/Assault Response and Prevention Training. The "Walk a Mile in Her Shoes" event was intended to "stop men's sexualized violence against women."[213]

The Military Police School at Fort McClellan, Alabama, devised a new method for handling training for women and their more delicate natures. Called "the LeBarge Touch," its doctrine can be summed up as "be nice." No shouting, no snarling, just smiles and rainbows and lots of encouragement. Women, insists the program, are *not* equal to men. They're *better* since they're not encumbered with a "macho mentality."

A hard-core Army officer put it this way: "If we go down to the University of Arkansas and tell them, 'You have a winning schedule, but this coming game you're going to have to put three women on the front line.'. . . guess what's going to happen. They're going to lose, and they're going to be the laughing stock of the NCAA. . . . Unfortunately, . . . the generals are too cowardly to say what is obvious."[214]

And *obvious* it should be—to anyone other than a Progressive. Combat demands tough men who bond in a warrior culture of self-sacrifice, not girls and hairdressers.

"Overwhelming evidence out there on physical, historical and medical reasons say no [to women in combat]," wrote retired Army Lt. Colonel Maginnis in *Deadly Consequences: How Cowards are Pushing Women into Combat.* "When we're talking about direct ground combat, I'm talking about smashing heads, shooting at short range, wrestling people in a death struggle to the ground. The question that ought to be asked is whether we want to be that kind of society that really puts women into ground combat. Are we that society, and what are the consequences for men and women and children?"[215]

A report in the federal government's own General Accounting Office listed reasons why women in combat units are an extremely bad bet: Women soldiers compared to male soldiers have higher rates of attrition and lower rates of retention; are three times more likely to be homosexual; are four times more likely to complain of physical ailments; have fourteen times the injury rate. In the course of a year, 10 to 17 percent of all female soldiers end up knocked up, with as high as 50 percent pregnant at any one time in smaller units, and are eight times more likely to be single parents. On the whole, women are less aggressive, less daring, less likely to suppress minor personal hurts, less aware of world affairs, less interested in military history, and less respectful of military tradition.[216]

However, as Brian Mitchell asserted in his testimony before the Presidential Commission on the Assignment of Women in the Armed Forces, women do seem to have a singular advantage: They are better behaved.

Even most women already serving in the military are against gender integration on the front lines. Take retired U.S. Marine gunnery sergeant Jessie Jane Duff:

> Women overall are not capable of performing to the same level as men are. We obviously, genetically, are designed completely differently. We have roughly 40–45 percent less muscle mass. We have less lung capacity . . . The female body breaks down faster . . . Do we want to start having quotas for the most important measures of our life—our national security, our combat readiness? Why would you want your daughters, your sisters, your mothers in hand-to-hand combat with ISIS? That's what it's going to boil down to.[217]

Throwing young men and women together with their hormones offers another predictable outcome in the new "androgynous" military. In November 1978, when the first women went to sea with the U.S. Navy on the repair ship *Vulcan*, three pregnant sailors had to return to shore before the ship even left port.

Congressman Robert Livingstone of Louisiana was outraged. "We expect young men and women to live together in the military without any distinction between the sexes? We've lost all common sense."[218]

I was assigned as first sergeant to an Army military police company during Operation Desert Storm, the first war in the Gulf. Before deployment, my supply sergeant returned from HQ with a Hefty bag full of condoms that were being issued to all overseas-bound units. He dumped them on my orderly room floor.

"The company that f--ks together stays together, Top," he quipped with a sardonic grin. "Make sure you tell our soldiers to keep the f--king within the company. No use raising the morale of some other outfit."

Even with the bag full of condoms, half my women subsequently ended up pregnant. One *soldier* had a miscarriage in the middle of deployment.

"Men and women in mixed-gender units . . . in which they are intermixed become completely ineffective on the battlefield," testified Colonel John H. Ripley before the President's Commission on the Assignment of Women in the Armed Forces. "[They] invite attack and destruction by the enemy, knowing that these are mixed-gender units. . . . If we see women as equal on the battlefield, you can be absolutely certain that the enemy do not see them as equal."[219]

Senior NCOs returning from deployment to Desert Storm were assigned in-service training at Fort Bliss, Texas. A female colonel paraded to the podium and looked out onto a sea of gnarled, weathered faces.

"Do you COO?" she asked forthrightly.

Stunned silence, followed by a guffaw. Indignant, the female colonel explained that COO was an acronym for "Consideration of Others." You had to grant her this: she had balls to stand up in front of senior sergeants, many of whom were combat vets, and propose to teach us to COO. It was bad enough having pregnant women waddling about on army posts in combat uniform. But to be forced to *COO* about it!

Weakness in the culture projected onto the world stage is a sure sign of social collapse. Previous empires throughout history fell when they lost the balls to defend themselves from enemies both internal and external. The soft hand of feminism when it comes to the military is a direct indicator of a society unable or unwilling to maintain the strength to do what is necessary to preserve freedom. In May 2016, the House Armed Services Committee approved an amendment to the National Defense Authorization Act that will require women to register with Selective Service to be drafted in the event the draft is reinstated.

In that same year, DOD also announced it would begin integrating women into elite special operations forces, like the Green Berets, Rangers, and SEALs. Statistics indicate women can't hack it in regular combat line outfits—so now we want to put them in special ops!

To paraphrase famed Israeli general Moshe Dayan, "Any society that will send its mothers, wives, and sisters to war is not a society worth preserving."

> *If you don't want a man unhappy politically, don't give him two sides to a question to worry him. Better yet, give him none.*
> —RAY BRADBURY IN FAHRENHEIT 451

A "WELL-REGULATED" PRESS

The press in the New World did not start out free. Massachusetts, for example, demanded a "well-regulated" press, not a "free press."

"License of the press is no proof of liberty. . . . When a people are corrupted, the press may be made an engine to complete their ruin," contended John Adams with astonishing precognitive foresight.[220]

Russia and China under Communism serve as the world's examples of a "well-regulated" press. Lenin and Stalin considered the various forms of media—limited in that age to the press and early radio—to be critical instruments of mass propaganda to help lead the Great Unwashed to socialism. Writers were "licensed" by government to ensure they walked the Party Line.

As recently as 2014, the Communist Chinese Government ordered its 250,000 "licensed" journalists to take annual training in "Marxist news values" and "correct journalism."

Vladimir Lenin referred to journalists as "engineers of the human soul" who would produce the New Soviet Man. After the 1917 Russian Revolution, he either executed or sent to the gulag to die nearly fifteen hundred "engineers of the human soul" for various "crimes against the people." They could serve government—or they would be destroyed. There was no middle road.

Russian author Boris Pasternak summed up the position of the tyrannical state when it comes to the media: "The technocrats want writers to be a sort of power for them. They want us to produce work which can be used for all kinds of social purposes."[221]

Progressives in the United States, through their hegemonic domination of TV, movies, magazines, newspapers, and culture, keep up a constant drumbeat of propaganda that determines what much of the public hears and thinks about critical social issues. Censorship through political correctness and control of the culture is nearly as effective as state censorship—and will ultimately lead to that. According to the World Press Freedom Index, the United States, due largely to the above factors, is now forty-sixth in the world when it comes to freedom of the press.

How can that possibly be?

"We are in a new inquisition," historian Victor Davis Hanson noted. He continued:

> Self-appointed censors try to stamp out any idea or word that they don't wish to be aired—in the pursuit of a new race, class, gender, and environment orthodoxy. . . . All of that them/us rhetoric has given a top-down green light to radical thought police to harass anyone who is open-minded about man-caused global warming, or believes that gay marriage needs more debate, or that supporting Israel is a legitimate cause, or that breaking federal immigration law is still a crime and therefore "illegal." Our civil liberties will not be lost to crude fascists in jackboots. More likely, the death of free speech will be the work of the new medieval Torquemadas who claim they destroyed

freedom of expression for the sake of "equality" and "fairness" and "saving the planet."[222]

"The Left," commentator Charles Krauthammer added, "is entering a new phase of ideological agitation—no longer trying to win the debate but stopping debate altogether, banishing from public discourse any and all opposition."[223]

The process begins with the media itself. Virtually all studies conclude that it is decidedly and perhaps irrevocably biased in favor of Progressivism. In 2013, only 7 percent of mainstream journalists described themselves as conservative, which explains why an overwhelming majority of them follow the Progressive line when it comes to government policy, politics, and social issues.[224]

Journalism colleges and most of academia preach the theology that Progressives are reasonable and morally correct on everything from guns to gay marriage, while the "fringe" is small-minded and bigoted and should shut up and let their betters tell them what to think.

Sandra Korn, a writer for the *Harvard Crimson*, opined that radical leftism should be the only permissible political philosophy on campus, that guaranteeing students and professors the right to hold controversial views puts liberalism in a bad light.

"If our university community opposes racism, sexism and heterosexism," she asked, "why should we put up with research that counters our goals? . . . If we give up our obsessive reliance on the doctrine of academic freedom, we can consider more thoughtfully what is just."[225]

"Hate speech," declared CNN's Chris Cuomo, "is excluded from protection [of the First Amendment.]"[226]

"Hate speech" as determined by whom?

A student at Wesleyan University penned an op-ed for the campus newspaper in which he mildly criticized the Black Lives Matter movement. A group of students, faculty, and alumni responded with a signed petition demanding the paper be defunded for "failing to provide a safe space for the voices of students of color." The paper's editor, naturally, groveled and expressed regret for "the wounds" created by publication of the op-ed.[227]

Progressives constantly contrive to shut down TV, radio, and print media opposition any way they can. A petition bearing more than 110,000 signatures demanded the *Washington Post* ban all articles that question global warming. Fox News Channel canceled the *Glenn Beck Show* after George Soros–funded Media Matters waged a full-scale attack on the show's advertisers.

Soros is one of the most powerful media figures on the planet. He controls or funds scores of media and other organizations. He has spent twenty-five years, Richard Poe wrote in *Canada Free Press*, "recruiting, training, indoctrinating and installing a network of loyal operatives in 50 countries, placing them in positions of influence and power in media, government, finance and academia . . . [through which he] continues undermining America's traditional Western values." The pressure he exerts runs deep, from the White House down to reporters in the newsrooms. When Soros speaks, generally behind the scenes, powerful people listen.[228]

Melissa Francis at CNBC-TV was ordered not to report negatively on President Barack Obama's socialized medicine scheme, a program Soros supports. "I was called into management," she explained, "where I was told I was disrespecting the office of the president by telling what turned out to be the absolute truth."[229]

Fox News has long been a thorn in the Progressive backside, criticized and attacked from the top of the Progressive food chain in the White House down to every two-bit politician.

"Fox News," raved Democrat Mike Dickinson while running for the Virginia House of Representatives, "does nothing but tell lies and mistruths. They have unqualified political analysts. We need the FCC to monitor and regulate them."[230]

If any media outlet has the temerity to move in the wrong direction, then, by golly, turn the government dogs loose on them. This is happening more and more regularly in the increasingly vicious battle for the soul and heart of America.

A friend inside the Obama White House warned Fox News anchor

Greta Van Susteren that reporter Jennifer Griffin's career could be ruined if she continued to "aggressively report" on the Benghazi scandal. Four Americans, including the U.S. ambassador, were murdered by jihadists in September 2012, resulting in a suspected cover-up of the facts by the White House and then secretary of state Hillary Clinton.[231]

In her book *Stonewalled,* former CBS reporter Sharyl Attkisson charged that the government hacked into her personal computer and CBS laptop after she began filing unflattering stories about Benghazi. Judicial Watch obtained an e-mail to White House deputy press secretary Eric Schultz from Tracy Schumaler, an aide to then attorney general Eric Holder, complaining that Attkisson was "out of control."

"I'm . . . calling Sharryl's [*sic*] editor," Schumaler's e-mail noted.

"Good," Schultz responded. "Her piece was really bad for the AG."

"They're simply executing a well-thought-out strategy to harass reporters and editors at the slightest air of negativity so as to impact the next news decisions," Attkisson noted. "To provide so much unpleasant static and interference that we may subconsciously alter the way we report stories. To consume so much of our time explaining and justifying what we're reporting that we begin to self-censor."[232]

The Internal Revenue Service has become a major government tool in silencing dissenters, as it proved with scandals involving the IRS persecution of conservative tax-exempt organizations such as the Tea Party. After Bill O'Reilly, host of Fox News' *The O'Reilly Factor*, was audited by the IRS two years in a row, his investigative reporting uncovered hundreds of other outspoken conservative journalists who were audited those same two years. The message couldn't have been clearer: *Keep your mouths shut and your pens silent unless we approve.*

Implying "criminal conspiracy," the U.S. Justice Department under Eric Holder subpoenaed the personal e-mail and phone records of at least two Fox News reporters and twenty Associated Press wire service reporters and editors in an intimidation campaign launched over an apparent leak within the CIA. Holder authorized a search warrant that identified Fox News' James Rosen as a "possible co-conspirator" in violation of the Espionage Act. Government lawyers attempted to force *New York Times* reporter James Risen to give up the concept of "reporters' privilege" and reveal his sources within the CIA who spoke out about botched efforts to stop Iran's pursuit of nuclear weapons.

Conservative author and filmmaker Dinesh D'Souza, who produced *2016*, a documentary film highly critical of the Obama administration, was indicted by the federal government for unknowingly exceeding a lawful campaign donation to Wendy Long, a candidate for a seat in the New York senate. His prosecution, said Gerald Molen, producer of the movie *Schindler's List*, "is the equivalent of prosecuting a political dissident in the Soviet Union for jaywalking. . . . The real point is that you're a political dissenter and the government wants to put you away."[233]

Government efforts to control the media never slack. One of government's first major encroachments upon freedom of the press occurred in 1949 with the so-called Fairness Doctrine Act, which required government-licensed radio and TV broadcasters to provide opposing viewpoints on all coverage of public issues—or the FCC would jerk their licenses. This was criticized as a blatant attempt to silence conservatives under the guise of "fairness."

"Our strategy," admitted Bill Ruder, President John F. Kennedy's assistant secretary of commerce, "was to use the Fairness Doctrine to challenge and harass right-wing broadcasters and hope that the challenges would be so costly to them that they would be inhibited and decide it was too expensive to continue."[234]

Although the Supreme Court abolished the Fairness Doctrine in 1987 as an intrusion on the First Amendment, the issue was not closed.

In May 2013, President Obama proposed a "News Police" plan wherein the Federal Communications Commission inspected TV and newspaper offices to interrogate reporters on how they made decisions about covering major news issues. The proposal failed—but it reappeared a year later in a bill introduced by Democratic senators Edward J. Markey and Hakeem Jeffries. Had the bill succeeded, it would have required researchers to comb through radio, cable and public-access TV, commercial mobile services, the Internet, and other electronic media to ferret out and act against "communications promoting violent acts and hate crimes."[235]

Failing in their "News Police" strategy, President Obama through New York senator Charles Schumer subsequently introduced a Free Flow of Information Act that, had it passed, would have opened the door to requiring all reporters down to bloggers to obtain a government license before they were allowed to "gather, prepare, collect, photograph, record, write, edit, report, or publish" any news.[236]

This, editorialized the *Washington Times*, was a road down which totalitarian and authoritarian states characteristically proceed in licensing only those who follow the official line.

In 2015, the FCC proposed to regulate the Internet after President Obama claimed bringing it under government purview was the only way to keep it "free." It was another back door to censoring the media. In 2014, China had shut down more than sixty thousand websites because of content.

A radical, Marxist-leaning organization known as Free Press, funded by George Soros, wrote a large portion of the new proposed FCC regulations. Free Press was created by Robert McChesney, an avowed socialist communications professor at the University of Illinois.

"Unless you have significant changes in the media," he is quoted as saying, "it will be vastly more difficult to have a revolution. . . Any serious effort to reform the media system would have to necessarily be part of a revolutionary program to overthrow the capitalist system itself . . . rebuilding the entire society on socialist principles . . . We need to do whatever we can to limit capitalist propaganda, regulate it, minimize it, and perhaps even eliminate it."[237]

Currently, the United States maintains control over the Internet, which it created through the military and NASA. Progressives, however, continue their campaigns to "free" it to world control—which means despotic nations like Russia and China will exert their own forms of control over it.

And for that lone voice of protest crying in the wilderness, for that one fool who will speak the truth, there is always the gulag or the firing squad.

7

GOVERNMENT INTERVENTIONISM

The great inlet by which a colour of oppression has entered the world is by
one man's pretending to determine concerning the happiness of another.

—EDMUND BURKE

"WE REALLY HAVE TO PROTECT PEOPLE FROM WRONG CHOICES," says Jonas in Lois Lowery's dystopian novel *The Giver*[1].

It is this attitude of protecting people from wrong choices that allows government intrusion into people's lives. "I'm from the government, and I'm here to help you."

"Of all tyrannies, a tyranny exercised for the good of its victims may be the most oppressive," wrote C. S. Lewis (1898–1963). "It may be better to live under robber barons than under omnipotent moral busybodies. The robber baron's cruelty may sometimes sleep, his cupidity may at some point be satiated; but those who torment us for our own good will torment us without end, for they do so with the approval of their consciences."[2]

GOVERNMENT TO THE RESCUE

America since at least the era of Woodrow Wilson has moved inexorably toward dependency on government. While Communism and fascism may have failed when they were initially implemented full force, they are on their way back through a watered-down version of collectivism, called "interventionism," which presumes to make decisions large and small for individuals. From the allowable ingredients in a bake sale cookie to what use you may make of your own property, the increasing power of the state wears away and eventually overrides constitutional restraint and the people's historical distrust of centralized power.

"Look at any part of economic and social life," challenged Richard Ebeling, "[and] try to find even one corner free from some form of direct or indirect government intrusion. Our lives are not our own anymore. We are the tools and victims of public policy that intend to construct brave new worlds concocted by intellectuals and political elites who still dream the utopian dream that they know better than us how lives should be lived."[3]

The natural progress of things is for liberty to yield and government to gain ground.

—THOMAS JEFFERSON

DEATH AND TAXES

It appears the old saw that the "only thing certain in life is death and taxes" bears fruit across human history.

While the word *tax* appeared first in the English language during the era of the Black Death, it commands a much longer history in actual operation. It is suggested in the Bible's book of Genesis that a fifth of all crops should go to Pharaoh (47:26). China levied taxes at least three thousand years ago. Julius Caesar in Rome imposed a sales tax; Augustus added an inheritance tax. The Mayan and Incan cultures developed forms of taxation. After the Normans invaded England in 1066, William the Conqueror commissioned the Doomsday Book to assess his new kingdom's tax potential.

If the American colonists thought taxation without representation was evil, what would they think today about taxation *with* representation? Over the more than two centuries since the United States declared independence, skillful politicians have overwhelmed people with a cataract of taxes in many forms—federal, state, and city income taxes; sales taxes; excise taxes; corporate taxes; gift taxes; payroll taxes; health care taxes; capital gains taxes; luxury taxes; personal property taxes; vehicle taxes; workers' compensation taxes . . . Not even the dead are exempt, as California proved by taxing gravesites.

THE TAX POEM

Tax his land, tax his bed, tax the table at which he's fed;

Tax his tractor, tax his mule, teach him taxes are the rule.

Tax his work, tax his pay, he works for peanuts anyway. . .

Tax his cigars, tax his beers. If he cries, tax his tears.

Tax his car, tax his gas. Find other ways to tax his ass.

—ANONYMOUS

The constitutionality of President Abraham Lincoln's first income tax, which he needed to fund the Civil War, was widely debated until the Sixteenth Amendment in 1913 allowed Congress to impose a nationwide income tax. President Woodrow Wilson promised the income tax would never exceed 3 percent. But, cautioned a lawyer named Joseph Choate, if government can seize 3 percent of an individual's income, what prevents it from confiscating 30 percent, 40 percent, even more?

"Who would levy such a tax?" sneered Senator William Borah from Idaho. "Whose equity, sense of fairness, of justice, of patriotism does Mr. Choate question?"[4]

During World War II, income taxes on top earners reached as high as 90 percent. U.S. corporations today are taxed up to 40 percent, the highest among the developed countries of the world. The average federal tax burden on the American family during the middle of the last century

CRUSHING the COLLECTIVE

was about 5 percent. It's now over 30 percent. In 1955, a wage earner worked until the first week of February to meet his federal, state, and local tax obligations for the year. In 2014, it took him 114 days, until nearly May, to fully pay his share of the tax burden.

Inevitably, taxation produces new government obligations as "fairness," "social justice," and "income inequality" begin to motivate the course of government.

An unwritten premise has risen among citizens that they owe unlimited obligation to government, a growing and never-ending debt to the state that is raised almost cavalierly. A politician's *need* for more revenue always trumps a citizen's *right* to his paycheck. The more of your paycheck government takes—and often wastes—the more it controls your life. Taxes have become so insidious that about one-third the price of a new house is due to taxes or government regulations. Tax, tax, and tax some more is the gateway to tyranny.

Contrary to the claim pushed by Occupy Wall Street that "the rich" do not pay their "fair share," facts show that the top 20 percent of income earners who produce 51.3 percent of all income pay 83.9 percent of all federal income tax. The bottom 50 percent pay almost nothing. The bottom 20 percent actually receive "refunds" through "earned income tax credits," which means a free handout.

During President Obama's tenure in office, he sought 442 new tax increases, raising taxes by $3 trillion.

CNBC's Steve Liesman asked him, "Is there a limit to how much you believe the government should take from an individual in terms of a top tax rate?"

"You know," Obama responded, "I don't have a particular number in mind."[5]

Yes, he does. All of it. In a 1998 speech, he stated, "I actually believe in [wealth] redistribution."[6]

Here are a few of the taxes that went up under the Obama administration:

Payroll taxes expanded from 4.2 percent to 6.2 percent.

Capital gains and dividend taxes increased from 15 percent to 20 percent.

Death taxes went up from 35 percent to 40 percent.

Taxes on business investment increased.

The "Obamacare" surtax of 3.8 percent kicked in for higher earners.

Wages don't really belong to citizens anyhow, according to Cass Sunstein, President Obama's then regulatory czar. "Without taxes," he said in an example of George Orwell's "doublethink," "there would be no liberty. Without taxes, there would be no property. Without taxes, few of us would have any assets worth defending. . . . There is no liberty without dependency."[7]

In *Inequality* magazine, Harvard professor Christopher Jencks urged government to become even more involved in the economic restructuring of American society: "We need to establish the idea that the federal government is responsible for not only the total amount of the national income, but for its distribution. . . . Some of those with high incomes must begin to feel ashamed of economic inequality. . . . We will have to establish political control over the economic institutions that shape our society."[8]

Render unto Caesar what is Caesar's, the Bible states (Mark 12:17). But what if Caesar wants it *all*?

Half the population of a nation cannot continue to support the other half without destroying individual self-reliance and eventually bringing on economic collapse. Even a Harvard professor should be able to understand that if you punish productivity and reward indolence, you get more indolence. There will come a time when the "rich" and successful will simply throw up their hands and stop laying the golden eggs.

"The personal income tax has made the individual vastly more dependent on the state and more avid for state handouts," wrote historian W. H. Chamberlain in 1958. "It has shifted the balance in

America from an individual-centered to a state-centered economic and social system."

Commandeering the fruits of a person's labor, he continued, "radically changes a person's life, effectively ensuring that he will be subjugated to government schools in his youth, reliance on government handouts in old age, and looking over his shoulder at the tax collectors for all the years in between."

Fifty years ago, Bertrand de Jouvenel warned of the consequences of "everyone of every class [trying] to rest his individual existence on the bosom of the state and [regarding] the state as the universal provider. . . . If the state is to guarantee to a man what the consequences of his actions shall be, it must take control of his activities."[9]

We can have a free society, or we can have a welfare nation. We cannot have it both ways.

> *Congress meets tomorrow morning. Let us pray to the Lord to give us strength to bear that which is about to be inflicted upon us.*
>
> —WILL ROGERS

THE REGULATORY STATE

"Today," observed Dr. Ben Carson, noted neurosurgeon and 2016 presidential candidate, "we have people who are simply over-governed, subject to taxation, regulations and intrusion by a massive federal government that our Founding Fathers would never have tolerated . . . It values political correctness over freedom, co-dependency over self-reliance, and redistribution over personal success."[10]

Columnist Jonah Goldberg noted how, in 1776, "the federal government's portfolio could have easily fit in a file folder: maintain an army and navy, a few federal courts, the post office, the patent office, and maybe a dozen or two other pretty obvious things."[11]

Since then, Congress has incrementally surrendered its constitutional mandate to defend limited government and allowed the administrative state to assume most government functions.

"The whole point," wrote Charles Kesler in *Claremont Review of Books*, "is to empower government officials, usually unelected and unaccountable bureaucrats, to bless or curse your petitions as they see fit. . . . When law ceases to be a common 'standard of right and wrong' and a 'common measure to decide all controversies,' then the rule of law ceases to be republican and becomes despotic. Freedom itself ceases to be a right and becomes a gift."[12]

The bloating of the administrative state creates departments, bureaus, agencies, divisions, boards, and other such entities that produce massive regulations that ignore legislative constraints and eventually serve as laws that require obedience. Regulations, in essence, function as the law of the land. If the EPA wills that you not take a leak in the forest, then you can go to jail for taking a leak in the forest.

"Social liberalism is the foremost, predominant, and in many instances the sole impulse for zealous regulation in this country," Jonah Goldberg continued. "[W]ho else do people think are behind the efforts to ban big sodas or sue hairdressers for charging women more than men? Who harasses little kids for making toy guns out of sticks, Pop Tarts, or their own fingers? Who wants to regulate the air you breathe, the food you eat . . .? Who wants to control your thermostat? Take your guns . . .? Who's in favor of speech codes on campus and 'hate crime' laws everywhere?"[13]

The number of civilian bureaucrats working for the executive branch alone is today nearly equal to the entire population of the United States in 1776. More than two million administrators in nearly a hundred thousand different government entities spend nearly $2 *trillion* annually to enforce and maintain almost 400 million federal regulations. Each law Congress passes requires an average of fifty-one new regulations to administer it. According to RegData, President Obama's first four-year term in office resulted in seventy-eight thousand new regulations. In one week alone, government published two thousand pages of new rules, regulations and proposals.

It is estimated that, due to regulations and rules, the average person commits three federal violations a day without realizing it.

Wyoming rancher Andy Johnson dug a stock pond on his property. The EPA threatened to fine him $75,000 a day for failing to first obtain permission from the Corps of Engineers.

The Health Department in Troy, Illinois, shut down Chloe Sterling's successful cupcake business for failure to obtain a government permit.

A woman was jailed for seventeen days for violating some obscure rule when she allowed her nine-year-old to play unsupervised in a public park.

Local and federal governments attempt various methods to discourage the use of tobacco, ranging from higher taxes to outright bans in certain locations. Oddly enough, they are legalizing marijuana at the same time. Toke 'em if you got 'em.

Among other things the federal government regulates are: lawn mowers, washing machines, toilets, dryers, dishwashers, detergents, pesticides, microwaves, showers, heating and cooling, refrigerators, freezers, ceiling fans, clothing, toys, baby cribs, pacifiers, toy balloons, matchbooks, televisions, radios, cell phones, swimming pools, toothpaste, hamburger meat, deodorants, dentures, fruit and vegetables, beef . . . It's difficult to name something that *isn't* regulated.

In 1920, only about thirty occupations in the United States required any sort of licensing. By the 1950s, about 5 percent of U.S. workers required licenses to perform their jobs—and that number has expanded enormously since then. Occupations requiring federal licensing include milk samplers, barbers, athletic trainers, auctioneers, and the list goes on and on.

At his discretion, an ambitious or willful official can always find a taxpayer, businessperson, homeowner, or self-employed entrepreneur in violation of some minute regulation that will extort from him fees or fines, shut him down, or lock him up.

When the defining history of the United States is written, it will conclude that the nation fell not by coup or revolution but instead by its weight of law and regulations.

There is all the difference in the world between treating people equally and attempting to make them equal.

—FRIEDRICH HAYEK

THE PUBLIC TROUGH

The *Wizard of Id* comic strip ran a sequence in which the Little Wizard is on his balcony, addressing a crowd. "Elect me," he says, "and I promise you free health care! Free housing! Free clothing! Food stamps! And jobs for everybody. Any questions?"

A voice from the crowd pipes up: "What do we need jobs for?"[14]

Formerly, rather than punishing the industrious and subsiding the indolent, the nation motivated people to become self-sustaining. Able-bodied Americans were once ashamed to accept charity, much less demand it. To do so brought a stigma upon one's character, a moral weakness, a strike against one's independence.

Not that early American society turned a blind eye to the legitimately needy. Distinction was made between the unworthy poor and those trying to better themselves. The community knew who was worthy and who was not. Compensation was made at the local level to assist orphans, the blind, disabled veterans, the deaf and mute, the crippled, and others in dire circumstances. Family and friends, supplemented by *private* charity, saw to their own. Society refused to tolerate the idea of pay without work for those who were able-bodied. Chronic dependency was not tolerated. Orphans became apprentices to local tradesmen; adults who could work became servants. Poverty and want served as an incentive to do better.

"The best way of doing good to the poor," Benjamin Franklin lectured in 1766, "is not making them easy in poverty, but leading or driving them out of it. . . . The more public provisions were made for the poor, the less they provided for themselves, and of course became poorer. And, on the contrary, the less was done for them, the more they did for themselves, and became richer. . . . More will be done for their happiness by inuring them to provide for themselves than could be done by dividing all your estates among them."[15]

Obviously, Franklin's wisdom was not inherited by the architects of the American entitlement state that followed. The Constitution was not even fifty years old when Congress proposed to appropriate $10,000 from the treasury to provide for the widow of a veteran. Congressman Davy Crockett objected.

"We have the right, as individuals, to give away as much of our own money as we please in charity," he argued, "but as members of Congress we have no right to appropriate even one dollar of the public's money."

He offered one week's pay from his own salary to the widow and challenged other Congressmen to do likewise. He later commented, "Not one of them responded to my proposition to put up their own money."[16]

The decline of a republic, Alexis de Tocqueville observed, begins when voters figure out they can vote themselves money from the public trough by electing politicians who promise to rob from the public treasure to reward them. Gradually, year by year, Congress after Congress, career politicians maneuvering to get themselves reelected, which is what politicians do, have brought the U.S. Treasury to bankruptcy by promising free stuff. Some are more blatant about it than others.

In his 1972 bid for the presidency, for example, George McGovern hatched a plan to buy votes by promising every voter a $1,000 windfall drawn, naturally, from the public trough.

A *Mallard Fillmore* comic strip showed a voter with his hand stuck out, a typical posture these days. The caption read, "I'll vote for you if you will say you'll take care of me in every way. If you stick by that principle, you'll be invincible . . . 'cause there's more folks like me every day."[17]

In 1960 when John Kennedy became president, the entire federal government supported only forty-five social programs. The JFK/LBJ administrations added 390 more. President Johnson's War on Poverty and his Great Society were Roosevelt's New Deal on steroids. The "entitlement" programs he pushed and the ones that followed succeeded in changing social norms and American character by destigmatizing dependency upon government and making it equivalent to productive work. One entitlement invariably leads to another.

Forgotten is the old maxim advising one to teach a man to fish rather than give him a fish. Progressives have given out so many fish—after first seizing them from other fishers—that they have created vast underclasses of millions dependent on government for most if not all their needs and who, in large part, have lost the ability to catch fish on their own and therefore must rely on government money, food, and shelter. Today, millions are feeding from the public trough and squealing for more. Roosevelt's "helping hand" has gradually become the "welfare hand that keeps on giving." If you are classified as "impoverished," you can live middle-class with the help of your neighbors. Why work when you can live off the fat of the land?

"Teach a man to fish," goes a revised Progressive mantra, "and we lose a voter."

According to the U.S. Census Bureau, 35 percent of the nation's population receives benefits from one or more separate overlapping and duplicative welfare programs that provide cash benefits, health care, food, child care, training, free cell phones, free computers, free lawyers, social services, housing, utility subsidies, and much more. Statistics from the 2012 census show that 83 million people are on Medicaid; 51 million receive food stamps; 22.5 million are on WIC (Women, Infants and Children) programs; 13.4 million live in subsidized housing.[18]

Americans on some form of welfare outnumber those who are actually working.

"In 2012," columnist Terence Jeffrey noted from census figures, "there were 103,087,000 full-time year-around workers. Welfare takers outnumber full-time workers by 6,544,000."[19]

Ten million men ages eighteen to twenty-four are not working because they can't find jobs that will pay them more than they receive by not working. In 1964, 80.6 percent of Americans were employed; fifty years later that number had dropped to 67.6 percent. During the eight-year period ending in 2016, the fastest-growing segment of the population enrolling for food stamps were able-bodied adults. In 2016, the government announced that food stamps could be used to have groceries delivered directly to a recipient's door.[20] The Obama administration explained that it was too much of a hardship for those on welfare to have to actually travel to the grocer.

"If converted to cash," said Robert Rector of the Heritage Foundation, "means-tested welfare spending is more than sufficient to bring the income of every lower-income American to 200 percent of the federal poverty level."[21]

Fifty years after its birth, the War on Poverty has cost more than $20 trillion and the poverty rate has continued to climb year by year. The Census Bureau reports that 27 percent of the American population between 2005 and 2007 lived in poverty. That percentage rose to 31.6 percent between 2009 and 2011, and continues to rise.

Ironically, while the U.S. Department of Agriculture touts the expansion of its food stamp program, the National Park Service displays signs reading, *Please Do Not Feed the Animals. . . . The animals will grow dependent on handouts and will not learn to take care of themselves.*

In government's latest entitlement, the Affordable Care Act, the Congressional Budget Office admitted socialist-style health care discourages individual independence and initiative and provides people an incentive to reduce their work hours and avoid full-time jobs that, if it is fully implemented, might move their income out of the subsidized range and add them to the welfare rolls. And this is only one of many entitlement programs.

"That," concluded the editorial, "is mostly a good thing, a liberating result of the law."[22]

In short, you can make more money by not working to make more money—and that is a "good thing"?

Expansion of programs "for the children" are even relieving parents of the responsibility to take care of their own kids. The Healthy Hunger-Free Kids Act of 2010 allows public school systems throughout the nation to offer *all* students two free meals a day, whether they are from poor families or not. The thinking is that offering free meals to everyone regardless of need erases the stigma that plagues students from poor families.

Receiving free meals, said Joshua Rivera, whose son is a second grader in Boston, is "one less burden for parents."[23]

And *that* is government's job?

The same philosophy of not stigmatizing applies to the replacement of food stamps with EBT debit cards for recipients going through checkout lines—to erase any negative stigma attached to welfare benefits.

The poverty lobby seems always ahead of the curve in devising new "empowerment" for the homeless and needy. In Tulsa, Oklahoma, pets of the needy are being fed and provided free veterinary care. The federal government ruled that food stamps may be used to purchase marijuana from legalized pot shops because "we don't want the poor to be deprived."[24] Street people in San Francisco are provided "hook-up" trucks to allow them to have sex in comfort, while a "shower bus" called Lava Mae, outfitted with private showers, clean toilets, soap, and towels, returns "a sense of dignity to those living on the streets."[25]

"Disability insurance" through the federal Social Security program was intended to provide those with legitimate physical and mental impairments at least a minimum living. It has grown and grown to become abused, abusive, corrupted, and increasingly expensive to maintain.

One thirty-four-year-old who held down a good industrial job for more than ten years decided he was "tired of working." He quit his job and received Social Security disability benefits on the grounds that he was "disabled" because he never learned how to read. It's so much *nicer,* he crowed, not to have to get up and go to work.

Jay Carney, former president Obama's mouthpiece, applauded the "opportunity created" by extended entitlements, because they allow "families in America to make a decision about how they will work, or *if* they will work."[26]

Workers unemployment benefits have followed the same pathway to bloat and abuse. The more extended the benefits, the less incentive people have to look for work. An unemployed person can now receive a check for up to *two years* for not working.

Out-of-work recipients have been quoted as exclaiming how unemployment checks "gave me time to find the right position . . . allowed me to take time off for myself. . . . I haven't had to look for work so hard."

Not surprisingly, North Carolina demonstrated during 2014 how slowing down the gravy train encourages people to go out and find jobs. The unemployment rate dropped dramatically when the state cut off long-term unemployment benefits.

"We would in theory," satirized *National Review*, "have the Federal Government deliver checks to every household and allow each and every one to follow his bliss as he sees fit. But the shelves of the grocery store would soon be empty."[27]

Empty grocery store shelves or not, studies show that no matter what most people *say*, they actually *want* the entitlements and benefits of Big Government. Fueled by movements that delegitimize individual accomplishment, we are bombarded with both blatant and subliminal messages that teach us we cannot make it without a government crutch.

Income inequality, declared President Obama in 2013, is "the defining challenge of our time. The combined trends of increasing inequality and decreasing mobility pose a fundamental threat to the American Dream, our way of life."[28]

Quite the contrary. Dependence on government is the fundamental threat to individual liberty and our way of life. The greed-envy-entitlement triad addicts people to government and entices us to want more of it. While the nation digs itself deeper and deeper into debt, unscrupulous and misguided "statesmen" continue crusades to implement socialism. There is no limit to the power they can accumulate if they can convince people to believe in utopian goals.

Problem is, sooner or later, the dam has to burst. And burst it will. The national debt now approaches $21 trillion. Progressives during Obama's eight years in office accumulated more debt than *all* previous presidents combined.

"You cannot bring about prosperity by discouraging thrift," twentieth-century Presbyterian leader William J. H. Boetcker warned. "You cannot strengthen the weak by weakening the strong. You cannot help small men by tearing down big men. You cannot lift the wage earner by pulling down the wage payer. You cannot help the poor by destroying the rich. . . . You cannot further the brotherhood of man by inciting class hatred. You cannot keep out of trouble by spending more than you earn. You cannot establish security on borrowed money. You cannot build character and courage by destroying men's initiative and independence. You cannot help men permanently by doing for them what they can and should do for themselves."[29]

That quote should be inscribed in bold letters above the doors of the White House, the U.S. Congress and Senate, and every state legislative house in the nation.

There will never be a perfectly racist-free society—on either side of the color line . . . What has always worked for me is a radical idea in comparison to today's standards: Do unto others as you would have others do unto you.[30]

—ARNOLD AHLERT

BACK ON THE PLANTATION

African-Americans have made remarkable progress in America's acceptance of their civil rights since slaves were first brought to the New World in the 1600s. Chicago and Los Angeles, among many other cities, have elected black mayors. Colin Powell and Condoleezza Rice became secretaries of state. In 2008, a black president was elected.

On the other hand, a large proportion of the nation's 40 million black people reside in urban ghettos, where crime and other social ills prevail.

The year of the 1964 Civil Rights Act, before the War on Poverty kicked in full force, I traveled across the United States for a year on an 80cc Yamaha motorbike, working odd jobs and talking with people.

I lived for a period with a black couple and their kids on a dirt farm in Mississippi. We went to church on Sundays and shared chores and responsibilities. The kids were expected to obey their parents and the Ten Commandments and grow up to become decent human beings. But things were already beginning to change.

"More and more," Papa said, "there's a new bunch that are being taught that Whitey owes 'em a living and they are gonna take what is owed 'em one way or another."

Horace Cooper, cochair of a board attached to the National Leadership Network of Black Conservatives, compared data points from the pre–civil rights and War on Poverty era to today. He discovered to the surprise of no one who will *listen* that before the 1960s the black illegitimacy rate of 14 percent was lower than in the rest of the nations. The black labor force was higher than the white. The black unemployment rate for sixteen- and seventeen-year-old black kids was under 10 percent, lower than for white teens. Black Americans were far less likely to be convicted and incarcerated as felons than were the broader community. In short, the pathology of poverty and crime in black communities is entirely recent in history.

Step forward to the present day.

Out-of-wedlock birth rates are the most visible symbol of the plague of social ills that infect inner-city black communities. Black illegitimate births now hover at around 70 percent, 80 percent in some cities, three times what it was in 1964. Most of the mothers are teens who end up on welfare. According to economist Mark Rosenzweig, every increase of 10 percent in welfare benefits increases the chances of out-of-wedlock births by 12 percent, thus perpetuating the cycle.[31] While the current poverty rate of a black household where both husband and wife work is a mere 2 percent, fully 85 percent of all black children in poverty live in a single-mother home.[32]

Social and psychological disadvantages as well as economic ones haunt family-deprived black children as compared to father-present families. Not only do out-of-wedlock childbirths cause more poverty, they also lead to other social maladies: dropping out of school; behavioral problems such as drug use and abuse; depression and low-self-esteem; early sexual activity; lower future earnings; cultural degradation, abuse and neglect; emotional disorders; a greater chance of being on welfare as adults; and a far greater chance of criminality.

While African-Americans are about 12 percent of the population, they commit 53 percent of all felony murders. By the age of 23, 49 percent of black males have been arrested at least once. Eighty-five percent of all youth in prison for crimes, including violent crimes, have absent fathers.

"The black family managed to survive several centuries of slavery and generations of the harshest racism and Jim Crow, to ultimately become destroyed by the welfare state," observed economist Walter E. Williams.

Crime statistics from black communities are commonly ignored, downplayed, or dismissed due to PC "cultural sensitivity." St. Louis, Missouri, might be used as an example of inner-city crime.

According to the city's official crime data for 2012, the St. Louis demographic was 49 percent black and 44 percent white. Yet, black suspects committed more than 82 percent of serious crimes, such as murder, aggravated assault, and robbery. Black males were responsible for 63.5 percent of all crimes; white males, 17 percent. Black females committed 14 percent of crimes, compared to 5.3 percent for white females. Nearly 98 percent of all homicides were committed by black people, whose victims were also overwhelmingly black.[33]

"Each year [in the United States]," columnist Walter E. Williams noted, "roughly 7,000 blacks are murdered. Ninety-four percent of the time, the murderer is another black person."[34]

In the media and among Progressives, there is constant knee-jerk lamenting over "disproportionate" representation of blacks in prisons and of too much "police presence" in inner cities. Police officers who work black communities see and recognize the pathology of violence better than any other segment of American society. Common sense understands that blacks are overrepresented in prison because they commit disproportionately more crimes. Likewise, it's common sense that cops patrol high-crime precincts more heavily than they do low-crime districts.

I was a cop for fourteen years—four in Miami, Florida, where I worked "salt-and-pepper" teams in the ghettos; ten in Tulsa, Oklahoma, where I was a homicide detective.

> [A street gang] stabbed a Puerto Rican one hundred times because he unwittingly took a shortcut across the Baby Browns' turf. Young junkies OD'd on heroin in some musty condemned building where cops had to kick the rats off the corpses. Ten-year-olds stole cars and snatched purses and shot twelve-year-olds . . . Kids ran as wild as little animals; girls thirteen years old gave birth in order to draw welfare, and everybody on the streets despised the cop because he was The Man. Mean dudes . . . clutched themselves in belligerent groups on the streets, dealing dope, and shouting, "Oink . . . SOOO-eee, pig!" when the police went by.
>
> —FROM *SHOOT TO KILL*[35]

When I'd arrive on the scene, women would often run up and hug me, with tears in their eyes. "Oh, God! Thank you, thank you!" they'd cry. "I'm afraid to go out of my house. Please throw these thieves and gangs and dopeheads in jail."

So what led to such deterioration in America's inner cities?

The answer is white liberal guilt and mass paternalistic dependency. The welfare state has destroyed the black man's self-reliance, his family, and his community by casting him back onto Big Government's plantation, where he is kept poor, ignorant, and resentful. Call it the "poor Negro" syndrome. Pat him on the head, give him a welfare check, tell him he can't win life's lottery without Progressive paternalism, that it's all Whitey's fault, and then—"Be sure to vote for Democrats in the next election."

One of the greatest sins a government can impose on its citizens, asserted rocker-turned-social commentator Ted Nugent, is "to provide for them, because it destroys their souls by creating dependency instead of self-reliance."[36]

Cadillac Progressives can't seem to help themselves when it comes to blaming the root of all black behavior or misbehavior on racism rather than on their own "remedies," which have repeatedly proved to destroy cultures and peoples. For a Progressive, racism dwells underneath the bed of every white, for which he must flagellate himself and offer endless reparations.

"The truly difficult work is looking deep within myself to recognize where my own reservoirs of whiteness reside and what value or burden they present to me," whimpered Democrat state lawmaker Graig Meyer from North Carolina. "My [white] guilt tends to creep up most when I'm forced to reflect on the power I wield."[37]

Most white Americans are so excoriated, mocked, and even punished for attempting to have an "honest conversation" about racial problems that they withdraw and keep their mouths shut. "Political correctness" assures that anyone who speaks the truth is viciously attacked for "insensitivity" and "racism." Heaven forbid that black communities become aware of and acknowledge that their true underlying problem is white paternalism that ensnares black people into depending on government to take care of them while excusing their bad behavior as the result of "white racism."

Wisconsin representative Paul Ryan, later U.S. Speaker of the House, was denounced as a racist and purveyor of hate when he dared comment how the "real cultural problem" of black inner city communities lay in a "tailspin . . . of men not working and just generations of men not even thinking about working or learning the value and culture of work."[38]

He can't say *that*. He's *white*. *Everyone* knows that only white people are racist. The phenomenon known as the "knockout game" is one of the most telling indications of how random *reverse* racial violence has infected many black areas.

The rules are simple: young black males, sometimes females, target

CRUSHING *the* COLLECTIVE

white strangers, often women and the elderly, and punch them in the face until they go down.

Such racial violence, explained prison psychologist Marlin Newburn, is perpetrated by black youth raised to view all nonblacks as the enemy who are "keeping my people down."[39] The more brutal the attack, the greater the attacker's social prestige and personal power status. The "game" plays out in malls, movie theaters, and other public venues, primarily in major cities, and has resulted in hundreds of injuries and deaths.

Twenty black teenage girls punched out a white man trying to catch a bus. "They ran straight at me and attacked me," said David Manz. "It was as if it was fun to them. Like it was a game."[40]

A group of black people in the Bronx beat Ralph Santiago so severely in 2013 that he sustained brain damage. A year later, three black thugs in Hoboken punched him out. He died from the attack.[41]

"It was something to do, it was fun," bragged one of a group of thirty perpetrators who dragged a twenty-eight-year-old white female into the bushes in New York's Central Park, where they hacked her with knives, pounded her face with a brick, bound her hands and gagged her, then raped her one by one.[42]

There were more than five hundred cases like these in more than a hundred American cities in 2013 alone. A former St. Louis police chief described it as an indication of general cultural degradation that is largely overlooked and excused by Progressive media and the power structure for fear of being labeled "racist" for even noticing that it is occurring. The *New York Times* dismissed the knockout game as an "urban myth."[43]

Black race hustlers like the "Reverends" Jesse Jackson and Al Sharpton, bolstered by the NAACP, the Congressional Black Caucus, and others, exploit black people for their own selfish ends by tolerating, excusing, and alibiing black criminality and antisocial behavior. They are commonly supported by opportunistic politicians and cheered on by guilt-harboring left-wing media.

Obama's first attorney general, Eric Holder, pressured public schools to be "more tolerant" of black misbehavior after the U.S. Department of Education discovered "racial disparity" in black children being disciplined in school at a higher rate than white children. Education secretary Arne Duncan seemed more disturbed by disciplinary action meted out by schools than by kids' rotten behavior, which included beating teachers, carrying concealed weapons, and smoking pot in bathrooms.

"Instead of kicking bullies and troublemakers out of classrooms," *Investors' Business Daily* summarized, "teachers will now have to join them in 'restorative justice' circles, where they'll chat about the racial 'root causes' of their misbehavior. Teachers will undergo training in 'cultural competency' and 'cultural responsiveness and institutional bias.' Those who over-discipline [read "discipline, period"] students of color will be singled out for rebuke."[44]

Teachers, shut up and take your lumps. No wonder high school graduates from inner-city schools (and many other schools, for that matter) can't read a menu or count change. It's a no-brainer for everyone except a Progressive that no learning can be accomplished without classroom discipline.

"This . . . carries over into nearly every other aspect of their daily lives since they've become conditioned to believe they're not responsible for anything," explained prison psychologist Marlin Newburn. "Can't read? It's the school's fault. No jobs? It's not because they have no skills, discipline, or sense of responsibility. It's because someone won't just give them one. . . . Resentment and chronic failure continue due to these disastrous failures."[45]

The case of eighteen-year-old Michael Brown in Ferguson, Missouri, is a telling example of how all these various racial pathologies, from "white guilt" and white condescension to black dependency and violence, play out in the national limelight.

Facts reveal that in August 2014, the six-four, 297-pound "gentle giant," as the press dubbed Brown, robbed a convenience store and roughed up the owner. High on marijuana, he was walking down the middle of a street minutes later when white police officer Darren

Wilson stopped him. Brown assaulted the cop and attempted to take the officer's gun. Wilson shot and killed him.

The policeman was automatically deemed guilty. The mainstream media, race hustlers like Al Sharpton, and politicians all the way up to the White House recognized an opportunity to pander and foment their litany of division and strike the white-guilt note. Far from being the unifier he promised to be during his campaign, President Obama and his administration have set back race relations a generation. Again and again in shooting from the lip, he has automatically let his alligator mouth overload his hummingbird ass.

Within days of the shooting, long before the investigation was completed, Obama sent Attorney General Holder to Missouri to seek "justice for the family of Michael Brown." Holder implied that failing to indict the policeman, whether or not he was guilty, would not be the end of the case; the federal Justice Department intended to indict him for civil rights violations.

Anger in Ferguson that Obama and Holder helped fan was "understandable," Obama said. Black Panthers chanted in the streets:

What do we want?

Darren Wilson.

How do we want him?

Dead.[46]

Rarely was it suggested in the mainstream media or by politicians that justice extended not only to Brown but also to the officer. Black citizens are being conditioned to automatically blame "racist" cops for all the ills in their communities. Police make visible scapegoats.

"A police officer shot and killed Michael Brown in broad daylight," lamented Missouri governor Jay Nixon. "People of all races and creeds are joining hands to pray for justice. . . . A vigorous prosecution must now be pursued. . . . We now have a responsibility to come together and do everything we can to achieve justice for this family. . . . So I ask that we continue to stand together as we work to achieve justice for Michael Brown."[47]

For pure sappiness, nothing compared to Episcopal minister Sarah Gaventa, who likened Brown's death to that of Jesus Christ. "[Jesus] is a living God who loved us so much . . . that he was willing to become human," she preached. "He became Michael Brown. He became the victim of our sins, so we wouldn't have to sacrifice each other anymore."[48]

In spite of the powerful political campaigning against him, Officer Wilson was found justified in shooting Brown. Rioting, as predicted, resulted. "Understanding" and "sensitivity" were the operative words as looting, gunfire, and arson spread across the little city. At least a dozen buildings burned to the ground, and scores of businesses were looted. Out of political correctness and fear of being dubbed racist, almost no one condemned it. The strongest and almost only censure came from a black minister, Rev. Jesse Lee Peterson.

"As I watch the social unrest," he said, "I can't help but compare the behavior of blacks in that city to that of spoiled rotten children. Blacks have been rioting and fighting with police after the shooting death of a thug, Michael Brown. And white political and law enforcement leaders have given in to their tantrums like weak parents."[49]

From Ferguson, rioting erupted in a wildfire across the nation, as it did in the 1960s—Baltimore, Charlotte, Seattle, Cleveland, Raleigh . . . Cops are accused of being murderers and waging a war of death against young black men. Organizations such as Black Lives Matter, composed of black activists and white radicals, take to the streets, chanting:

Pigs in a blanket!

Fry 'em like bacon!

Anarchy is celebrated. People cheer when cops are murdered. Ultimately, an environment that rewards irresponsibility and dependency while stirring up bitterness among targeted "oppressed" groups by convincing them they cannot receive a square deal will drag the nation into the dark pits of collectivism and total government rule to control the unrest Progressives and their hangers-on have themselves nurtured.

> *The one absolutely certain way of bringing this nation to ruin, of preventing all possibility of its continuing to be a nation at all, would be to permit it to become a tangle of squabbling nationalities.*[50]
>
> —THEODORE ROOSEVELT

THE DUMPING GROUNDS

> *Give me your tired, your poor,*
>
> *Your huddled masses yearning to breathe free,*
>
> *The wretched refuse of your teeming shore.*
>
> *Send these, the homeless, tempest-tost to me.*
>
> *I lift my lamp beside the golden door!*

Emma Lazarus's 1883 poem appears on a bronze plaque installed on the Statue of Liberty. It embodies the noble sentiment of a "melting pot" and *e pluribus unum*—"out of many, one." Today, the "melting pot" has become a dumping ground. Barbarians are not simply waiting outside the gates; they are being invited to come inside the walls.

"During the collapse of Western Civilization the first time," historian Victor Davis Hanson pointed out, "the Roman Empire could not or would not define their borders. . . . So when people started coming from northern Europe [the Romans] thought, 'Well, they're not coming in very big numbers,' or 'We're so much more sophisticated that we will assimilate them quickly,' or 'They're coming because they want to be like us . . .' All these assumptions proved pretty naïve."[51]

Basic rules for the survival of any society include a common or accepted language; a shared history; a sense of community and family; patriotism; and a feeling of similarity and kinship. Modern America has turned multiracial, multilingual, multiethnic, and multicultural. Immigrants centered in many large cities refuse to learn English and to accept American history and society. In fact, they openly oppose assimilation. It is not uncommon to watch *illegal* immigrants on TV, protesting, in foreign languages, for their "rights."

From 1675 until recent years, the native-born population of the United States, about 80 percent of which were of British stock, never fell below 85 percent. According to the U.S. Census Bureau, *legal* emigrants into the United States from 1921 to 1970 averaged approximately 195,000 annually. They were screened according to a quota system that emphasized cultural and economic compatibility to the existing U.S. society. Nine of every ten Americans in 1960 were professed Christians who traced their ancestry to Europe.[52]

In 1965, Progressive president Lyndon Johnson signed the Hart–Celler Act, which did away with the quota system in order to make the system "fair." Foreign-born people in the United States quadrupled. The Congressional Budget Office revealed that in 2012, 40 million immigrants legally resided in the United States, 13 percent of the total population,[53] while according to the Immigration and Naturalization Service, an uncounted number of other foreign-born estimated as high as 38 million reside here illegally.[54] Researchers for the Center for Immigration Studies estimated the number of *legal* immigrants may increase to 58.3 million by 2022. It is projected that white Americans of European ancestry will be a minority by 2042.[55]

Call it cultural redistribution. Progressive elites commonly reject the idea of a "melting pot" on the grounds that it is nativist bigotry against people different from the general run of American crackers with IQs in the lower carrot range. Through "sensitivity" to treat all cultures as equal, they encourage "multicultural separation" within the nation and ignore various dysfunctions and contradictory values.

Researchers from Eagle Forum and the Center for Immigration Studies drew up a profile of current waves of immigrants entering the United States either legally or illegally. Overall, they are an influx of the poor from Third World countries with attendant high rates of illegitimacy, spousal and child abuse, crime, and incarceration, whose governments are rooted in social welfare philosophies. Which means they like Big Government, said Steve Camarota, Center for Immigration Studies. They like Obamacare, gun control, the rich paying more taxes, more environmental regulations. A Pew Poll found that 55 percent of Hispanics view capitalism negatively and that 75 percent prefer bigger government that provides them more services.[56]

The average household headed by an immigrant uses 41 percent more welfare benefits (such as cash, food, and Medicaid) than the average native-headed household. Over half of all immigration households—both legal and illegal—use at least one welfare program.[57]

"There isn't a wall high enough to stop illegal immigrants from sneaking across the border," commentator Ann Coulter asserted, "when the reward waiting on the other side is free health care, jobs, driver's licenses and college tuition subsidized by American taxpayers."[58]

Nonetheless, defying both immigration law and common sense, Progressives rise in strident support of all immigration, whether legal or illegal. The 2016 DNC platform argued that U.S. borders are not open wide enough to ensure equal treatment for "all Americans—regardless of immigration status."[59]

Huntington Park, California, even appointed two illegal immigrants to its city commission. Illegals in California are even allowed to practice law, a bit of irony lost on most Progressives.

Apparently, judging from crime rates, the United States has so few homegrown criminals that it must import fresh ones. According to the U.S. Sentencing Commission, illegal immigrants represent 36.7 percent of all federal crime sentencings. That includes 74.1 percent of all drug possession cases; 20 percent of kidnapping and hostage-taking offenses; 16.8 percent of drug trafficking cases; 12.3 percent of money laundering incidents; and 12 percent of all murders.[60] The FBI Gang Report of 2013 reported that criminal gangs of illegals account for 95 percent of all crimes committed with firearms in 65 jurisdictions nationwide.[61]

Most criminal aliens are allowed to stay in the United States—even if they are apprehended and convicted of serious crimes. In fiscal 2015, ICE (Immigration and Custom Enforcement) officers released 30,558 criminal aliens inside the United States after their convictions.[62]

"The reality is that unless you commit multiple crimes," U.S. representative Michael McCaul from Texas commented, "the chances of your being removed from the country are close to zero."[63]

While violence surging across the southern border is generally the common criminal variety, of even greater peril to national security are jihadists immigrating illegally—or legally—from ISIS and al-Qaeda terrorist networks. Former FBI director James Comey said the FBI is investigating nearly one thousand cases of potential terrorists residing in the United States while a number of ISIS terrorists have been killed by U.S. police. That jihadist terrorists are present in America and plotting and committing terrorist acts became even more evident in 2015–16 as the number of such incidents soared.

The objective of terrorism is to so intimidate targeted peoples that they cease to resist out of fear. Well-intentioned fantasies of multiculturalism, diversity, and tolerance, warned terrorism expert Robert Spencer, are permitting radical Islam to claim a greater power than it might ordinarily exert.[64]

"Most Americans are more afraid of violating the rules of PC than they are of another 9/11 occurrence," social commentator William Kilpatrick noted.[65]

Out of some bizarre sensitivity, even the president of the United States, Barack Obama, refused to name ISIS members as "Islamist terrorists" and never missed an opportunity to publicly praise Islam. He thanked Muslims for "building the very fabric of our nation and strengthening the core of our democracy. Islam has been a part of America. . . . American Muslims have made extraordinary contributions to our country."[66]

Can he be so ignorant of history that he doesn't know that not a single mosque was erected in the United States until 1934? That not until LBJ liberalized immigration in the 1960s did large numbers of Muslims arrive, their presence then totaling fewer than 150,000?

However, Muslim refugees now arriving in the United States from hot spots in the Middle East increase their numbers each year and are expected to soon boost the U.S. Muslim population to nearly seven million. Far from assimilating as Americans, they seem to work against society.

A 2015 poll conducted by the Center for Security Policy revealed that 51 percent of U.S. Muslims seek sharia law over the U.S. Constitution. One in four Muslims believes "it is legitimate to use violence to punish those who give offense to Islam" and to pursue a sharia-based political order.[67] Only 39 percent believe Muslims in the United States should be subjected to American courts.[68] Sufi leader Sheikh Muhammed Hisham Kabbani testified before the U.S. State Department that the Islam extremist ideology has taken over 80 percent of mosques established in the United States.[69]

Statistics speak for themselves. While the so-called moderate Muslim community may not actually participate in violent jihad, rarely does it oppose it.

The "Caliphate" launched out of Syria and Iraq is a two-pronged jihad to subjugate the West. The first prong is terrorism and violence such as that experienced in Paris, Beirut, Holland, and in San Bernardino, Orlando, Boston, New York, and other cities in the United States.

The second prong of the jihadist strategy is to overwhelm the system through long-term immigration, a process whereby America could be conquered and Islamized through a slow and steady process of "absorption" such as that which is now occurring in Europe.

"Stealth jihad," said William Kilpatrick, ". . . is an attempt to turn a culture in an Islamic direction by infiltrating and influencing key institutions such as schools, courts, churches, media, government, and the entertainment industry. . . . Stealth jihad is already a fact in America. Its influence can be seen in textbooks and on college campuses, in the media, and even in the movies."[70]

Out of naïveté, political correctness, ignorance, or perhaps some motive much darker, American leaders continue to allow questionable Muslims entry into the nation. Even while thousands of Islam immigrants and refugees legally or illegally overwhelmed our borders, a number of whom are assuredly jihad terrorists biding their time, President Obama went before the United Nations and blithely declared that "the future must not belong to those who slander the prophet of Islam."[71]

You'll be shot or beheaded if you do.

As with Rome's barbarians, the "huddled masses" from the unsettled Third World are inside the gates of the world's last chance for freedom—and are changing and overwhelming it.

8

THE COLLECTIVE WORLD

The deterioration of every government begins with the decay of the principles on which it was founded.

—FRENCH PHILOSOPHER CHARLES-LOUIS DE SECONDAT

FOLLOWING ONE OF JOSEPH STALIN'S ENDLESS SPEECHES, his congregation of true believers rose for the obligatory standing ovation. Anxiety increased as applause continued on and on, each member of the audience afraid to be the first to stop clapping upon possible penalty of being shipped off to the gulag for lack of proper enthusiasm. Collectivism is like that. Once the clapping starts, no one has the courage or the individual fortitude to stop. It goes on and on.

THE COLLECTIVE WORLD
When the Berlin Wall fell, followed by the collapse of Communism in the Soviet Union, the initial response of the free world was that Soviet

socialism had been catastrophic and murderous, so good riddance. However, Marxist ideas and the collectivist philosophies that drive socialism continue to rise from the grave like Dracula to suck out the blood of liberty. The Marxist ideology still convinces people that only government can manage social and economic affairs better and wiser than can free peoples in their messy ways.

Since, historically, the average empire lasts for about two centuries, virtually every society has deteriorated year by year into some form of collectivism and tyranny. Since people are susceptible to arguments of peace and security, argued Niccolò Machiavelli in his sixteenth-century *The Prince*, it is therefore easy to persuade them. However, it is difficult to fix them in that persuasion. "Thus," he said, "it is necessary to take such measures that, when they believe no longer, it may be possible to make them believe by force."

"The wave of the future isn't a wave at all," proclaimed a *National Review* op-ed, "but an eternal tide that champions of freedom must fight against constantly. For if they stop, even briefly, the tide will push them back to the shores of the natural human condition, and the state of nature is not liberal democratic capitalism, but tribal, thuggish authoritarianism."[1]

History is, indeed, little more than the register of the crimes, follies, and misfortunes of mankind.

—EDWARD GIBBON

DYSTOPIA

Chinese Communist Mao Tse-tung (1893–1976), the most powerful dictator who ever lived, ruled a billion people for a quarter century. His philosophy for success was a simple one: "Political power grows out of the barrel of a gun."[2]

Mao's methods of collectivist tyranny were the same in practice as those of Pheidon of Argos in Greece (died circa 660 BC), in whose honor the word *tyrant* seems to have been coined. Human nature being what it is, tyranny has remained virtually unchanged throughout history. A dagger or an AK-47 more often than not hides beneath the slickest smiles and the grandest promises.

"The apparent inability of the West to see the danger [of collectivist ideologies] . . . leads us to reject the logical and historical conclusion to be drawn from facts," observed Dutch politician Geert Wilders in 2010. "What is wrong with modern Western man that we make the same mistakes over and over again?"[3]

> Little by little, states become monstrous and all-powerful divinities. They force people to study, to work, to fight. They no longer let them sleep, they grind them down and fleece them mercilessly in the name of socialism, of the people, of the proletariat.
>
> —ITALIAN HISTORIAN GUGLIELMO FERRERO

The word *dystopia* means a very bad place, a place opposite utopia.

Fact may indeed be stranger than fiction as the dystopian world of novels morphs into an actual dystopian world. The monster of state totalitarianism that crushes individuality and obliterates diversity keeps rising out of its grave to create dystopian societies of order through brutality. Collectivist despots and tyrants always call for strong governments and weak people.

The world today is more perilous than at perhaps any other period in history as both the Far Left (Communism) and the Far Right (fascism)—both collectivist and oppressive—clamor to replace capitalism and individual freedom with central planning and economic nationalism. In the continuing cycle of history repeated, we are back to the era leading into World War II—except nations now possess nuclear weapons.

All the old, jaundiced players have returned to the stage, only with different faces. Vladimir Putin of Russia is rising as a new Hitler in scheming to achieve his dream of building another great socialist utopia to dominate the world from Moscow, resetting the European continent to the 1930s, when isolated and disunified nations could be picked off one by one.

Communist China is flexing her military muscle while at the same time buying up tons of gold with the aim of eventually collapsing the West economically and changing the world's center of power.

The rise of Islam through Iran's soon-to-be-developed nuclear capabilities, along with the explosion of terror through ISIS and the violent resurrection of a "New Caliphate," are not new. Islam has raged across the Middle East, Africa, and Europe through several historical eras. America's first foreign war was with Islam's Barbary pirates in 1801. In the 1970s, the Soviet KGB sent four thousand Marxists to the Islamic world to stir up hatred against the United States and Israel, continuing a similar policy introduced by Hitler in the 1930s and 1940s. Seeds planted then bear poisoned fruit today as jihadists savage the globe with beheadings, eviscerations of women and children, sexual slavery, and other public atrocities that reach new levels of barbarity.

In Europe, and increasingly in America, Muslim immigrations form enclaves of dissent and rebellion, "no go" zones where extremists and terrorists plot and openly talk of one day casting aside the Western legal system to replace it with harsh sharia.

Once again, as in the 1930s and as in the centuries before, the Jews have returned as universal scapegoat, however irrationally they are targeted. Anti-Semitism is on the rise even in the United States, most notably among Progressives targeting Israel.

All this is reminiscent of the world of the 1920s and 1930s and presages history repeating itself. While Islamic terrorism is perhaps the greatest threat the world has failed to confront since Nazism in World War II, is in fact a form of fascism, reaction to it from European populations in fear of losing their culture to an alien civilization is resulting in the appearance of competing fascism throughout Europe. Fascism and Communism are once more clawing at each other in the streets for souls and minds as they seek a "final solution" to humankind's differences. The outcome can only be chaos, war, and ultimate tyranny from both sides.

As Hitler did in the 1930s with Germany, Vladimir Putin is now linking Russia to nearly every major right-wing group in Europe. The Ataka Party in Bulgaria reports directly to the Russian embassy; the "New Force" in Italy meets with Putin and the Russian Duma; the Russian bank donated €9 million to the French National Front to help put fascist candidate Marine Le Pen in power.

And in the United States, socialists of a wide range, from Marxists to fascists, flirt with reducing America to one more failing welfare state—and it too is in chaos as collectivism takes over hearts, minds, and bodies.

Historians Warren Carroll and Mike Djordjevich, the latter a refugee from Yugoslavian Communism, compiled a list of "Fourteen Signposts" on the Road to Totalitarianism, among them the following. The United States seems to be on that well-traveled road:

abolition of private ownership of guns

detention of individuals without judicial process

requirement that private financial transactions be keyed to Social Security numbers so government can record them

use of compulsory education laws to forbid attendance at presently existing private schools

compulsory nonmilitary service

compulsory psychological treatment for nongovernment workers or public school children

an official declaration that anticommunist organizations (such as the Tea Party) are subversive and subsequent legal action taken to suppress them

laws limiting the number of people allowed to meet in a private home

wage and price controls

compulsory registration of individuals' places of employment restricted movement of individuals within the United States

new major laws by executive decree[4]

Toward the end of the downfall of any nation, observed Leonard Peikoff in *The Ominous Parallels*, the symptoms are wild-eyed mobs; bookstores flaunting pornography; promiscuity; orgies; drug addiction; destruction of cultural institutions; disintegration of the family; government corruption; anti-Semitism; murder in the streets.[5]

Liberty lies in the hearts of men and women; when it dies there, no constitution, no law, no court can save it; no constitution, no law, no court can even do much to help it.

—JUDGE LEARNED HAND

AS ROME WENT

During its golden period, Rome was such a great republic that people actually purchased citizenship. Then, after thriving as the world's greatest republic for roughly four hundred years, the first really large community in history and the first free community larger than a city, Rome began to decay.

Again and again, successful societies have risen and declined along Alexander Tytler's Liberty-Tyranny Cycle, disintegrations notable for the stark insight they provide into modern Western civilization and its journey through the cycle.

After 167 BC in Rome, the monopoly over the political system devolved into the hands of the richest families, since only people of considerable fortune could afford to seek office. Even though the will of the people was theoretically sovereign, for all practical matters a political elite through the senate exercised almost total control over government and thus over the people. Corruption followed power, as it always does.

The economy and culture began showing signs of crisis. Poets and philosophers such as Petronius and Tacitus referred to excessive wealth, corruption, and a closed, top-heavy government as factors leading to disintegration. Roman poet Juvenal described how emperors bribed upper-class families and distracted the masses by providing free food and entertainment while the nation became more shallow, corrupt, and pleasure-crazed.[6] By the time of Marcus Aurelius, as many as 135 yearly holidays featured magnificent public displays of chariot races and gladiators and other games to keep the masses excited, entertained, and distracted. More than three hundred thousand male citizens received public welfare relief at the expense of the state by the time of Julius Caesar. Free food, Juvenal noted, was the best way to conquer and domesticate animals—and people.

Solid family life, the cornerstone of Roman social structure, began to dissipate. The sanctity of the home and the dignity of work were gradually undermined. Sexual perversions, common immorality, and social degeneracy followed as citizens chose security and a comfortable lifestyle over freedom. Men became effeminate, cowardly, and indolent, and looked to barbarian mercenaries to defend them.

By the third century AD, government had grown so huge that taxes and natural resources could no longer support it. Commerce and industry declined. Workers became increasingly restless and rebellious. Soldiers mutinied. Barbarians invaded. Epidemics ravaged the nation in the wake of war and plundering.

Faced with increasing demands for services because of economic collapse, government survived by tightening controls and increasing the use of military and police to enforce order and obedience. What ultimately remained was a destroyed or languishing private industry, failing commerce, fallow fields and poor production, cultural stagnation, a general feeling of hopelessness and malaise—and a totalitarian state.

Historian Edward Gibbon summed up the causes behind the fall of the Roman Empire:

undermining of the dignity and sanctity of home and family

military buildups against enemies outside, when the real decadence was within a mad craze for pleasure and entertainment

decay of religion and spirituality

weakened people prone to outsourcing their duties to immigrants and barbarian mercenaries

men becoming too effeminate and cowardly to live a tougher, "manly" lifestyle

inflation and all-consuming taxation

a top-heavy and expanded bureaucracy

concentrated political power and accompanying corruption

loss of historical traditions

general immorality and sexual perversions

a welfare state

government oppression

redistribution of dwindling wealth

reliance on military force to maintain power

debasement of currency

failure to provide incentives for intellectual and economic efforts

A list to describe the condition of Western civilization might look a lot like this one.[7]

The inherent vice of capitalism is the unequal sharing of the blessings. The internal virtue of Socialism is the equal sharing of misery.[8]

—WINSTON CHURCHILL

THE REPLAYS

If collectivism, particularly socialism, is such a utopia, why do millions of people worldwide risk their lives climbing walls, thrusting themselves against barbed wire, braving gunfire, and swimming seas to escape it? Nations around the world seek utopia through the collective state and find, instead, tyranny.

CUBA: More than one million Cubans, approximately 10 percent of the population, have fled the "island paradise" since the late Fidel Castro seized power in 1959. Parents smuggled out their young children to foster care in the United States to prevent their living under Communism. Thousands of desperate *balseros* risked the ninety miles of rough seas in the Florida Straits between Cuba and Miami in order to escape. Hundreds, perhaps thousands, perished in the attempt.

VENEZUELA: In the early twentieth century, oil propelled Venezuela into a modern nation of wealth, with the largest economy in Latin America. Like his comrades in Latin America, the late Hugo Chávez used the electoral process in 1998 to install himself as dictator to establish a socialist vision so admired by American Progressives.

The result was predictable in a pattern repeated again and again on the planet. Devaluation of currency and default on the national debt produced a fiscal crisis. Inflation accelerated to the highest in the world. Poverty increased by as much as 53 percent. Basic staples, such as flour and cooking oil, became scarce, with other shortages of everything from electricity to medical equipment. Foreign journalists who failed to take a pro-government stance were expelled. The country had the highest homicide rate in the world in 2013.

Chavez's successor, Nicolás Maduro, continued his mentor's failed socialist policies. In 2015, for the second year in the row, an international survey determined that Venezuela was the most miserable nation on the planet. Maduro's establishment of a "Vice Ministry of Supreme Social Happiness" prompted one housewife to comment that, rather than having a new government ministry, she would be satisfied merely to be able to buy basic groceries.

CHINA: In *Life and Death in Shanghai*, Nien Cheng described a particularly poignant incident during his political imprisonment by the Communist Chinese when he asked a guard for a cake of soap.

"When are you going to get rid of your capitalistic way of wanting more than other people?" the guard snapped. "You are lucky to be allowed one cake per month. In many places, the people are only allowed one cake per family."[9]

Chinese Communism under Mao Tse-tung followed the same pathway taken by Russia under Lenin and Stalin. Communist fellow travelers in the United States and throughout the world applauded Mao's utopian aims while the "Cultural Revolution" and the "Great Leap Forward" claimed a death toll of at least 20 million people.

During President Obama's early tenure as president, the White House Christmas tree included an ornament bearing a likeness of Mao Tse-tung.

NORTH KOREA: The deranged Marxist policies of three successive generations of equally deranged despots—Kim Il-Sung, his son Kim Jong Il, and current psycho-in-residence Kim Jong-Un, the first Kim's grandson—have left the country desolate, repressive, and ugly. Claiming a mandate from history to achieve full socialism on his own terms, the current Kim maintains power through state terrorism while people literally starve to death.

Survivors tell of unspeakable torture, imprisonment, and forced labor for daring to criticize the government. "State enemies" are rounded up periodically and shipped off to prison camps. Women are sometimes forced to murder their own newborns.

Author David Horowitz, himself a former "Red diaper baby," points out that U.S. celebrities seem to always side with collectivist nations. He noted how singer Barbra Streisand's "political advisor," Robert Scheer, "organized a radical political junket to North Korea . . . and returned to Berkeley saying he had seen the future that worked and praising the brain-dwarfing thoughts of Kim Il-Sung."[10]

SWEDEN: Sweden, described as living a "soft socialism," was once lauded as the "most successful society on the planet." In 1976, *Time* magazine cheered it as a veritable utopia.

"It is a country," *Time* effused, "whose very name has become a synonym for a materialistic paradise. . . . Swedes enjoy free public education through college, four weeks' annual vacation and comprehensive retraining programs if they want to switch careers. . . . In pursuit of new ways to ease the angst of life, a local politician actually proposed that the government provide free sex partners for the lonely"[11]

Like all welfare states, with their egalitarian ethos, Sweden is now consumed by taxes, government expenditures, corruption and dysfunction, top-heavy public sectors, and the loss of an individual work ethic. The "most successful society on the planet" is now on the skids and heading toward inevitable tyranny due to old mistakes that have repeatedly plagued the world.

THE EUROPEAN UNION: Socialism as "a good example," David Horowitz wrote, "does not exist in the world. It has provided nothing other than famine, fear, and chronic backwardness."[12] The lesson is apparent in the economic and social deterioration of European culture under the unelected ruling body of the European Union, through which people are sacrificing their individuality and liberty in a compact with the devil.

Europe suffers rigid centralization of governments, flagrant corruption, unaffordable entitlements, cradle-to-grave welfare, more and more dependency on an immigrant workforce, and threats of impending bankruptcy and economic implosion. Six countries in the Eurozone violated "sound fiscal policy" rules in 2014 by exceeding debt-to-GDP limits. Six of the nations exceeded limits by over 100 percent, accumulating debt beyond their ability to pay.[13]

In short, the EU is falling apart. In 2016, Great Britain voted to separate from the EU, which it did. Other EU nations, most notably France and Germany, may soon follow suit, as they deal not only with an economic crisis caused by socialism but also by a refugee crisis of large numbers of Muslims pouring in from the Middle East to completely transform the European nations.

In these examples, as elsewhere around the globe, champions of collectivism from all points of the political spectrum continue to build webs of deceit and control. Eradicating them is like playing the children's game Whac-A-Mole. Whack one here, another two or three pop up over there.

As there is but one God in Heaven, there ought to be but one ruler on Earth.

—TAMERLANE[14]

ONE WORLD COLLECTIVE

Humankind's tendency from the beginning has been to expand from small groupings to larger ones while conceding along the way certain personal liberties for the good of the whole. Alexander Wendt, professor of political science at Ohio State University, states that a one-world government is inevitable due to the tendency of systems to develop from less-organized entities to more-organized ones.[15] Individuals and groups, he said, move through five stages: a system of states; a society of states; world society; collective security; and the world state.

The idea of a one-world government is not a recent concept. Francisco de Vitorin (1483–1546), the "founder of global political philosophy," proposed a plan for a "Republic of the Whole World." In 1771, Adam Weishaupt formed the concept of a "New World Order" that abolished all sovereign governments and established communal *everything*.

Trends toward relinquishing sovereignty to world organizations moved into a "golden age" during the Cold War mind-set following World War II. A number of books, such as *One World*, written by presidential hopeful Wendell Wilkie, and *The Anatomy of Peace* by Emery Reves argued in favor of a federal world government.

Prominent people such as Albert Einstein, Bertrand Russell, and even Winston Churchill called on government to take gradual steps toward creating a world government. Others followed their lead.

President Richard Nixon, a California congressman in 1950, went on record favoring a world supreme court and a world police force. As a presidential candidate in 1968, he responded to a letter from the United World Federalists with, "Your organization can perform an important service by continuing to emphasize that world peace can only come through world law."[16]

The League of Nations, founded as a result of the Treaty of Versailles, which ended the Great War, seemed to be the internationalists' crowning achievement. However, without its own armed forces, the League had no way to enforce its edicts and proved incapable of preventing aggression by Axis powers in the 1930s. The United Nations replaced it on April 20, 1946, following the end of World War II. Although initially designed to fulfill a limited advisory role with a goal of preventing deadly international conflict, and to work on international law, international security, world economic development, human rights, social programs, and eventual world peace, it soon developed higher aspirations for superseding national governments in a federalized central system.

To achieve world government, said Brock Chisolm, director of the UN World Health Organization, it is necessary first to "remove from the minds of men their individualism, loyalty to family tradition, national patriotism, and religious dogmas."[17]

From its inception, the UN has been dominated by a type of "socialist liberation theology" that largely opposes free enterprise capitalism in favor of government planning. In its Declaration on Establishment of a New International Economic Order, the UN recommended that "prevailing disparities in the world . . . be banished."[18] John Podesta, former chief of staff to President Bill Clinton and founder of Center for American Progress, which is largely funded by George Soros, conspired with the UN to implement a so-called universal sustainable development agenda, which is essentially food stamps for the world's poor, paid for by Americans—another Marxist scheme to seize from "the rich" to give to the poor.

In an *SCP Journal* article, Progressive journalist Tal Brooke took one-world a step further by advocating a one-world religion. "A generic spirituality is necessary to fuse diverse, even hostile cultures and faiths into a unity. To fight the world together, religious boundaries must be eliminated."[19]

For those who are Christians, this is a chilling reminder of the New Testament book of Revelation and the coming of the Antichrist.[20]

In embracing one-world aspirations, the environmental movement has more to do with social and political control, with taking over the world and remaking it, than it does with clean air and water.

"The origin of global warming lies in capitalism," asserted Bolivian president Evo Morales at the UN Climate Change Conference in Lima. "If we could end capitalism then we would have a solution."[21]

Lord Christopher Monckton of Britain, a delegate to the UN-backed Dona Climate Conference of 2012, tried to point out the one-world socialist agenda behind the global warming movement.

"International climate treaties," he said, "may yet prove a greater threat to liberty than fascism or communism. For it is the same threat writ global, albeit with the jackboots and guns very carefully hidden—for now."

He was booed for his temerity and banned from all future conferences.[22]

Barack Obama declared with stunning hubris future generations would say his election to the presidency was "the moment when the rise of the oceans began to slow and our planet began to heal."[23] Through executive orders and his policies, rules and regulations, Obama backed freedom into a corner by imposing limits not only on environmental issues but also on everything else, from political speech to gun ownership. Increasingly, he championed the UN's inserting itself into affairs that have traditionally belonged to individual nations and which have put the United States on the short road to world government.

While the UN so far lacks the absolute power to execute its policies, the Western world philosophically accepts much of its agenda and proceeds to give up more and more of its sovereignty.

During the 2012 presidential elections in the United States, the UN dispatched poll watchers to make sure voting in Kansas and Ohio and other states was conducted fairly.

With Obama's backing, the UN's "Arms Trade Treaty" was an effort to regulate firearms worldwide. Congress eventually rejected it—but it is not yet a dead issue.

In 2014, Obama pushed to ratify the UN Law of the Sea Convention, which would allow UN international law to control the world's oceans and seas—and eventually its rivers and other bodies of water, all the way down to farm ponds.

"I believe we are now reaching a tipping point," warned Fox News and History Channel contributor Paul McGuire. "The U.N. is already in control of a great deal, but we are going to see the U.N. come out of the shadows and openly exercise its authority over the United States . . . I believe the elites are ready to bring global government out of the closet."[24]

The Obama administration appeared to be opening the closet door.

Attorney General Loretta Lynch voiced support for Obama's "Strong Cities Network," which he announced before the UN in September 2015. The goal of this move is to plug local police departments through the UN into an international network of police that will train together and share intelligence in order to combat "violent extremism," which could include everything from an ISIS terrorist cell to a riot such as that which occurred in Ferguson, Missouri.

"Under Obama," cautioned John Whitehead, a constitutional lawyer and founder of the Rutherford Institute, "we've moved closer and closer to federalizing the police. . . . With the Strong Cities program we see the goal is to have global police. . . . It's saying the U.N. is going to be a global police force."[25]

Other measures in play are equally threatening to American sovereignty.

From 2012 to 2016, the Obama administration secretly negotiated a free trade agreement between the United States and eleven other nations, from Canada and Mexico to Australia, Japan, and Vietnam. The White House refused to provide Congress a draft of the Trans-Pacific Pact (TPP), insisting only that it be ratified "fast track" when it appears.

If funded, TPP would bring more than 60 percent of the global economy into the "largest ever economic treaty," predicted to eclipse national sovereignty. It covers everything from food safety to fracking, from financial markets and medical prices to copyright rules and Internet freedom.[26] The longest section of the agreement, entitled "Enforcement," details police measures that pose serious implications for individual rights and civil liberties.

Public schools, colleges, and universities in the United States are busy indoctrinating children and young adults in their roles as citizens of the world. Dozens of educational institutions support entire departments offering classes in planning "alternative futures" for the world, which means agitating for a one-world government. New generations of young Americans with their heads full of Orwellian newspeak and value-neutral thinking are perfect candidates for the Brave New World.

9

THE DECLINE

"Tolerance and apathy are the last virtues of a dying society."

—ARISTOTLE

UTOPIAN COLLECTIVISTS hold a common myopic view of the world, if not a total blindness to reality. In their minds they see a perfect society where happy citizens sing "Kumbaya" and dance through tulips while Big Brother watches with a benign smile to make sure everyone stays in step. U.S. Army Major Euell White, who served in Berlin before the Wall fell, provided an eerie glimpse into that reality should utopianists prevail.

EPIC MISERY
He described how each Sunday morning, two women "appeared at the same time on either side of The Wall, just stood there gazing at one another, crying. . . . They were mother and daughter. Afraid to wave or do anything other than just look at one another because communist

police would punish the woman on the East Berlin side. Terrorized by a society where even the most innocent human behavior could be construed as anti-social."[1]

In the midst of his election campaign against Britain's socialist Labour Party, Winston Churchill predicted dire consequences if his opponents won, because "they do not see where their theories are leading them."[2]

That is as true of today's American collectivist radicals as it was of the fascists and Communists of Churchill's day. They do not see where their theories are leading them, although they have to be blind not to.

The so-called radical revolution of the 1960s was a revolution not of the proletariat but of the spoiled privileged on a Marxist rampage. They are still with us—they and their spawn. And they *are* the government. Their legacy of rock 'n' roll, drugs, free sex, and Marxism infiltrated the American mainstream and put these foolish young people in control of social, cultural, and political institutions all the way up to the White House. Focused on political processes and the vulnerabilities of the two-party political system, they exploit the future in Marxist terms through the Big Lie that socialism protects the downtrodden masses and that it is therefore inevitable. Ours has become the government our Founders warned us against.

"You wondered whether this Western culture could survive," one of novelist Saul Bellows characters comments in *Mr. Sammler's Planet*, "or whether the worst enemies of civilization might not prove to be its petted intellectuals who attacked it at its weakest moments."

Here comes the orator! With his flood of words, and his drop of reason.
—BENJAMIN FRANKLIN

HAIL THE MESSIAH

When President Barack Obama announced his candidacy for president of the United States in 2007 and subsequently voiced his desire to

"fundamentally transform" the nation,[3] most people were either ignorant of his intentions or, as in the case of Progressives, supported them.
During his eight years in office, he moved the United States more rapidly and completely toward socialist collectivism than any other force in
history. Obama is a creature created for the time by Progressives, socialists, Marxists, one-worlders, and the U.S. media. Grounds of freedom
lost under his reign may never be recovered.

So how did he do it?

The mainstream media quite simply refused to vet the candidate
and his background. Throughout his presidency, his college and law
school records remained sealed, his career as "community organizer"
obfuscated, his family background overlooked, his friends undercover,
his ideological influences unexplored and unexplained, even his eligi-
bility for office largely left unquestioned.

As the nation's first black president, Obama wasn't merely elected;
he was *anointed*. Progressives and their fellow travelers threw an orgy
of adulation.

"We thought that he was going to be . . . the next messiah," Barbara
Walters confided to Piers Morgan on CNN.[4]

"In a way Obama's standing above the country . . . above the world.
He's sort of God," effused Evan Thomas, editor of *Newsweek,* under a
banner that hailed "the Second Coming."[5]

MSNBC's Chris Matthews described how thrills ran up his leg when
he heard the president speak.[6]

Actress Gwyneth Paltrow hosted an Obama Hollywood fund-raiser
during which she gushed over how handsome he was, asserting, "It
would be wonderful if we are able to give this man all the power he
needs to pass the things he needs to pass."[7]

Although in his White House bio Obama noted how his story
was "the American story—values from the heartland, a middle-class
upbringing in a strong family," the truth in his upbringing might best
be described as dysfunctional. His father was an African Communist
who deserted Obama's white mother and was rarely heard from again.

His mother remarried an Indonesian Muslim. Obama as a child attended a madras and went to mosque regularly. He later described the sound of the Muslim call to prayers as one of "the prettiest sounds on earth at sunset."[8]

Obama was still a young child when his irresponsible Communist mother dumped him on her parents in Hawaii to raise. Obama's grandfather was likely a Communist as well.

In *Dreams from My Father*, Obama's autobiography, he admitted to hanging around with his "choom gang" of pot smokers and "the more politically active black students. The foreign students. The Chicanos. The Marxist professors and structural feminists and punk-rock performance poets. . . . When we ground out our cigarettes in the hallway carpet or set our stereos so loud that the walls began to shake, we were resisting the bourgeois society's stifling constraints. We weren't indifferent or careless or insecure. We were alienated."[9]

Frank Chapman, an activist with a Communist front group known as the World Peace Council, described Obama as a "mole" while explaining how Marx "once compared revolutionary struggle with the work of the mole, who sometimes burrows so far beneath the ground that he leaves no trace of his movement on the surface."[10]

After his election as president, Obama the mole emerged with collectivist policies and actions that included socialized medicine, open borders, wealth redistribution, fascistic merging of government and private enterprise, attacks on the Constitution, circumventing law and the Constitution through executive orders and bureaucratic regulations, denigrating America at home and abroad, expanding dependency on government, assaulting capitalism, siding with socialist governments, refusing to act against jihad terrorists, utilizing government agencies such as the IRS and NSA to attack political opponents. . . . on and on.

"I never thought we would be looking so soon at the prospect of a one-party state," David Horowitz wrote.

Those words may sound hyperbolic, but take a moment to think about it. If you have transformed the taxing agency of the state into a political weapon—and Obama has; if you are setting up a massive government program to gather the financial and health information of every citizen, and control their access to care; and if you have a spy agency that can read the mail and listen to the communications of every individual in the country, you don't really need a secret police to destroy your opponents. Once you have silenced them, you can proceed with your plans to remake the world in your image.[11]

Obama's danger extends beyond his two terms in office in that they have provided a blueprint for future Progressive takeovers that will leave people yearning for the days when government largely left us alone.

"As democracy is perfected," H. L. Mencken once noted, "the office [of the president] represents, more and more closely, the inner soul of the people. . . . On some great and glorious day the plain folks of the land will reach their heart's desire at last and the White House will be adorned by a downright moron."[12]

It is difficult to free fools from the chains they revere.

—VOLTAIRE

THE LIST

You shall know a man by the company he keeps. And the company Barack Obama keeps is a clear indication of who he is and what he intended as president. The following are only a few of those he allowed to ride him like an old whore, who followed him into power, supported or influenced him, possibly even controlled him to some degree, and whose convictions they borrowed from the likes of Marx, Lenin, Stalin, Hitler, Mao, and others to infect the United States with the fatal virus of ultimate decline.

FRANK MARSHALL DAVIS: A well-known black Communist journalist and poet, a former agent of the Soviet Union under FBI scrutiny for two decades, who apparently introduced Barack Obama to

Communism. Davis was a friend of Obama's maternal grandfather, upon whom Obama's footloose mother dumped him when he was still a child. Davis mentored young Barack during his formative years in Hawaii and bent the twig in the direction the tree was to grow.

"Anti-Americanism," economist Dr. Tom Sowell noted, "is the rule among Obama's mentors over the years."[13]

SAUL ALINSKY: Alinsky (died 1972) authored *Rules for Radicals* as a modern instruction manual for fundamentally transforming social institutions in order to implement Marx's manifesto. In it, he gave an "over-the-shoulder acknowledgment to the very first radical . . . Lucifer."[14] Among his converts were President Barack Obama and 2016 presidential hopeful Hillary Clinton.

"[Alinsky] was the education that was seared into my brain," Obama crowed at the Iowa Citizens Action Network. "It was the best education I have ever had, better than anything I got at Harvard Law School."[15]

Hillary Clinton offered her seventy-five-page senior thesis at Wellesley College as a tribute to him.

Alinsky's premise was a simple one: Americans will never accept violent revolution. At least not yet. Therefore, the radical must trade in his beard, ponytail, and pot for a three-piece suit and infiltrate the system as a wolf in sheep's clothing. Or, as Frank Chapman put it, a "mole" hiding his true intentions behind a curtain of "social justice" and "peace."

Alinsky delineated eight levels of control that must be seized in order to create a socialist state:

1. Health care: Control it and you control the people.

2. Poverty: Poor people are easy to control if they depend upon government to provide their livelihood.

3. Debt: Increase the national debt to an unsustainable level, which justifies increasing taxes and thus more government control over individuals.

4. Gun control: Restrict the capability of citizens to defend themselves against government incursion.

5. Welfare: Control every aspect of life—food, income, housing . . . and you control life itself.

6. Religion: God is a rally point for opponents of socialism. Therefore, renounce Him, destroy Him.

7. Education: Control schools, universities, the media, pop culture [and today the Internet], and you control politics.

8. Class warfare: Divide and conquer by creating discontent.[16]

Lying, cheating, *anything* is permissible to advance the cause and win the prize. To summarize Alinsky's message, "Don't telegraph your goals; infiltrate [the] institutions and subvert them; moral principles are disposable fictions; the end justifies the means; and never forget that your political goal is always *power*."[17]

"A revolutionary organizer must shake up the prevailing pattern of [people's] lives—agitate, create disenchantment and discontent with the current values, to produce, if not a passion for change, at least a passive, affirmative, non-challenging climate. . . . [People] must feel so frustrated, so defeated, so lost, so futureless in the prevailing system that they are willing to let go of the past and change the future."[18]

People who refuse to be converted will be demonized, punished, neutralized, ridiculed, and destroyed. A society becomes ripe for takeover once they give up and drop out.

Lucifer must be grinning his fool head off at the way things are playing out.

RICHARD CLOWARD AND FRANCES FOX PIVEN: In 1966, Columbia University professor Richard Cloward and his research assistant, Frances Fox Piven, penned an article in the *Nation* entitled "The Weight of the Poor: A Strategy to End Poverty."[19] The two later married.

Their theory, known as the Cloward–Piven strategy, called for Communist "organizers" to collapse capitalism by leading the masses to overload the government bureaucracy with a flood of impossible demands that would put the nation into crisis and cause its collapse. Society could then be fundamentally transformed.

Think Occupy Wall Street, with its impossible demands for free *everything*.

"The Cloward–Piven strategy," noted Right Side News, utilizes "mass movements . . . to draft poor people into service as revolutionary foot soldiers. . . . The flood of demands [is] calculated to break the budget, jam the bureaucratic gears into gridlock, and bring the system crashing down. Fear, turmoil, violence and economic collapse would accompany such a breakdown—providing perfect conditions for fostering radical change."[20]

The dynamic duo from Columbia enlisted a black militant named George Wiley to try out the theory. Wiley formed the National Welfare Rights Organization (NWRO) in 1967, which was heavily funded by socialist billionaire George Soros. NWRO followers invaded welfare offices all across the United States to bully social workers and demand every penny to which the law "entitled" them.

In New York, reported the *City Journal*, "single-parent households on welfare soared from 4.3 million to 10.8 million despite mostly flush economic times."[21]

One person was suddenly on welfare for every two working. The overload forced the city to declare bankruptcy in 1975.

Cloward–Piven is still in play today. Think Detroit, Chicago, Baltimore . . . Former New York mayor Rudy Giuliani credits Cloward–Piven with changing cultural attitudes toward welfare from a temporary expediency to a lifetime "entitlement."[22]

In 1973, the ideas of Cloward and Piven became part of presidential nominee George McGovern's platform at the Democratic National Convention. Cloward died in 2001, but his wife was known to visit the White House and President Obama.

GEORGE SOROS: Multibillionaire one-worlder George Soros plays the tune by which the socialist, collectivist marionettes in the United States dance. This Nefarious Puppeteer sits on his high throne, with strings attached to almost every nation on the globe. Having "earned" his billions through manipulating hedge funds and speculating in currency, he is truly a kingmaker, with the power to determine the fate of virtually every human being on earth.

"By his own admission," Discover the Networks reported, "he helped engineer coups in Slovakia, Croatia, Georgia and Yugoslavia. When Soros targets a country for 'regime change,' he begins by creating a shadow government—a fully formed government-in-exile ready to assume power when the opportunity arises. The Shadow Party he has built in America greatly resembles those he created in other countries prior to instigating a coup."[23]

It has been suggested that Obama may be a player in the U.S. Shadow Government.

Soros's mission, said social critic L. Brent Bozell, is to fundamentally transform America into a second-rate socialist state in a one-world government by destroying the conservative movement and its leaders; neutering the U.S. Constitution; erasing Judeo-Christian values and morality; and establishing government-controlled and government-funded "new" organizations to propagandize the population.

His propaganda machine consists of some thirty major news organizations that reach more than 300 million people around the globe. Cash from his various foundations is funneled into Columbia University's School of Journalism, the nation's primary journalism school, and partly supports major journalism associations, such as the National Federation of Community Broadcasters, the National Association of Hispanic Journalists, and the Committee to Protect Journalists. "Top journalists" in the United States are attracted to his media enterprises.

The fourteen-member Journalist Advisory Board of Soros's "Pro Politico," which attacks oil and gas companies, private schools, the private health care industry, banks, and the U.S. military, includes, or has included, prominent media figures such as CNN's David Gergen; *New York Times* executive editor Jill Abramson; *Boston Globe* editor Martin Baron; and *Atlanta Journal Constitution*'s editorial page editor, Cynthia A. Tucker.

The advisory board for the "Center for Public Integrity" includes, or has included, ABC's Christiane Amanpour; *Huffington Post* founder Arianna Huffington; and NBC universal's vice president and chief diversity officer, Paul Madison.

"Watchdog groups" such as Media Matters, founded by David Brock with funds supported by Soros, launches character assassination attacks against conservative media figures like Rush Limbaugh, Sean Hannity, Glenn Beck, Michael Savage, and Bill O'Reilly. It partnered with the Obama White House in an ongoing campaign to smear and destroy Fox News.

Soros's other organizations and front groups are equally dedicated to smashing opposition to his socialist agenda. The Tides Foundation, which he and various government grants support, created an entity called "Imagining America," which is like a department of arts and culture that floods dough into "our cultural communities."

"[It] 'looks uncomfortably . . . [like] the Ministry of Propaganda and Public Enlightenment' [that] used to enforce and regulate the culture of Nazi Germany," Glenn Beck pointed out. "So we have the government, radicals, and the universities, and some of their affili-ates are actually public officials. They actually hold conferences and presentations about how to re-author American history—and it's [funded] by you. . . . This is exactly what Germany was doing. They re-imagined history with a look to the social frontier. . . . teaching and influencing your children [through] art and music and film and history books."[24]

In 1997, the National Popular Vote (NPV) campaign received seed money from the Joyce Foundation, a nonprofit on whose board Barack Obama sat, in an effort to transform the nation from a republic to a democracy by changing the way presidents are elected. The Soros-funded Center for Voting and Democracy joined the campaign, which means, if successful, electing a president will bypass the Electoral College in favor of a nationwide popular vote. The heavily populated Progressive coasts and the Northeast would determine who becomes president from now on.

During the nationwide racial and anti-police rioting that began with Ferguson in 2014 and continues in cities throughout the nation, groups supported by Soros forked out millions of dollars to send activists to foment chaos along the teachings of Saul Alinsky and Cloward–Piven. Among those Soros-funded groups marching in the streets, burning, looting, shooting, and shouting, "Hands up; don't shoot!" were the Open Society Foundation, the Drug Policy Alliance, Equal Justice U.S., and Community Change in Washington.

Soros's hand can be found inserted into every area of American politics. In *Guilty,* Ann Coulter refers to Soros as the "Daddy Warbucks of the Democratic Party" who, she says, spends millions to fund phony "grassroots" left-wing organizations such as MoveOn. Org, the Association of Community Organizations for Reform Now (ACORN), and the ACLU. "These are the organizations that call the shots in the Democratic Party."[25]

One of Soros's foundations, the Apollo Alliance, helped conceive and design Obama's failed financial stimulus plan. It also played a major role in drafting the socialist-style Affordable Care Act, known as "Obamacare."

Politicians listen when George Soros speaks. As president, Barack Obama faithfully stressed issues in economic and environment that Soros outlined and approved. Soros himself has his eyes set on the goal of bringing the world's population to heel. He is the perfect James Bond villain. He is now in his eighties, but his influence will likely continue after his death through his son Jonathan, who is reportedly posed to take the puppet strings and make the nations continue to dance and sing the Soros way.

VALERIE JARRETT: Valerie Jarrett, former president Obama's senior White House adviser, was sometimes referred to as the power and the brains behind the throne. She and her family were all Communists, according to author and former Communist David Horowitz.

"The president, his chief operative Valerie Jarrett and his chief political strategist David Axelrod all came out of the same communist left and the same radical new left as I did," Horowitz noted. ". . . Instead of calling themselves communists or socialists, they call themselves liberals and progressives. This camouflage is very old. I never once heard my parents and their Party friends refer to themselves as communists. They were *progressives*—and registered Democrats."[26]

MICHELLE OBAMA: Barack Obama met his future bride in the summer of 1989 at the Chicago law firm of Sidley Austin, where she, an attorney of the firm, was assigned to mentor him after his first year at Harvard Law School. They visited a community center on their first date, where, as Michelle later recalled, Obama "talked to the residents . . . about two concepts. He told about 'the world as it is' and 'the world as it should be.'"[27]

These were themes he later tossed about during his presidential campaign, themes explored in Saul Alinsky's *Rules for Radicals*.

BILL AYERS: Bill Ayers, a former radical member of SDS (Students for a Democratic Society) and a cofounder of the violent Weather Underground movement, is most noted for terrorist bombings and for leading the "Days of Rage" in Chicago during the 1968 Democratic National Convention. In his memoir, *Fugitive Days*, he described how he and the Weather Underground bombed New York City police headquarters in 1970, the U.S. Capitol Building in 1971, and the Pentagon in 1972.

"I don't regret setting bombs," he confided in the *New York Times* in 2001. "I feel we didn't do enough."[28]

An FBI informant named Larry Grathwohl attended a Weather Underground meeting during which Ayers and others discussed a future Communist takeover of the United States. According to this scenario, the Soviet Union, Cuba, North Korea, and China would occupy various parts of the United States and establish "reeducation centers" to prevent a counterrevolution. At least 24 million "diehard capitalists" would have to be eliminated.

"When I say 'eliminate,' I mean 'kill,'" Grathwohl stated during his testimony. "I want you to imagine sitting in a room with 25 people, most of which have graduate degrees, from Columbia and other well-known educational centers, and hear them figuring out the logistics for the elimination of 25 million people. They absolutely believed they, along with the international revolutionary movement, would cause the collapse of the United States and they would be in charge."[29]

Ayers and fellow revolutionary Bernardine Dohrn went underground in 1970 after they were indicted on various charges. The two eventually married and continued their terrorist rampage while on the run.

They remained on the lam until they surfaced to face charges in 1982. Ayers was exonerated only because police had used illegal wire taps to gather evidence. Incredibly, in an example of the state of American education, Ayers went on to become a professor of education at the University of Illinois.

Word leaked out about a possible association between Ayers and Barack Obama when Obama launched his bid for the White House. Obama shrugged it off, insisting on a number of occasions how he barely knew the man. Ayers was "just a guy who lived in the neighborhood." Their relationship, as it turned out, was much more than that.[30]

An avowed Communist named Alice Palmer, who groomed Obama to run for her vacated Senate seat in Illinois, reportedly introduced the two men. Apparently, she felt the two might be compatible. For the next several years leading up to Obama's campaigning for the presidency, the two worked together to employ Alinsky methods in a variety of forums. They appeared together as speakers for several public events, such as the 1997 University of Chicago Panel on

Children and in 2002 an event sponsored by the University of Illinois, titled: "Intellectuals: Who Needs Them?"

Obama served on the Joyce Foundation's board from 1974 to 2002. During that time, the foundation provided start-up capital to Chicago's Annenberg Challenge (CAC), an education "reform" group headed by Bill Ayers. CAC's sole purpose for existence seemed to be granting money to radical left-wing activists. Obama was subsequently appointed chairman of the board at CAC.

BERNARDINE DOHRN: Dohrn served as the only woman national committee member of SDS. She linked up with Bill Ayers and Jeff Jones to found a Weather Underground offshoot. FBI director J. Edgar Hoover dubbed her "the most dangerous woman in America" after she and Kathy Boudin placed explosives in the women's bathroom of the Senate building in Washington.[31]

In December 1969, the year before she and Ayers fled underground to avoid criminal prosecution, she reacted to details of the Charles Manson murders: "Dig it! First they killed those pigs, then they ate dinner in the same room with them. They even shoved a fork into the victim's stomach. Wild!"[32]

After resurfacing from being on the run with now-husband Bill Ayers in 1982, she was convicted of a single felony and soon released to become a paralegal in the Chicago law firm of Sidley Austin, where, coincidentally, the future Mrs. Obama also worked. Restricted from taking the bar exam because of her felony convictions, she ended up as an associate professor of law at Northwestern University.

CASS SUNSTEIN: A Harvard law professor, Sunstein believed, as he argued along with coauthor Richard Thaler in their 2009 book, *Nudge*, that government granted citizens their rights—and therefore could retract them.

President Obama selected him as "regulatory czar" while appointing his wife, Samantha, as ambassador to the United Nations. As an official presidential adviser, Sunstein used federal regulations to chip away the power and freedom of individuals while the state increased its control. In *Nudge*, reported the *New York Times*, he explained "how government and other organizations could induce people to avoid common errors"[33] to nudge them in the "right" direction. A kinder, gentler tyranny in engineering people toward making "correct" moral and social choices the Progressive way.

WADE RATHKE: Like Bill Ayers and Bernardine Dohrn, Rathke was a member of SDS. He was also a disciple of George Wiley, whom Cloward and Piven used to "crash" the welfare system. In 1970, Rathke and Gary Delgado founded ACORN, the Association of Community Organizations for Reform Now, which Rathke headed. At its peak, ACORN was the largest radical group in the United States, with more than a half million members working on such projects as voter registration, affordable housing, and health care.

ACORN received 40 percent of its funding from the federal government, much of the rest from George Soros's Open Society Institute. Its big push was in voter registration, not only in registering Democrats to vote, but in fomenting crisis, Cloward–Piven-style. ACORN's goal was to so overwhelm the system with registrations, multiple entries, dead voters, and random and contrived names that it would become impossible to police. That would essentially lead to no rules at all. Everyone would vote, legal or not. Multiple times. Shocking how many Democrats subsequently rose from their graves to vote. During the 2004–2006 election cycles, ACORN was accused of widespread voter fraud in twelve different states.

According to the *Wall Street Journal*, eight of the nineteen terrorist hijackers of 9/11 were registered to vote. As Democrats, no doubt.

In the early 1980s, Barack Obama was an ACORN community organizer who headed an ACORN affiliate, Project Vote! ACORN claimed to have played a major role in Barack Obama's election to the White House. Obama lauded its members for their efforts. "I've been fighting alongside ACORN on issues you care about my entire career," he said. "Even before I was an elected official, ACORN was smack dab in the middle of it, and we appreciate your work."[34]

A year after Obama's election, filmmaker James O'Keefe exposed voter fraud and other criminal activities involving ACORN. ACORN and its officials were cited for being a criminal enterprise and forced to shut down operations in 2010 and splinter into smaller, statewide organizations. Rathke subsequently cofounded the Soros-funded Tides Foundation, became head of a local SEIU chapter, and chaired an AFL-CIO organizers forum.

In retaliation for his audacity, it would seem, O'Keefe has been audited twice by the IRS.

RAHM EMANUEL: It was Rahm Emanuel who uttered the administration's most infamous line: "You never want a serious crisis to go to waste. . . . It's an opportunity to do things that you . . . could not do before."[35]

Obama apparently heeded his advice. Everything in the Obama administration was a crisis—banking, auto companies, health care, gun control, the economy, immigration, global warming, race relationships . . .

"They overstate a problem," Rush Limbaugh explained, "and work society into a frenzied state in order to justify their invariable big government solutions."[36]

PETER DREIER: Dreier is a former ACORN strategist and *Huffington Post* columnist whose 1979 essay in *Social Policy* called for introducing "unmanageable strains into the capitalist system, strains that precipitate an economic and/or political crisis."[37] He was Barack Obama's 2008 campaign adviser.

ERIC HOLDER: Appointed U.S. attorney general by President Obama, Holder was perhaps the most controversial figure ever to occupy the position. Under his and Obama's watch, the Justice Department refused to enforce federal laws with which they disagreed—laws on immigration, drugs, gay marriage, and others.

Holder also apparently stonewalled a number of Congressional investigations of corruption involving Obama's heir apparent, Hillary Clinton.

JOHN KERRY: Kerry replaced Hillary Clinton as secretary of state during Obama's second presidential term. He and his wife, Teresa Heinz Kerry, the "Ketchup Queen,"[38] have contributed generously to practically every radical group in the nation, many of which are also funded by George Soros.

JOHN PODESTA: Previously chief of staff for President Bill Clinton, Podesta moved back to the White House as an Obama strategist. A founder of the Soros-funded Center for American Progress, he wrote the foreword for a report titled *The Power of the President: Recommendations to Advance Progressive Change*, in which he and others subtly suggested the right president could circumvent Congress and essentially become a king.[39]

VAN JONES: After graduating from law school in the early 1900s, Jones moved to San Francisco to become a member of STORM (Standing Together to Organize a Revolutionary Movement). STORM members, he wrote in conjunction with other radical authors in *Reclaiming Revolution*, "have a political commitment to the fundamental ideas of Marxism-Leninism. . . . We found inspiration and guidance in the insurgent revolutionary strategies developed by Third World revolutionaries like Mao Tse-tung."[40]

President Obama selected him as the White House's adviser on environmental matters, a "green czar." He lasted less than a year before being exposed by TV personality Glenn Beck as a Communist revolutionary. The exposure, of course, did nothing to damage his reputation among Progressives.

He subsequently worked with MoveOn.Org and became a member of the board of the Center for American Progress, on which John Podesta also served. Both are Soros enterprises. He hosted CNN's *Crossfire* and holds a joint appointment at Princeton

University in the Center for African-American studies, and at the Woodrow Wilson School of Public and International Affairs.

CHUCK HAGEL: George Soros was a chief advocate of Hagel's being appointed as President Obama's secretary of defense. Before his appointment, Hagel served on the board of Soros's Ploughshares, which the *Washington Post* reports is the "largest grant-making foundation in the United States focusing exclusively on peace and security issues."[41] A proponent for a "nuclear weapons–free world,"[42] Ploughshares opposes American development of a missile defense system and contributes funds to radical groups that protest the U.S. military and U.S. foreign policy. It is a partner of the Marxist-oriented Institute for Policy Studies.

ANTOIN REZKO: It is said Barack Obama would never have gotten to the White House without Tony Rezko. A Chicago crook with a gambling problem, Rezko was a big Obama fund-raiser until he was convicted in 2008 on sixteen counts of fraud, money laundering, aiding and abetting bribery, and summarily living off the government grid while corrupting public officials.

During the seventeen-year relationship between Obama and Rezko, their two families purchased adjoining properties and often dined together. Tim Novak of the *Chicago Sun-Times* noted that Obama as state senator performed official acts for Rezko for certain considerations.

AHMED YOUSEF: Yousef is a former political adviser for Hamas, which is listed by the U.S. State Department as a terrorist organization. As an Obama White House adviser, he publicly stated that Hamas supported Obama's foreign policy issues.[43]

CAROL BROWNER: Browner served as Obama's "global warming czar." She was one of fourteen leaders of the Socialist International Commission for a Sustainable World Society, an organization that promotes a one-world movement.

MARK RUDD: Another SDS alumni, and subsequently an educator in Albuquerque and a Progressives for Obama supporter, he penned a blog following Obama's election in which he reassured Progressives that, although Obama was elected by campaigning in the center, he would now move to the left end of the scale.

HUMA ABEDIN: Abedin was secretary of state Hillary Clinton's chief foreign policy adviser on Muslim Affairs, and remained Hillary's closest adviser as she campaigned for the presidency in 2016. Before Abedin moved up to the State Department, she worked twelve years for Abdullah Omar Naseef, a top funder for al-Qaeda terrorist leader Osama bin Laden. Naseef remains a fugitive from the U.S. government for his role in the 9/11 attacks on the World Trade Center and the Pentagon.

DRUMMOND PIKE: An avowed socialist, Pike helped found the Tides Foundation, which supports "environmental extremism, exclusion of humans from public and private wildlands, banning of guns, abolition of the death penalty, abortion, and gay rights."[44] Two of Tides' largest financial contributors are George Soros and Teresa Heinz.

ELENA KAGAN: President Obama nominated Kagan to the U.S. Supreme Court. One of her most notable comments illustrates the direction toward which the United States is moving: "Government can restrict speech if it believes that speech can cause harm, either directly or by inciting others to do harm."[45]

* * *

These few listed radicals, Communists, and socialist riffraff were only the most notable ones associated with President Obama and his administration. There were many more, both known and unknown, who, like termites, gnawed incessantly at the fabric of a free society. Progressivism works not in fell swoops but in baby steps, over time. Obama did what he could during his reign to increase government control—over health care, the environment, immigration, and economics. Now it's the duty of the next Progressive president to move the cause another few steps along.

The truth that makes men free is for the most part the truth that men prefer not to hear.

—HERBERT SEBASTIEN AGAR

THE POD PEOPLE

"Pod People" in the old sci-fi movie *Invasion of the Body Snatchers* were aliens planted among humans to snatch their bodies to use in taking over the world. Progressives are new "Pod People," seeded among us with their slick predatory rhetoric to "fundamentally transform" the world.

"It's clear to all but the most obtuse and deceived among us," columnist Gina Miller noted, "that the United States of America has been taken over by Marxist enemies within."[46]

The movement to dismantle the American system did not spring up overnight. It is the product of a century of gradual encroachment upon American society to allow socialist themes to enter the American mainstream and conquer it.

Although Communism appeared to die out in the 1950s for a number of reasons previously discussed, it reemerged during the 1960s and 1970s to reach new influence in a more muted, underground incarnation. Ignoring the high human cost of tyranny that had stolen the lives of hundreds of millions during Marxism's relatively short history, subversives were willing to bring back the evil and do it all over again while pretending that the human destruction it brought the first time had never occurred. As in any garden where pests and predators are allowed to wreak havoc, Communism and its fellow weed, socialism, became pervasive in American institutions, cropping up in education and among intellectuals and political elites experimenting with and pushing the false ideologies of redistribution, "social justice," and envy.

The secret to "reformed" socialism's success is to make small gains in institutions that have political influence—like churches, labor unions, and universities—and spread out from there to infiltrate and control mainstream political parties and institutions. Through deceptive organizations, alliances, and consortiums, socialism has become respectable, making societal transformation all the easier.

Gus Hall, chairman of the Communist Party of the United States of America, explained how it worked as early as 1972 in his book, *A Lame Duck in Turbulent Waters* (New Outlook, 1972). Initiating Communism into the United States, he said, was like a three-legged stool that could not stand on its own. Until the first two legs of the stool—the Communist Party and the "forces of political independence"—were strong enough to bear their own weight, the "one operating leg would be the liberal wing of the Democratic Party."[47]

For the past fifty years, a fifth column of socialist and authoritarian radicals have systematically infiltrated America through various organizations dedicated to undermining every free institution from your children's kindergarten class to the White House.

COMMUNIST PARTY USA (CPUSA): Established in 1919, CPUSA is the largest Communist party in the United States, funded by the Soviet Union until the USSR collapsed in 1989. Its membership has declined precipitously since then by fanning out to various other socialist and Progressive venues. CPUSA still supports the usual socialist causes.

In spite of its loss of members, CPUSA over the past thirty years through its various offshoots, labor unions, and universities, has succeeded in electing hundreds of "Progressive" politicians to positions ranging from school board members to the U.S. Congress.

An official report issued through the fourteenth International Meeting of Communists and Workers Party in Beirut, Lebanon, in 2014 stated, "The Communist Party USA not only welcomes the election of President Barack Obama, but actively engaged in the electoral campaign for his reelection and for the election of many Democratic Party congressional candidates. We regarded the 2012 election as the most important in the United States since 1932."[48]

THE COMMUNIST PARTY LEGISLATIVE ACTION NETWORK: As an "All Peoples Front," it was organized to aid Communists seeking election to public office.

YOUNG COMMUNIST LEAGUE USA (YCLUSA): This organization sprang up to enroll young people in the political process of installing Communists in public office.

"Currently, conditions rarely if ever allow us to run open communists for office," a YCLUSA member wrote in 2010. "When members do run for office, it is within the auspices of the Democratic Party."[49]

U.S. PEACE COUNCIL: This group launched in 1979 as the U.S. component of the World Peace Council, a Soviet front. Its executive board included prominent Democrats, among them future Illinois senator Alice Palmer, an important mentor to Barack Obama.

WORKERS WORLD PARTY (WWP): Founded in 1959, the WWP remains one of the most hard-core Marxist organizations in the United States, working to replace the U.S. Constitution with a Marxist plan.

SOCIALIST INTERNATIONAL (SI): SI is a worldwide organization of some 170 socialist democratic, socialist, and labor parties. SI's leadership includes, or has included, Democratic Party figures such as former Clinton secretary of state Madeleine Albright, former senator Tom Daschle, and former Democratic National Committee chairman Howard Dean.

DEMOCRATIC SOCIALISTS OF AMERICA (DSA): An affiliate of Socialist International, it was organized in 1982 by former SDS and CPUSA members who merged with the Democratic Socialist Organizing Committee and the New American Movement. It follows the philosophy of Italian Communist Party theoretician Antonio Gramsci, who preached that Communism could best be achieved by infiltrating civil society and turning its institutions into revolutionary vehicles.

THE PROGRESSIVE PARTY: Former president Theodore Roosevelt founded the Progressive Party in 1912 to counter the increasingly conservative policies of President William Howard Taft, who succeeded Roosevelt. The new party's platform called for a national health service; a form of Social Security; a minimum wage law; farm relief; workers' compensation; an inheritance tax; and a federal income tax.

By 1918, the Progressive wing of the Republican Party had all but vanished. Former Progressives flocked to the New Deal Democratic Party coalition of President Franklin Roosevelt in the 1930s. Not until the later part of the twentieth century did "Progressive" become a widely recognized category of politician.

PROGRESSIVE DEMOCRATS OF AMERICA (PDA): Established by affiliates of Democratic Socialists of America (DSA) and the Institute for Policy Studies, PDA "was founded . . . to transform the Democratic Party and our country" by driving Democrats further to the left.[50]

CONGRESSIONAL PROGRESSIVE CAUCUS (CPC): Openly socialist Bernie Sanders, a 2016 Democratic candidate for president, founded CPC in 1991, with guidance and assistance from Democratic Socialists of America and the Institute for Policy Studies. Lynn Woolsey, House chair of CPC in 2010, told the *Huffington Post* that the number of CPC members in the House of Representatives numbered eighty-three and that "it is clear that we represent the heart and soul of the Democratic Party."[51]

LABOR UNIONS: In 1824, the House of Commons in England granted workers the right to "collective bargaining," which led to development of trade and labor unions. The idea of unions spread to the United States and other nations, where socialists/Communists subverted it such that it became a means of "fundamentally transforming" the system.

Communists were prohibited from holding office in major labor unions until 1995, when Progressives took over the U.S. government, removed the clause banning Communists, and installed Democratic Socialists of America member John Sweeney as president of the AFL-CIO. Socialists now dominate every major union in the United States.

INSTITUTE FOR POLICY STUDIES (IPS): Membership in this oldest and most influential far left "think tank" in Washington, D.C., includes many former or current members of Congress, including Leon Panetta (D-CA), who served as secretary of defense and head of the CIA under President Obama. At the height of the Cold War in 1978, the late historian Brian Crozier described the IPS in a *National Review* article as the "perfect intellectual front for Soviet activities which would be resisted if they were to originate openly from the KGB."[52]

CAMPAIGN FOR AMERICA'S FUTURE (CAF): CAF is another project from the combined efforts of Democratic Socialists of America and the Institute for Policy Studies. CAF helps coordinate the U.S. Progressive movement through annual conferences held in Washington, known variously as 'Take Back America," Take Back the American Dream," or "America's Future Now," that attract thousands of Progressives, socialists, Communists, labor unionists, politicians and left-wing activists. Notable speakers at the gatherings in recent years included former Speaker of the House (now minority leader) Nancy Pelosi; "Green Czar" Van Jones; and President Barack Obama.

TAX-EXEMPT FOUNDATIONS: Foundations such as Ford, Rockefeller, and the Carnegie Endowment for International Peace, the latter of which was once headed by convicted Soviet spy Alger Hiss, have long proved to be cash cows for Progressive, socialist, and Communist fronts. In 1953, representative B. Carroll Reece of Tennessee called a special committee to investigate them. The committee "concluded that tax-exempt foundations were deliberately using wealth and privilege to attack the basic structure of the U.S. Constitution."[53]

DEPARTMENT OF DEFENSE EQUAL OPPORTUNITY MANAGEMENT INSTITUTE (DEOMI): The Progressive-dominated culture, whose hedonism, amorality, and degeneracy reminds author and conservative talk show host Michael Savage of Germany's Weimar Republic, has insinuated its tentacles into perhaps the last remaining institution of traditional values—the military—and is in the process of dismantling it.[54] DEOMI, originally formed in 1971 to address racial inequality in the armed services, has grown into a Progressive attack dog to push radical feminism, gay and transgender "rights," same-sex marriage, and a myriad of other questionable policies down the military's throat, turning the Navy, Army, Air Force, and Marines into an extension of the social laboratory experiments from the society at large.

The Marxist movement, Savage continued, holds an inherent distrust of strong males. To a Progressive, they are emblematic of capitalism's civil power and must therefore be brought down and replaced by "victims" of society. Exactly what the military needs— *victims* defending freedom and the Constitution.[55]

Pink berets and Tupperware parties may be at hand.

AMERICAN CIVIL LIBERTIES UNION (ACLU): Founded in 1920 by Roger Baldwin, an avowed communist who later rejected Soviet-style communism, the ACLU was nonetheless founded as a communist organization. In 1927, Baldwin visited the Soviet Union and wrote a laudatory book about it, *Liberty Under the Soviets*. He stated of the ACLU, "Communism is, of course, the goal."

AGENDA 21: The "climate change" movement and its conglomerates of organized fanatics and true believers is more about government control over individuals and the economy than it is about "saving the planet." It intends to use this pretext to control everything from your backyard grill to the economy.

Former vice president Al Gore, guru of the ever-present "the sky is falling" bunch, suggested that those who deny "global warming" should pay a price. Others of his ilk are more explicit about what this price should be.[56]

"I wish there were a law you could punish them with," Robert F. Kennedy Jr. said.[57]

Austrian professor Richard Parncutt suggested the death penalty as an "appropriate punishment for influential [global warming] deniers."[58]

These people are *serious* and are supported by much of the mainstream media, most educational institutions, powerful congressional lobbies—and George Soros. Agenda 21 or some variant may be the result if these people have their way.

Agenda 21 was the "sustainable development" brainchild of the United Nations Conference on Environment and Development held in Brazil in 1992. The "21" refers to the twenty-first century. Essentially, what the plan calls for is authoritarianism at its most extreme. Its goal is government control of all land, water, minerals, plants, and animals, along with all means of production, all energy sources, all education, all information, and all human beings. Individual rights to ownership must give way to the needs of the community. This is necessary because people are not good stewards of the earth—and government naturally knows best.

The push is to get people off the land and packed into urban human settlements near employment centers and mass transportation, where they will become more dependent. Get them out of private houses and into condos, out of private vehicles and onto bicycles and public transportation. Even the jeans you wear won't be yours.

On top of all this, the plan sees American affluence as a major problem that needs correction. The United States and other prosperous nations must lower their standards of living so people in poorer countries will have more. Call it "social justice." Call it equal worldwide poverty. Call it 1930s USSR on a global scale.

President George W. Bush was one of 178 heads of government who signed on to adopt the nonbinding program. Today, twelve hundred U.S. cities promote "sustainable development" at a local, first-stage level.

* * *

There can be little doubt that the United States is being infiltrated and "fundamentally transformed" from within by radical Pod People working through their foundations and organizations and the Democratic Party. Once America is transformed, the combined collectives of tyranny will carve up what's left of the world among themselves—a process in which America appears to be losing the courage to protect either herself or what remains of the free world.

> *He that troubleth his own house shall inherit the wind."*
>
> —PROVERBS 11:29

THE LAST DAYS

During the last days of a failing society appear prophets who try to warn of the precipice ahead in the darkness. "If our guiding lights are ever extinguished," Alexis de Tocqueville noted, "they would grow dim gradually and, as it were, of their own accord. . . . We should not, therefore, complacently think that the barbarians are still far away for, if some nations allow the torch to be snatched from their hands, others stamp it out themselves."[59]

According to a Gallup survey, 91 percent of Americans were satisfied with their level of personal freedom in 2006. Less than a decade later, that percentage had fallen to 79 percent.[60] Other polls reveal that 69 percent of the American population believes the United States is in decline.[61]

In 1972, Don McLean's pop hit "American Pie" was No. 1 on the charts. Some four decades later, McLean said the song "was not a parlor game. . . . Basically, in 'American Pie,' things are heading in the wrong direction. . . . I was around in 1970 and now I am around in 2015 . . . There is no poetry and very little romance in anything anymore, so it is really like the last phase of 'American Pie.'"[62]

Here are some of the lyrics from McLean's timeless song:

And while Lenin read a book on Marx

The quartet practiced in the park.. .

And as the flames climbed high into the night . . .

I saw Satan laughing with delight

The day the music died[63]

During Rome's final days, when "the music died," people were so distracted by cultural garbage that they failed to notice their rights and liberties were being dismantled. No one remembered and stood up for traditional values. Little evils left unchecked and largely unnoticed destroyed the Romans as it did the Greeks. As it has destroyed other nations and empires since then. Moral and social decadence, weariness, suspicion, laziness, preoccupation with self, hedonism, materialism, and rejection of truth are a few unmistakable signs of decline.

Jim Nelson Black, author of *When Nations Die*, listed a number of symptoms that indicate a dying society:

an overcentralized government

heavy taxation

a top-heavy government bureaucracy

the rise of liberal opinions, attitudes, and policies controlled by sentiment rather than sound moral judgment

a general increase in lawlessness

loss of economic discipline and self-restraint

excessive government regulations

loss of respect for established religion

erosion in the quality and relevancy of education

increased materialism

immorality

decline in the value of human life[64]

During the twentieth century, before America was yet two centuries old, social engineers cropped up in continuing reverberations from Karl Marx. In rapid sequence America experienced the beginning of the Progressive Era, the Great Society, the War on Poverty, "Change you can believe in." The federal government gradually stepped in to control our lives—and we willingly turned them over in exchange for "entitlements" and "security."

In "fundamentally transforming" Russia into the USSR, Lenin employed divide-and-conquer tactics to create rifts between kulaks and peasants, bourgeoisie and proletarians, intelligentsia and workers, and so on. Progressive politicians such as Obama, Sanders, and Hillary Clinton in the United States have employed the same tactics in pitting people against each other along social, gender, sexual, religious, and economic lines in a divide-and-conquer blitzkrieg to keep them disorganized and susceptible to "change."

"When Lenin set out to . . . fundamentally transform Russia," David Horowitz wrote, "he didn't say he was going to kill 40 million people, create famines and concentration camps . . . He said he was going to give them bread, land, and peace."[65]

Economics professor Dr. Thomas Sowell warned that "as long as millions of Americans vote on the basis of who gives them free stuff, look for their freedom—and all our freedom—to be eroded away, bit by bit. Our children and grandchildren may yet come to see the Constitution as just some quaint words from the past that people once took seriously."[66]

Social commentator Alice Russie recognized a disturbing correlation between the rise of Hitler and what is occurring now in the United States.

She described how in the spring of 1933, Hitler passed a series of laws that made it impossible for anyone to challenge his power. "The Reich President Elect for the Protection of People and State" took away rights that in the United States are guaranteed by the First Amendment. In America today, "executive orders" issued by the president increasingly usurp the power of the legislative branch and provide a breeding ground for the dissolution of the Constitution and its protections.[67]

Hitler's "Treachery Law" decreed that anyone who opposed the Nazis was a traitor to the country and to the Party. In the United States today, take a principled stand against the actions of government when it comes to issues such as religion, same-sex marriage, women in combat, euthanasia, abortion, immigration, and so forth, and you are promptly labeled a hate monger . . . bigot . . . homophobe . . . racist . . . sexist . . . Just short of being a traitor to the country and to the [Progressive] Party.

"I guarantee that many people—too many people—would kill their neighbors if their government told them to do it," Michael Savage wrote in *Trickle Down Tyranny.* "That is the danger of this type of thinking. Many people, if given a uniform and the authority, would round up innocent citizens who happen to belong to an unpopular party or religious sect and kill them."[68]

Incredibly, most Germans at first thought Hitler's new measures were good for the country. Likewise, as restrictions on the rights and freedoms of Americans become more pervasive, citizens seem willing to go along and exchange liberty for perceived security.

The internal decline of American society combined with its loss of power and influence around the globe reduces America as a force for freedom and stability in the world. The collapse of American power that is under way has predictable geopolitical repercussions, as indicated by the rise of Islamic terrorism, aggression between nations, the growth of Hitler-like socialism, and a general withdrawal of Western civilization.

In such a climate, columnist Barret Moore believes, conflict between the largest and most powerful nations becomes inevitable. It could be a real World War III, in which satellites fall from the sky, ships sink, and

CRUSHING *the* COLLECTIVE

life is lost to a magnitude that few people alive today can comprehend. War that will literally turn the world into a giant dump and penal colony where the strong dominate and the weaker submit or die.[69]

"Ultimately," Mark Steyn has concluded, "we're talking about a total civilizational collapse—basically, that the civilization that built the modern world is actually in retreat."[70]

"Our world includes entire nations that resemble insane asylums where the most deluded and dangerous people are those in positions of authority," author David Kupelian observed. "In the case of major utopian systems like communism, Nazism, and Islamism, millions are brainwashed into not only embracing impossibly irrational, degrading and destructive beliefs, but also believing that they are required to force everyone else on Earth to adopt their beliefs—or else be subjugated or slaughtered."[71]

It may be too late to save a free United States of America, as it was too late to save Rome or any of the other empires that collapsed, or are now on the way to collapse through the same process. The torch is burning out in America. "Socially, culturally, morally," Patrick J. Buchanan concluded, "America has taken on the aspect of a decadent society and a declining nation."[72]

"Have too many among us already surrendered or been conquered?" author and radio commentator Mark Levin wondered. "Can the people overcome the constant and relentless influences of ideological indoctrination, economic manipulation, and administrative coerciveness, or have they become hopelessly entangled in and dependent on a ubiquitous federal government? Have the Pavlovian appeals to radical egalitarianism, and the fomenting of jealousy and faction through class warfare and collectivism conditioned the people to accept or even demand compulsory uniformity as just and righteous?"[73]

Anita Dittman, eighty-seven-year-old Holocaust survivor of Hitler's concentration camps, speaks to audiences all over the United States, telling people what happened once so that it need never happen again.

"The [United States] that I came to in 1946 was very different. . . .

When I started speaking in 1978–79, people would ask me, 'Do you think it [a Hitlerian takeover] could happen in this country?' And I said, 'Oh no, people are used to so much freedom in this country, it could never happen here.' . . . When they ask that question now, I say, 'It is already happening.'"[74]

Lord Byron the poet (1788–1824) has the final word in a twist on Alexander Tytler's axiom:

There is the moral of all human tales:

'Tis but the same rehearsal of the past.

First Freedom, and then Glory—when that fails,

Wealth, vice, corruption—barbarism at last.[75]

THE END

SELECTED BIBLIOGRAPHY

Alexander, Mark. "Derailing ObamaCare and DemoDebt: The Conservative Strategy." *Patriot Post*, September 19, 2013. https://patriotpost.us/alexander/20184.

———. "Ending Liberty by Undermining Faith and Family." *Patriot Post*, August 22, 2013. https://patriotpost.us/alexander/19661.

———. "Mastering the Art of the Big Lie." *Patriot Post*, December 12, 2013. https://patriotpost.us/alexander/22209.

———. "ObamaCare Success? Unfortunately Yes. Obama's OCA Agenda Moving Forward." Patriot Post, November 7, 2013. https://patriotpost.us/alexander/21491.

———. "Populist Socialism on the Rise." *Patriot Post*, November 3, 2011. https://patriotpost.us/alexander/11684.

———. "The Real Tragedy in Ferguson—and Across the Nation: Unintended Consequences of 'The Great Society.'" *Patriot Post* August 20, 2014. https://patriotpost.us/alexander/28379.

———. "Tank Man: Genuine Courage v Juvenile Cowardice." *Patriot Post*, November 17, 2011. https://patriotpost.us/alexander/11805.

Allen, Gary, with Larry Abraham. *None Dare Call It Conspiracy*. N.p.: Concord Press, 1972.

Ambrose, Jay. "The Progressives Are Waging War on Equality." *Tulsa World*, January 4, 2014.

Arn, Larry. "A Rebirth of Liberty and Learning," *Imprimis* 42, no. 12, 2013. https://imprimis.hillsdale.edu/a-rebirth-of-liberty-and-learning/.

Attkinson, Sharyl. *Stonewalled: My Fight for Truth Against the Forces of Obstruction, Intimidation, and Harassment in Obama's Washington*. New York: HarperCollins, 2014.

Avrich, Paul. *Sacco and Venzetti: The Anarchist Background*. Princeton University Press, 1991.

Bagwell, Tyler E. "The Jekyll Island Duck Hunt that Created the Federal Reserve." Jekyll Island History. March 23, 2014. http://www.jekyllislandhistory.com/federalreserve.shtml.

Bailey, Steve. "No Children Need Apply," *Boston Globe*, July 4, 2007.

Barber, Matt. "Gay Marriage and the Easter Bunny," *Whistleblower*, January 2015.

———. "Left's New Crusade: Adult-Kid Sex," WND, October 11, 2013. http://www.wnd.com/2013/10/lefts-new-crusade-adult-kid-sex/.

———. "Raunch: Huffington Post Says Friends Should Have Casual, Meaningless Sex," BarbWire, March 24, 2014. http://barbwire.com/2014/03/21/huffington-post-true-friends-casual-meaningless-sex/.

———. "Sexual Predator Honored with U.S. Postage Stamp," WND, October 25, 2013. http://www.wnd.com/2013/10/sexual-predator-honored-with-u-s-postage-stamp/.

———. "You 'Must Be Made' to Obey," Townhall, May 18, 2015. http://townhall.com/columnists/mattbarber/2015/05/17/draft-n1999950.

Barr, Bob. "The UN Comes After America's Guns," *Washington Times*, August 26, 2013. http://www. washingtontimes.com/news/2013/aug/19/barr-the-un-comes-after-americas-guns/.

Baggett, Jay. "Florida City Spies on Churches, Demands Licenses," WND, February 25, 2015. http:// www.wnd.com/2015/02/u-s-city-spies-on-churches-demands-licenses/.

Bastiat, John. "SCOTUS Endorses Same-Sex Marriage," *Patriot Post*, June 26, 2015, https://patriotpost. us/articles/36045.

Bauman, Michael. *Man and Marxism: Religion and the Communist Retreat.* N.p.: Hillsdale College Press, 1991.

Beck, Glenn. *Control: Exposing the Truth About Guns.* New York: Threshold, 2013.

———. *It Is About Islam: Exposing the Truth About ISIS, Al Qaeda, Iran, and the Caliphate.* New York: Threshold, 2015.

———. *Liars: How Progressives Exploit Our Fears for Power and Control.* New York: Threshold, 2016.

———. "You Won't Believe the Advice a Nebraska Elementary School Gave Students About Bullying," GlennBeck.com, April 17, 2014, http://www.glennbeck.com/2014/04/17/you-wont-believe-the-advice-a-nebraska-elementary-school-gave-students-about-bullying/.

Beer, Samuel H. *Marx and Engels: The Communist Manifesto.* N.p.: AHM, 1955.

Bellow, Adam, ed. *New Threats to Freedom.* West Conshohocken, PA: Templeton Press, 2010.

Bennett, William J. *De-Valuing of America: Fight FOR Our Culture and Our Children.* N.p.: Touchstone, 1992.

Bennetts, Marc. "Who's Godless Now? Russia Says It's U.S." *Washington Times.* January 28, 2014. http:// www.washingtontimes.com/news/2014/jan/28/whos-godless-now-russia-says-its-us/.

Bergman, Jerry. *Hitler and the Nazi Darwinian Worldview.* N.p.: Joshua Press, 2012.

Bevard, James. *Lost Rights: The Destruction of American Liberty.* New York: St. Martin's, 1992.

BillOReilly.com Staff. "America in Decline," Bill O'Reilly website. October 27, 2011, http://www. billoreilly.com/newslettercolumn?pid=34433.

Black, Edwin. *War Against the Weak: Eugenics and America's Campaign to Create a Master Race.* N.p.: Four Walls Eight Windows, 2003.

Black, Jim Nelson. *When Nations Die: Ten Warning Signs of a Culture in Crisis.* N.p.: Tyndale, 1994.

Blum, John Morton. *Woodrow Wilson and the Politics of Morality.* Boston: Little Brown, 1956.

Boak, Arthur and Edward Romilly. *A History of Rome to 565 A.D.* N.p.: McMillan, 1965.

Boorstin, Daniel J. *The Americans: The Colonial Experience.* N.p: Vintage, 1958.

Boortz, Neal. *Somebody's Gotta Say It.* New York: HarperCollins, 2007.

Bork, Robert H. *Slouching Towards Gomorrah: Modern Liberalism and American Decline.* N.p.: Simon & Schuster, 1996.

Bornick, Evan. "A Tank on Every Corner? Why Police Departments Are Acquiring Armored Vehicles and What to Do About It." *Daily Signal*, February 10, 2014. http://dailysignal.com/2014/02/10/ tank-every-corner-police-departments-acquiring-armored-vehicles/.

Bovard, James. *Lost Rights: The Destruction of American Liberty.* New York: St. Martin's, 1994, 1995.

Boychuk, Ben. "Ben Boychuk: Is Legalizing Marijuana Inevitable?" *Tulsa World*, March 30, 2014. http://www.tulsaworld.com/opinion/editorials/ben-boychuk-is-legalizing-marijuana-inevitable/ article_4c23e093-1eaa-5b00-9c15-d669d2b8687f.html.

Bradbury, Ray. *Fahrenheit 451.* N.p.: Ballantine, 1953.

Branstetter, Ziva. "Execution Halt Being Pushed by ACLU," *Tulsa World*, May 20, 2014.

Bremmer, Paul. "Step 2: Left's Next Target After 'Gay Marriage,'" WND, July 5, 2015

Bridenbaugh, Carl. *Mitre and Sceptre: Transatlantic Faiths, Ideas, Personalities, and Politics, 1689-1775.* Oxford Press, 1962.

Brinton, Crane. *A History of Civilization.* N.p. Prentice-Hall, 1967.

Brinton, Crane, John B. Christopher, and Robert Lee Wolff. *A History of Civilization: Prehistory to 1735.* Vol. 1. N.p.: Prentice-Hall, 1976.

Brown, Michael. "My Gender Is Fill in the Blank,'" Townhall, February 28, 2015, http://townhall.com/columnists/michaelbrown/2015/02/28/my-gender-is-fill-in-the-blank-n1963298.

Brown, Susan Stamper. "Who's Responsible for the Moral Decline?" Townhall, June 3, 2015, http://townhall.com/columnists/susanstamperbrown/2015/06/02/whos-responsible-for-the-moral-decline-n2007035.

Bruce, Tammy. *The Death of Right and Wrong: Exposing the Left's Assault on Our Culture and Values.* New York: Crown, 2004.

———. "Raising a Police State Army," *Washington Times,* June 23, 2014.

———. "Saying 'So Long' to the First Amendment," *Washington Times,* March 23, 2015, http://www.washingtontimes.com/news/2015/mar/16/tammy-bruce-net-neutrality-kills-first-amendment/.

Buchanan, Patrick J. "America: Microcasm of a World on Fire," *Whistleblower,* August 2014.

———. *The Death of the West: How Dying Populations and Immigrant Invasions Imperil Our Country and Civilization.* New York: St. Martin's, 2002.

———. "Is Third World America Inevitable?" Townhall, June 18, 2015, http://townhall.com/columnists/patbuchanan/2015/06/16/is-third-world-america-inevitable-n2012900.

———. "Is This End of Line for the Welfare State?" *Tulsa World,* February 12, 2014.

———. "It Is Freedom That Produces Inequality," Tulsa World, January 3, 2014.

———. *Suicide of a Superpower.* New York: St. Martin's, 2011.

———. "It Is Freedom That Produces Inequality." *Tulsa World,* January 3, 2014.

Burnham, James. *Suicide of the West: An Essay on the Meaning and Destiny of Liberalism.* New York and London: Encounter Books, 1964.

Caldwell, Erskine. *God's Little Acre.* N.p.: Viking, 1933.

Calvocoressi, Peter, and Guy Wint. *Total War: Causes and Courses of The Second World War.* N.p.: Pantheon, 1972.

Carson, Dr. Ben. "A Plea for Constitutional Literacy on Constitution Day," *Washington Post,* September 22, 2014.

Carter, Jimmy. *A Call to Action.* New York: Simon & Schuster, 2014.

Cawthorne, Nigel. *The Crimes of Stalin: The Murderous Career of the Red Tsar.* Kindle edition. N.p.: Arcturus, 2011.

———. *Tyrants: History's 100 Most Evil Despots & Dictators.* N.p.: Metro Books, 2012.

Chafets, Zev. *Rush Limbaugh: An Army of One.* N.p.: Sentinel, 2010.

Chang, Gordon G. "Tiananmen? Never Heard of It." *National Review,* June 2014. https://www.nationalreview.com/nrd/articles/378033/tiananmen-never-heard-it.

Charen, Mona. "Obama and The Grievance Industry." *Washington Times,* February 10, 2014

Chumley, Cheryl. "Withdraw $5,000 from Bank, Get Cops Called on You." WND, March 24, 2015. http://www.wnd.com/2015/03/banks-to-call-police-on-customers/.

Clements, Kendrick A. *The Presidency of Woodrow Wilson.* N.p.: Standard Scholarly Survey, 1922.

Codevilla, Angela M. *The Character of Nations: How Politics Makes and Breaks Prosperity, Family, and Civility.* New York: Basic Books, 1997.

Collier, Peter, and David Horowitz. *Destructive Generation: Second Thoughts About the '60s.* N.p.: Summit Books, 1989.

Cooke, Charles C. W. "Locked In at Last," *National Review,* September 2, 2013. https://www.nationalreview.com/nrd/articles/355858/locked-last.

Cooper, John Milton. *Reconsidering Woodrow Wilson: Progressivism, Internationalism, War, and Peace.* N.p.: John Hopkins University Press, 2008.

Corombos, Greg. "Black Leader: Obama's Policies Stoking Ferguson Anger," WND, August 23, 2014. http://www.wnd.com/2014/08/black-leader-obamas-policies-stoking-ferguson-anger/.

———. "Commander: 'Cowards' Pushing Women into Combat." WND, December 7, 2013. http://www.wnd.com/2016/05/lady-marine-huge-mistake-to-put-women-into-combat/.

———. "Lady Marine: Huge Mistake to Put Women in Combat," WND, May 21, 2016. http://www.wnd.com/2016/05/lady-marine-huge-mistake-to-put-women-into-combat/.

———. "Navy SEALs 'Feel Politicized Under Obama.'" WND, March 16, 2014. http://www.wnd.com/2014/03/674241/.

———. "Obama Hatches Plan to Explode Welfare," WND, August 24, 2014. http://www.wnd.com/2014/08/obama-hatches-plan-to-explode-welfare/.

Corrigan, Gordon. *The Second World War: A Military History.* N.p.: St. Martin's, 2010.

Corsi, Jerome R. "Congressman: Obama Using 'Cloward-Piven' Maneuver," WND, June 11. 2014. http://www.wnd.com/2014/06/congressmen-obama-using-cloward-piven-maneuver/.

———. "Harvard Housing Satanic 'Black Mass,'" WND, May 9, 2014. http://www.wnd.com/2014/05/harvard-hosting-satanic-black-mass/.

———. "Marriage Supporters Warned of Wave of McCarthyism," WND, June 1, 2014. http://www.wnd.com/2014/05/marriage-supporters-warned-of-wave-of-mccarthyism/.

———. "National ID Headed for Your Wallet, Purse," WND, December 30, 2013. http://www.wnd.com/2013/12/national-id-headed-for-your-wallet-purse/.

———. "Obama Inviting 'Invasion of Murderers, Gang Members,'" WND, July 28, 2014. http://www.wnd.com/2014/07/obama-inviting-invasion-of-murderers-gang-members/.

———. *The Obama Nation.* New York: Threshold, 2008.

———. "'Schindler's List' Producer: Obama Wants to Lock Up Foes," WND, May 21, 2014. http://www.wnd.com/2014/05/critic-obama-thinks-political-opponents-are-enemies/.

———. "WikiLeaks Reveals Secret Trans-Pacific Trade Deal," WND, November 13, 2013. http://www.wnd.com/2013/11/wikileaks-reveals-secret-trans-pacific-trade-deal/.

Coulter, Ann. "As Long as Obama Brought Up the Cost of College," Townhall, January 17, 2015. http://townhall.com/columnists/anncoulter/2015/01/14/as-long-as-obama-brought-up-the-cost-of-college-n1943204.

———. *Guilty: Liberal "Victims" and Their Assault on America.* New York: Crown Forum, 2015.

———. *Treason: Liberal Treachery from the Cold War to the War on Terrorism.* New York: Crown Forum, 2003.

Cox, Jack. *Requiem in the Tropics: Inside Central America.* N.p.: UCA Books, 1987.

Cox, Kenneth. *Revelation Pure and Simple.* N.p.: 3ABN Books, 2012.

Crawford, Thomas M. "Liberal Agenda Seeks Return to Middle Ages," *Washington Times*, January 20, 2014.

Critchlow, Donald T., and Agnieszka Critchlow. *Enemies of The State: Personal Stories from the Gulag.* Chicago: Ivan R. Dee, 2003.

Crowley, Monica. *The Monica Crowley Show* (radio), May 10, 2014.

———. "The Stranger in The White House." *Washington Times*, March 2, 2015.

Crum, William. "OKC Play Draws Religious Backlash," *Tulsa World*, December 2, 2013.

Cruz, Ted. "Fahrenheit 451 Democrats," *Washington Times*, July 14, 2014.

———. "The Miracle of Freedom," *Imprimis*, May/June 2013. https://www.scribd.com/document/168476659/The-Miracle-of-Freedom-Imprimus-Magazine.

D'Souza, Dinesh. "America: Exceptionally Good or Exceptionally Evil?" WND, August 2, 2014. http://www.wnd.com/2014/08/america-exceptionally-good-or-exceptionally-evil/.

Dastell, Johanna. "Homosexual Activist Says 'Marriage' Isn't About Equality, It's About Destroying Marriage," LifeSiteNews.com, October 22, 2013, https://www.lifesitenews.com/news/vatican-next-synod-will-not-tackle-women-deacons-married-priests.

DeManus, Doyle. "Evangelicals Return to Seeking Souls, Not Votes," *Tulsa World*, April 6, 2014.

De Witt, Benjamin P. *The Progressive Movement.* N.p.: MacMillian, 2015.

DeWitt, Jason. "Somali 'Refugees' on Lifetime Welfare Demand Their Free Food Adhere to Islamic Law." Quoted in "Fw: Minnesota Food Bank," Google Groups. November 18, 2015. https://groups.google.com/forum/#!topic/akers-follett-ssl-study-group/U22zr7rYmY0.

Dinan, Stephen. "ICE Releases 30,000 Immigrants with Criminal Records," *Washington Times*, March 23, 2015.

———. "Study: Little Hope for GOP on Immigration," Washington Post, April 21, 2014.

Discoverthenetworks.org. "Breakdown of the Black Family, and its Consequences," accessed November 28, 2014. http://www.discoverthenetworks.org/viewSubCategory.asp?id=1261.

Dobson, James. "I Fear Judgment Befalling America," WND, June 26, 2015. http://www.wnd.com/2015/06/i-fear-judgment-befalling-america/.

Doherty, Daniel. "Left-Leaning Pundits on 2016: 'Democrats Should Be Very Worried," Townhall, February 10, 2015, http://townhall.com/tipsheet/danieldoherty/2015/02/09/van-jones-dems-in-2016-should-be-very-worried-n1954802.

Donnelly, Elaine. "Taking Diversity to Extremes." *Washington Times*, June 29, 2015.

Ebeling, Richard M. "The Free Market and the Interventionist State," *Imprimis*, August 1997. https://imprimis.hillsdale.edu/the-free-market-and-the-interventionist-state/.

Ebeling, Richard. *The Global Failure of Socialism.* Hillsdale, MI: Hillsdale Press, 1992.

———. "Is the 'Specter of Communism' Still Haunting the World?" FEE, March 2006, https://fee.org/resources/is-the-spectre-of-communism-still-haunting-the-world/.

Ebenstein, William. *Today's Isms.* New York: Prentice-Hall, 1967.

English Online. "African Americans." History from Slavery to the Civil Rights Movement. Accessed November 25, 2014. http://www.english-online.at/history/african-americans/history-of-african-americans.htm.

Erickson, Erick. "Too Soon to Go Full Totalitarian," Townhall, April 10, 2015. http://townhall.com/columnists/erickerickson/2015/04/10/too-soon-to-go-full-totalitarian-n1983007.

Erier, Edward J. "The Second Amendment as an Expression of First Principles," *Imprimis*, March 2013. https://imprimis.hillsdale.edu/the-second-amendment-as-an-expression-of-first-principles/.

Ernst, Douglas. "Report: 6 Syrians Caught at Texas Border," WND, November 18, 2015. http://www.wnd.com/2015/11/report-8-syrians-caught-at-texas-border/.

Evans, M. Stanton, and Herbert Romerstein. *Stalin's Secret Agents: The Subversion of Roosevelt's Government.* New York: Threshold, 2012.

Farah, Joseph. "The Criminalization of Christianity Is Here," WND, October 26, 2014. http://www.wnd.com/2014/10/the-criminalization-of-christianity-is-here/.

———. "Islam's Rapid, Bloody Empire Building," *Whistleblower*, October 2014.

———. "The Obamanation Explained," WND, August 2014. http://www.wnd.com/2014/07/the-obamanation-explained/.

Fernandez-Armesto, Felipe. *Millennium: A History of the Last Thousand Years.* N.p.: Scribner, 1995.

Finn, Peter, and Petra Couvée. *The Zhivago Affair.* New York: Pantheon, 2014.

Flaherty, Colin. "Black Biker Gang Behind SUV Attack in NYC," WND, October 2, 2013. http://www.

wnd.com/2013/10/black-biker-gang-beats-suv-driver-in-nyc/.

———. "Black-on-White Beatings Leave More Dead," WND, September 24, 2013. http://www.wnd.com/2013/09/black-on-white-beatings-leave-3-more-dead/.

———. "Killer's Family to Victim's Kin: 'We Hate You,'" WND, February 8, 2014. http://www.wnd.com/2014/02/killers-family-to-victims-kin-we-hate-you/.

———. "'Lefty' Librarian Beaten to Pulp in Knockout Game,", WND, December 3, 2013. http://www.wnd.com/2013/12/knockout-game-victim-i-no-longer-trust-blacks/.

———. "Pack of Black Youth Terrorize City," WND, October 14, 2013. http://www.wnd.com/2013/10/pack-of-black-youth-terrorize-city/.

———. "Take a Stroll, Wake Up in Hospital Thanks to Black Mob," WND, October 14, 2013. http://www.wnd.com/2013/10/take-a-stroll-wake-up-in-hospital-thanks-to-black-mob/.

Forstmann, Theodore J. "Statism: The Opiate of The Elites," *Imprimis*, May 1997. https://imprimis.hillsdale.edu/statism-the-opiate-of-the-elites/.

Freddoso, David. *The Case Against Barack Obama: The Unlikely Rise and Unexamined Agenda of the Media's Favorite Candidate*. Washington, DC: Regnery, 2008.

Free Republic. "Poverty and Culture," September 7, 2006. http://www.freerepublic.com/focus/f-news/1697491/posts.

Friedman, Lawrence M. *A History of American Law*. New York: Simon & Schuster, 1973.

Frye, Northrop. *Northrop Frye on Modern Cultures*. Edited by Ian Gorak. Toronto: U. of Toronto Press, 2003.

Fukuyama, Francis. *The End of History and the Last Man*. New York: Avon, 1992.

Funny.com. "Funny Jokes: The Tax Poem," accessed October 29, 2014. http://www.funny.com/cgi-bin/WebObjects/Funny.woa/wa/funny?fn=CL3FE&Funny_Jokes=The_Tax_Poem.

Gable, John Allen. *The Bullmoose Years: Theodore Roosevelt and the Progressive Party*. N.p.: Kennikat Press, 1978.

Gellately, Robert. *Against Leviathan*. Independent Institute, 2004.

———. *Lenin, Stalin and Hitler*. Alfred A. Knopf, 2007.

Gentry, Kurt. *J. Edgar Hoover: The Man and His Secrets*. New York and London: W. W. Norton, 1991.

Gera, Vanessa. "At Auschwitz, Leader Warns Jews Are Again Targets," *Tulsa World*, January 28, 2015.

Gertz, Bill. Editorial, *Washington Post*, April 21, 2014.

Gibbon, Edward. *The History of the Decline and Fall of the Roman Empire* (1776–1789), vol. 1. London: Strahan & Cadell, 1776. Digitized 2008.

Gibbs, Douglas. "The Leftist Assault on American Football," Conservative Action Alert, January 27, 2014.

Giles, Doug. "Rachel Dolezal: Is a Dude Playing a Dude Disguised as Another Dude?" Townhall, June 15, 2015. http://townhall.com/columnists/douggiles/2015/06/14/rachel-dolezal-is-a-dude-playing-a-dude-disguise-as-another-dude-n2012211.

Glenn Beck program, Blaze TV. "The Root of The Problem—Russia," part 3. January 14, 2015. Transcript at http://www.glennbeck.com/2015/01/14/the-root-of-the-problem-russia-part-2/.

Goldberg, Bernard. *Arrogance: Rescuing America from the Media Elite*. N.p.: Warner Books, 2003.

Goldberg, Jonah. "The Grievance Game." *National Review*, January 26, 2015. https://www.nationalreview.com/nrd/articles/395995/grievance-game.

Goldberg, Robert Alan. *Enemies Within: The Culture of Conspiracy in Modern America*. N.p.: Yale University Press, 2001.

Goodman, Joshua. "Venezuela Crackdown Spurs Uncertainty." Yahoo! News, November 13, 2013. https://www.yahoo.com/news/venezuela-appliances-crackdown-spurs-uncertainty-204221319--finance.html?ref=gs.

GOPUSA.COM. "U.S. Military Can't Do Churches—But Gay Parades OK?" August 4, 2014, https://www.onenewsnow.com/national-security/2014/08/01/us-military-cant-do-churches-but-gay-parades-ok.

Gordon, John Steele. "Entrepreneurship in American History," *Imprimis*, February 2014. https://imprimis.hillsdale.edu/entrepreneurship-in-american-history/.

Greenfield, Daniel. *The Emperor President.* N.p.: David Horowitz Freedom Center, 2014.

Gregory, Paul Roderick. "Why the Fuss? Obama Has Long Been on the Record in Favor of Redistribution." *Forbes.* September 23, 2012. http://www.forbes.com/sites/paulroderickgregory/2012/09/23/why-the-fuss-obama-has-long-been-on-record-in-favor-of-redistribution/#3114fee75db6.

Griffith, Robert. *The Politics of Fear: Joseph R. McCarthy and the Senate.* Amherst: University of Massachusetts Press, 1970.

Guinn, Jeff. *Manson: The Life and Times of Charles Manson.* New York: Simon & Schuster, 2013.

Gutfield, Greg. *Not Cool: The Hipster Elite and Their War on You.* New York: Crown Forum, 2014.

Hamburger, Philip. "The History and Danger of Administrative Law," *Imprimis*, September 2014. https://imprimis.hillsdale.edu/the-history-and-danger-of-administrative-law/.

Hanks, Bill. "Addiction: The Great Marijuana Debate," *Tulsa World*, January 23, 2014.

Hanson, Victor Davis. "Why Do Societies Give up?" *Washington Times*, February 25, 2013.

Harper, Jennifer. "Inside the Beltway," *Washington Times*, July 28, 2014.

Hawkins, John. "How Much Should We Tolerate?" Townhall, December 30, 2014. http://townhall.com/columnists/johnhawkins/2014/12/27/how-much-should-we-tolerate-n1936093.

Haynes, John Earl, and Harvey Klehr. *In Denial: Historians, Communism, and Espionage.* N.p.: Encounter Books, 2003.

———. *Venona: Decoding Soviet Espionage in America.* N.p.: Yale Press, 2000.

Helms, Jesse. *"When Free Men Shall Stand"* Grand Rapids: Zondervan, 1976.

Hendershott, Ann. "No Apology Necessary," *Washington Times*, June 30, 2014.

Hentoff, Nat. "The History and Possible Revival of the Fairness Doctrine," *Imprimis*, January 2006. https://imprimis.hillsdale.edu/the-history-and-possible-revival-of-the-fairness-doctrine/.

Higgs, Robert. *Against Leviathan: Government Power and a Free Society.* Oakland, CA: Independent Institute, 2004.

Hohmann, Leo. "Ben Carson Uncorks on What's Wrong with America," WND, July 6, 2014. http://www.wnd.com/2014/07/ben-carson-uncorks-on-whats-wrong-with-america/.

———. "Holocaust Survivor Booted from Public Schools," WND, January 29, 2015. http://www.wnd.com/2015/01/holocaust-survivor-booted-from-public-schools/.

———. "Is World War III Coming Soon?" WND, April 12, 2015. http://www.wnd.com/2015/04/is-world-war-iii-coming-soon/.

———. "LGBT Activists: Marriage Was Never the 'End Game.'" WND, June 30, 2014. http://www.wnd.com/2015/06/lgbt-activists-marriage-was-never-the-end-game/.

———. "Meet New Victims of So-Called 'Marriage Equality,'" WND, October 12, 2014. http://www.wnd.com/2014/10/christian-vendors-locked-out-of-wedding-business/.

———. "Obama Brings 1,500 Terrorists to U.S.," WND, September 29, 2015. http://www.wnd.com/2015/09/obama-brings-1500-terrorists-to-u-s/.

———. "Obama's U.N. Plan: Globalize Cops Against 'Violent Extremists,'" WND, October 6, 2015. http://www.wnd.com/2015/10/obamas-u-n-plan-globalize-cops-against-violent-extremists/.

———. "Secret Weapon to Take Over America Revealed," WND, September 21, 2014. http://www.wnd.com/2014/09/secret-weapon-to-take-over-america-revealed/.

———. "Top Sheriff: America's Now Ruled by Oligarchy," WND, July 2, 2015. http://www.wnd.com/2015/07/top-sheriff-americas-now-ruled-by-oligarchy/.

Hornberger, Jacob G. and Richard M. Ebeling. *The Tyranny of Gun Control*. Fairfax, VA: Future of Freedom Foundation, 1997.

Horowitz, David. *The Black Book of the American Left: The Collected Conservative Writings of David Horowitz*. N.p.: Heritage Foundation, 2013.

———. *Fight Fire with Fire*. Kindle edition. N.p.: David Horowitz Freedom Center, 2013.

———. *Left Illusions: An Intellectual Odyssey*. N.p.: Spence, 2003/

———. *The Professors: The 101 Most Dangerous Academics in America*. Washington, D. C., Regnery, 2006.

Horrock, Nicholas M. "Communists in 1950s," *New York Times*, December 17, 1978

Hough, Jerry F. "Soviet Succession and Policy Choices," Bulletin of Atomic Scientists 38, no. 9 November 1982.

House to House, Heart to Heart. "I'm Looking for a Church That Is Not So . . ." April 2014. http:// housetohouse.com/im-looking-for-a-church-that-is-not-so/.

Hurt, Charles. "Race Pimps and War Tanks," *Washington Times*, August 25, 2014.

Huxley, Aldous. *Brave New World*. New York: Harper & Row, 1946.

Ingraham, Laura. *The O'Reilly Factor*, Fox News, May 8, 2014.

Jackson, Nate. "Gates: BSA Must Surrender to Homosexual Agenda." *Patriot Post*, May 22, 2015. https:// patriotpost.us/articles/35374.

Jeffrey, Terence. "36% of Generation Turning 21 This Year Born to Unmarried Mothers." *Patriot Post*, September 3, 2014. https://patriotpost.us/opinion/28763.

Jessup, Kathy. "Still Radical, Still Influential." Townhall, March 2012.

Johnson, Lyndon Baines. Speeches & Films. LBJ Presidential Library. http://www.lbjlibrary.org/lyndon-baines-johnson/speeches-films/.

Jones, Mike. "Are We One?" *Tulsa World*, February 23, 2014.

Kant, Garth. "Crowd Declares '2nd Revolution' Outside White House," WND, November 21, 2013. http://www.wnd.com/2013/11/crowd-declares-2nd-revolution-outside-white-house/.

———. "Palin: Washington Buying Bullets for US," WND, March 1, 2013. http://www.wnd. com/2013/02/palin-washington-buying-bullets-for-us/.

———. "Ticking Time Bomb About to Explode on GOP," WND, December 30, 2014. http://www. wnd.com/2014/12/ticking-time-bomb-about-to-explode-on-gop/.

Karoliszyn, Henrick, and Rich Shapiro. "Taking Protest 101," *New York Daily News*, November 6, 2011.

Keene, David A. "A License to Censor," *Washington Times*, April 7, 2014.

Kengor, Paul. "Reagan's 'Evil Empire' Turns 30," *American Spectator*, February 5, 2014. https://spectator. org/33780_reagans-evil-empire-turns-30/.

Kesler, Charles R. "Limited Government: Are the Good Times Really Over?" Imprimis, March 2008. https://imprimis.hillsdale.edu/limited-government-are-the-good-times-really-over/.

Kissinger, Henry. "The Chance for A New World Order," *New York Times*, January 12, 2009.

Klein, Aaron. "Big Chill: Feds Want to Scour Net Media for 'Hate Speech,'" WND, April 29, 2014. http://www.wnd.com/2014/04/big-chill-feds-want-to-scour-net-media-for-hate-speech/.

———. "'December Surprise' for Next Presidential Race," WND, November 12, 2014. http://www.wnd. com/2014/11/december-surprise-for-next-presidential-race/.

———. "Defense Secretary Directed 'Nuclear-Free Activist Group." WND. November 15, 2014, http:// www.wnd.com/2014/11/defense-secretary-directed-nuclear-free-activist-group/.

———. "FBI Data Backs Up Trump's Claims on Illegals and Crime," WND, July 9, 2015. http://www. wnd.com/2015/07/fbi-data-backs-up-trump-claims-on-illegals-and-crime/.

———. "Now Obama Gets 'Executive Power' Czar," WND, December 11, 2013. http://www.wnd. com/2013/12/now-obama-gets-executive-power-czar/.

———. "Obama Pushes Scheme to Cede U.S. Oceans to UN," WND, June 19, 2014. http://www.wnd. com/2014/06/obama-pushes-scheme-to-cede-u-s-oceans-to-u-n/.

———. "Obama Secretly Signing Away U.S. Sovereignty," WND, October 16, 2013. http://www.wnd. com/2013/10/obama-secretly-signing-away-u-s-sovereignty/.

———. "'Obama's Army' Deploys to Tel Aviv to Topple Netanyahu," WND, January 27, 2015. http:// www.wnd.com/2015/01/obama-army-deploys-to-tel-aviv-to-topple-netanyahu/.

———. "Pardon Me? Obama, Bill Ayers, Crack Cocaine," WND, April 24, 2014. http://www.wnd. com/2014/04/pardon-me-obama-bill-ayers-crack-cocaine/.

———. "Unions, Internet Giants Plan to Revolutionize Voting," WND, September 28, 2014. http:// www.wnd.com/2014/09/unions-internet-giants-plan-to-revolutionize-voting/.

Knight, Amy W. *How the Cold War Began: The Igor Gouzenko Affair and the Hunt for Soviet Spies.* New York: Carroll & Graf, 2006.

Knight, Robert H. *The Age of Consent: The Rise of Relativism and the Corruption of Popular Culture.* N.p.: Spence, 1998.

———. "Aiding and Abetting the New Slavery," *Washington Times*, March 31, 2014.

———. "Banning Free Speech Until the Cows Come Home," *Washington Times*, May 5, 2014.

Koire, Rosa. "Sounds Like Science Fiction—or Some Conspiracy Theory—but It Isn't." Democrats against Agenda 21 website, accessed March 19, 2015. http://www.democratsagainstunagenda21. com/.

Kovacs, Joe. "Harvard Writer: Abolish Free Speech." WND. February 25, 2014. http://www.wnd. com/2014/02/harvard-writer-free-speech-threatens-liberalism/.

———. "Radio Stars Fired for Whacking Unusual Dem Policy," WND, May 28, 2014. http://www. wnd.com/2014/05/radio-stars-fired-for-non-p-c-clowning/.

Krauthammer, Charles. *Things That Matter: Three Decades of Passions, Pastimes and Politics.* New York: Crown Forum, 2013.

Krieg, Dr. Adrian H. *Oz in the New Millennium.* N.p.: A2Z Press, 2010.

Krupskaya, Nadezhda. *On Labour-Oriented Education and Instruction.* Moscow: Progress, 1982.

Kupelian, David. "America, Land of 1,000 Addictions," WND, June 29, 2014. http://www.wnd. com/2014/06/america-land-of-1000-addictions/.

———. "Amputating Healthy Organs, The New Morality," WND, October 24, 2013. http://www.wnd. com/2013/10/amputating-healthy-organs-the-new-normal/.

———. "The Caliphate and Me," *Whistleblower*, October 2014.

———. "Chaos Theory," *Whistleblower*, January 2015.

———. "Faith Crimes," *Whistleblower*, May 2015.

———. "How America Morphed into 'Bizarro World,'" WND, September 18, 2013. http://www.wnd. com/2013/09/how-america-morphed-into-bizarro-world/.

———. "Interpreting the King's Dreams," *Whistleblower*, January 2015.

———. *The Marketing of Evil.* Washington, WND Books, 2005.

———. "Meet the New Fascists—and Their Victims," WND, May 22, 2014. http://www.wnd. com/2014/05/meet-the-new-fascists-and-their-victims/.

———. "Messiahs False and True," *Whistleblower*, June 2014.

LaBarbera, Peter. "Gay Power vs. Religious Liberty," WND, November 29, 2013. http://www.wnd. com/2013/11/gay-power-vs-religious-liberty/.

Landsberg, Mitchell. "Searching for NATO," *Los Angeles Times*, May 22, 2003.

Larson, Reed E. "Government-Granted Coercive Power: How Big Labor Blocks the Freedom Agenda," *Imprimis*, April 2000. https://imprimis.hillsdale.edu/governmentgranted-coercive-power-how-big-labor-blocks-the-freedom-agenda/.

Levin, Mark R. *Ameritopia.* New York: Threshold, 2012.

Levin, Mark R. *Liberty and Tyranny: A Conservative Manifesto.* New York: Threshold, 2009.

Lewis, Patrice. "Hope and Change: Bread and Circuses," *Whistleblower,* June 2014.

Lileks, James. "Economics for Dummies," *National Review,* January 27, 2014. https://www.nationalreview.com/nrd/articles/367993/economics-dummies.

———. "Puttin' in the Ritz," *National Review,* May 2, 2014. https://www.nationalreview.com/nrd/articles/364982/puttin-ritz.

Limbaugh, David. *Crimes Against Liberty: An Indictment of President Barack Obama.* Washington, D.C.: Regnery, 2010.

Limbaugh, Rush. "My Conversation with Victor Davis Hanson, Historian," *Limbaugh Letter,* October 2015.

———. "Surrounded by Ignorance," *Limbaugh Letter,* April 2015.

———. "The Common Core Debacle," *Limbaugh Letter,* January 2014.

———. "The Last Bastion of American Toughness," *Limbaugh Letter,* June 2015.

———. "The Left Goes Totalitarian," *Limbaugh Letter,* August 2015.

———. *Limbaugh Letter,* April 1998.

———. January 1999.

———. January 2000.

———. November 1999.

———. *The Rush Limbaugh Show* (radio). January 16, 2014.

———. February 6, 2014.

———. February 20, 2014.

Loewen, James W. *Lies My Teacher Told Me: Everything Your American History Textbook Got Wrong.* New York: Touchstone Books, 1995.

Loudon, Gina. "Communist 'Recipe' for U.S. Revealed," WND, September 29, 2014. http://www.wnd.com/2014/09/communist-recipe-for-u-s-revealed/.

———. "Obama Firing Off More Executive Orders," WND, September 17, 2013. http://www.wnd.com/2013/09/obama-firing-off-more-executive-orders/.

Lowry, Lois. *The Giver.* Giver Quartet Series. N.p.: Laurel-Leaf, 1993/.

Luebke, Frederick C. *Bonds of Loyalty: German Americans and World War I.* N.p.: Northern Illinois University Press, 1974.

Lutzer, Erwin, with Steve Miller. *The Cross in the Shadow of the Crescent: An Informed Response to Islam's War with Christianity.* Eugene, OR: Harvest House, 2013.

Lyons, Eugene. *Assignment in Utopia: An Autobiography.* N.p.: Harcourt, Brace, 1937.

Mac Donald, Heather. "Practical Thoughts on Immigration," *Imprimis,* February 2015. https://imprimis.hillsdale.edu/practical-thoughts-on-immigration/.

Machiavelli, Niccoli. *The Prince.* New York: Penguin, 1960.

Maginnis, Bob. *Deadly Consequences: How Cowards Are Pushing Women into Combat.* Washington, D.C.: Regnery, 2013/.

Malkin, Michelle. *Culture of Corruption: Obama and His Team of Tax Cheats, Crooks, and Cronies.* Washington, D.C.: Regnery, 2009.

Maloof, F. Michael. "Obama Building 'Compliant Officer Class,'" WND, November 13, 2012. http://www.wnd.com/2013/11/obama-building-compliant-officer-class/.

———. "Obama 'Gutting Military' by Purging Generals," WND, October 29, 2013. http://www.wnd.com/2013/10/obama-gutting-military-by-purging-generals/.

————. "'Purge Surge:' Obama Fires Another Commander," WND, November 5, 2013. http://www.wnd.com/2013/11/purge-surge-obama-fires-another-commander/.

Marchione, Marilynn. "Global Study: Kids Today Are in Worse Shape Than Their Parents Were." *Business Insider*, November 20, 2013.

Marcuse, Herbert. "Repressive Tolerance." Essay. Marcuse.org, 1965. http://www.marcuse.org/herbert/pubs/60spubs/65repressivetolerance.htm.

Marini, John. "Budget Battles and the Growth of the Administrative State," *Imprimis*, October 2013. https://imprimis.hillsdale.edu/budget-battles-and-the-growth-of-the-administrative-state/.

————. "Frank Capra's America and Ours," *Imprimis*, March 2015. https://imprimis.hillsdale.edu/frank-capras-america-and-ours/.

Mathis, Joel. "Joel Mathis: Is Legalizing Marijuana Inevitable?" *Tulsa World*, March 30, 2014. http://www.tulsaworld.com/opinion/editorials/joe-mathis-is-legalizing-marijuana-inevitable/article_272618d0-b7eb-11e3-a77e-0017a43b2370.html.

Matlock, Jack F. *Reagan and Gorbachev: How the Cold War Ended*. New York: Random House, 2004.

McCain, Robert Stacy. "The Worst Idea in the World," *American Spectator*, February 5, 2014. https://spectator.org/57691_worst-idea-world/.

Milburn, John. "Bradley Is Chelsea Now: Judge Grants Manning Permission to Change Name." Johnson City Press, April 23, 2014. http://www.johnsoncitypress.com/Local/2014/04/23/Bradley-is-Chelsea-now-Judge-grants-Manning-permission-to-change-name.

Miller, Emily. "D.C. Gun Owners Face Registrations," *Washington Times*, January 6, 2014.

Miller, Gina. "U.S. Military Could Stop Obama, So He's Destroying It." *Military* magazine. February 2014.

Minor, Jack. "Doc Faces Boot for Citing 'Gay Health Dangers,'" WND, June 27, 2015. http://www.wnd.com/2015/06/doc-faces-boot-for-citing-gay-health-dangers/.

Mitchell, Brian. *Weak Link: The Feminization of The American Military*. Washington, D.C.: Regnery, 1989.

————. *Women in the Military: Flirting with Disaster*. Washington, D.C.: Regnery, 1998.

Monkton, Lord. "1 Year from Now, Freedom Dies Worldwide," WND, December 14, 2014. http://www.wnd.com/2014/12/1-year-from-now-freedom-dies-worldwide/.

Moore, Art. "Amusing Ourselves to Death," *Whistleblower*, June 2014.

————. "Democrat Wants FCC to Stifle Fox News," WND, February 20, 2014. http://www.wnd.com/2014/02/democrat-candidate-wants-fcc-to-stifle-fox-news/.

Moore, Barrett. "War and Chaos Ahead: How Mega-Rich are Preparing," WND, March 20, 2015. http://www.wnd.com/2015/03/war-and-chaos-are-coming-how-mega-rich-are-preparing/.

Moore, Stephen. "Welfare in America: A $1 Trillion Tab and Rising," *Whistleblower*, June 2014.

————. "Welfare Is the New Look," *New York Times*, August 8, 2016.

Morlan, Kent. "We're Not No. 1—but We Need to Be," *Tulsa World*, January 8, 2014.

Morris, Lewis. "Venezuela: When Free Stuff Runs Out, State Power Remains." *Patriot Post*, May 26, 2016. https://patriotpost.us/articles/42805.

Murchison, William. "The Problem Isn't Obama, But Dependency," *Washington Times*, October 7, 2013.

Murphy, Bridget. "Boston Makes Free Meals Available to All Students," *Tulsa World*, September 7, 2013.

Murphy, Sean. "Group Unveils Satan Statue Design for Oklahoma," Yahoo! News, January 6, 2014. https://www.yahoo.com/news/group-unveils-satan-statue-design-oklahoma-224102124.html?ref=gs.

Murray, Charles. *Coming Apart: The State of White America, 1960–2010*. New York: Crown Forum, 2013.

Napolitano, Andrew P. *It's Dangerous to Be Right When the Government Is Wrong: The Case for Personal Freedom*. Nashville: Thomas Nelson, 2010.

———. "What Freedom of Speech?" *Washington Times.* January 14, 2015. http://www.washingtontimes. com/news/2015/jan/14/what-freedom-of-speech/.

New Internationalist. "A Short History of Taxation," October 1, 2008. https://newint.org/ features/2008/10/01/tax-history/.

Newcomb, Jerry. "Tracing the Marxist Roots of The Assault on the Family," Townhall, June 18, 2015. http://townhall.com/columnists/jerrynewcombe/2015/06/17/tracing-the-marxist-roots-of-the-assault-on-the-family-n2012948.

Newman, Alex. "Schools Propose: Let Boys into Girls Locker Rooms," WND, November 11, 2014. http://www.wnd.com/2014/11/schools-propose-let-boys-into-girls-locker-rooms/.

Nordlinger, Jay. "The Spirit of Struggle." *National Review*, December 22, 2014. http://www. nationalreview.com/sites/default/files/nordlinger_juancarlos122214.html.

ONeill, Jim. "Soros: Republic Enemy #1." *Canada Free Press*, September 15, 2009. http://canadafreepress. com/article/soros-republic-enemy-1.

O'Reilly, Bill. "Here Comes Socialism." Talking Points Memo. October 23, 2013. http://www.billoreilly. com/b/Bill-OReilly:-Here-comes-socialism/119030328151050951.html.

———. "Why Entitlement Culture Has Exploded," *Tulsa World*, 2014.

O'Reilly, Bill, and Michael Dugard. *Killing Jesus: A History.* New York: Henry Holt, 2013.

Obama, Barack. *Dreams from My Father: A Story of Race and Inheritance.* N.p.: Broadway Books, 2004.

Ohlemacher, Stephen. "Investigators: 36K Get Improper Disability Pay," *Tulsa World*, September 15, 2013.

———. "Report: Improperly OK'd Disability Claims Cot $3B." *Tulsa World*, November 15, 2014.

Olmstead, Kathryn S. *Red Spy Queen: A Biography of Elizabeth Bentley.* Chapel Hill and London: University of North Carolina Press, 2002.

Orwell, George. *1984.* N.p.: Signet, 1950.

Oshinsky, David M. *A Conspiracy So Immense: The World of Joe McCarthy.* New York: Oxford University Press, 1983.

Paul, Ron. "Drafting Women Would Mean Equal Bondage." *Tulsa World*, May 6, 2016.

Paulson, Steven K. "Colorado Boy, 6 Years Old, Suspended for Kissing a Girl." CTV News, December 11, 2013. http://www.ctvnews.ca/world/colorado-boy-6-suspended-for-kissing-a-girl-1.1584425.

Pavlich, Katie. "Gun Crime Soars in England Where Guns Are Banned," Townhall, June 1, 2014. http://townhall.com/tipsheet/katiepavlich/2012/12/11/gun-crime-soars-in-england-where-guns-are-banned-n1464528.

Peikoff, Leonard. *The Ominous Parallels.* N.p.: Stein & Day, 1982.

Peterson, Jesse Lee. "Black Fatherless Homes, Left Creating Cop Killers," WND, July 20, 2014. http:// www.wnd.com/2014/07/black-fatherless-homes-and-left-creating-cop-killers/.

———. "Houston's Lesbian Mayor Turns Tyrant," WND, October 19, 2014. http://www.wnd .com/2014/10/houstons-lesbian-mayor-turns-tyrant/.

———. "What If White American Just Said 'No!'" WND, August 24, 2014. http://www.wnd .com/2014/08/what-if-white-america-just-said-no/.

Porter, Nathan. "Atheists Find Shelter from Christianity in 'Secular Safe Zones.'" *Washington Times*, October 7, 2013.

Powers, Kirsten. *The Silencing.* Washington, D.C.: Regnery, 2015.

Prager, Dennis. "American Decay Is Speeding Up," Townhall. April 8, 2015. http://townhall.com /columnists/dennisprager/2015/04/07/americas-decay-is-speeding-up-n1981613.

Prelutsky, Burt. "The New and Improved Iron Curtain." *Los Angeles Times*, December 6, 2009. http:// www.burtprelutsky.com/2009/12/new-and-improved-iron-curtain.html.

Reagan, Ronald. "Evil Empire Speech," delivered March 8, 1983.

———. "A Time for Choosing Speech," delivered October 27, 1964.

Rees, Laurence. *Auschwitz.* N.p.: MJF, 2005.

Reeves, Thomas. *The Life and Times of Joe McCarthy: A Biography.* N.p.: Madison Books, 1982.

Richardson, Joel. "What a New Caliphate Means for the World," *Whistleblower,* October 2014.

Riddell, Kelly. "Children of The State." *Washington Times,* September 19, 2016.

———"Liberal Billionaire Funds Ferguson Protests, Hopes to Spur Civil Action," *Washington Times.*

Ringer, Robert. "Following in Rome's Footsteps," *Whistleblower,* June 2014.

Robertson, Pat. *The New World Order.* N.p.: Word, 1991.

Robinson, Peter. "Looking Again at Reagan and 'Tear Down This Wall.'" *Wall Street Journal,* November 2009.

Rosin, Hanna. "Men Are Obsolete: Five Reasons We Are Definitely Witnessing the End of Men," *Time,* January 2, 2014.

Rossiter, Clinton. *The American Presidency.* N.p.: New American Library, 1960.

Samuelson, Robert J. "Nation Also Suffering from Family Deficit," *Tulsa World,* November 6, 2014.

Savage, Michael. *The Enemy Within: Saving America from the Liberal Assault on Our Churches, Schools, and Military.* Nashville: WND, 2003.

———. *Stop the Coming Civil War.* New York: Center Street, 2014.

———. *Trickle Down Tyranny: Crushing Obama' Dream of the Socialist States of America.* N.p.: William Morrow, 2012.

Scarborough, Rowan. "French Muslims Carve Out Own Mini-States." *Washington Times,* January 12, 2015.

———. "Lesbian Affection Case Likely to End Soldier's Career." *Washington Times,* November 17, 2014.

———. "Pentagon Issues Sex Change Manual, Allows Extended Time Off for Process." *Washington Times,* July 18, 2016.

Schallbern, Kaitlyn. "California City Council Meeting Erupts After Two Illegal Immigrants Are Appointed to Commission," TheBlaze, August 5, 2015. http://www.theblaze.com/ stories/2015/08/05/california-city-council-meeting-erupts-after-two-illegal-immigrants-are-appointed-to-commissions-you-are-out-of-order/.

Schilling, Chelsea. "Radical Black Activist Issues Cop-Kill Predictions," WND, January 1, 2015. http:// www.wnd.com/2015/01/radical-black-activist-issues-cop-kill-prediction/.

Schrecker, Ellen. "Soviet Espionage in America: An Oft-Told Tale." *Reviews in American History* 38, no. 2 (June 2010).

Shedlock, Mike. "The Downward Spiral of The Eurozone." Townhall, February 14, 2015.

Shank, John D. *Military.* "Editor's Log," April 2014.

Shannon, T. W. "Chapel for Founders, History, Faith and Freedom." *Tulsa World,* November 26, 2013.

Shapiro, Ben. *How to Debate Leftists and Destroy Them: 11 Rules for Winning the Argument.* N.p.: Truth Revolt, 2014.

Sherman, Bill. "Christian Apologist Decries Cultural Shift," *Tulsa World,* November 16, 2013.

———. "Religious Persecution Rising." *Tulsa World,* January 25, 2014.

———. "Word Explosion Speaker Says U.S. Freedoms Eroding," *Tulsa World,* August 9, 2014

Shlaes, Amity. "The Legacy of the 1936 Election," *Imprimis,* September 2006. https://imprimis.hillsdale. edu/the-legacy-of-the-1936-election/

Siegel, Fred. *The Revolt Against the Masses.* New York: Encounter, 2014.

Sikma, Brian. "Sen. Baldwin: 1st Amendment Doesn't Apply to Individuals," Media Trackers, July 2, 2015. http://mediatrackers.org/wisconsin/2015/07/02/sen-baldwin-1st-amendment-doesnt-apply-individuals.

Skousen, W, Cleon. *The Naked Communist.* N.p.: CreateSpace, 1958.

Smith, Robin. "Having Dispensed with God, Leftists Now Aim for Christians." *Patriot Post*, June 29, 2015. https://patriotpost.us/articles/36076.

Snyder, Timothy. *Bloodlands: Bloodlands.* New York: Basic, 2010.

Solzhenitsyn, Aleksandr. *The Gulag Archipelago.* New York: Harper & Row, 1974/.

Somers, Meredith. "Southern Baptists Cite Threats to Religious Freedom in World." *Washington Times*, June 23, 2014.

Sorlin, Pierre. *The Soviet People and Their Society: The Soviet People and Their Society.* N.p.: Frederick A. Praeger, 1968.

Sowell, Thomas. "Freedom Is Never Free." *Washington Times*, March 10, 2014.

———. "The War Against Achievement." *Washington Times*, November 25, 2013.

Sparrow Project. "The Declaration of the Occupation of New York City," Sparrow Project, 2011, https://www.sparrowmedia.net/declaration/.

Spence, Gerry. *From Freedom to Slavery: The Rebirth of Tyranny in America.* New York: St. Martin's, 1993.

Spencer, Robert. "Obama's Immigration Fiasco and National Security." *Frontpage Magazine,* October 2014.

Starnes, Todd. "Catholic University Marquette Suspends Professor Over Anti-Gay Marriage Controversy." Townhall, December 20, 2014. http://townhall.com/columnists/toddstarnes/2014/12/18/catholic-university-marquette-suspends-professor-over-antigay-marriage-controversy-n1933853.

——— "Hey, Boy Scouts—Don't Squirt." Townhall, May 22, 2015. http://townhall.com/columnists/toddstarnes/2015/05/20/hey-boy-scouts--dont-squirt-n2001710.

——— "U.S. Army Defines Christian Minority as 'Domestic Hate Group.'" Fox News, October, 15, 2013. http://www.foxnews.com/opinion/2013/10/14/us-army-defines-christian-ministry-as-domestic-hate-group.html.

Steyn, Mark. *After America.* Washington, D.C.: Regnery, 2011.

———. "Live Free or Die." *Imprimis*, April 2009. https://imprimis.hillsdale.edu/live-free-or-die/.

———. "Where the Action Is," *National Review*, Mach 10, 2014. https://www.nationalreview.com/nrd/articles/371573/where-action.

STORM. *Reclaiming Revolution: History, Summation & Lessons from the Work of Standing Together to Organize a Revolutionary Movement.* N.p.: STORM, 1994.

Sumner, William Graham. *The Forgotten Man and Other Essays.* Trinity, AL: Sparklight, 2009.

Tapson, Mark. *Obama's 1984.* N.p.: David Horowitz Freedom Center, 2013.

Thatcher, Margaret. "All Beginnings Are Hopeful: Challenges Facing the 21st Century." *Imprimis*, April 2007. https://imprimis.hillsdale.edu/all-beginnings-are-hopeful-challenges-facing-the-21st-century/.

Tucker, William. *Marriage and Civilization.* Washington, D.C.: Regnery, 2014.

Tzouliadis, Tim. *The Forsaken: An American Tragedy in Stalin's Russia.* New York: Penguin, 2008.

Unruh, Bob. "Activist Judges Push 'Gay Marriage.'" WND, July 19, 2014. http://www.wnd.com/2014/07/gay-marriage-push-driven-by-activist-judges/.

———. "Appeals Court: States Can define Marriage as 1 Man 1 Woman." WND, November 7, 2014. http://www.wnd.com/2014/11/appeals-court-states-can-define-marriage-as-1-man-1-woman/.

———. "Armed Fed Raid Prompted by Safety Rules." WND, April 17, 2014. http://www.wnd.com/2014/04/armed-fed-raid-prompted-by-safety-rules/.

———. "Army Sued over Plan to Put Women on Front Lines of Combat." WND, April 4, 2015. http://www.wnd.com/2015/04/army-sued-over-plan-to-put-women-on-front-lines-of-combat/.

———. "Black Mob Attacks Victim 'Like It Was a Game.'" WND, May 30, 2014. http://www.wnd.com/2014/05/black-teens-attack-victims-like-it-was-a-game/.

———. "Businesses Fire Back Against Ban on the Word 'Gun.'" WND, November 11, 2014. http://www.wnd.com/2014/11/now-the-word-gun-and-images-of-guns-get-banned/.

———. "Christian Girl Given Zeroes for Her Beliefs." WND, May 4, 2015. http://www.wnd.com/2015/05/christian-girl-given-zero-grades-for-her-beliefs/.

———. "Churches Warned: Tidal Wave of Gay Theology." WND, August 23, 2014. http://www.wnd.com/2014/08/churches-warned-tidal-wave-of-gay-theology-looming/.

———. "Confirmed Non-Citizen Voters Boosting Democrats." WND, October 30, 2014. http://www.wnd.com/2014/10/confirmed-illegal-ballots-by-non-citizens-boost-democrats/.

———. "Criticize 'Gays,' Get Sued for 'Crime Against Humanity.'" WND, April 20, 2014. http://www.wnd.com/2014/04/criticize-gays-get-sued-for-crime-against-humanity/.

———. "'Gay' National Monuments to Rewrite American History." WND, May 30, 2014. http://www.wnd.com/2014/05/gay-national-monuments-to-rewrite-americas-history/.

———. "'Ghoulish' Plan to Grab Guns When Owner Dies." WND, November 14, 2014. http://www.wnd.com/2014/11/plan-to-grab-guns-when-owner-dies-labeled-ghoulish/.

———. "Gov't in Massive Crush of Religious Freedom." WND October 22, 2013. Government in Massive Crush of Religious Freedom.

———. "Horror 'More Dangerous Than Terrorist Groups.'" WND, February 9, 2014. http://www.wnd.com/2014/11/horror-more-dangerous-than-terrorist-groups/.

———. "ISIS Running Training Camp on Texas Border." WND, April 14, 2015. http://www.wnd.com/2015/04/isis-running-training-camp-on-texas-border/.

———. "ISIS Terrorists: We're Here in Ferguson." WND, August 19, 2014. http://www.wnd.com/2014/08/isis-terrorists-were-here-in-ferguson/.

———. "Judge Says Ordinary Tools Actually Are 'Weapons.'" WND, April 19, 2014. http://www.wnd.com/2014/04/judge-says-ordinary-tools-actually-are-weapons/.

———. "Lawsuit Targets Atheist's Influence with Pentagon." WND, September 28, 2013. http://www.wnd.com/2013/09/lawsuit-targets-atheists-influence-with-pentagon/.

———. "Nazareth Rejects Jesus, Gets Sued." WND, April 9, 2014. http://www.wnd.com/2014/04/nazareth-rejects-jesus-gets-sued/.

———. "New Hanky Panky for Transgender Bathrooms." WND, February 25, 2014. http://www.wnd.com/2014/02/new-hanky-panky-for-transgender-bathrooms/.

———. "Obama 'Threatens Fox News Reporter's Career.'" WND, January 22, 2014. http://www.wnd.com/2014/01/fox-anchor-team-obama-threatened-benghazi-reporter/.

———. "Ron Paul Predicts BLM Overreach 17 Years Ago." WND, April 29, 2014. http://www.wnd.com/2014/04/1997-ron-paul-warned-of-bureaucrats-with-guns/.

———. "Shock Claim: Obama Worse Than a Communist." WND, December 9, 2013. http://www.wnd.com/2013/12/shock-claim-obama-not-a-communist/.

———. "Shock Prayer: City Calls on Allah, Zeus, Satan." WND, October 26, 2014. http://www.wnd.com/2014/12/city-meeting-calls-on-allah-zeus-satan/.

———. "State 'Weeding Out' Christian Beliefs." WND, September 28, 2013. http://www.wnd.com/2013/09/state-official-weed-out-conservatives-seeking-to-adopt/.

———. "State Nanny Plan Makes 'Good Parents' Fair Game." WND, February 9, 2014. http://www.wnd.com/2014/02/state-nanny-plan-makes-good-parents-fair-game/.

———. "Supreme Court Green Lights Detention of Americans." WND, April 30, 2014. http://www.wnd.com/2014/04/supreme-court-green-lights-detention-of-americans/.

———. "Threats Target Church After Stand for Bible." WND, November 28, 2013. http://www.wnd. com/2011/11/368929/.

———. "Warning: Gun Confiscation Coming Soon." WND, January 13, 2014. http://www.wnd. com/2014/01/americans-warned-gun-confiscation-coming/?cat_orig=us.

———. "Washington Still Sucking Up Ammo Supplies." WND, August 21, 2013. http://www.wnd. com/2013/08/washington-still-sucking-up-ammo-supplies/.

———. "White Lawmaker 'Ashamed He's White.'" WND, September 29, 2014. http://www.wnd. com/2014/09/white-democrat-lawmaker-ashamed-hes-white/.

Vespa, Matt. "Insanity: The Word 'Man' Is Banned at Princeton University," Townhall, September 10, 2016. http://townhall.com/tipsheet/mattvespa/2016/08/20/insanity-the-word-man-is-banned-at-princeton-n2207565.

Voegeli, William. "The Case Against Liberal Compassion." Imprimis, October 2014. https://imprimis. hillsdale.edu/the-case-against-liberal-compassion/.

Wade, Jarrel. "Feeding Furry Friends." Tulsa World, November 4, 2014.

Wang, Jessica Ching-Sze. John Dewey in China: To Teach and Learn. Albany: State University of New York Press, 2007.

Wells, H. G. The New World Order. N.p.: Hesperides, 2006.

———. The Outline of History. N.p.: Garden City Books, 1961.

———. The Time Machine. Dover Thrift Editions. N.p.: Dover, 1995.

Wendt, Alexander. "Why a World State Is Inevitable." European Journal of International Relations 9, no. 4 (2003).

West, Allen. "Navy Losing Sailors and SEALs over Emphasis on Social Issues." Allen B. West website. April 28, 2014. http://www.allenbwest.com/allen/navy-losing-sailors-seals-emphasis-social-issues.

West, Diana. American Betrayal. New York: St. Martin's, 2013.

Wetzstein, Cheryl. "Same-Sex Couples' Children Tell Court of Ham." Washington Times, January 12, 2015.

———. "Till Death Do Us Part, or Just Till Contract Ends." Washington Times, October 6, 2014.

White, Euell, "Why Has Our Position on Communism Changed?" Military, April 2014.

Widlanski, Michael. Battle for Our Minds: Western Elites and the Terror Threat. New York: Threshold, 2012.

Wieland, Carl. One Human Family: The Bible, Science, Race and Culture. N.p.: Creation Publishers, 2011.

Wikipedia. "Agenda 21," accessed March 19, 2015.

———. "Association of Community Organizations for Reform Now," accessed March 4, 2015.

———. "Communist Party USA," accessed March 21, 2015.

———. "Francis Fox Piven," accessed October 30, 2013.

———. "History of Immigration to the United States," accessed December3, 2014.

———. "Kim Jong-Un," accessed February 3, 2015.

———. "League of Nations," accessed October 21, 2014.

———. "List of School Shootings in the United States," accessed June 2, 2014.

———. "The New Colossus," accessed December 3, 2014.

———. "Van Jones," Accessed October 30, 2013.

———. "World Government," accessed February 6, 2015.

Will, George. "How to Keep Them Down on the Farm." St. Louis Post-Dispatch, March 16, 2014. http://www.stltoday.com/news/opinion/columns/george-will/george-will-how-to-keep-them-down-on-the-farm/article_d26935e5-4bdf-56aa-92bd-0f80618a9c38.html.

———. "LBJ's Bifurcated Legacy," *St. Louis Post-Dispatch*, May 18, 2014. http://www.stltoday.com/news/opinion/columns/george-will/george-will-lbj-s-bifurcated-legacy/article_c475c259-b2d9-5cef-8fdf-eefe8f25fe21.html.

———. "What Political Ignorance Delivers," *St. Louis Post-Dispatch*, January 2, 2014. http://www.stltoday.com/news/opinion/columns/george-will/george-will-what-political-ignorance-delivers/article_cde4fce9-1f94-56e4-8d18-4b4f79f879fe.html.

Will, George F. *Suddenly: The American Idea Abroad and at Home 1986 to 1990*. New York: Free Press, 1990.

Williams, Walter E. "Black Progressives and Retrogression." Townhall, December 25, 2014. Black Progressives and Retrogression.

Williamson, Kevin D. *The Politically Incorrect Guide to Socialism*. Washington, D.C.: Regnery, 2011.

WND. "Doctors Urged to Amputate Healthy Limbs." WND. June 22, 2015. http://www.wnd.com/2015/06/prof-doctors-should-amputate-healthy-limbs/.

———. "'Duck' Censorship a Warning to Ministers." WND. December 20, 2013. http://www.wnd.com/2013/12/duck-censorship-a-warning-to-ministers/.

———. "Founding Fathers Rip Obama's Muslim 'Fabric.'" WND. August 3, 2015. http://www.wnd.com/2014/08/founding-fathers-refute-obamas-muslim-fabric/.

———. "'Gay' U.S. Soldiers Caught in Astonishing Act." WND. March 3, 2014. http://www.wnd.com/2014/03/gay-u-s-soldiers-sing-dance-in-drag/.

———. "A Government Every American Should Fear." WND. April 7, 2014. http://www.wnd.com/2014/04/a-government-every-american-should-fear/.

———. "Librarians Confronted over Ban on Books." WND. September 21, 2013. http://www.wnd.com/2013/09/librarians-confronted-over-ban-on-books/.

———. "Michael Savage: We've Lost the Battle." WND. October 22, 2015. http://www.wnd.com/2015/10/michael-savage-weve-lost-the-battle/.

———. "Network Face: 'I Want My Kid to Be Gay Too.'" WND. February 23, 2015. http://www.wnd.com/2015/02/cnn-commentator-i-want-my-kid-to-be-gay-too/.

———. "New Inquisitions: Punish Climate Change 'Deniers.'" WND. March 21, 2015. http://www.wnd.com/2015/03/new-inquisition-punish-climate-change-deniers/.

———. "NSA Ops 'Walk in Park' Next to Plans to Track Kids." WND. January 20, 2014. http://www.wnd.com/2014/01/nsa-ops-walk-in-park-next-to-plans-to-track-kids/.

———. "Push to Court-Martial General for Thanking God," WND, May 17, 2015. http://www.wnd.com/2015/05/push-to-court-martial-general-for-mentioning-god/.

———. "The Real Zombie Apocalypse." WND. February 5, 2014. http://www.wnd.com/2014/02/the-real-zombie-apocalypse/.

———. "Revealed: Obama Policy to Use Military Against Citizens." WND. May 29, 2014. http://www.wnd.com/2014/05/revealed-obama-policy-to-use-military-against-citizens/.

———. "Rush Limbaugh Accuses Critics of Mass Deception." WND. September 23, 2014. http://www.wnd.com/2014/09/rush-limbaugh-charges-critics-with-mass-deception/.

———. "Schoolchildren Exposed to Sex Games at Cal Berkeley." WND. February 22, 2014. http://www.wnd.com/2014/02/schoolchildren-exposed-to-sex-games-at-cal-berkeley/.

———. "They Want to Know Who You Are, What You Have." WND. April 27, 2014. http://www.wnd.com/2014/04/they-want-to-know-who-you-are-what-you-have/.

———. "University Stung by Jury Verdict over Religious Retaliation." WND. March 21, 2014. http://www.wnd.com/2014/03/university-stung-by-jury-verdict-in-retaliation-case/.

———. "U.S. Thrusts 'Gay' Agenda Upon World." WND. June 16, 2014. http://www.wnd.com/2014/06/u-s-thrusts-gay-agenda-upon-world/.

Wong, Gillian. "In China, Brutality Yields Confessions of Graft." *Salon*. March 10, 2014. http://www.salon.com/2014/03/10/in_china_brutality_yields_confessions_of_graft-2/.

Zagier, Alan Scher. "Holder Says He Understands Mistrust of Police." *LowellSun.com*. August 21, 2014. http://www.lowellsun.com/todaysheadlines/ci_26370027/.

Zahn, Drew. "Black-Crime Explosion: 'America's Worst City Revealed.'" WND. November 24, 2014. http://www.wnd.com/2014/11/black-crime-explosion-americas-worst-city-revealed/.

———. "Ex-CBS News Star Reveals Why Media Still Cover for Obama." WND, June 20, 2014. http://www.wnd.com/2014/06/ex-cbs-news-star-spills-secrets-on-right-wing-nuts/.

———. "'Gay' Columnists Blast Same-Sex Marriage." WND. November 18, 2013. http://www.wnd.com/2013/11/gay-columnist-blasts-same-sex-marriage/.

———. "General: Border Crisis Threatens U.S. Existence." WND, July 6, 2014. http://www.wnd.com/2014/07/general-border-crisis-threatens-u-s-existence/.

———. "Hitler Survivor Tells America: Buy More Guns." WND, January 4, 2014. http://www.wnd.com/2014/01/hitler-survivor-tells-americans-buy-more-guns/.

———. "Lefty Journalist: Obama Seeks 'State Media.'" WND, December 7, 2013. http://www.wnd.com/2013/12/lefty-journalist-obama-seeks-state-media/.

———. "Knock This Out: Media Absurd Claim on Black Mobs." November 26, 2014. http://www.wnd.com/2013/11/knock-this-out-media-make-absurd-claim-on-black-mobs/.

———. "VA Sued for Harassing Christian Chaplains." WND, November 11, 2013. http://www.wnd.com/2013/11/va-sued-for-harassing-christian-chaplains/.

NOTES

Introduction

1. See JB Williams, "From Apathy Back into Bondage," Canada Free Press, March 10, 2008, http://canadafreepress.com/article/from-apathy-back-into-bondage.
2. Aldous Huxley, *Brave New World*, repr. ed. (London: Everyman's Library, 2013), 229.

Chapter 1: Beginnings

1. H. G. Wells, *The Outline of History* (Illustrated and Annotated), 401 (CreateSpace, 2014), 401.
2. Jonathan Mayhew, "A Discourse Concerning Unlimited Submission and Non-Resistance to the Higher Powers," sermon (1750), National Humanities Center, http://nationalhumanitiescenter.org/pds/becomingamer/american/text5/mayhewsubmission.pdf, p. 1.
3. E. A. Bucchianieri, *Faust: My Soul Be Damned for the World*, vol. 2, repr. (Bloomington, IN: AuthorHouse, 2014), 536.
4. Amanda Carpenter, "Clinton: 'Something Has to Be Taken Away from Some People,'" Townhall, June 4, 2007, http://townhall.com/columnists/amandacarpenter/2007/06/04/clinton_something_has_to_be_taken_away_from_some_people.
5. Adolf Hitler, quoted in Leonard Peikoff, *The Cause of Hitler's Germany* (New York: Plume, 1982; repr., 2014) , chap. 1.
6. Plato, *Laws*, bk. 5, (written 360 BC), trans. Benjamin Jowett, http://classics.mit.edu/Plato/laws.5.v.html.
7. Derived from Plato's *Republic*.
8. Leonard Peikoff, *The Ominous Parallels* (New York: Stein & Day, 1982). 35.
9. John MacCormack, "Pelosi on Occupy Wall Street Protesters: 'God Bless Them,'" *Weekly Standard*, October 6, 2011, http://www.weeklystandard.com/pelosi-on-occupy-wall-street-protesters-god-bless-them/article/595117.
10. James Rosen, "Obama Voices Empathy with 'Frustration' Behind Anti-Wall Street Protests," Fox News Politics, October 6, 2011, http://www.foxnews.com/politics/2011/10/06/obama-empathizes-anti-wall-st-protests.html.
11. Joseph Stromberg, "Starving Settlers in Jamestown Colony Resorted to Cannibalism," Smithsonian.com, April 30, 2013, http://www.smithsonianmag.com/history/starving-settlers-in-jamestown-colony-resorted-to-cannibalism-46000815/.
12. Ellie Hall, "Cannibal Colonists Devoured 14-Year-Old Girl at Jamestown," BuzzFeed, May 2, 2013, https://www.buzzfeed.com/elliehall/cannibal-colonists-devoured-14-year-old-girl-at-jamestown?utm_term=.ju8MY2n8VD#.fblJ83RM0w.

13. "Account of the First Harvest Feast and Thanksgiving," *Patriot Post*, November 25, 2009, https://patriotpost.us/articles/4194.

14. Aristotle, *Politics*, bk. 2, pt. 3.

15. The Founders' Constitution, vol. 1, chap. 16, doc. 1, University of Chicago Press, http://press-pubs.uchicago.edu/founders/documents/v1ch16s1.html.

16. "The History and Legacy of Thanksgiving," *Patriot Post*, accessed January 12, 2017, https://patriotpost.us/pages/284.

17. The Founders' Constitution, vol. 1, chap. 4, doc. 1, http://press-pubs.uchicago.edu/founders/documents/v1ch4s1.html.

18. Joshua Charles, "The Nexus Between Illicit Sex and Luxury," WND, July 24, 2015, http://www.wnd.com/2015/07/the-nexus-between-illicit-sex-and-luxury/.

19. The Founders' Constitution, vol 1, chap. 17, doc. 9, http://press-pubs.uchicago.edu/founders/documents/v1ch17s9.html.

20. Quoted in Francis R. Aumann, *The Changing American Legal System: Some Selected Phrases* (Columbus: Ohio State University Press, 1940), 13.

21. A reference to Engels's use of the phrase "withering away of the state" in his 1878 work *Anti-Dühring*.

22. For the full text of the *Manifesto*, see Karl Marx and Frederick Engels, *Manifesto of the Communist Party* (1848) at https://msuweb.montclair.edu/~lebelp/MarxEngelsTheCommunistManifesto1848.pdf. Citations in this chapter are from this edition.

Chapter 2: Collectivism: The Expansion

1. Dean Koontz, *Life Expectancy: A Novel*, mass market ed. (New York: Bantam, 2012), 200.

2. Dmitri Volkogonov, *Lenin: Life and Legacy*, trans. Harold Shukman (N.p.: HarperCollins, 1994), 182.

3. John Reed, *Ten Days That Shook the World* (public domain), chap. 11.

4. Aleksandr I. Solzhenitsyn, *The Gulag Archipelago* (New York: Harper & Row, 1974), 37.

5. Ibid, 31.

6. V.I. Lenin, *Lenin Collected Works* (Wareham, Mass.: Omni, 1962).

7. Arsene de Goulévitch, *Czarism and Revolution: From the Past to the Future of Russia* (N.p.: Omni Publications, 1962).

8. Timothy Snyder, *Bloodlands* (New York: Basic Books, 2010), 380.

9. F. A. Hayek, *The Road to Serfdom*, 2nd ed. (Abingdon, UK: Routledge, 2001), 155.

10. Chuck Morse, *Was Hitler a Leftist?* Kindle ed. (N.p.: City Metro Enterprises, 2013).

11. Aleksandr Solzhenitsyn, *The Gulag Archipelago Abridged: An Experiment in Literary Investigation* (New York: Harper, 2007), 9.

12. Tim Tzouliadis. *The Forsaken* (New York: Penguin, 2008), 173.

13. Varlam Shalamov, *Kolyma Tales* (New York and London: Penguin, 1995), 32.

14. Nigel Cawthorne, *The Crimes of Stalin* (Arcturus, 2011), 104.

15. Modern History Sourcebook: Hymn to Stalin, Fordham University website, accessed January 12, 2017, http://sourcebooks.fordham.edu/halsall/mod/stalin-worship.asp.

16. Tim Tzouliadis, *The Forsaken* (New York: Penguin, 2008), 1.

17. Alexander Solzhenitsyn, *Foreign Affairs*, Spring 1980, 797, quoted in Harry Antonides, "Has Communism Been Defeated? *Comment* magazine, January 1, 1990, https://www.cardus.ca/comment/article/1722/has-communism-been-defeated/.

18. *New York Times*, March 31, 1933, 13, quoted in Arnold Beichman, "Pulitzer-Winning Lies," *Weekly Standard*, June 12, 2003.

19. Marco Carynnyk, "'Deliberate,' 'diabolical' starvation" Malcolm Muggeridge on Stalin's Famine," *Ukrainian Weekly*, May 29, 1983, http://www.ukrweekly.com/old/archive/1983/228321.shtml, reprinted on the Free Republic website, http://freerepublic.com/focus/f-news/3338192/posts.

20. Joseph Stalin, speech on agrarian policy, December 27, 1929, online on the website of Hanover College, http://history.hanover.edu/courses/excerpts/111stalin.html.

21. Aleksandr Solzhenitsyn, *The Gulag Archipelago, 1918–1956: An Experiment in Literary Investigation*, vol. 1 (New York: Harper & Row, 1974), 76.

22. Nigel Cawthorne, *The Crimes of Stalin* (London: Arcturus, 2011), 112.

23. Revolutionary Holocaust: Genocide by Famine: "The Famine of 1932–1933: A Genocide by Other Means," a special to the e-mail newsletter by Taras Hunczak, GlennBeck.com, accessed January 13, 2017, http://www.glennbeck.com/content/articles/article/198/35215/.

24. Timothy Snyder, *Bloodlands: Europe Between Hitler and Stalin* (New York: Basic, 2010, 2012), 50, 51.

25. Ibid., 50.

26. Ibid., 51.

27. Marco Carynnyk, "The Famine the 'Times' Couldn't Find," *Commentary* magazine, November 1, 1983, https://www.commentarymagazine.com/articles/the-famine-the-times-couldnt-find/.

28. Solzhenitsyn, *The Gulag Archipelago, 1918–1956*, 178.

29. Franklin D. Roosevelt, first inaugural address, March 4, 1933, Bartleby.com, http://www.bartleby.com/124/pres49.html.

30. Diana West, *American Betrayal* (New York: St. Martin's, 2013), 192.

31. Quoted in Tim Tzouliadis, *The Forsaken: An American Tragedy in Stalin's Russia* (New York: Penguin, 2008), 10.

32. M. Ilin, *New Russia's Primer*, in ibid., 5.

33. Tzouliadis, *The Forsaken*, 6.

34. Ibid., 26.

35. Ibid., 61.

36. Ibid., 23, 24.

37. George Orwell, *Nineteen Eighty-Four*, pt. 3, chap. 3, posted by Project Gutenberg Australia, August 2001, updated November 2008, http://gutenberg.net.au/ebooks01/0100021.txt.

38. Mark Alexander, "Mastering the Art of The Big Lie, (quoting *Mein Kampf*), *The Patriot Post*, December 12, 2013.

39. Page editor, "Hitler Survivor Tells Americans: 'Buy More Guns!'" *Desert Sun*, January 6, 2014, http://www.thedesertreview.com/hitler-survivor-tells-americans-buy-more-guns/.

40. Walter Laqueur, "A Look Back at the Weimar Republic—the Cry Was, 'Down with the System,'" *New York Times*, August 16, 1970, http://www.nytimes.com/1970/08/16/archives/a-look-back-at-the-weimar-republic-the-cry-was-down-with-das-system.html?_r=0.

41. Hermann Rauschning, *Hitler Speaks: A Series of Political Conversations with Adolf Hitler on His Real Aims* (N.p.: Kessinger, 2006), 222.

42. Fred Hechinger, "About Education," *New York Times*, May 15, 1979, http://www.nytimes.com/1979/05/15/archives/about-education-educators-seek-to-teach-context-of-the-holocaust.html.

43. Orwell, *Nineteen Eighty-Four*, pt. 1, chap. 1.

44. Charles W. Sasser, Personal conversation at OWS in 2011, New York.

45. Charles Darwin, *The Descent of Man*, Shine Classics (N.p.: CreateSpace, 2014), 67.

46. Daniel J.Kevles, *In the Name of Eugenics: Genetics and the Uses of Human Heredity* (New York: Knopf, 1985), 91.

47. George W. Hunter, *A Civic Biology, Presented in Problems* (New York: Dossier, 2016; CreateSpace, 2016), 139.

48. Theodore Roosevelt, letter to Charles B. Davenport, January 3, 1913, reproduced at https://www.dnalc.org/view/11219-T-Roosevelt-letter-to-C-Davenport-about-degenerates-reproducing-.html.

49. *Buck v. Bell*, 274 U.S. 200, at 207.

50. Margaret Sanger, *Woman and the New Race* (New York: Brentanos, 1922), chap. 5.

51. Margaret Sanger, "Is Race Suicide Probable?" *Colliers*, August 15, 1925.

52. Duncan W. McKim, *Heredity and Human Progress* (New York and London: G. P. Putnam's Sons, 1900).

53. William J. Robinson, *Eugenics, Marriage and Birth Control (Practical Eugenics)* (New York: The Critic and Guide Company, 1917), 74.

54. Edwin Black, "The Horrifying American Roots of Nazi Eugenics," History News Network, September 2003, http://historynewsnetwork.org/article/1796.

55. Kevles, *In the Name of Eugenics*, chap. 5.

56. "Scientists: 'Look, One-Third of the Human Race Has to Die for Civilization to Be Sustainable, So How Do We Want to Do This?'" the Onion website, January 26, 2012, http://www.theonion.com/article/scientists-look-one-third-of-the-human-race-has-to-27166.

Chapter 3: Struggle for Individualism

1. Frederick Jackson Turner, *The Significance of the Frontier in American History* (State Historical Society of Wisconsin, 1894; Penguin UK: 2008). Citation is to the Penguin edition.

2. Robert Penn Warren, *All the King's Men* (Orlando: Harcourt, 1946, 1974), 405.

3. Ralph Raico, in *American Conservatism: An Encyclopedia*, ed. Bruce Frohnen, Jeremy Beer, Jeffrey O. Nelson (Wilmington, DE: ISI Books, 2006), 498.

4. Adam Smith, *The Wealth of Nations*, repr. (CreateSpace, 2015), 190.

5. Ibid., 292.

6. Benito Mussolini, quoted in Neal Boortz, *Somebody's Gotta Say It* (New York: HarperCollins, 2007), 23.

7. Robert Higgs, *Against Leviathan: Government Power and A Free Society* (Washington, DC: Independent Institute, 2004), 132.

8. Jeffrey Rogers Hummel, *Emancipating Slaves, Enslaving Free Men: A History of the American Civil War*, 2nd ed. (Chicago: Open Court, 2013), 328.

9. David Wagner, *The New Temperance: The American Obsession with Sin and Vice* (Boulder, CO: Westview, 1997), 18.

10. Alexis de Tocqueville, *Democracy in America*, vol. 2, bk. 4, chap. 6, at http://xroads.virginia.edu/~HYPER/DETOC/ch4_06.htm.

11. John B. Judis, "Homeward Bound," *New Republic*, March 2, 2003, https://newrepublic.com/article/66760/herbert-croly-new-republic-liberalism.

12. Leonard Peikoff, *The Ominous Parallels* (New York: Stein & Day, 1982), 285.

13. Barack Obama, quoted in Victor Davis Hanson, "From Energy to Foreign Policy to the Presidency Itself, Obama's Agenda Rolls Along," *National Review*, October 1, 2013, http://www.nationalreview.com/article/359967/obama-transforming-america-victor-davis-hanson.

14. Leonard Peikoff, *The Ominous Parallels* (New York: Stein & Day, 1982), 282.

15. "The Supreme Court: The Power to Tax," *Time*, March 17, 1958.

Chapter 4: Leviathan Emerges

1. Woodrow Wilson, *The New Freedom: A Call For the Emancipation of the Generous Energies of a People* (Library of Alexandria, 1961).

2. Karl Marx and Frederick Engels, *Manifesto of the Communist Party* (1848), p. 26, at https://msuweb. montclair.edu/~lebelp/MarxEngelsTheCommunistManifesto1848.pdf.

3. Federal Reserve Act (ch. 6, 38 Stat. 251; see http://legisworks.org/sal/38/stats/STATUTE-38-Pg251a.pdf.

4. Gary Allen, with Larry Abraham, *None Dare Call It Conspiracy*, repr. (N.p.: Dauphin, 2013), 40–41.

5. Michael Linfield, *Freedom Under Fire: U.S. Civil Liberties in Times of War* (Boston: South End Press, 1999), 57.

6. The Nobel Peace Prize for 2009, Nobelprize.org, accessed January 13, 2017, http://www.nobelprize. org/nobel_prizes/peace/laureates/2009/press.html.

7. Nikki Schwab, "POLITICS: Fred Thompson Says His Politics Haven't Lost Him a Part," *U.S. News & World Report*, March 7, 2014, http://www.usnews.com/news/blogs/washington-whispers/2014/03/07/fred-thompson-says-his-politics-havent-lost-him-a-part.

8. Ludwig von Mises, auoted in Richard M. Ebelin, "The Free Market and the Interventionist State," *Imprimus* 26, no. 8 (August 1997): 2, http://imprimisarchives.hillsdale.edu/file/archives/pdf/1997_08_Imprimis.pdf.

9. Clinton L. Rossiter, *Constitutional Dictatorship: Crisis Government in the Modern Democracies* (Princeton: Princeton University Press, 1948), 295.

10. Leonard Peikoff, *The Ominous Parallels: The End of Freedom in America,* (New York: Stein & Day, 1982), 289.

11. Ibid., 133.

12. Ibid., 290.

13. Paul R. Hollrah, "The Passion of Political Movements," *Banner,* August 10, 2016.

14. Amity Shlaes, "The Legacy of The 1936 Election," *Imprimis,* September 2007.

15. From Franklin D. Roosevelt's State of the Union address, January 11, 1944, on the website of the Heritage Foundation, accessed January 13, 2017, http://www.heritage.org/initiatives/first-principles/primary-sources/fdrs-second-bill-of-rights.

16. Robert Higgs, *Against Leviathan: The End of Freedom in America* (New York: Stein & Day, 1982), 36–38.

17. Amity Shlaes, "The Legacy of The 1936 Election," *Imprimis,* September 2007.

18. Shlaes, "The Legacy of the 1936 Election," *Imprimis,* September 2007.

19. Mark R. Levin, *Liberty & Tyranny* (New York: Threshold, 2009), 88.

20. Mark R. Levin, *Ameritopia* (New York: Threshold, 2012), 206.

21. Viktor Suvorov, *The Chief Culprit: Stalin's Grand Design to Start World War II* (Annapolis, MD: Naval Institute Press, 2008), 1905.

22. Judge Andrew P. Napolitano, *It's Dangerous To Be Right When The Government is Wrong* (Nashville: Thomas Nelson, 2011), 163.

Chapter 5: Communism Arrives

1. Diana West, *American Betrayal* (New York: St. Martin's, 2013), 2.

2. Ibid, 3.

3. Ibid.

4. Ibid, 16.

5. Friedrich Hayek. *The Road to Surfdom* (London: Routledge, 1956), preface.

6. Viktor Kravchenko, *I Chose Freedom: The PersonalaAnd Political Life of a Soviet Official* (N.p.: Pickle Partners, 2016).

7. M. Stanton Evans, *Blacklisted by History: The Untold Story of Senator Joe McCarthy and His Fight Against America's Enemies* (New York: Three Rivers Press, 2009), 49–50.

8. History.com staff, "McCarthy Says Communists Are in State Department," History.com, accessed January 16, 2017, http://www.history.com/this-day-in-history/mccarthy-says-communists-are-in-state-department.

9. M. Stanton Evans and Herbert Romerstein, *Stalin's Secret Agents* (New York: Threshold, 2012), 100.

10. Cicero, "The Traitor."

11. Ann Coulter, *Treason* (New York: Crown Forum, 2003), 18.

12. Whittaker Chambers, *Witness*, repr. ed. (Washington, DC: Regnery History, 2014), 455.

13. Diana West, *American Betrayal* (New York: St. Martin's, 2013), 131.

14. Diana West, "On This Day in 2013," the website of Diana West, July 8, 2014, http://dianawest.net/Home/tabid/36/EntryId/2868/On-This-Day-in-2013.aspx.

15. Richard M. Fried, *Nightmare in Red: The McCarthy Era in Perspective*, repr. ed. (New York: Oxford University Press, 1991), 128.

16. Ibid., 156.

17. See "'Reds under the Bed,'" Alpha History, accessed January 16, 2017, http://alphahistory.com/coldwar/reds-under-the-bed/.

18. Ann Coulter, *Treason* (New York: Crown, 2003), 20.

19. Ibid, 21.

20. Janny Scott, "Alger Hiss, Divisive Icon of the Cold War, Dies at 92," *New York Times*, November 16, 1996, http://www.nytimes.com/1996/11/16/nyregion/alger-hiss-divisive-icon-of-the-cold-war-dies-at-92.html.

21. Nikita Khrushchev, quoted in Will Gragido and John Pirc, *Cybercrime and Espionage: An Analysis of Subversive Multi-Vector Threats* (Burlington, MA: Syngress, 2011), 101.

22. David M. Oshinsky, *A Conspiracy So Immense: The World of Joe McCarthy* (New York: Oxford University Press, 2005), 463.

23. Eugene Lyons, *The Red Decade: The Stalinist Penetration of America* (Garden City, NY: Bobbs-Merrill, 1941), 12.

24. Peter Collier and David Horowitz, *Destructive Generation: Second Thoughts About the Sixties* (2005), 203.

25. Peter Collier; David Horowitz. *Destructive Generation* (Charlottesville: Summit, 1989), 168–192.

26. West, "On This Day in 2013."

27. Ann Coulter, *Treason* (New York: Crown, 2003), 96.

28. Ibid, 95–96.

29. Diana West, *American Betrayal* (New York: St. Martin's, 2013), 87.

30. David Horowitz, *McCarthyism: The Last Refuge of the Left*, *Commentary* magazine, https://www.commentarymagazine.com/articles/mccarthyism-the-last-refuge-of-the-left/.

31 Peter Collier: David Horowitz. *Destructive Generation* (Charlottesville: Summit, 1989), 166–167.

32. Ann Coulter, *Treason* (New York: Crown, 2003), 6.

33. Diana West, *American Betrayal* (New York: St. Martin's, 2013), 53.

34. Edward Dmytryk, *Odd Man Out: A Memoir of the Hollywood Ten* (N.p.: Southern Illinois University Press, 1996), 158.

35. Chamberlain, quoted on the Sources of British History page at Britannia.com, accessed January 16, 2017, http://www.britannia.com/history/docs/peacetime.html.

36. From Matthew 24:6.

37. Clinton Rossiter, *The American Presidency* (New York: New American Library, 1960), 36.

38. Peter Collier and David Horowitz, *Destructive Generation* (Charlottesville: Summit, 1989), 223.

39. Jack Cox, *Requiem in The Tropics* (Conway, AR: UCA Books, 1987), 8.

40. Peter Collier and David Horowitz, *Destructive Generation* (Charlottesville: Summit, 1989), 312.

41. Jack Cox. *Requiem in The Tropics* (Conway, AR: UCA Books, 1987), 215.

42. "Transcript of President's Speech on the U.S. Response to Soviet Force in Cuba," special to the *New York Times*, October 2, 1979, http://www.nytimes.com/1979/10/02/archives/transcript-of-presidents-speech-on-the-us-response-to-soviet-force.html.

43. Stefan Kanfer, "Peace at any Prize," *City Journal*, October 17, 2002, http://www.city-journal.org/html/peace-any-prize-9965.html.

44. Exchange on CNBCs *The News with Brian Williams*, October 11, 2002, cited by Media Research Center on their profile of Brian Williams, http://www.mrc.org/profiles-bias/brian-williams.

45. James H. Hansen, *Radical Road Maps: Uncovering the Web of Connections Among Far-Left Groups in America* (Nashville: Thomas Nelson, 2006), 206.

46. Ann Coulter, *Treason* (New York: Crown, 2003), 174.

47. Peter Collier and David Horowitz. *Destructive Generation* (Conway, AR: Summit, 1989), p. 310–311.

48. Carl Limbacher and the newsMax.com staff, "Moore: Americans are 'The Dumbest People on the Planet,'" Newsmax.com, posted on the Free Republic website by "kattracks," June 26, 2004.

49. "NYT's David Carr: 'Middle Places' Home Of 'Low-Sloping Foreheads,'" Real Clear Politics Video, June 24, 2011, http://www.realclearpolitics.com/video/2011/06/24/nyts_david_carr_middle_places_home_of_low_sloping_foreheads.html.

50. John Earl Haynes, "The Cold War Debate Continues: A Traditionalist View of Historical Writing on Domestic Communism and Anti-Communism," *Journal of Cold War Studies* 2, no. 1 (January 2000): 76–115, http://www.johnearlhaynes.org/page67.html.

51. Ibid.

52. David Horowitz, *Left Illusions* (Leesburg, VA: Spence, 2003), 317.

53. Robert Higgs, *Against Leviathan: Government Power and A Free Society* (Washington, DC: Independent Institute, 2004), 42–43.

54. "How the Alger Hiss Case Explains the Tea Party," Bloomberg View, October 29, 2013, https://www.bloomberg.com/view/articles/2013-10-29/how-the-alger-hiss-case-explains-the-tea-party.

55. Gary Alan and Larry Abraham, *None Dare Call It Conspiracy* (Cape Girardeau, MO: Concord, 1971), 27.

56. Rafael Cruz, "Freedom Rising" presentation. ORU Mabee Center, Tulsa, Oklahoma, November 3, 2013.

57. Chambers, *Witness*, xli.

58. M. Stanton Evans; Romerstein, Herbert. *Stalin's Secret Agents* (New York: Threshold, 2012), 19.

59. Ann Coulter, *Treason* (New York: Crown, 2003), 154–157.

60. Paul Kengor, "Hot Words in the Cold War," *Christian History*, no. 99 (2008), https://www.christianhistoryinstitute.org/magazine/article/hot-words-in-the-cold-war/.

61. Al Fuller, "Winning The Cold War, Part I—The "Evil Empire" Speech. *http://history.com*. January 23, 2011.

62. Ibid.

63. Romesh Ratnesar, "80 Days That Changed the World: Bedeviling an Empire," *Time*, March 31, 2003, http://content.time.com/time/specials/packages/article/0,28804,1977881_1977895_1978704,00.html.

64. Ann Coulter, *Treason: Liberal Treachery from the Cold War to the War on Terrorism* (New York: Crown Forum, 2004), 166.

65. Ibid., 159.

66. Ibid.

67. Ibid., 160.

68. "Remarks on East-West Relations at the Brandenburg Gate in West Berlin," June 12, 1987, Ronald Reagan Presidential Library, accessed January 17, 2017, https://reaganlibrary.archives.gov/archives/speeches/1987/061287d.htm.

69. Dinesh D'Souza, "Russian Revolution: How Reagan Won the Cold War," *National Review*, June 6, 2004, http://www.nationalreview.com/article/210955/russian-revolution-dinesh-dsouza.

70. Jeffrey Lord, "Chief Justice Neville Chamberlain," *American Spectator*, July 10, 2012, https://spectator.org/35200_chief-justice-neville-chamberlain/.

71. Bill O'Reilly, *The O'Reilly Factor*, "Talking Points, *Fox News*, February18, 2014.

72. Adapted from W. Cleon Skousen, *The Naked Communist*, Political Freedom Series, vol. 1 (Salt Lake City: Izzard Ink, 2013), 282–302.

73. Mark Steyn, "Live Free or Die," *Imprimis*, April 2009.

74. Aldous Huxley, quoted in *Bloom's Guides: Aldous Huxley's "Brave New World,"* ed. Aislinn Goodman (Broomall, PA: Chelsea House, 2004), 14–15.

Chapter 6: Fundamental Transformation of Culture and Institutions

1. Alfredo Rocco, "The Political Doctrine of Fascism," reprinted in *Readings on Fascism and National Socialism*, ed. Alan Swallow (N.p.: CreateSpace, 2013), 23.

2. Bernard Goldberg. *100 People Who Are Screwing Up America* (New York: Harper Collins, 2005), 28.

3. Michael Medved, *Hollywood vs America: Popular Culture and the War on Traditional Values* (New York: Harper Perennial, 1993), 279.

4. "The Way You Look Tonight" by Dorothy Fields and Jerome Kern in *Swing Time* with Fred Astaire (1936), rerecorded by the Lettermen in 1961, 7" single.

5. Nine Inch Nails, "Big Man with a Gun," on *The Downward Spiral*, Nothing Records and Interscope Records (U.S.); Island Records (Europe), 1994. Album.

6. D. James Kennedy; Jerry Newcombe. *What if America were A Christian Nation Again?* (Nashville: Nelson, 2003).

7. "Obsessed with Sex," WND, November 18, 2004, http://www.wnd.com/2004/11/27466/.

8. James Bovard, *Lost Rights* (New York: St. Martin's, 1992), 159.

9. Charles Krauthammer, "The Mayor, the Museum, and the Madonna," *Weekly Standard*, October 11, 1999, http://www.weeklystandard.com/the-mayor-the-museum-and-the-madonna/article/11946.

10. Dana Rohrabacher, "Shield the Taxpayers from Funding Trash," *USA Today*, March 27, 1990, 10A, quoted in Bill Kauffman, "Subsidies to the Arts: Cultivating Mediocrity," Cato Institute *Policy Analysis*, no. 137 (August 8, 1990), https://object.cato.org/sites/cato.org/files/pubs/pdf/pa137.pdf.

11. Ian Daley, "You Call That Poetry?!" Poetry Foundation website, accessed January 18, 2017, https://www.poetryfoundation.org/features/articles/detail/68913.

12. Bill O'Reilly, *The O'Reilly Factor*, "Talking Points," Fox News, April 8, 2014.

13. Bill Hanks, "Addiction: The Great Marijuana Debate," *Tulsa World* editorials, January 23, 2014.

14. Jaime Fuller, "Gov. Jerry Brown on legalized marijuana: 'How many people can get stoned and still have a great state?'" *Washington Post*, March 2, 2014, https://www.washingtonpost.com/news/post-politics/wp/2014/03/02/gov-jerry-brown-on-legalized-marijuana-how-many-people-can-get-stoned-and-still-have-a-great-state/?utm_term=.2346bad422a3.

15. David Kupelian, "The Real Zombie Apocalypse," *Whistleblower*, February 4, 2014, http://www.wnd.com/2014/02/the-real-zombie-apocalypse/.

16. Ibid.

17. Manon McKinnon, "Defending Deviancy Down," *American Spectator*, June 22, 2011, https://spectator.org/37376_defending-deviancy-down/.

18. Quin Hillyer, "At Sea in an Alien Culture, Where 'Normal' Is Defined as 'Deviant,'" *National Review*, May 25, 2015, http://www.nationalreview.com/article/418830/sea-alien-culture-where-normal-defined-deviant-quin-hillyer.

19. Viagra TV commercial, video posted in 2012 on iSpot.tv, https://www.ispot.tv/ad/7LUL/viagra-knowing-what-youre-made-of.

20. Helen Kennedy, "Doc Billed Her for 120 Personalities," *New York Daily News*, February 12, 1997, http://www.nydailynews.com/archives/news/doc-billed-120-personalities-article-1.766795.

21. Charles W. Sasser, *Going Bonkers: The Wacky World of Cultural Madness* (AWOC, 2004), 9–11.

22. Neal Boortz, *Somebody's Got To Say It* (New York: Harper, 2007), 26.

23. Associated Press, "Sexual Harassment? 6-Year-Old Suspended for Kiss on Hand," *USA Today*, December 10, 2013, http://www.usatoday.com/story/news/nation/2013/12/10/first-grade-kiss-suspension/3963813/.

24. Rob Long, "Tolerant and Progressive Commencement Speeches, 2014," *National Review*, May 5, 2014, https://www.nationalreview.com/nrd/articles/375968/tolerant-and-progressive-commencement-speeches-2014.

25. John Stossel, "Longing to Be a Victim," *Townhall*, October 16, 2013, http://townhall.com/columnists/johnstossel/2013/10/16/longing-to-be-a-victim-n1724550.

26. "Doctors Urged to Amputate Healthy Limbs," WND, June 22, 2015, http://www.wnd.com/2015/06/prof-doctors-should-amputate-healthy-limbs/.

27. Ibid.

28. Franklin D. Roosevelt, radio address, Albany, NY, April 7, 1932, reprinted at http://newdeal.feri.org/speeches/1932c.htm.

29. Amity Shlaes, "The Legacy of the 1936 Election," *Imprimis*, September 2007, https://imprimis.hillsdale.edu/the-legacy-of-the-1936-election/.

30. Allan Bloom, The Closing of the American Mind (New York: Simon and Schuster, 1987).

31. "Public school system designed for failure," *News-Times* (Danbury, CT), June 13, 2004, http://www.newstimes.com/news/article/Public-school-system-designed-for-failure-251575.php.

32. David Kupelian, *The Marketing of Evil* (Washington, DC: WND, 2005), 157.

33. Chuck Morse, "The Four Horsemen of the Frankfort School," *Free Republic*, January 12, 2002, http://www.freerepublic.com/focus/fr/606886/posts.

34. Fred Lucas, "'What is Government?' Elementary Students Taught It's Your 'Family,'" *TheBlaze*, August 30, 2013, http://www.theblaze.com/stories/2013/08/30/what-is-government-elementary-students-taught-its-your-family/.

35. "The Educational System Was Designed to Keep Us Uneducated and Docile," Information Clearing House, accessed January 18, 2017, http://www.informationclearinghouse.info/article11693.htm.

36. Milan Kundera, *The Book of Laughter and Forgetting* (New York: Knopf, 1980).

37. Michelle Malkin, "'Social Justice' for Grade-Schoolers: The Howard Zinn Education Project," MichelleMalkin.com, December 8, 2009, http://michellemalkin.com/2009/12/08/social-justice-for-grade-schoolers-the-howard-zinn-education-project/.

38. David Horowitz, *The Professors* (Washington DC: Regnery, 2006), 358–364.

39. Robby Soave, "Philadelphia City Council Wants Socialism Taught in Schools," *Daily Caller*, October 27, 2013, http://dailycaller.com/2013/10/27/philadelphia-city-council-wants-socialism-taught-in-schools/.

40. Dean Kalahar, "Common Core: Nationalized State-Run Education," *American Thinker*, April 12, 2013, http://www.americanthinker.com/articles/2013/04/common_core_nationalized_state-run_education.html.

41. Jeffrey Lord, "Common Core: ObamaCare for Education," *American Spectator*, May 15, 2014, https://spectator.org/59227_common-core-obamacare-education/.

42. Rush Limbaugh, "The 'Common Core' Debacle, *Limbaugh Letter*, July 2014, http://www.thelimbaughletter.com/thelimbaughletter/january_2014?pg=14#pg14.

43. "Claim: Christians Sin by Putting Kids in Public School, WND, May 17, 2014, http://www.wnd.com/2014/05/claim-christians-sin-by-putting-kids-in-public-school/.

44. "Education? No, It's about Data-Mining," WND, May 10, 2014, http://www.wnd.com/2014/05/education-no-its-about-data-mining/.

45. Ibid.

46. Tom Christoffel, David Finkelhor, and Dan Gilbarg, *Up against the American Myth* (New York(?): Holt Rinehart Winston, 1970), 1.

47. Charles C. W. Cooke, "Revolution in Dotage," *National Review*, November 11, 2013.

48. Ann Coulter, "As Long as Obama Brought Up the Cost of College . . . ," Townhall, January 14, 2015, http://townhall.com/columnists/anncoulter/2015/01/14/as-long-as-obama-brought-up-the-cost-of-college-n1943204.

49. David Horowitz, *Left Illusions* (Dallas: Spence, 2003), 214–228.

50. Coulter, "As Long as Obama Brought Up the Cost of College."

51. Todd Starnes, "Catholic University Marquette Suspends Professor over Anti-Gay Marriage Controversy," Fox News, December 19, 2014, http://www.foxnews.com/opinion/2014/12/19/catholic-university-marquette-suspends-professor-over-anti-gay-marriage.html.

52. Todd Starnes, "Teacher to Student: If You Don't Support Gay Marriage, Drop My Class," Fox News, November 22, 2014, http://www.foxnews.com/opinion/2014/11/22/teacher-to-student-if-dont-support-gay-marriage-drop-my-class.html.

53. Diana West, *American Betrayal* (New York: St. Martin's, 2013), 81.

54. Ann Coulter, "Some 9/11 Lessons & Remembrances Excluded God, Patriotism," *Education Reporter*, October 2002, http://eagleforum.org/educate/2002/oct02/9-11-lessons.shtml.

55. Thomas G. West, "The Theology of the United States," *CRB*, December 1, 1996, http://www.claremont.org/crb/basicpage/the-theology-of-the-united-states/.

56. Kirsten Powers, *The Silencing* (Washington, DC: Regnery, 2015), 86.

57. Lisa Leff, "'Trigger Warnings' Stir Debate in Universities," *Tulsa World*, Associated Press, April 29, 2014.

58. David French, "The P.C. Police Aren't Fragile; They're Vengeful and Malicious," the *Corner* (*National Review* blog), March 24, 2015, http://www.nationalreview.com/corner/415885/pc-police-arent-fragile-theyre-vengeful-and-malicious-david-french.

59. David French, "'When People Have the Freedom to Choose, They Choose Wrong:' Watching *The Giver,* the *Corner*, August 12, 2014, http://www.nationalreview.com/corner/385251/when-people-have-freedom-choose-they-choose-wrong-watching-giver-david-french.

60. Kirsten Powers, *The Silencing* (Washington, DC: Regnery, 2015), 79–80.

61. John Leo, "College Campuses' Feelings-Based Tyranny," the *Corner*, December 19, 2014, http://www.nationalreview.com/corner/395108/college-campuses-feelings-based-tyranny-john-leo.

62. Kirsten Powers, *The Silencing* (Washington, DC: Regnery, 2015), 79–80.

63. Non-Discrimination and Anti-Harassment Policy and Complaint Procedures for Students, NYU website, accessed January 19, 2017, http://www.nyu.edu/about/policies-guidelines-compliance/policies-and-guidelines/non-discrimination-and-anti-harassment-policy-and-complaint-proc.html.

64. Foundation for Individual Rights in Education, "Spotlight: College of the Holy Cross," FIRE website, accessed January 19, 2017, https://www.thefire.org/schools/college-of-the-holy-cross/.

65. Kirsten Powers, *The Silencing* (Washington, DC: Regnery, 2015), 81.

66. Ibid.

67. Jennifer Kabbany, "Schoolchildren Exposed to Giant Penis, Sex Games at UC Berkeley," the College Fix, February 20, 2014, http://www.thecollegefix.com/post/16425/.

68. "Today's Nuze: May 10, 2004," *Nealz Nuze: Latest Blogs and Rants from Neal Boorz*, WSB Radio, http://www.wsbradio.com/weblogs/nealz-nuze/2004/may/10/2004-05-10/.

69. Richard Pérez-Peña and Tanzina Vega, "Brandeis Cancels Plan to Give Honorary Degree to Ayaan Hirsi Ali, a Critic of Islam," *New York Times*, April 8, 2014, https://www.nytimes.com/2014/04/09/us/brandeis-cancels-plan-to-give-honorary-degree-to-ayaan-hirsi-ali-a-critic-of-islam.html.

70. Robert H. Bork, *Slouching Towards Gomorrah* (New York: Simon & Schuster, 1996), 259.

71. Bill O'Reilly, *The O'Reilly Factor, Fox News*, March 24, 2015.

72. Mona Charen, "Termites at Work on American History," *Townhall.com*, December 13, 2014.

73. *An Examination of the Leading Principles of the Federal Constitution* (1787).

74. Philip B. Kurland and Ralph Lerner, eds., *The Founders' Constitution*, vol. 3, art. 1, sec. 8, clause 12, doc. 27, http://press-pubs.uchicago.edu/founders/documents/a1_8_12s27.html.

75. Richard Henry Lee, *Pennsylvania Gazette*, February 20, 1788.

76. Niccolò Machiavelli, *The Prince and the Art of War*, rev. ed. (London: Collector's Library, 2004), 221.

77. "Taming the Monster: Get Rid of the Guns : More Firearms Won't Make America Safer—They Will Only Accelerate and Intensify the Heartache and Bloodshed," *Los Angeles Times*, December 28, 1993, http://articles.latimes.com/1993-12-28/local/me-6058_1_gun-violence.

78. Richard Harris, "A Reporter at Large: Handguns," *New Yorker*, July 26, 2976, http://www.newyorker.com/magazine/1976/07/26/handguns.

79. Steven Reinberg, "U.S. Murder Toll From Guns Highest in Big Cities," *U.S. News:Healthday*, May 12, 2011.

80. Judy McLeod, "CCRKBA Blasts Buffalo Police Gun Grab from Bereaved Families," Canada Free Press, November 14, 2014, http://canadafreepress.com/article/ccrkba-blasts-buffalo-police-gun-grab-from-bereaved-families.

81. Catherine J. Frompovich, "The Feds "Assault" On U.S. War Veterans You Won't Believe," *Activist Post*, July 19, 2016, http://www.activistpost.com/2016/07/feds-assault-u-s-war-veterans-wont-believe.html.

82. Gina Loudon, "Obama Firing Off More Executive Orders," WND, September 17, 2013, http://www.wnd.com/2013/09/obama-firing-off-more-executive-orders/.

83. Edward J. Erler, "The Second Amendment As An Expression of First Principles," *Impromis*, March 2013.

84. "Another Look at the Federal Raid of Bozeman Brass Company," Before It's News, April 15, 2014, http://beforeitsnews.com/survival/2014/04/another-look-at-the-federal-raid-of-bozeman-brass-company-2518678.html.

85. James Bovard, *Lost Rights: The Destruction of American Liberty* (New York: St. Martin's, 1992), 217–218.

86. Kelsey Harkness, "Meet Four Business Owners Squeezed by Operation Choke Point," *Daily Signal*, August 12, 2014, http://dailysignal.com/2014/08/12/meet-four-business-owners-squeezed-by-operation-choke-point/.

87. FoxNews.com, "Gun Dealers Sue over California Law Barring Window Displays," Fox News, November 11, 2014, http://www.foxnews.com/politics/2014/11/11/gun-dealers-sue-over-california-law-barring-window-displays.html.

88. *The Patriot Post*, "Daily Digest," November 13, 2014.

89. Associated Press, "Congressman: Obama Wants Gestapo-Like Force," NBCNews.com, updated November 11, 2008, http://www.nbcnews.com/id/27655039/ns/politics-white_house/t/congressman-obama-wants-gestapo-like-force/#.WIYcVfkrKUk.

90. Bob Unruh, "Washington Sucking Up Ammo Supplies," WND, August 21, 2013.

91. "Feds Building 100 Years Worth of Ammo," WND, March 11, 2013, http://www.wnd.com/2013/03/feds-buying-100-years-worth-of-ammo/.

92. Jeff Poor, "Levin: US Preparing for Societal Collapse by Buying Up Billions of Rounds of Ammo [AUDIO]," *Daily Caller*, February 16, 2013, http://dailycaller.com/2013/02/16/levin-u-s-govt-preparing-for-civil-societys-collapse-by-buying-up-billions-of-rounds-of-ammo/.

93. "A Federal Police Force Is Unconstitutional: A Speech by Rep. Ron Paul," special to the *Libertarian Enterprise*, September 17, 1997, http://ncc-1776.org/tle1997/le971225-11.html.

94. "Defense Support of Civil Authorities (DSCA): A Proposed Rule by the Defense Department on 12/04/2008," *Federal Register* website, accessed January 23, 2017, https://www.federalregister.gov/documents/2008/12/04/E8-28706/defense-support-of-civil-authorities-dsca.

95. Leo Hohmann, "Obama UN Plan: Globalize Cops Against 'Violent Extremists,'" WND, October 6, 2015.

96. Rafael Cruz, "Freedom Rising" Presentation, ORU Mabee Center, Tulsa, Oklahoma, November 3, 2013.

97. Justin Butterfield and Bryan Clegg, eds., *Undeniable: The Survey of Hostility to Religion in America*, 2013 ed. (Plano, TX: Liberty Institute, 2013), iv.

98. See Ed Pilkington, "Obama Angers Midwest Voters with Guns and Religion Remark," *Guardian* (UK), April 14, 2008, https://www.theguardian.com/world/2008/apr/14/barackobama.uselections2008.

99. Byron York, "Iowa Democrat Prays: Dear God, Thank You for Abortion," *Washington Examiner*, August 21, 2013, http://www.washingtonexaminer.com/iowa-democrat-prays-dear-god-thank-you-for-abortion/article/2534969.

100. John Culhane, "What Today's Gay Marriage Victory in Pennsylvania Means for the Rest of America," *Slate*, May 20, 2014, http://www.slate.com/blogs/outward/2014/05/20/whitewood_v_wolf_what_the_pennsylvania_gay_marriage_victory_means_for_the.html.

101. Kerry Picket, "Hillary on Abortion: 'Deep-Seated Cultural Codes, Religious Beliefs and Structural Biases Have to Be Changed,'" *Daily Caller*, April 23, 2015, http://dailycaller.com/2015/04/23/hillary-on-abortion-deep-seated-cultural-codes-religious-beliefs-and-structural-biases-have-to-be-changed/.

102. "Claim: Christians Sin by Putting Kids in Public School," WND, May 17, 2014, http://www.wnd.com/2014/05/claim-christians-sin-by-putting-kids-in-public-school/.

103. Norman Geisler and Frank Turek, *I Don't Have Enough Faith to Be an Atheist* (Wheaton, Ill.: Crossway, 2004).

104. Eric Owens, "First-Grade Teacher Seizes Christian Kid's Candy Canes, Says 'Jesus Is Not Allowed in School,'" *Daily Caller*, January 8, 2014, http://dailycaller.com/2014/01/08/first-grade-teacher-seizes-christian-kids-candy-canes-says-jesus-is-not-allowed-in-school/.

105. Stone v. Graham, 449 U.S. 39 (1980); "Ten Commandments in America (Radio)," Probe for Answers, October 9, 2006, https://www.probe.org/ten-commandments-in-america-radio/.

106. Jim Patterson, "Expert: Stop Complaining about the Moral Decline of Western Society," Research News @ Vanderbilt, April 3, 2015, https://news.vanderbilt.edu/2015/04/03/expert-stop-complaining-about-the-moral-decline-of-western-society/.

107. Book of Lucifer 3, pars. 37–38.

108. CBSNewYork/AP, "N.Y. Group Applies To Build Satan Statue At Oklahoma State Capitol," CBS New York, January 6, 2014, http://newyork.cbslocal.com/2014/01/06/n-y-group-applies-to-build-satan-statue-at-oklahoma-state-capitol/.

109. Hemant Mehta, "Atheists Launch Political Action Committee," *Friendly Atheist* (blog), September 18, 2013, http://www.patheos.com/blogs/friendlyatheist/2013/09/18/atheists-launch-political-action-committee/.

110. "What Happened During This City Council Meeting Should Leave You Outraged," GlennBeck.com, December 10, 2014, http://www.glennbeck.com/2014/12/10/what-happened-during-this-city-council-meeting-should-leave-you-outraged/.

111. Jeff Schogol, "Group Wants Two-Star Court-Martialed for Speech," *Air Force Times*, May 15, 2015, https://www.airforcetimes.com/story/military/2015/05/15/group-wants-two-star-court-martialed-for-speech/27317903/.

112. Todd Starnes, "US Army defines Christian Ministry as 'Domestic Hate Group,'" Fox News Opinion, October 14, 2013, http://www.foxnews.com/opinion/2013/10/14/us-army-defines-christian-ministry-as-domestic-hate-group.html.

113. Katherine Weber, "Military Chaplains Banned FROM Using Jesus' Name, Reciting Bible; Lawsuit Filed in Calif.," *Christian Post*, November 14, 2013, http://www.christianpost.com/news/military-chaplains-banned-from-using-jesus-name-reciting-bible-lawsuit-filed-in-calif-108734/.

114. Heather Clark, "Kentucky Governor Vetoes Religious Freedom Bill Citing Public Safety, Homosexual 'Rights' Concerns," Christian News, March 24, 2013, http://christiannews.net/2013/03/24/kentucky-governor-vetoes-religious-freedom-bill-over-public-safety-homosexual-rights-concerns/.

115. Bob Unruh, "State 'Weeding Out' Christian Beliefs," WND, September 28, 2013, http://mobile.wnd.com/2013/09/state-official-weed-out-conservatives-seeking-to-adopt/.

116. "Religious Groups: IRS Scrutinized Us," CBS News, May 15, 2013, http://www.cbsnews.com/news/religious-groups-irs-scrutinized-us/.

117. Leo Hohmann, "Ben Carson: America Now in 'Pre-Fascist' Era," WND, July 6, 2014, http://www.wnd.com/2014/07/ben-carson-uncorks-on-whats-wrong-with-america/.

118. Jacob Laksin, "The Church of the Latter-Day Leftists," *FrontPage Magazine*, January 13, 2005, http://archive.frontpagemag.com/readArticle.aspx?ARTID=9938.

119. Lisa Cherry, "'Noah' Controversy: It's Not about the Movie," WND, April 6, 2014, http://www.wnd.com/2014/04/noah-controversy-its-not-about-the-movie/.

120. Susan Stamper Brown, "Who's Responsible for The Moral Decline?" *Standard Examiner*, June 7, 2015, http://www.standard.net/National-Commentary/2015/06/07/Who-s-responsible-for-the-moral-decline.

121. Marc Bennetts, "Who's 'Godless' Now? Russia Says It's U.S.," *Washington Times*, January 28, 2014, http://www.washingtontimes.com/news/2014/jan/28/whos-godless-now-russia-says-its-us/.

122. T.W. Shannon, "Chapel for Founder, History, Faith, and Freedom," *Tulsa World* Editorial Page," November 26, 2013.

123. Major Family-Related UN Documents, Including Reservations, "Key Family Provisons: Beijing + 5, 60," Family Policy Center, accessed January 26, 2017, http://www.familypolicycenter.org/id35. html.

124. Terence P. Jeffrey, "36% of Generation Starting to Turn 21 This Year Born to Unmarried Mothers," cnsnews.com, September 3, 2014, http://www.cnsnews.com/commentary/terence-p-jeffrey/36-generation-starting-turn-21-year-born-unmarried-mothers.

125. Robert J. Samuelson, "Nation Also Suffering from Family Deficit," *Tulsa World,* "Editor's Page," November 6, 2014, http://www.tulsaworld.com/nation-also-suffering-from-family-deficit/article_01cfe031-a6fa-5beb-ab92-5965a0b359f0.html.

126. Jerry Newcombe, "Tracing the Marxist Roots of The Assault on The Family," *Christian Post,* June 17, 2015, http://www.christianpost.com/news/tracing-the-marxist-roots-of-the-assault-on-the-family-140484/.

127. "The Unbreakable Katy Perry: Inside Rolling Stone's New Issue," *Rolling Stone* website, July 30, 2014, http://www.rollingstone.com/music/news/the-unbreakable-katy-perry-inside-rolling-stones-new-issue-20140730.

128. Valerie Solanas, SCUM Manifesto (Paris: Olympia Press, 1967).

129. "Sex, Society, and the Female Dilemma," *Saturday Review*, June 14, 1975.

130. Kelly Riddell, "Children of the State: Hillary Thinks You're So Deplorable the Government Should Raise Your Children," *Washington Times*, September 15, 2016, http://www.washingtontimes.com/news/2016/sep/15/hillary-clinton-believes-state-can-raise-children-/.

131. Katherine Connell, "How to Consciously Uncouple," *National Review*, March 26, 2014, http://www.nationalreview.com/article/374291/how-consciously-uncouple-katherine-connell.

132. Paul Rampell," A High Divorce Rate Means It's Time to Try 'Wedleases,'" *Washington Post*, August 4, 2013, https://www.washingtonpost.com/opinions/a-high-divorce-rate-means-its-time-to-try-wedleases/2013/08/04/f2221c1c-f89e-11e2-b018-5b8251f0c56e_story.html?utm_term=.cb093f66696e.

133. D. A. Wolf, "5 Benefits of Having a Friend With Benefits," *Huffington Post*, March 17, 2014, http://www.huffingtonpost.com/2014/03/17/friends-with-benefits-_n_4944757.html.

134. David Kupelian, "America: Land of 1,000 Addictions," *WND,* June 29, 2014, http://www.wnd.com/2014/06/america-land-of-1000-addictions/.

135. Molly Young, "He & He & He," *New York* magazine, July 29, 2012, http://nymag.com/news/features/sex/2012/benny-morecock-throuple/.

136. Angi Becker Stevens, "My Two Husbands," *Salon*, August 4, 2013, http://www.salon.com/2013/08/05/my_two_husbands/.

137. Mark Oppenheimer, "Married, with Infidelities," *New York Times*, June 30, 2011, http://www.nytimes.com/2011/07/03/magazine/infidelity-will-keep-us-together.html.

138. Jacob Appel, "Legalize Prostitution, Polygamy, Bestiality and Incest" (video and transcript), Big Think, accessed January 26, 2017, http://bigthink.com/videos/legalize-prostitution-polygamy-bestiality-and-incest.

139. Molly Wharton, "Australian Judge Says Incest Is No Longer Taboo," *The Corner* (blog), July 11, 2014, http://www.nationalreview.com/corner/382543/australian-judge-says-incest-no-longer-taboo-molly-wharton.

140. Jon Henley, "Paedophila: Bringing Dark Desires to Light," *Guardian* (UK), January 3, 2013, https://www.theguardian.com/society/2013/jan/03/paedophilia-bringing-dark-desires-light.

141. Matt Barber, "Sexual Anarchy," Townhall, September 3, 2011, http://townhall.com/columnists/mattbarber/2011/09/03/sexual_anarchy.

142. Urvashi Vaid et al., " What's Next for the LGBT Movement?" *Nation*, June 27, 2013, https://www.thenation.com/article/whats-next-lgbt-movement/.

143. "The Tragedy of Fatherless Homes," accessed February 3, 2017, http://cog-onlinestudy.com/World_Tomorrow/Tragedy%20Of%20Fatherless%20Homes.htm.

144. Jeffrey, "36% of Generation Turning 21 This Year Born to Unmarried Mothers."

145. Father Absence + Involvement | Statistics, © 2016 National Fatherhood Statistics, accessed January 27, 2017, http://www.fatherhood.org/fatherhood-data-statistics.

146. William Tucker, *Marriage and Civilization: How Monogamy Made Us Human* (Washington, DC: Regnery: 2014), 232.

147. Ibid., 230.

148. Dewey Cornell et al., "Characteristics of Adolescents Charged with Homicide," *Behavioral Sciences and the Law* 5 (1987): 11–23.

149. Charles Krauthammer, *Things That Matter* (New York: Crown Forum, 2013), 137–138.

150. See Jessica Gavora, "Opinions: Obama's 'Julia' Ad and the New Hubby State," *Washington Post*, May 11, 2012, https://www.washingtonpost.com/opinions/obamas-julia-ad-and-the-new-hubby-state/2012/05/11/gIQAcRdoIU_story.html?utm_term=.e937ea5dbcdf.

151. *Tulsa World. Scene,* "Movie Review: *300: Rise of An Empire,*" March 7, 2014, http://www.tulsaworld.com/scene/moviereviews/review-rise-of-an-empire/article_3109b4c2-e322-56c4-8457-2287e24e4b8a.html.

152. United Nations Human Rights Office of the High Commissioner, "Every Woman's Right to Water, Sanitation and Hygiene," OHCHR website, March 14, 2014, http://www.ohchr.org/EN/NewsEvents/Pages/Everywomansrighttowatersanitationandhygiene.aspx#sthash.JmJF5XYg.dpuf.

153. Mark Steyn, *After America* (Washington, DC: Regnery, 2011), 175.

154. Christin Scarlett Milloy, "Don't Let the Doctor Do This to Your Newborn," *Outward* (blog), June 26, 2014, http://www.slate.com/blogs/outward/2014/06/26/infant_gender_assignment_unnecessary_and_potentially_harmful.html.

155. Rush Limbaugh, *The Limbaugh Letter,* November 2013.

156. Chuck Ross, "Boy Admonished for Playing This Popular Childhood Game," *Daily Caller,* June 13, 2014, http://dailycaller.com/2014/06/13/boy-admonished-for-playing-this-popular-childhood-game/.

157. Zach Noble, "'The Most Unsafe of All the Playground Equipment': Schools in One Town Are Nixing an Iconic Childhood Activity," TheBlaze, October 4, 2014, http://www.theblaze.com/news/2014/10/04/the-most-unsafe-of-all-the-playground-equipment-schools-in-one-town-are-nixing-an-iconic-childhood-activity/.

158. See Katherine Timpf, "Boy Scouts Ban Water-Gun Fights Because Squirt Guns Are 'Simulated Firearms,'" *National Review*, May 19, 2015, http://www.nationalreview.com/article/418635/boy-scouts-ban-water-gun-fights-because-squirt-guns-are-simulated-firearms-katherine.

159. Marilynn Marchione, "Study: Kids Running Slower," *Associated Press,* November 20, 2003.

160. Michael Goodwin, "Mourning the Loss of Freedom to Fail," Fox News, July 13, 2010, http://www.foxnews.com/opinion/2010/07/13/michael-goodwin-wall-street-big-fail-lehman-depression-new-york-city-education.html.

161. Rebecca "Burt" Rose, "Nebraska School Gives Most Idiotic Advice Ever to Deal with Bullies," *Jezebel* (blog), April 16, 2014, http://jezebel.com/nebraska-school-gives-most-idiotic-advice-ever-to-deal-1564016234?utm_campaign=socialfow_jezebel_twitter&utm_source=jezebel_twitter&utm_medium=socialflow.

NOTES

162. Matt Vespa, "Insanity: The Word 'Man' Is Banned at Princeton University," Townhall, August 20, 2016, http://townhall.com/tipsheet/mattvespa/2016/08/20/insanity-the-word-man-is-banned-at-princeton-n2207565.

163. H. G. Wells, *The Time Machine* (New York: Henry Holt, 1895), chap. 5.

164. Bob Unruh, "Activist Judges Push 'Gay Marriage,'" *WND,* October 14, 2013, http://www.wnd.com/2014/07/gay-marriage-push-driven-by-activist-judges/.

165. Bob Unruh, "Ex-Surgeon General Promoting Transsexuals in Military," WND, March 13. 2014, http://www.wnd.com/2014/03/joycelyn-elders-promoting-transsexuals-in-military/.

166. Andrea L. Roberts, M. Maria Glymour, and Karestan C. Koenen, "Does Maltreatment in Childhood Affect Sexual Orientation in Adulthood?" *Archives of Sexual Behavior* 42, no. 2 (February 2013): 161–171, doi 10.1007/s10508-012-0021-9.

167. Bob Unruh, "Winning 'Gay' Battles May Come at Incredible Cost—the Supreme Court," WND, December 10, 2016, http://www.wnd.com/2016/12/winning-gay-battles-may-come-at-incredible-cost-the-supreme-court/#m7B6WaSc6xE6VTIY.99.

168. Gregory a. Freeman, "Bug Chasers: The Men Who Long to be HIV+," *Rolling Stone*, February 6, 2013, online at https://www.scribd.com/document/88696440/Bug-Chasers.

169. Belinda Robinson, "'I'm Gay. And I Want My Kid to Be Gay Too': Lesbian CNN Pundit Admits She Does Not Want Her Daughter, 6, to Be Straight and Is 'Disappointed' That She Is Already 'Boy Crazy,'" *Daily Beast*, February 22, 2015, http://www.dailymail.co.uk/news/article-2964063/Gay-mom-says-gay-want-daughter-gay-too.html.

170. Jack Minor, "Doc Faces Boot for Citing 'Gay Health Dangers,'" WND, June 27, 2015, http://www.wnd.com/2015/06/doc-faces-boot-for-citing-gay-health-dangers/.

171. Walter Williams, "Things I Don't Understand," *(Hernando, MS) DeSoto Times-Tribune*, December 23, 2016, http://www.desototimes.com/opinion/columns_editorials/things-i-don-t-understand/article_05ca75d0-c94c-11e6-99a5-7f7199203992.html.

172. Michael W. Chapman, "Johns Hopkins Psychiatrist: Transgender Is 'Mental Disorder;' Sex Change 'Biologically Impossible,'" cnsnews.com, June 2, 2015, http://www.cnsnews.com/news/article/michael-w-chapman/johns-hopkins-psychiatrist-transgender-mental-disorder-sex-change.

173. Clara Moskowitz, "High Suicide Risk, Prejudice Plague Transgender People," *Live Science,* November 19, 2010, http://www.livescience.com/11208-high-suicide-risk-prejudice-plague-transgender-people.html.

174. Mona Charen, "Our Crazed Sexuality Standards," *National Review*, January 14, 2014, http://www.nationalreview.com/article/368337/our-crazed-sexuality-standards-mona-charen.

175. Michael Savage, *The Enemy Within* (Washington DC: WND Books, 2003), 127–128.

176. Henry Makow, "How America Went Gay," HenryMakow.com, February 8, 2014, https://www.henrymakow.com/2014/02/how-america-went-gay.html.

177. Justin Wm. Moyer, "Why Some Critics Don't Think Caitlyn Jenner Deserved the Arthur Ashe Courage Award," *Washington Post*, July 16, 2015, https://www.washingtonpost.com/news/morning-mix/wp/2015/07/16/why-some-critics-dont-think-caitlyn-jenner-deserved-the-arthur-ashe-courage-award/?utm_term=.7d615ef9ecd7.

178. Robert Gehl, "Teachers Ordered To Call Students 'Purple Penguins,' not 'boys and girls'," Downtrend.com, October 9, 2014, http://downtrend.com/robertgehl/teachers-ordered-to-call-students-purple-penguins-not-boys-and-girls.

179. Alex Newman, "Schools Propose: Let Boys Into Girls Locker Rooms," WND, November 11, 2014, https://www.google.com/url?sa=t&rct=j&q=&esrc=s&source=web&cd=1&ved=0ahUKEwjh6POD7-zSAhUf3YMKHX5DC8wQFggaMAA&url=http%3A%2F%2Fwww.wnd.com%2F2014%2F11%2Fschools-propose-let-boys-into-girls-locker-rooms%2F&usg=AFQjCNEU9htwwFZaFQA_xmOIeXael_Detg&sig2=2TJtj_sFx7lv0jvakHo_LA&bvm=bv.150475504,d.amc&cad=rja.

180. Admission of Transgender Students, Mount Holyoke website, accessed January 30, 2017, https://www.mtholyoke.edu/policies/admission-transgender-students.

181. Jonah Goldberg, "China Syndrome Liberalism," *National Review*, January 31, 2016, http://www.nationalreview.com/g-file/413087/china-syndrome-liberalism-jonah-goldberg.

182. Makow, "How America Went Gay."

183. Bob Unruh, "'Gay' National Monuments to Rewrite America's History," WND, May 29, 2014, http://www.wnd.com/2014/05/gay-national-monuments-to-rewrite-americas-history/.

184. "Protect your children from 'Harvey Milk Gay Day,'" SaveCalifornia.com, accessed January 30, 2017, http://savecalifornia.com/harvey-milk-day.html.

185. ICRA, "Myths and Facts about Homosexuality," TrueNews.org, accessed January 30, 2017, http://www.truenews.org/Homosexuality/homosexual_myths_and_facts.html.

186. Peter Kurth, "The Trouble with Normal' by Michael Warner" (12/08/99), *Salon*, Letters to the Editor, December 15, 1999, http://www.salon.com/1999/12/15/sullivan/.

187. FoxNews.com, "Carrie Prejean Says Answer to Gay Marriage Question Cost Her Miss USA Crown," Fox News, April 20, 2009, http://www.foxnews.com/story/2009/04/20/carrie-prejean-says-answer-to-gay-marriage-question-cost-her-miss-usa-crown.html.

188. Ethan Thomas, "25 Questions About Michael Sam, the NFL and Homophobia," *The Blog*, May 16, 2014, http://www.huffingtonpost.com/etan-thomas/25-qsts-about-michael-sam_b_5336486.html.

189. David Limbaugh, "Political Correctness Doesn't Only Threaten Speech," *Townhall.com,* September 16, 2016, https://townhall.com/columnists/davidlimbaugh/2016/09/16/political-correctness-doesnt-only-threaten-speech-n2218651.

190. Scott Lively, "An Open Letter to Christian Leaders in America," BarbWire, August 20, 2014, http://barbwire.com/2014/08/20/open-letter-christian-leaders-america/.

191. "Not Just Another Sin" (brochure) Defend the Family International, Scott Lively.com, accessed January 31, 2017, http://www.scottlively.net/wp-content/uploads/2014/08/NJAS-brochure-Final_print.pdf.

192. Rush Limbaugh, "The Left Goes Totalitarian," *The Limbaugh Letter,* August 2015.

193. LifeSiteNews.com, "Court Orders Christian Mother to Not Expose Her Child to 'Homophobic' Religious Upbringing," LifeSite, October 30, 2003, https://www.lifesitenews.com/news/court-orders-christian-mother-to-not-expose-her-child-to-homophobic-religio.

194. See Human Rights First, "International Human Rights Defense Act," accessed January 31, 2017, http://www.humanrightsfirst.org/sites/default/files/IHRDA-Final-One-pager.pdf.

195. Bob Unruh, "Criticize 'Gays,' Get Sued for 'Crime Against Humanity,'" WND, April 19, 2014, http://www.wnd.com/2014/04/criticize-gays-get-sued-for-crime-against-humanity/.

196. Ted Lapkin, "Weakening the ADF in the Name of Equality," ABC (AU), June 29, 2011, http://www.abc.net.au/news/2011-06-29/lapkin---weakning-the-adf-in-the-name-of-equality/2776294.

197. Madeline Morris, "By Force of Arms: Rape, War and Military Culture," *Duke Law Journal* 45 (1996): 653, quoted in David W. Lutz, "Unit Cohesion and Organizational Change" (presentation at the Joint Services Conference on Professional Ethics XX, National Defense University, Fort McNair, WA), January 29–30, 1998, http://isme.tamu.edu/JSCOPE98/LUTZ98.HTM.

198. Chris Johnson, "'Don't Ask, Don't Tell' Is Gone," *Washington Blade*, September 20, 2011, http://www.washingtonblade.com/2011/09/20/dont-ask-dont-tell-is-gone/.

199. Rowan Scarborough, "Pentagon Celebrates Gay Troops," *Washington Times*, June 25, 2013, http://www.washingtontimes.com/news/2013/jun/25/pentagon-celebrates-gay-troops/.

200. Ibid.

201. Ibid.

202. E. Michael Maloof, "'Purge Surge': Obama Fires Another Commander," WND, November 4, 2013, http://www.wnd.com/2013/11/purge-surge-obama-fires-another-commander/.

203. Travis J. Tritten, "Gay, Lesbian Troops Perform in Drag at Kadena Air Base Fundraiser," *Stars & Stripes*, March 2, 2014, http://www.stripes.com/news/gay-lesbian-troops-perform-in-drag-at-kadena-air-base-fundraiser-1.270747.

204. Ibid.

205. John Milburn, "Soldier Convicted in WikiLeaks Case Gets New Name," Military.com, April 23, 2014, http://www.military.com/daily-news/2014/04/23/soldier-convicted-in-wikileaks-case-gets-new-name.html.

206. E. Michael Maloof, "Obama Building' Compliant Officer Class,'" WND, November 12, 2013, http://www.wnd.com/2013/11/obama-building-compliant-officer-class/.

207. "Boot Camp or Summer Camp?   Restoring Rigorous Standards to Basic Training," Heritage Foundation *Backgrounder #1147*, November 6, 1997, http://www.heritage.org/research/reports/1997/11/boot-camp-or-summer-camp.

208. Dave Philipps, "Raised-Fist Photo by Black Women at West Point Spurs Inquiry," *New York Times*, May 6, 2016, https://www.nytimes.com/2016/05/07/us/raised-fist-photo-by-black-women-at-west-point-spurs-inquiry.html?_r=0.

209. Brian Mitchell, *The Feminization of The American Military* (Washington, DC: Regnery, 1989), 5.

210. Ibid.

211. Greg Corombos, "Commander: 'Cowards Pushing Women into Combat," WND Radio, December 7, 2013, http://www.wnd.com/2013/12/commander-cowards-pushing-women-into-combat/.

212. Rowan Scarborough, "Israeli Women's Combat Roles Exaggerated, Military Traditionalists Say," *Washington Times*, May 25, 2015, http://www.washingtontimes.com/news/2015/may/25/womens-combat-roles-in-israel-defense-forces-exagg/.

213. NewMedia, "Army HUMILIATES Male Soldiers, Forces Them to Wear Women's Clothing as Part of Mandatory Training," UFP News, April 20, 2015, http://ufpnews.com/army-humiliates-male-soldiers-forces-them-to-wear-womens-clothing-as-part-of-training/.

214. Corombos, "Commander."

215. Robert L. MacGinnis, *Deadly Consequences: How Cowards are Pushing Women into Combat* (Washington, D.C.: Regnery, 2013).

216. "Women in the Military: More Military Jobs Can Be Opened Under Current Statutes," U.S. Government Accountability Office, Sep 7, 1988, http://www.gao.gov/products/NSIAD-88-222.

217. Greg Corombos, "Lady Marine: Huge Mistake to Put Women into Combat," WND, May 21, 2016, http://www.wnd.com/2016/05/lady-marine-huge-mistake-to-put-women-into-combat/.

218. Brian Mitchell, *Women In The Military* (Washington, DC: Regnery, 1998), 335.

219. Testimony of Col. John W. Ripley to the Presidential Commission on the Assignment of Women in the Armed Forces, June 26, 1992, posted on the website of the American Society for the Defense of Tradition, Family and Property, http://www.tfp.org/testimony-of-col-john-w-ripley-to-the-presidential-commission-on-the-assignment-of-women-in-the-armed-forces/.

220. Daniel J. Boorstin, *The Colonial Experience* (New York: Vintage, 1958), 331.

221. Peter Finn; Petra Couvee, *The Zhivago Affair* (New York: Pantheon, 2014).

222. Victor Davis Hanson, "The New Inquisition," Townhall, April 10, 2014, http://townhall.com/columnists/victordavishanson/2014/04/10/the-new-inquisition-n1821994.

223. Charles Krauthammer, "Thought Police on Patrol," *National Review*, April 10, 2014, http://www.nationalreview.com/article/375544/thought-police-patrol-charles-krauthammer.

224. Kelly Riddell, "Republicans' media bias claims boosted by scarcity of right-leaning journalists," *Washington Times*—Sunday, November 8, 2015, http://www.washingtontimes.com/news/2015/nov/8/republicans-media-bias-claims-boosted-by-scarcity-/.

225. Sandra Korn, "The Doctrine of Academic Freedom," *Harvard Crimson*, February 18, 2014, http://www.thecrimson.com/column/the-red-line/article/2014/2/18/academic-freedom-justice/?page=single.

226. Eddie Scarry, "CNN's Chris Cuomo: Hate speech 'Excluded from Protection' in Constitution," *Washington Examiner*, May 6, 2015, http://www.washingtonexaminer.com/cnns-chris-cuomo-hate-speech-excluded-from-protection-in-constitution/article/2564066.

227. Frederick M. Hess, "Lukewarm Column on 'Black Lives Matter' Sparks Demands for Reeducation," National Review, September 23, 2015, http://www.nationalreview.com/article/424483/lukewarm-column-black-lives-matter-sparks-demands-reeducation-frederick-m-hess.

228. Jim ONeill, "Soros: Republic Enemy #1," Canada Free Press, September 15, 2009, http://canadafreepress.com/article/soros-republic-enemy-1.

229. "BOMBSHELL: Francis 'Silenced' by CNBC for Criticizing ObamaCare," *Fox News Insider*, November 16, 2014, http://insider.foxnews.com/2014/11/16/bombshell-melissa-francis-says-she-was-silenced-cnbc-criticizing-obamacare.

230. "Hannity Takes on Dem Candidate Who Wants FCC to Regulate Fox News," *Fox News Insider*, February 25, 2014, http://insider.foxnews.com/2014/02/25/hannity-takes-democratic-congressional-candidate-mike-dickinson-who-wants-fcc-regulate.

231. Bob Unruh, "Obama 'Threatens Fox News Reporter's Career," WND, 22 January 2014, http://www.wnd.com/2014/01/fox-anchor-team-obama-threatened-benghazi-reporter/.

232. Sharyl Attkisson, *Stonewalled* (New York: Harper, 2014), 321.

233. Jerome R. Corsi, "Schindler's List' Producer: Obama Wants to 'Lock Up' Foes," WND, May 20, 2014, http://www.wnd.com/2014/05/critic-obama-thinks-political-opponents-are-enemies/.

234. Robert Zelnick, "Politics and the Fairness Doctrine," *Boston Globe*, March 7, 2009, http://archive.boston.com/bostonglobe/editorial_opinion/oped/articles/2009/03/07/politics_and_the_fairness_doctrine/.

235. Aaron Klein, "Big Chill: Feds Want to Screen Net, Media for 'Hate Speech'," WND, April 29, 2014, http://mobile.wnd.com/2014/04/big-chill-feds-want-to-scour-net-media-for-hate-speech/.

236. David A. Keene, "A License to Censor," *Washington Times*, April 7, 2014, http://www.washingtontimes.com/news/2014/mar/31/keene-a-license-to-censor/.

237. *The Western Center for Journalism*, "Obama Orders Radio Station to Stop Broadcasting Rush Limbaugh," April 1, 2015.

Chapter 7: Government Interventionism

1. Lois Lowery, *The Giver* (New York: Laurel-Leaf, 1993), 99.

2. C. S. Lewis, *God in the Dock*, repr. ed. (Grand Rapids: Eerdmans, 1972), 292.

3. Richard M. Ebeling, *Imprimis*, "The Free Market and The Interventionist State,' August 1997.

4. U.S. Senator Jesse Helms: *When Free Men Shall Stand* (Grand Rapids: Zondervan, 1976), 48.

5. "CNBC Transcript: CNBC Exclusive: CNBC Senior Economics Reporter Steve Liesman Interviews President Barack Obama Today, Thursday, July 24th at 5PM ET" (news release), CNBC, July 24, 2014, http://www.cnbc.com/2014/07/24/cnbc-transcript-cnbc-exclusive-cnbc-senior-economics-reporter-steve-liesman-interviews-president-barack-obama-today-thursday-july-24th-at-5pm-et.html.

6. "Redistribution: AUDIO: 1998 Recording Captures Obama Embracing 'Redistribution,'" Fox News, September 19, 2012, http://nation.foxnews.com/president-obama/2012/09/18/obama-n-1998-i-actually-believe-redistribution.

7. "Stephan Holmes & Cass R. Sunstein, Why We Should Celebrate Paying Taxes, in the *Chicago Tribune*, at 19 (April 14, 1999)," http://home.uchicago.edu/~csunstei/celebrate.html.

8. Robert Higgs, *Against Leviathan: Government Power and A Free Society* (Washington, DC: Independent Institute, 2004), 4.

9. Bertrand de Jouvenel, *On Power: The Natural History of Its Growth* (Indianapolis: Liberty Fund, 1993; original French edition 1945), 388–89.

10. Ben S. Carson, "A Plea For Constitutional Literacy on Constitution Day," *Washington Times,* September 22, 2014, http://www.washingtontimes.com/news/2014/sep/16/carson-a-plea-for-constitutional-literacy-on-const/.

11. Jonah Goldberg, "Government Is a Giant Twinkie We Apparently Can't Live Without," *New York Post*, November 8, 2013, http://nypost.com/2013/11/08/government-is-a-giant-twinkie-we-apparently-cant-live-without/.

12. Jon Marini, "Abandoning the Constitution," *CRB* 12, no. 2 (Spring 2012), http://www.claremont.org/crb/article/abandoning-the-constitution/.

13. Jonah Goldberg, "The Myth of Live-and-Let-Live Liberalism," *National Review*, September 11, 2013, http://www.nationalreview.com/article/358147/myth-live-and-let-live-liberalism-jonah-goldberg.

14. Brant Parker and Johnny Hart, *Wizard of Id* cartoon strip, reproduced in "Obama's Plans Refuted in 'Wizard of Id' Cartoon," on the Everyday Christian website, November 12, 2008, https://sanctification.wordpress.com/2008/11/12/obamas-plans-refuted-in-wizard-of-id-cartoon/.

15. Steve Straub, "Benjamin Franklin, On the Price of Corn and Management of the Poor, November 1766," the Federalist Papers Project, accessed February 3, 2017, http://thefederalistpapers.org/founders/franklin/benjamin-franklin-on-the-price-of-corn-and-management-of-the-poor-november-1766.

16. "David Crockett: Crockett on the Power to Make Charitable Donations," Constitution Society, accessed February 6, 2017, http://www.constitution.org/cons/crockett.htm.

17. *Mallard Fillmore*, image 103109, Cartoonistgroup.com, accessed February 6, 2017, http://cartoonistgroup.com/store/add.php?iid=103109.

18. Greg Corombos, "Obama Hatches Plan to Explode Welfare," *WND,* August 24, 2014, http://www.wnd.com/2014/08/obama-hatches-plan-to-explode-welfare/.

19. Terence Jeffrey, "The 35.4 Percent: 109,631,000 on Welfare," *Washington Examiner*, August 21, 2014, http://www.washingtonexaminer.com/the-35.4-percent-109631000-on-welfare/article/2552288.

20. Elizabeth Cook, "Editorial: Food Stamp Realities for Able-Bodied Adults," *Salisbury Post,* February 1, 2016, http://www.salisburypost.com/2016/02/04/editorial-food-stamp-realities-for-able-bodied-adults/.

21. Robert Rector, "Examining the Means-tested Welfare State: 79 Programs and $927 Billion in Annual Spending: Testimony before Committee on the Budget United States House of Representatives," Heritage House, April 17, 2012, http://budget.house.gov/uploadedfiles/rectortestimony04172012. pdf.

22. The Editorial Board, "Freeing Workers from the Insurance Trap," *New York Times*, February 4, 2014, https://www.nytimes.com/2014/02/05/opinion/freeing-workers-from-the-insurance-trap. html?_r=0.

23. Bridget Murphy, "Family Income Not a Factor as Students Eat Free," *Herald-Sun* (Durham, NC), September 9, 2013, http://www.heraldsun.com/lifestyles/family-income-not-a-factor-as-students-eat-free/article_6a7af8f4-156b-5556-b13d-cf954878102c.html.

24. Bill O'Reilly. *The O'Reilly Factor,* January 16, 2014.

25. Associated Press, "Bus Offers Showers for San Francisco Homeless," CBS News, July 20, 2014, http://www.cbsnews.com/news/bus-offers-showers-for-san-francisco-homeless/.

26. Michael Goodwin, "Obama Democrats' Troubling View on Work," *New York Post*, February 9, 2014, http://nypost.com/2014/02/09/obama-democrats-troubling-view-on-work/, emphasis added.

27. The Editors, "The CBO's Obamacare Scorecard," *National Review*, February 5, 2014, http://www. nationalreview.com/article/370367/cbos-obamacare-scorecard-editors.

28. "Remarks by the President on Economic Mobility," White House, Office of the Press Secretary, December 4, 2013, https://obamawhitehouse.archives.gov/the-press-office/2013/12/04/remarks-president-economic-mobility.

29. Dave Mikkelson, "Prosperity Disparity," Snopes.com, upd. August 8, 2016, http://www.snopes. com/quotes/lincoln/prosperity.asp; *Wikipedia*, s.v. "William J. H. Boetcker," accessed February 6, 2013, https://en.wikipedia.org/wiki/William_J._H._Boetcker.

30. Arnold Ahlert, "A Racist-Free Society?" *Patriot Post*, May 27, 2014, https://patriotpost.us/posts/26066.

31. "Poverty & Culture," *Free Republic,* September 7, 2006, http://www.freerepublic.com/focus/f-news/1697491/posts.

32. *Discoverthenetworks.org.* "Breakdown of the Black Family and its Consequences," Accessed, February22, 2017, http://www.discoverthenetworks.org/viewSubCategory.asp?id=1261.

33. "Black-Crime Explosion: 'America's Worst City" Revealed," WND, November 24, 2014, http:// www.wnd.com/2014/11/black-crime-explosion-americas-worst-city-revealed/.

34. Walter E. Williams, "Should Black People Tolerate This?," Townhall, May 23, 2012, http:// townhall.com/columnists/walterewilliams/2012/05/23/should_black_people_tolerate_this.

35. Charles W. Sasser, *Shoot to Kill: Cops Who Have Used Deadly Force* (New York: Pocket Books, 1994), 22.

36. Colin Stutz, "Ted Nugent Rails on Liberals, 'Thugs,' 'Welfare Crack' in Rightist Essay," *Billboard*, October 3, 2014, http://www.billboard.com/articles/news/6274050/ted-nugent-rails-on-liberals-thugs-welfare-crack-in-rightist-essay.

37. TPNN, "Liberal Nonsense: Dem Lawmaker Claims He's Ashamed to be White," TeaParty. org, September 29, 2014, http://www.teaparty.org/liberal-nonsense-dem-lawmaker-claims-hes-ashamed-white-58099/.

38. Charles W. Blow, "Paul Ryan, Culture and Poverty," *New York Times*, March 21, 2014, https:// www.nytimes.com/2014/03/22/opinion/blow-paul-ryan-culture-and-poverty.html.

39. Colin Flaherty, "'Lefty' Librarian Beaten to Pulp in Knockout Game," WND, December 3, 2013, http://www.wnd.com/2013/12/knockout-game-victim-i-no-longer-trust-blacks/.

40. Bob Unruh, "Black Mob Attacks Victims 'Like It Was a Game,'" WND, May 29, 2014, http://www.wnd.com/2014/05/black-teens-attack-victims-like-it-was-a-game/.
41. Colin Flaherty, "Black-on-White Beatings Leave More Dead," WND, September 23, 2013, http://www.wnd.com/2013/09/black-on-white-beatings-leave-3-more-dead/.
42. George F. Will, *Suddenly* (New York: The Free Press, 1990), 25–27.
43. Cara Buckley, "Police Unsure if Random Attacks Are Rising Threat or Urban Myth," *New York Times*, November 22, 2013, http://www.nytimes.com/2013/11/23/nyregion/knockout-game-a-spreading-menace-or-a-myth.html.
44. "D.C. Bans School Suspensions, Declaring Them Racist," editorial, *Investors' Business Daily*, July 17, 2014, http://www.investors.com/politics/editorials/district-of-columbia-bans-school-suspensions-citing-racism/.
45. Colin Flaherty, "Killer's Family to Victim's Kin: 'We Hate You,'" WND, February 8, 2014, http://www.wnd.com/2014/02/killers-family-to-victims-kin-we-hate-you/.
46. Ryan Lovelace, "Ferguson Protesters Erupt Outside Police Department: 'What Do We Want? Darren Wilson! How Do We Want Him? Dead!'" *The Corner* (blog), November 21, 2014, http://www.nationalreview.com/corner/393195/ferguson-protesters-erupt-outside-police-department-what-do-we-want-darren-wilson-how.
47. "Gov. Nixon Calls For 'Vigorous Prosecution' in Brown Shooting," *Fox News Insider*, August 19, 2014, http://insider.foxnews.com/2014/08/19/read-gov-nixon-calls-vigorous-prosecution-michael-brown-shooting.
48. Joseph Farah, "The Michael Brown Cult," WND, September 1, 2014, http://www.wnd.com/2014/09/the-michael-brown-cult/.
49. Jesse Lee Peterson, "What If White America Just Said 'No'?" WND, August 24, 2014, http://www.wnd.com/2014/08/what-if-white-america-just-said-no/.
50. "Roosevelt Bars the Unhyphenated," *New York Times*, October 13, 1915, http://query.nytimes.com/mem/archive-free/pdf?res=9901E0DD1239E333A25750C1A9669D946496D6CF.
51. Rush Limbaugh, "My Conversation With Victor Davis Hanson, historian," *The Limbaugh Letter,* October 2015.
52. Garth Kant, "Ticking Time Bomb to Explode on GOP," WND, December 30, 2014, http://www.wnd.com/2014/12/ticking-time-bomb-about-to-explode-on-gop/.
53. Douglas W. Elmendorf, Congressional Budget Office, "A Description of the Immigrant Population—2013 Update," report to Paul Ryan, May 8, 2013, https://www.cbo.gov/sites/default/files/113th-congress-2013-2014/reports/44134_Description_of_Immigrant_Population.pdf.
54. James H. Walsh, "Illegal Aliens: Counting the Uncountable," *Social Contract* 17, no. 4, accessed February 7, 2017, http://www.thesocialcontract.com/artman2/publish/tsc_17_4/tsc_17_4_walsh.shtml.
55. Patrick J. Buchanan, "America: Microcosm of A World on Fire," *Whistleblower,* August 2014.
56. Garth Kant, "Chris Matthews Admits: Dems Want Illegals for Votes," WND, July 8, 2015, http://www.wnd.com/2015/07/top-tv-host-admits-dems-want-illegals-for-votes/.
57. Caroline May, "Report: Immigrants Use $6,234 in Welfare Benefits per Household, 41 Percent More than Non-Immigrant Households," Breitbart, May 9, 2016, http://www.breitbart.com/big-government/2016/05/09/report-immigrant-use-6-2k-welfare-benefits-per-household-41-native-households/.
58. Ann Coulter, "A Bridge Too Far-Fetched," the Ann Coulter website, February 5, 2014, http://www.anncoulter.com/columns/2014-02-05.html.

59. FAIR (Federation for American Immigration Reform), "Legislative Update: 8/2/2016," FAIR, August 2, 2016, http://www.fairus.org/legislative-updates/legislative-update-8-2-2016.
60. Caroline May, "Illegal Immigrants Accounted for Nearly 37 Percent of Federal Sentences in FY 2014," Breitbart, July 7, 2015, http://www.breitbart.com/big-government/2015/07/07/illegal-immigrants-accounted-for-nearly-37-percent-of-federal-sentences-in-fy-2014/.
61. Aaron Klein, "FBI Data Backs Up Trump Claims on Illegals and Crime," Americans for Legal Immigration PAC, July 10, 2015, https://www.alipac.us/f12/fbi-data-backs-up-trump-claims-illegals-crime-321112/.
62. Stephen Dinan, "DHS Released Another 30,000 Criminal Aliens onto Streets," *Washington Times*, March 18, 2015, http://www.washingtontimes.com/news/2015/mar/18/dhs-released-another-30000-criminal-aliens-streets/.
63. Michael McCaul, "Chairman McCaul Opening Statement at Hearing on the Impact of Presidential Amnesty on Border Security," Homeland Security Committee, December 2, 2014, https://homeland.house.gov/press/chairman-mccaul-opening-statement-hearing-impact-presidential-amnesty-border-security/.
64. Joseph Farah, "Islam's Rapid, Bloody Empire Building," *Whistleblower,* October 2014.
65. William Kilpatrick, "The Big Picture: ISIS in Context," *FrontPageMag*, September 3, 2014, http://www.frontpagemag.com/fpm/240092/big-picture-isis-context-william-kilpatrick.
66. White House Office of the Press Secretary, "Statement by the President on the Occasion of Eid-al-Fitr" (press release), July 27, 2014, https://obamawhitehouse.archives.gov/the-press-office/2014/07/27/statement-president-occasion-eid-al-fitr; "Statement by the President on the Occasion of Ramadan" (press release), August 11, 2010, https://obamawhitehouse.archives.gov/the-press-office/2010/08/11/statement-president-occasion-ramadan.
67. Jim Hoft, "SHOCK POLL: 51% of US Muslims Want Sharia Law—25% Okay with Violence against Infidels," Gateway Pundit, September 22, 2015, http://www.thegatewaypundit.com/2015/09/shock-poll-51-of-muslims-want-sharia-law-25-okay-with-violence-against-infidels/.
68. "Center for Security Policy: Poll of U.S. Muslims Reveals Ominous Levels of Support for Islamic Supremacists' Doctrine of Shariah, Jihad" (press release). Center for Security Policy, June 23, 2015, http://www.centerforsecuritypolicy.org/2015/06/23/nationwide-poll-of-us-muslims-shows-thousands-support-shariah-jihad/.
69. "Muhammad Hisham Kabbani—Islamic Extremism: A Viable Threat to U.S. National Security, An Open Forum at the U.S. Department of State—Islamic Supreme Council of America (ISCA), January 7, 1999, cited on *WikiIslam*, s.v. "Muslim Statistics (Mosques)," accessed February 8, 2017, http://wikiislam.net/wiki/Muslim_Statistics_-_Mosques#cite_note-17.
70. Kilpatrick, "The Big Picture."
71. Barack Obama, "Remarks by the President to the UN General Assembly" (press release), White House Office of the Press Secretary, September 25, 2012, https://obamawhitehouse.archives.gov/the-press-office/2012/09/25/remarks-president-un-general-assembly.

Chapter 8: The Collective World
1. Jonah Goldberg, "Days of Future Past," *National Review*, October 2, 2014, http://www.nationalreview.com/article/388860/days-future-past-jonah-goldberg.
2. "Problems of War and Strategy" in *Selected Works of Mao Tse-tung*, vol. 2, 224, online at https://www.marxists.org/reference/archive/mao/selected-works/volume-2/mswv2_12.htm#p1.
3. Robert Spencer, "Geert Wilders: Speech in Berlin Yesterday," *Jihad Watch,* October 2, 2010, https://www.jihadwatch.org/2010/10/geert-wilders-speech-in-berlin-yesterday.

4. Adapted from "Fourteen Signposts to Slavery," by Warren Carroll and Mike Djordjevich, in Gary Allen, *None Dare Call It Conspiracy*, with Larry Abraham, repr. (n.p.: Dauphin, 2013), 106.

5. Leonard Peikoff, *The Ominous Parallels: The End of Freedom in America* (N.p.: Plume, 1983).

6. David Kupelian, "America: Land of 1,000 Addictions," WND, June 29, 2014, http://www.wnd.com/2014/06/america-land-of-1000-addictions/.

7. Robert Ringer, "Following in Rome's Footsteps," *Whistleblower,* June 2014.

8. Winston Churchill, speech in the House of Commons, October 22, 1945, http://hansard.millbanksystems.com/commons/1945/oct/22/demobilisation#S5CV0414P0_19451022_HOC_300.

9. Nien Cheng, *Life and Death in Shanghai* (New York: Penguin, 1988), 302.

10. Ann Coulter, *Treason* (New York: Crown, 2003), 239.

11. Kevin D. Williamson, *The Politically Incorrect Guide to Socialism* (Washington, DC: Regnery, 2011), 99.

12. Peter Collier; David Horowitz *Destructive Generation* (Charlottesville: Summit, 1989), 237.

13. Mike Shedlock, "The Downward Spiral of the Eurozone," *Townhall,* February 3, 2015, http://finance.townhall.com/columnists/mikeshedlock/2015/02/03/the-downward-spiral-of-the-eurozone-n1951971.

14. "The Conqueror," TV Tropes, accessed February 13, 2017, http://tvtropes.org/pmwiki/pmwiki.php/Main/TheConqueror.

15. *Stanford Encyclopedia of Philosophy: plato.stanford.edu/entries/world government.* "World Government," Revised July 2, 2012.

16. Gary Allen; Larry Abraham, *None Dare Call It Conspiracy* (Concord, NH: Concord Press, 1972), 122–123.

17. Quoted in Llewellyn B. Davis, *Going Home to Schools*, rev. ed. (N.p.: Elijah Co., 1991), 69.

18. United Nations, 3201 (S-VI). Declaration on the Establishment of a New International Economic Order, May 1, 1974, http://www.un-documents.net/s6r3201.htm.

19. Pat Robertson, *The New World Order* (Tusla: World Publishing, 1991), 168.

20. See Revelation 13.

21. Jordan Candler, "Pouring Cold Water on 'Hottest Year Ever'," *Patriot Post*, December 18, 2014, https://patriotpost.us/articles/31844.

22. Lord Monckton, "1 Year from Now, Freedom Dies Worldwide," WND, December 14, 2014, http://www.wnd.com/2014/12/1-year-from-now-freedom-dies-worldwide/.

23. "George F. Will: As the Oceans Rise," *Newsweek*, June 7, 2008, http://www.newsweek.com/george-f-will-oceans-rise-90915.

24. Leo Hohmann, "Obama's U.N. Plan: Globalize Cops against 'Violent Extremists'," WND, October 6, 2015, http://www.wnd.com/2015/10/obamas-u-n-plan-globalize-cops-against-violent-extremists/.

25. Ibid.

26. Jerome R. Corsi, "Wikileaks Reveals Secret Trans-Pacific Trade Deal," WND, November 15, 2013.

Chapter 9: The Decline

1. Major Euell White, U.S. Army (retired), "Why Has Our Position on Communism changed?" *Military,* April 2014, http://www.euelltwhite.info/ComCh.pdf.

2. Thomas Sowell, "Ignoring Facts and Attacking Character," *National Review*, January 14, 2014, http://www.nationalreview.com/article/369184/ignoring-facts-and-attacking-character-thomas-sowell.

3. Based on Obama's statement on October 30, 2008, when he said, ""We are five days away from fundamentally transforming the United States of America," quoted in Victor Davis Hanson, "Obama: Transforming America," National Review, October 1, 2013, http://www.nationalreview. com/article/359967/obama-transforming-america-victor-davis-hanson.

4. Cheryl K. Chumley, "Barbara Walters Admits 'We' Thought Obama Was 'the Next Messiah'," Washington Times, December 18, 2013, http://www.washingtontimes.com/news/2013/dec/18/ barbara-walters-admits-we-thought-obama-was-next-m/.

5. Paul Bedard, "Newsweek: Obama Is 'The Second Coming'," Washington Examiner, January 19, 2013, http://www.washingtonexaminer.com/newsweek-obama-is-the-second-coming/ article/2519111. This article links to the Newsweek cover image, at http://contentviewer.adobe. com/s/Newsweek/c5cabc60bd7a45d4a6b493fc0ba1ffcf/com.newsweek.20130118/00_cover_03. html.

6. "Chris Matthews: "I Felt This Thrill Going Up My Leg" As Obama Spoke," Huffington Post, upd. May 25, 2011, http://www.huffingtonpost.com/2008/02/13/chris-matthews-i-felt-thi_n_86449. html.

7. Darlene Superville, "Gwyneth Paltrow: 'Would Be Wonderful' to Give Obama 'All the Power He Needs'," cnsnews.com, October 9, 2014, http://www.cnsnews.com/news/article/gwyneth-paltrow-would-be-wonderful-give-obama-all-power-he-needs.

8. Nicholas Kristof, "Obama: Man of the World," New York Times, March 6, 2007, http://www. nytimes.com/2007/03/06/opinion/06kristof.html.

9. Barack Obama, Dreams from My Father (N.p.: Broadway Books, 2004), 100–1.

10. Cliff Kincaid, "Obama's Communist Mentor," Accuracy in Media, February 18, 2008, https:// www.aim.org/aim-column/obamas-communist-mentor/.

11. David Horowitz, "The Threat We Face," FrontPage Mag, October 9, 2013, http://www. frontpagemag.com/fpm/206712/threat-we-face-david-horowitz.

12. H. L. Mencken, On Politics: A Carnival of Buncombe (Baltimore and London: John Hopkins University Pres, 1996), 21.

13. "The Root of Obama's Anti-Americanism," Patriot Post, April 1, 2014, https://patriotpost.us/ posts/24511.

14. Saul Alinsky, Rules for Radicals: A Practical Primer for Realistic Radicals (New York: Vintage, 1989), ix.

15. Beth Fouhy, "Obama Addresses Question of Experience," Washington Post, April 21, 2007, http:// www.washingtonpost.com/wp-dyn/content/article/2007/04/21/AR2007042100650.html.

16. Saul D. Alinsky, Rules for Radicals (New York: Vintage Books, 1989).

17. David Horowitz, "The Threat We Face."

18. Alinsky, Rules for Radicals, xxi–xxii, xix.

19. Frances Fox Piven and Richard A. Cloward, "The Weight of the Poor: A Strategy to End Poverty," Nation, May 2, 1966, http://www.commondreams.org/news/2010/03/24/weight-poor-strategy-end-poverty.

20. "Collapsing the System . . . on Purpose," Right Side News, August 11, 2011, http://www. rightsidenews.com/us/politics/collapsing-the-system-on-purpose/.

21. Sol Stern, "ACORN's Nutty Regime for Cities," City Journal, Spring 2003, https://www.city-journal.org/html/acorn%E2%80%99s-nutty-regime-cities-12414.html.

22. James Simpson, "Barack Obama and The Strategy of Manufactured Crisis," American Thinker, September 28, 2008, http://www.americanthinker.com/articles/2008/09/barack_obama_and_ the_strategy.html.

23. Quoted in Jim ONeill, "Soros: Republic Enemy #1," Canada Free Press, September 15, 2009, http://canadafreepress.com/article/soros-republic-enemy-1.

24. Erica Ritz, "Glenn Beck 'Horrified' by 'America's Latest Propaganda Machine,'" TheBlaze, October 17, 2013, http://www.theblaze.com/news/2013/10/17/glenn-beck-horrified-by-americas-latest-propaganda-machine/.

25. Ann Coulter, Guilty: Liberal "Victims" and Their Assault on America (New York: Crown, 2009), 237.

26. Horowitz, "The Threat We Face."

27. Aaron Klein, "Obama Quotes Alinsky in Speech to Young Israelis," WND, March 21, 2013, http://www.wnd.com/2013/03/obama-quotes-alinsky-in-speech-to-young-israelis/.

28. Dinitia Smith, "No Regrets for a Love of Explosives; In a Memoir of Sorts, a War Protester Talks of Life with the Weathermen," New York Times, September 11, 2001, http://www.nytimes.com/2001/09/11/books/no-regrets-for-love-explosives-memoir-sorts-war-protester-talks-life-with.html.

29. Art Moore, "Bama Friend Tried to Overthrow U.S. Government," WND, July 1, 2014, http://www.wnd.com/2014/07/obama-pal-admits-being-revolutionary-communist/.

30. Kathy Jessup, "Still Radical, Now Influential," Townhall, March 2012.

31. John W. Fountain, "Northwestern Alumni to End Donations if Ex-Radical Stays," New York Times, November 4, 2001, http://www.nytimes.com/2001/11/04/us/northwestern-alumni-to-end-donations-if-ex-radical-stays.html.

32. Andrew C. McCarthy, "Bill Ayers: Unrepentant LYING Terrorist," The Corner (blog), August 27, 2008, http://www.nationalreview.com/corner/167989/bill-ayers-unrepentant-lying-terrorist-andrew-c-mccarthy.

33. David Brooks, "The Nudge Debate," New York Times, August 8, 2013, http://www.nytimes.com/2013/08/09/opinion/brooks-the-nudge-debate.html.

34. James Walsh, "Obama, Voter Fraud & Mortgage Meltdown," NewsMax, September 22, 2008, http://www.newsmax.com/Politics/obama-voter-fraud/2008/09/22/id/325456/.

35. "Rahm Emanuel on the Opportunities of Crisis," YouTube video, 2:47, "Rahm Emanuel, chief of staff for president-elect Barack Obama, outlines the opportunities for bipartisan reform that he says the financial crisis presents at the Wall Street Journal CEO Council in Washington, D.C.," posted by the Wall Street Journal, November 19, 2008, https://www.youtube.com/watch?v=_mzcbXi1Tkk.

36. "Rush Limbaugh in See, I Told You So," OntheIssues.org, accessed February 14, 2017, http://www.ontheissues.org/Archive/Told_You_So_Rush_Limbaugh.htm.

37. Michael Knox Beran, "A Cautionary Election Note," City Journal, November 3, 2010, https://www.city-journal.org/html/cautionary-election-note-10778.html.

38. See Brad Hamilton, "Kerry's Ketchup Queen; Heiress Adds Sauce to Husband's Campaign," New York Post, February 1, 2004, http://nypost.com/2004/02/01/kerrys-ketchup-queen-heiress-adds-sauce-to-hubbys-campaign/.

39. John Podesta, in Center for American Progress Staff and Senior Fellows, The Power of the President: Recommendations to Advance Progressive Change, comp. Sarah Rosen Wartell (Center for American Progress, November 2010), ix, for example.

40. STORM members, Reclaiming Revolution: History, Summation and Lessons from the Work of Standing Together to Organize a Revolutionary Movement (STORM) (Spring 2004), http://webpages.charter.net/westerfunk/STORMSummation.pdf, 51.

41. Patricia Sullivan, "Sally Lilienthal, 87; Created Peace Fund," Washington Post, October 27, 2006, http://www.washingtonpost.com/wp-dyn/content/article/2006/10/26/AR2006102601603.html.

42. Rashmi Kanti, "Ploughshares Funds to the Organisations Working for Nuclear Weapons-Free World," FundsforNGOs, March 26, 2015, https://www.fundsforngos.org/peace-conflict-resolution/ploughshares-funds-to-the-organisations-working-for-nuclear-weapons-free-world/.

43. David Freddoso, *The Case Against Baack Obama* (Washginton, DC: Regnery, 2008), 138.

44. Gretchen Randall and Tom Randall, "The Tides Foundation: Liberal Crossroads of Money and Ideas," *Foundation Watch*, December 2003, http://www.winningreen.com/site/files/621/41804/163246/225444/Tides_Foundation.pdf, 1.

45. Seton Motley, "SCOTUS Nominee Kagan for 'Redistribution of Speech' (Diversity Czar Lloyd Must be Thrilled)," mrc NewsBusters, May 12, 2010, http://www.newsbusters.org/blogs/nb/seton-motley/2010/05/12/scotus-nominee-kagan-redistribution-speech-diversity-czar-lloyd.

46. Gina Miller, "Obama Impeachment Fear: Nationwide 'Ferguson'?" RenewAmerica, November 19, 2014, http://www.renewamerica.com/columns/miller/141119.

47. Alex Newman, "Top U.S. Communist Boasts That Party 'Utilizes' Democrats," *New American*, January 28, 2015, https://www.thenewamerican.com/usnews/politics/item/19997-top-u-s-communist-boasts-that-party-utilizes-democrats.

48. Ibid.

49. Ibid.

50. PDA website, accessed February 14, 2017, http://pdamerica.org/about-pda/.

51. Earl Ofari Hutchinson, "Progressive House Democrat Co-Chair Vows Democrats Won't Roll Over to the GOP," *Huffington Post: The Blog*, upd. May 25, 2011, http://www.huffingtonpost.com/earl-ofari-hutchinson/progressive-house-democra_b_783414.html.

52. Christian Gomez, "Leon Panetta and the Institute for Policy Studies<" *New American*, June 11, 2011, https://www.thenewamerican.com/usnews/congress/item/2354-leon-panetta-and-the-institute-for-policy-studies.

53. Pat Robertson, *The New World Order* (Tulsa: Word Publishing, 1991), 141–142.

54. Michael Savage, *The Savage Nation radio program,* November 24, 2008.

55. Ibid.

56. "Al Gore: Climate Change Deniers Should Pay 'A Price,'" *Newsmax,* March 16, 2015, http://www.newsmax.com/Newsfront/gore-climate-change-deniers/2015/03/16/id/630426/.

57. Marc Morano, "Update: Video: Robert F. Kennedy Jr. Wants to Jail His Political Opponents—Accuses Koch Brothers of 'Treason'—'They Ought to Be Serving Time for It'," Climate Depot, September 21, 2014, http://www.climatedepot.com/2014/09/21/robert-f-kennedy-jr-wants-to-jail-his-political-opponents-accuses-koch-brothers-of-treason-they-ought-to-be-serving-time-for-it/.

58. Daniel Greenfield, "Progressive Professor Demands Death Penalty for Global Warming Skeptics and the Pope," *FrontPage Mag*, December 25, 2012, http://www.frontpagemag.com/point/170948/progressive-professor-demands-death-penalty-global-daniel-greenfield.

59. Alexis de Tocqueville, *Democracy in America and Two Essays on America*, trans. Gerald E. Bevan, 13th printing (London and New York: Penguin Classics, 2003), 537.

60. Jon Clifton, "Americans Less Satisfied with Freedom," Gallup, July 1, 2014, http://www.gallup.com/poll/172019/americans-less-satisfied-freedom.aspx.

61. Mike Lillis, "Polls," *The Hill*, October 24, 2011, http://thehill.com/polls/189273-the-hill-poll-most-voters-say-the-us-is-in-decline.

62. Justin William Moyer, "Gloomy Don McLean Reveals Meaning of 'American Pie'—and Sells Lyrics for $1.2 Million," *Washington Post*, April 8, 2015, https://www.washingtonpost.com/news/morning-mix/wp/2015/04/08/gloomy-don-mclean-reveals-meaning-of-american-pie-and-sells-lyrics-for-1-2-million/?utm_term=.b43430825a56.

63. Don McLean, "American Pie," in *American Pie*, United Artists Records, 1971, vinyl, quoted in ibid. (as transcribed by azlyrics.com).

64. Jim Nelson Black, *When Nations Die* (Carol Stream, Ill.: Tyndale, 1994), 16.

65. Erica Ritz, "The Horrific Story That Prompted David Horowitz's Conservative Transformation," TheBlaze, December 3, 2013, http://www.theblaze.com/news/2013/12/03/the-horrific-story-that-prompted-david-horowitz-conservative-transformation/.

66. Thomas Sowell, "Freedom Is Not Free," *Spectator*, March 4, 2014, https://spectator.org/57985_freedom-not-free/.

67. Alice Russie, "Commentary," *Military*, October 2014.

68. Michael Savage, *Trickle Down Tyranny: Crushing Obama's Dream of the Socialist States of America* (New York: William Morrow, 2012), 61.

69. Barret Moore, "War and Chaos Ahead: How Mega-Rich are Preparing," *NC Renegade*, March 21, 2015, http://ncrenegade.com/editorial/war-and-chaos-ahead-how-mega-rich-are-preparing/.

70. Rush Limbaugh, "Interview with Mark Steyn," *The Limbaugh Letter*, November 2014

71. David Kupelian, "Messiahs False and True," WND, December 23, 2014, http://www.wnd.com/2014/12/messiahs-false-and-true/.

72. Patrick J. Buchanan, *Suicide of a Superpower: Will America Survive to 2025?* (New York: Thomas Dunne, 2011), front matter.

73. Mark R. Levin, *Ameritopia: The Unmaking of America*, repr. ed. (New York: Threshold Editions, 2012), 246.

74. Leo Hohmann, "Holocaust Survivor Booted from Public Schools," WND, January 29, 2015, http://www.wnd.com/2015/01/holocaust-survivor-booted-from-public-schools/.

75. Lord Byron, *Childe Harold's Pilgrimage* (n.p.: CreateSpace, 2009), canto 4, st. 108.

INDEX

Hegel, Georg, 8. 13, 16
Heinz, Teresa, 252, 254
Henry, Patrick, 49
Herbert, David, 44
high schoolers, number who are
    ambivalent about the First
    Amendment, 122
Hispanics, percent who view capitalism
    negatively, prefer bigger
    government, 216
Hiss, Donald, 75, 76
Hiss, Alger, 75, 76, 78, 79, 80, 97, 128,
    259
History of the United States, A (high
    school text), 82
Hitchcock, James (author, *The Pope
    and the Jesuits*), 89
Hitler, Adolf, 6, 7, 19, 38–41, 43, 44,
    67, 73, 84, 109, 120, 124, 147,
    150, 223–24, 240, 264, 265, 266
Hobbes, Thomas, 13, 14, 46
Ho Chi Minh, 97
Hoffer, Eric, 108, 125
Holder, Eric, 187, 210–11, 212, 251–52
Hollrah, Paul R., 63
Hollywood, 82, 84, 91, 95, 110, 138,
    159, 167, 238
Hollywood Ten, 84
Holmes, Oliver Wendall, Jr., 43, 52
Holocaust, 44, 124, 266
Home Owners Loan Corporation;
    Deposit Insurance Corporation;
    Security and Exchange
    Commission; Fair Labor
    Standards Act, etc., 64
homosexuality, 105, 148, 150, 156,
    163–65, 167, 171, 172

"hooking up," 154
Hoover, Herbert, 61, 96
Hoover, J. Edgar, 68, 74, 78, 80, 249
Hopkins, Harry, 76, 77, 79, 80, 96
Horowitz, David, 132, 229, 230, 239–
    40, 247, 264
Hottel, Guy, 74
Houghton Mifflin, 83
House Armed Services Committee, 183
House Un-American Activities
    Committee (HUAC), 73, 74,
    77–79
Huffington, Arianna, 245
Huffington Post, 154, 170, 251, 258
Hummel, Jeffrey Rogers, 50
Hunter, George William, 42
Huxley, Aldous, 3, 107, 110, 113, 115
Huxley, Thomas, 41

I

ICE (Immigration and Custom
    Enforcement), 217
Ickes, Harold L., 63
illegal immigrants, 215, 216
    percent of all federal crime
        sentencings represented by, 216
imperialism, 9, 24, 92–93
incest, 155, 156, 157, 164
inclusion, 121, 166
individualism. *See especially chapter
    3, "Struggle for Individualism"
    (46–55). See also* 19, 120, 124,
    132, 232
Inequality magazine, 195
"inferior racial groups," 44
Institute for Policy Studies (IPS), 91,
    253, 258, 259

Pope, Barbara, 178

pop music, 110–11

pornography, 39, 83, 105, 111, 112, 146, 225

   percent of men and women who watch Internet, 154–55

posse comitatus law, 140

Posner, Michael, 173

pot, percent of increase of use since legalization began, 114

poverty

   percent of all black children from a single-mother home who live in, 206

   percent of American population who live in, 202

Powell, Colin, 205

power, three classic (Marxist) methods of gaining, 24

Pravda, 21

prayer, 103, 105, 142, 143–44, 170

Prejean, Carrie, 169

Presidential Commission on Assignment of Women in the Armed Forces, 178

   testimony of Brian Mitchell before the, 181

   testimony of Col. John H. Ripley before the, 182

presidents or vice presidents who have made the Nobel Peace Prize list, 59

press, regulation of the, 183–90

Princeton University, 162, 252

private property, 7, 8, 16, 17, 18, 21, 47, 63, 123

Progressive Era, 50, 51, 55, 264

Progressive Democrats, 79–80

Progressive Democrats of America, 258

Progressive Party, 82, 98–99, 258, 265

Progressives, five motivating factors for, 52–53

Progressivism, 42, 47, 51, 53, 54, 185, 254

proletariat, 10, 17–18, 20, 67, 87, 91, 222, 237, 264

promiscuity, 105, 106, 158, 169, 225

Proposition 8, 170

"proselytizing," 147

Province of Georgia. *See* Georgia colony

psychiatric profession, 105

public education, 119–25, 230

public schools, top seven disruptive problems in (1940s and 2015, compared), 157–58

Public Works Administration (PWA), 63–64

Putin, Vladimir, 222, 224

Q

Quindel, Jessica, 128–29

quota system, 215

R

racism, 117, 124, 185, 207, 209

radio, 68, 105, 183, 186, 188, 198

Radosh, Ronald, 82, 91

Raico, Ralph, 47

Raleigh, Walter, 11

Rathke, Wade, 250–51

Ray, Kimberly, 170